William Robertson

The History of the Reign of the Emperor Charles V.

Volume I.

William Robertson

The History of the Reign of the Emperor Charles V.
Volume I.

ISBN/EAN: 9783742824066

Manufactured in Europe, USA, Canada, Australia, Japa

Cover: Foto ©ninafisch / pixelio.de

Manufactured and distributed by brebook publishing software (www.brebook.com)

William Robertson

The History of the Reign of the Emperor Charles V.

THE
HISTORY
OF THE
REIGN
OF THE
EMPEROR CHARLES V.

WITH

A VIEW of the PROGRESS of SOCIETY in EUROPE, from the Subverſion of the ROMAN EMPIRE, to the Beginning of the SIXTEENTH CENTURY.

IN FOUR VOLUMES.

By WILLIAM ROBERTSON, D. D.
PRINCIPAL of the Univerſity of EDINBURGH, and HISTORIOGRAPHER to his MAJESTY for SCOTLAND.

THE SECOND EDITION.

VOL. I.

LONDON:
Printed for W. STRAHAN; T. CADELL, in the Strand; and J. BALFOUR, at Edinburgh.
MDCCLXXII.

TO THE

KING.

SIR,

I PRESUME to lay before your Majesty the History of a Period, which, if the abilities of the Writer were equal to the dignity of the Subject, would not be unworthy the attention of a Monarch, who is no less a Judge than a Patron of Literary Merit.

HISTORY claims it as her prerogative to offer instruction to KINGS, as well as to their people. What reflections the Reign of the Emperor

DEDICATION.

CHARLES V. may fuggeſt to Your Majeſty, it becomes not me to conjecture. But your Subjects cannot obſerve the various calamities, which that Monarch's ambition to be diſtinguiſhed as a Conqueror, brought upon his dominions, without recollecting the felicity of their own times, and looking up with gratitude to their Sovereign, who, during the fervour of youth, and amidſt the career of victory, poſſeſſed ſuch ſelf-command, and maturity of judgment, as to ſet bounds to his own triumphs, and prefer the bleſſings of peace to the ſplendour of military glory.

POSTERITY will not only celebrate the Wiſdom of Your Majeſty's choice, but will enumerate the many Virtues, which render Your Reign conſpicuous for a ſacred regard to all the duties incumbent

DEDICATION.

Incumbent on the Sovereign of a Free People.

It is our happiness to feel the influence of these Virtues; and to live under the dominion of a Prince, who delights more in promoting the Public Welfare, than in receiving the just Praise of his royal beneficence. I am,

SIR,

YOUR MAJESTY's

Most faithful Subject,

And most dutiful Servant,

WILLIAM ROBERTSON.

THE
PREFACE.

NO period in the history of one's own country can be considered as altogether uninteresting. Such transactions as tend to illustrate the progress of its constitution, laws, or manners, merit the utmost attention. Even remote and minute events are objects of a curiosity, which, being natural to the human mind, the gratification of it is attended with pleasure.

BUT, with respect to the history of foreign States, we must set other bounds to our desire of information. The universal progress of science during the two last centuries, the art of printing, and other obvious causes, have filled Europe with such a multiplicity of histories, and with such vast collections of historical materials, that the term of human life is too short for the study or even the perusal of them. It is necessary, then, not only for those who are called to conduct

PREFACE.

the affairs of nations, but for such as inquire and reason concerning them, to remain satisfied with a general knowledge of distant events, and to confine their study of history in detail chiefly to that period, in which the several States of Europe having become intimately connected, the operations of one power are so felt by all, as to influence their councils, and to regulate their measures.

Some boundary, then, ought to be fixed in order to separate these periods. An æra should be pointed out, prior to which, each country, little connected with those around it, may trace its own history apart; after which, the transactions of every considerable nation in Europe become interesting and instructive to all. With this intention I undertook to write the history of the Emperor Charles V. It was during his administration that the powers of Europe were formed into one great political system, in which each took a station, wherein it has since remained with less variation, than could have been expected after the shocks occasioned by so many internal revolutions, and
so

PREFACE

so many foreign wars. The great events which happened then have not hitherto spent their force. The political principles and maxims, then established, still continue to operate. The ideas concerning the balance of power, then introduced or rendered general, still influence the councils of nations.

The age of Charles V. may therefore be considered as the period at which the political state of Europe began to assume a new form. I have endeavoured to render my account of it, an introduction to the history of Europe subsequent to his reign. While his numerous Biographers describe his personal qualities and actions; while the historians of different countries relate occurrences the consequences of which were local or transient, it hath been my purpose to record only those great transactions in his reign, the effects of which were universal, or continue to be permanent.

As my readers could derive little instruction from such a history of the reign of Charles V. without some information concerning

PREFACE

cerning the state of Europe previous to the sixteenth century, my desire of supplying this has produced a preliminary volume, in which I have attempted to point out and explain the great causes and events, to whose operation all the improvements in the political state of Europe, from the subversion of the Roman Empire to the beginning of the sixteenth century, must be ascribed. I have exhibited a view of the progress of society in Europe, not only with respect to interior government, laws and manners, but with respect to the command of the national force requisite in foreign operations; and I have described the political constitution of the principal states in Europe at the time when Charles V. began his reign.

In this part of my work I have been led into several critical disquisitions, which belong more properly to the province of the lawyer or antiquary, than to that of the historian. These I have placed at the end of the first volume, under the title of Proofs and Illustrations. Many of my readers will, probably,

probably, give little attention to such researches. To some they may, perhaps, appear the most curious and interesting part of the work. I have carefully pointed out the sources from which I have derived information, and have cited the writers on whose authority I rely with a minute exactness, which might appear to border upon ostentation, if it were possible to be vain of having read books, many of which nothing but the duty of examining with accuracy whatever I laid before the public, could have induced me to open. As my inquiries conducted me often into paths which were obscure or little frequented, such constant recourse to the authors who have been my guides, was not only necessary for authenticating the facts which are the foundations of my reasonings, but may be useful in pointing out the way to such as shall hereafter hold the same course, and in enabling them to carry on their researches with greater facility and success.

EVERY intelligent reader will observe one omission in my work, the reason of which it is necessary to explain. I have given no account of the conquests of Mexico and Peru, or of the establishment of the Spanish colonies in the continent and islands of America. The history of these events I originally intended to have related at considerable length. But upon a nearer and more attentive consideration of this part of my plan, I found that the discovery of the new world; the state of society among its ancient inhabitants; their character, manners, and arts; the genius of the European settlements in its various provinces, together with the influence of these upon the systems of policy or commerce in Europe, were subjects so splendid and important, that a superficial view of them could afford little satisfaction; to treat of them as extensively as they merited, must produce an episode, disproportionate to the principal work. I have therefore reserved these for a separate history; which, if the performance now offered to the public shall receive its approbation, I propose to undertake.

Though, by omitting such considerable but detached articles in the reign of Charles V. I have

PREFACE.

I have circumscribed my narration within more narrow limits, I am yet persuaded, from this view of the intention and nature of the work which I thought it necessary to lay before my readers, that the plan must still appear to them too extensive, and the undertaking too arduous. I have often felt them to be so. But my conviction of the utility of such a history prompted me to persevere. With what success I have executed it, the public must now judge. I wait, in sollicitude, for its decision; to which I shall submit with a respectful silence.

DIRECTIONS to the BINDER.

Place the Head of the Author before the Title
 Vol. I.
The Head of Charles V. before the Title Vol. II.
——————— Francis before the Title Vol. III.
Charles V. expiring, before the Title Vol. IV.

A VIEW

A VIEW
OF THE
PROGRESS OF SOCIETY
IN
EUROPE,
FROM THE
SUBVERSION OF THE ROMAN EMPIRE,
TO THE
BEGINNING OF THE SIXTEENTH CENTURY.

SECTION I.

View of the Progress of Society in Europe, with respect to interior Government, Laws and Manners.

TWO great revolutions have happened in the political state, and in the manners of the European nations. The first was occasioned by the progress of the Roman power; the second by the subversion of the Roman Empire. When the spirit of conquest led the armies of Rome beyond the Alps, they found all the countries which they invaded, inhabited by people whom they denominated barbarians, but who were never-

Sect. I. The effects of the Roman power on the state of Europe.

SECT. I. nevertheless brave and independent. These defended their ancient possessions with obstinate valour. It was by the superiority of their discipline, rather than of their courage, that the Romans gained any advantage over them. A single battle did not, as among the effeminate inhabitants of Asia, decide the fate of a state. The vanquished people resumed their arms with fresh spirit, and their undisciplined valour, animated by the love of liberty, supplied the want of conduct as well as of union. During these long and fierce struggles for dominion or independence, the countries of Europe were successively laid waste, a great part of their inhabitants perished in the field, many were carried into slavery, and a feeble remnant, incapable of further resistance, submitted to the Roman power.

The desolation which it occasioned.

THE Romans having thus desolated Europe, set themselves to civilize it. The form of government which they established in the conquered provinces, though severe, was regular, and preserved public tranquillity. As a consolation for the loss of liberty, they communicated their arts, sciences, language, and manners, to their new subjects. Europe began to breathe, and to recover strength after the calamities which it had undergone; agriculture was encouraged; population increased; the ruined cities were rebuilt; new towns were founded; an appearance of prosperity succeeded, and repaired, in some degree, the havock of war.

The improvements which it introduced.

THIS

THIS state, however, was far from being happy, or favourable to the improvement of the human mind. The vanquished nations were difarmed by their conquerors, and overawed by soldiers kept in pay to restrain them. They were given up as a prey to rapacious governors, who plundered them with impunity; and were drained of their wealth by exorbitant taxes, imposed with so little attention to the situation of the provinces, that the impositions were often increased in proportion to their inability to support them. They were deprived of their most enterprizing citizens, who resorted to a distant capital in quest of preferment, or of riches; and were accustomed in all their actions to look up to a superior, and tamely to receive his commands. Under all these depressing circumstances, it was impossible that they could retain vigour or generosity of mind. The martial and independent spirit, which had distinguished their ancestors, became extinct among all the people subjected to the Roman yoke; they lost not only the habit but even the capacity of deciding for themselves, or of acting from the impulse of their own minds; and the dominion of the Romans, like that of all great Empires, degraded and debased the human species [A].

SECT. I.
The bad consequences of their dominion.

A SOCIETY in this state could not subsist long. There were defects in the Roman government, even in its most perfect form, which threatened its dissolution. Time ripened these original seeds of corruption,

The Irruption of the barbarous nations.

[A] NOTE I.

Sect. I. corruption, and gave birth to many new diforders. A conftitution, unfound, and worn out, muft have fallen in pieces of itfelf, without any external fhock. The violent irruption of the Goths, Vandals, Huns, and other barbarians haftened this event, and precipitated the downfal of the Empire. New nations feemed to arife, and to rufh from unknown regions, in order to take vengeance on the Romans for the calamities which they had inflicted on mankind. Thefe fierce tribes either inhabited the various provinces in Germany which had never been fubdued by the Romans, or were fcattered over the vaft countries in the north of Europe, and north-weft of Afia, which are now occupied by the Danes, the Swedes, the Poles, the fubjects of the Ruffian Empire, and the Tartars. Their condition, and tranfactions, previous to their invafion of the Empire, are but little known. All our information with refpect to thefe is derived from the Romans; and as they did not penetrate far into countries which were at that time uncultivated and uninviting, the accounts of their original ftate given by them are extremely imperfect. The rude inhabitants themfelves, deftitute of fcience, and of records, without leifure, or curiofity to enquire into remote events, retained, perhaps, fome indiftinct memory of recent occurrences, but beyond thefe, all was buried in oblivion, or involved in darknefs, and in fable [B].

State of the countries into which they allied.

THE prodigious fwarms which poured in upon the Empire from the beginning of the fourth century

[B] NOTE II.

tury to the final extinction of the Roman power, have given rise to an opinion that the countries whence they issued were crowded with inhabitants; and various theories have been formed to account for such an extraordinary degree of population as hath procured these countries the appellation of The Storehouse of Nations. But if we consider, that the countries possessed by the people who invaded the Empire were of vast extent; that a great part of these was covered with woods and marshes; that some of the most considerable of the barbarous nations subsisted entirely by hunting or pasturage, in both which states of society large tracts of land are required for maintaining a few inhabitants; and that all of them were strangers to the arts, and industry, without which population cannot increase to any great degree, it is evident, that these countries could not be so populous in ancient times as they are at present, when they still continue to be less peopled than any other part of Europe or of Asia.

But if these circumstances prevented the barbarous nations from becoming populous, they contributed to inspire, or to strengthen the martial spirit by which they were distinguished. Inured by the rigour of their climate, or the poverty of their soil, to hardships, which rendered their bodies firm, and their minds vigorous; accustomed to a course of life which was a continual preparation for action; and disdaining every occupation but that of war; they undertook, and prosecuted their

The people fit for daring enterprises.

SECT. I. military enterprizes with an ardour and impetuosity, of which men softened by the refinements of more polished times can scarcely form any idea [C].

The motives of their first excursions.

THEIR first inroads into the Empire proceeded rather from the love of plunder, than from the desire of new settlements. Roused to arms by some enterprizing or popular leader, they sallied out of their forests; broke in upon the frontier provinces with irresistible violence; put all who opposed them to the sword; carried off the most valuable effects of the inhabitants; dragged along multitudes of captives in chains; wasted all before them with fire or sword; and returned in triumph to their wilds and fastnesses. Their success, together with the accounts which they gave of the unknown conveniencies and luxuries that abounded in countries better cultivated, or blessed with a milder climate than their own, excited new adventurers, and exposed the frontier to new devastations.

Their reasons for settling in the countries which they conquered.

WHEN nothing was left to plunder in the adjacent provinces, ravaged by frequent incursions, they marched farther from home, and finding it difficult, or dangerous to return, they began to settle in the countries which they had subdued. The sudden and short excursions in quest of booty, which had alarmed and disquieted the Empire, ceased; a more dreadful calamity impended. Great bodies of armed men, with their wives and

[C] NOTE III.

children,

children, and slaves and flocks, issued forth, like regular colonies, in quest of new settlements. People who had no cities, and seldom any fixed habitation, were so little attached to their native soil, that they migrated without reluctance from one place to another. New adventurers followed them. The lands which they deserted were occupied by more remote tribes of barbarians. These, in their turn, pushed forward into more fertile countries, and, like a torrent continually increasing, rolled on, and swept every thing before them. In less than two centuries from their first irruption, barbarians of various names and lineage, plundered and took possession of Thrace, Pannonia, Gaul, Spain, Africa, and at last of Italy, and Rome itself. The vast fabrick of the Roman power, which it had been the work of ages to perfect, was in that short period overturned from the foundation.

The extent of their settlements.

MANY concurring causes prepared the way for this great revolution, and ensured success to the nations which invaded the Empire. The Roman commonwealth had conquered the world by the wisdom of its civil maxims, and the rigour of its military discipline. But, under the Emperors, the former were forgotten or despised, and the latter was gradually relaxed. The armies of the Empire in the fourth and fifth centuries bore scarcely any resemblance to those invincible legions which had been victorious wherever they marched. Instead of freemen, who voluntarily took arms from the love

The circumstances which occasioned the downfal of the Roman Empire.

Sect. I. love of glory, or of their country, provincials and barbarians were bribed or forced into service. They were too feeble, or too proud to submit to the fatigue of military duty. They even complained of the weight of their defensive armour, as intolerable, and laid it aside. Infantry, from which the armies of ancient Rome derived their vigour and stability, fell into contempt; the effeminate and undisciplined soldiers of later times could hardly be brought to venture into the field but on horseback. These wretched troops, however, were the only guardians of the Empire. The jealousy of despotism had deprived the people of the use of arms; and subjects oppressed and rendered incapable of defending themselves, had neither spirit nor inclination to resist their invaders, from whom they had little to fear, because their condition could hardly be rendered more unhappy. As the martial spirit became extinct, the revenues of the Empire gradually diminished. The taste for the luxuries of the East increased to such a pitch in the Imperial court, that great sums were carried into India, from which money never returns. By the vast subsidies paid to the barbarous nations a still greater quantity of species was withdrawn from circulation. The frontier provinces wasted by frequent incursions became unable to pay the customary tribute; and the wealth of the world, which had long centered in the capital of the Empire, ceased to flow thither in the same abundance, or was diverted into other channels. The limits of the Empire continued to be as extensive as ever,

while

while the spirit requisite for its defence declined, Sect. I.
and its resources were exhausted. A vast body,
languid, and almost unanimated, became incapable of any effort to save itself, and was easily overpowered. The Emperors, who had the absolute direction of this disordered system, sunk in the softness of eastern luxury, shut up within the walls of a palace, ignorant of war, unacquainted with affairs, and governed entirely by women and eunuchs, or by ministers equally effeminate, trembled at the approach of danger, and under circumstances which called for the utmost vigour in counsel as well as in action, discovered all the impotent irresolution of fear, and of folly.

In every respect, the condition of the barbarous nations was the reverse of that of the Romans. Among them, the martial spirit was in full vigour; their leaders were hardy and enterprizing; the arts which had enervated the Romans were unknown among them; and such was the nature of their military institutions, that they brought forces into the field without any trouble, and supported them at little expence. The mercenary and effeminate troops stationed on the frontier, astonished at their fierceness, either fled at their approach, or were routed in the first onset. The feeble expedient to which the Emperors had recourse, of taking large bodies of the barbarians into pay, and of employing them to repel new invaders, instead of retarding, hastened the destruction of the Empire. They soon turned their arms against their masters,

The circumstances which contributed to the success of the barbarous nations.

and

Sect. I. and with greater advantage than ever: for, by serving in the Roman armies, they had acquired all the discipline, or skill in war, which the Romans still retained; and, upon adding these to their native ferocity, they became altogether irresistible.

The spirit with which they carried on war.

But though from these, and many other causes, the progress and conquests of the nations which over-ran the Empire, became so extremely rapid, they were accompanied with horrible devastations, and an incredible destruction of the human species. Civilized nations which take arms upon cool reflection, from motives of policy or prudence, with a view to guard against some distant danger, or to prevent some remote contingency, carry on their hostilities with so little rancour, or animosity, that war among them is disarmed of half its terrors. Barbarians are strangers to such refinements. They rush into war with impetuosity, and prosecute it with violence. Their sole object is to make their enemies feel the weight of their vengeance, nor does their rage subside until it be satiated with inflicting on them every possible calamity. It is with such a spirit that the savage tribes in America carry on their petty wars. It was with the same spirit that the more powerful and no less fierce barbarians in the north of Europe, and of Asia, fell upon the Roman Empire.

The desolation which they brought upon Europe.

Wherever they marched, their rout was marked with blood. They ravaged or destroyed all around them. They made no distinction between what was sacred, and what was profane. They respected no age, or sex, or rank. What escaped the fury of the first inundation, perished in those which followed it. The most fertile and populous provinces were converted into deserts, in which were scattered the ruins of villages and cities, that afforded shelter to a few miserable inhabitants whom chance had preserved, or the sword of the enemy, wearied with destroying, had spared. The conquerors who first settled in the countries which they had wasted, were expelled or exterminated by new invaders, who coming from regions farther removed from the civilized parts of the world, were still more fierce and rapacious. This brought new calamities upon mankind, which did not cease until the north, by pouring forth successive swarms, was drained of people, and could no longer furnish instruments of destruction. Famine and pestilence, which always march in the train of war, when it ravages with such inconsiderate cruelty, raged in every part of Europe, and completed its sufferings. If a man were called to fix upon the period in the history of the world, during which the condition of the human race was most calamitous and afflicted, he would, without hesitation, name that which elapsed from the death of Theodosius the Great, to the establishment of the Lombards in Italy [a]. The contemporary authors who beheld that scene of desolation, labour and are at a

---

[a] Theodosius died A. D. 395. the reign of Alboinus in Lombardy began A. D. 571; so that this period was 176 years.

loss

Sect. I. loss for expressions to describe the horror of it. *The scourge of God, The destroyer of nations,* are the dreadful epithets by which they distinguish the most noted of the barbarous leaders; and they compare the ruin which they had brought on the world, to the havock occasioned by earthquakes, conflagrations, or deluges, the most formidable and fatal calamities which the imagination of man can conceive.

The universal change which they occasioned in the state of Europe.

But no expressions can convey so perfect an idea of the destructive progress of the barbarians as that which must strike an attentive observer, when he contemplates the total change, which he will discover in the state of Europe after it began to recover some degree of tranquillity towards the close of the sixth century. The Saxons were by that time masters of the southern, and more fertile provinces of Britain; the Franks of Gaul; the Huns of Pannonia; the Goths of Spain; the Goths and Lombards of Italy and the adjacent provinces. Scarce any vestige of the Roman policy, jurisprudence, arts, or literature, remained. New forms of government, new laws, new manners, new dresses, new languages, and new names of men and countries, were every where introduced. To make a great or sudden alteration with respect to any of these, unless where the ancient inhabitants of a country have been almost totally exterminated, has proved an undertaking beyond the power of the greatest conquerors [D]. The total change which the settlement of the barbarous nations occasioned

[D] NOTE IV.

in the state of Europe, may, therefore, be considered as a more decisive proof, than even the testimony of contemporary historians, of the destructive violence with which these invaders carried on their conquests, and of the havock which they had made from one extremity of this quarter of the globe to the other [E].

In the obscurity of the chaos occasioned by this general wreck of nations, we must search for the seeds of order, and endeavour to discover the first rudiments of the policy and laws now established in Europe. To this source, the historians of its different kingdoms, have attempted, though with less attention and industry than the importance of the enquiry merits, to trace back the institutions and customs peculiar to their countrymen. It is not my province to give a minute detail of the progress of government and manners in each particular nation, whose transactions are the object of the following history. But, in order to exhibit a just view of the state of Europe at the opening of the sixteenth century, it is necessary to look back, and to contemplate the condition of the northern nations upon their first settlement in those countries which they occupied. It is necessary to mark the great steps by which they advanced from barbarism to refinement, and to point out those general principles and events which, by their uniform as well as extensive operation, conducted all of them

From this state of disorder the laws of government now established must be traced.

[E] NOTE V.

Sect. I. to that degree of improvement in policy and in manners which they had attained at the period when Charles V. began his reign.

The principles on which the northern nations made their settlements in Europe.

WHEN nations subject to despotic government make conquests, these serve only to extend the dominion and the power of their master. But armies composed of freemen conquer for themselves, not for their leaders. The people who overturned the Roman Empire, and settled in its various provinces, were of the latter class. Not only the different nations that issued from the north of Europe, which has always been considered as the seat of liberty, but the Huns and Alans who inhabited part of those countries which have been marked out as the peculiar region of servitude [b], enjoyed freedom and independence to such a high degree as seems to be scarcely compatible with a state of social union, or with the subordination necessary to maintain it. They followed the chieftain who led them forth in quest of new settlements, not by constraint, but from choice; not as soldiers whom he could order to march, but as volunteers who offered to accompany him [F]. They considered their conquests as a common property, in which all had a title to share, as all had contributed to acquire them [G]. In what manner, or by what principles, they divided among them the lands which they seized, we cannot now determine with any

[b] De L'esprit des loix, liv. 17. ch. 3.

[F] NOTE VI.   [G] NOTE VII.

certainty.

certainty. There is no nation in Europe whose records reach back to this remote period; and there is little information to be got from the uninstructive and meagre chronicles, compiled by writers ignorant of the true end, and unacquainted with the proper objects of history.

THIS new division of property, however, together with the maxims and manners to which it gave rise, gradually introduced a species of government formerly unknown. This singular institution is now distinguished by the name of the *Feudal system*: and though the barbarous nations which framed it, settled in their new territories at different times, came from different countries, spoke various languages, and were under the command of separate leaders, the Feudal policy and laws were established, with little variation, in every kingdom of Europe. This amazing uniformity hath induced some authors [e] to believe that all these nations, notwithstanding so many apparent circumstances of distinction, were originally the same people. But it may be ascribed with greater probability to the similar state of society and of manners to which they were accustomed in their native countries, and to the similar situation in which they found themselves on taking possession of their new domains.

As the conquerors of Europe had their acquisitions to maintain, not only against such of the

[e] Procop. de Bello Vandal. ap. Script. Byz. edit. Ven. vol. i. p. 345.

SECT. I.

National defence the great object of feudal policy.

ancient inhabitants as they had spared, but against the more formidable inroads of new invaders, self-defence was their chief care, and seems to have been the sole object of their first institutions and policy. Instead of those loose associations, which, though they scarcely diminished their personal independence, had been sufficient for their security while they remained in their original countries, they saw the necessity of confederating more closely together, and of relinquishing some of their private rights in order to attain publick safety. Every freeman, upon receiving a portion of the lands which were divided, bound himself to appear in arms against the enemies of the community. This military service was the condition upon which he received and held his lands, and as they were exempted from every other burden, that tenure, among a warlike people, was deemed both easy and honourable. The King or general, who led them to conquest, continuing still to be the head of the colony, had, of course, the largest portion allotted to him. Having thus acquired the means of rewarding past services, as well as of gaining new adherents, he parcelled out his lands with this view, binding those on whom they were bestowed, to follow his standard with a number of men in proportion to the extent of the territory which they received, and to bear arms in his defence. His chief officers imitated the example of the sovereign, and in distributing portions of their lands among their dependants, annexed the same condition to the grant. Thus a feudal kingdom resembled a military establishment, rather than a civil institution. The victorious army, cantoned out in the country which it had seized, continued ranged under its proper officers, and subordinate to military command. The names of a soldier and of a freeman were synonimous[d]. Every proprietor of land, girt with a sword, was ready to march at the summons of his superior, and to take the field against the common enemy.

BUT though the Feudal policy seems to be so admirably calculated for defence against the assaults of any foreign power, its provisions for the interior order and tranquillity of society were extremely defective. The principles of disorder and corruption are discernable in that constitution under its best and most perfect form. They soon unfolded themselves, and spreading with rapidity through every part of the system, produced the most fatal effects. The bond of political union was extremely feeble; the sources of anarchy were innumerable. The monarchical and aristocratical parts of the constitution, having no intermediate power to balance them, were perpetually at variance, and justling with each other. The powerful vassals of the crown soon extorted a confirmation for life of those grants of land, which being at first purely gratuitous, had been bestowed only during plea-

The feudal government defective in its provisions for interior order in society.

[d] Du Cange Glossar. voc. *Miles.*

sure.

Sect. I. fure. Not satisfied with this, they prevailed to have them converted into hereditary possessions. One step more completed their usurpations, and rendered them unalienable [H]. With an ambition no less enterprizing, and more preposterous, they appropriated to themselves titles of honour, as well as offices of power or trust. These personal marks of distinction, which the publick admiration bestows on illustrious merit, or which the publick confidence confers on extraordinary abilities, were annexed to certain families, and transmitted like fiefs, from father to son, by hereditary right. The crown vassals having thus secured the possession of their lands and dignities, the nature of the Feudal institutions, which though founded on subordination verged to independence, led them to new, and still more dangerous encroachments on the prerogatives of the sovereign. They obtained the power of supreme jurisdiction both civil and criminal within their own territories; the right of coining money; together with the privilege of carrying on war against their private enemies in their own name, and by their own authority. The ideas of political subjection were almost entirely lost, and frequently scarce any appearance of feudal subordination remained. Nobles who had acquired such enormous power, scorned to consider themselves as subjects. They aspired openly at being independent: the bonds which connected the principal members of the constitution with the crown, were dissolved. A kingdom considerable

[H] NOTE VIII.

in

in name and in extent, was broken into as many separate principalities as it contained powerful barons. A thousand causes of jealousy and discord subsisted among them, and gave rise to as many wars. Every country in Europe, wasted or kept in continual alarm during these endless contests, was filled with castles and places of strength, erected for the security of the inhabitants, not against foreign force, but against internal hostilities. An universal anarchy, destructive, in a great measure, of all the advantages which men expect to derive from society, prevailed. The people, the most numerous as well as the most useful part of the community, were either reduced to a state of actual servitude, or treated with the same insolence and rigour as if they had been degraded into that wretched condition [1]. The King, stripped of almost every prerogative, and without authority to enact or to execute salutary laws, could neither protect the innocent, nor punish the guilty. The nobles, superior to all restraint, harassed each other with perpetual wars, oppressed their fellow-subjects, and humbled or insulted their sovereign. To crown all, time gradually fixed, and rendered venerable this pernicious system, which violence had established.

Such was the state of Europe with respect to the interior administration of government from the seventh to the eleventh century. All the external operations of its various states, during this period, were, of course, extremely feeble. A kingdom

It prevented nations like these from acting with vigour in their external operations.

[1] NOTE IX.

Sect. I. dismembered, and torn with dissention, without any common interest to rouze, or any common head to conduct its force, was incapable of acting with vigour. Almost all the wars in Europe, during the ages which I have mentioned, were trifling, indecisive, and productive of no considerable event. They resembled the short incursions of pirates or banditti, rather than the steady operations of a regular army. Every baron, at the head of his vassals, carried on some petty enterprize, to which he was prompted by his own ambition, or revenge. The state itself, destitute of union, either remained altogether inactive, or if it attempted to make any effort, that served only to discover its impotence. The superior genius of Charlemagne, it is true, united all these disjointed and discordant members, and forming them again into one body, restored to government that degree of activity which distinguishes his reign, and renders the transactions of it, objects not only of attention but of admiration to more enlightened times. But this state of union and vigour, not being natural to the feudal government, was of short duration. Immediately upon his death, the spirit which animated and sustained the vast system which he had established, being withdrawn, it broke into pieces. All the calamities which flow from anarchy and discord, returning with additional force, afflicted the different kingdoms into which his Empire was split. From that time to the eleventh century, a succession of uninteresting events; a series of wars, the

motives

STATE OF EUROPE.

motives as well as the consequences of which were equally unimportant, fill and deform the annals of all the nations in Europe.

To these pernicious effects of the feudal anarchy, may be added its fatal influence on the character and improvement of the human mind. If men do not enjoy the protection of regular government, together with the certainty of personal security, which naturally flows from it, they never attempt to make progress in science, nor aim at attaining refinement in taste, or in manners. That period of turbulence, oppression, and rapine, which I have described, was ill suited to favour improvement in any of these. In less than a century after the barbarous nations settled in their new conquests, almost all the effects of the knowledge and civility which the Romans had spread through Europe disappeared. Not only the arts of elegance which minister to luxury, and are supported by it, but many of the useful arts, without which life can scarcely be considered as comfortable, were neglected or lost. Literature, science, taste, were words hardly in use during the ages we are contemplating; or if they occur at any time, eminence in them is ascribed to persons and productions so contemptible, that it appears their true import was little understood. Persons of the highest rank, and in the most eminent stations, could not read or write. Many of the clergy did not understand the breviary which they were obliged daily

Sect. I.

The fatal effects of this state of society on sciences and arts.

Sect. I. to recite; some of them could scarcely read it [K]. All memory of past transactions was lost, or preserved in annals filled with trifling events, or legendary tales. Even the codes of laws published by the several nations which established themselves in the different countries of Europe, fell into disuse, while, in their place, customs, vague and capricious, were substituted. The human mind neglected, uncultivated, and depressed, sunk into the most profound ignorance. Europe did not produce, during four centuries, one author who merits to be read, either on account of the elegance of his composition, or the justness and novelty of his sentiments. There is hardly one invention useful or ornamental to society of which that long period can boast.

upon religion;

Even the Christian religion, though its precepts are delivered, and its institutions are fixed in scripture with a precision which should have exempted them from being misinterpreted or corrupted, degenerated during those ages of darkness into an illiberal superstition. The barbarous nations when converted to Christianity changed the object, not the spirit of their religious worship. They endeavoured to conciliate the favour of the true God by means not unlike to those which they had employed in order to appease their false deities. Instead of aspiring to sanctity and virtue, which alone can render men acceptable to the great author of

[K] NOTE X.

order

order and of excellence, they imagined that they satisfied every obligation of duty by a scrupulous observance of external ceremonies [L]. Religion, according to their conception of it, comprehended nothing else; and the rites, by which they persuaded themselves that they could gain the favour of heaven, were of such a nature as might have been expected from the rude ideas of the ages which devised and introduced them. They were either so unmeaning as to be altogether unworthy of the Being to whose honour they were consecrated; or so absurd as to be a disgrace to reason and humanity [M]. Charlemagne in France, and Alfred the Great in England, endeavoured to dispel this darkness, and gave their subjects a short glimpse of light and knowledge. But the ignorance of the age was too powerful for their efforts and institutions. The darkness returned, and settled over Europe more thick and heavy than formerly.

As the inhabitants of Europe during these centuries were strangers to the arts which embellish a polished age, they were destitute of the virtues which abound among people who continue in a simple state. Force of mind, a sense of personal dignity, gallantry in enterprize, invincible perseverance in execution, contempt of danger and of death, are the characteristic virtues of uncivilized nations. But these are all the offspring of equa-

Upon the character and virtues of the human mind.

[L] NOTE XI. [M] NOTE XII.

lity

Sect. I. lity and independence, both which the feudal institutions had destroyed. The spirit of domination corrupted the nobles; the yoke of servitude depressed the people; the generous sentiments inspired by a sense of equality were extinguished, and nothing remained to be a check on ferocity and violence. Human society is in its most corrupted state at that period when men have lost their original independence and simplicity of manners, but have not attained that degree of refinement which introduces a sense of decorum and of propriety in conduct, as a restraint on those passions which lead to heinous crimes. Accordingly, a greater number of those atrocious actions which fill the mind of man with astonishment and horror, occur in the history of the centuries under review, than in that of any period of the same extent in the annals of Europe. If we open the history of Gregory of Tours, or of any contemporary author, we meet with a series of deeds of cruelty, perfidy, and revenge, so wild and enormous as almost to exceed belief.

From the beginning of the eleventh century government and manners begin to improve.

But, according to the observation of an elegant and profound historian [*], there is an ultimate point of depression, as well as of exaltation, from which human affairs naturally return in a contrary progress, and beyond which they seldom pass either in their advancement or decline. When defects, either in the form, or in the administration

[*] Hume's History of England, vol. ii. p. 441.

STATE OF EUROPE.

of government, occasion such disorders in society as are excessive and intolerable, it becomes the common interest to discover and to apply such remedies as will most effectually remove them. Slight inconveniencies may be long overlooked or endured, but when abuses grow to a certain pitch, the society must go to ruin, or must attempt to reform them. The disorders in the feudal system, together with the corruption of taste and manners consequent upon these, which had gone on increasing during a long course of years, seem to have attained their utmost point of excess towards the close of the eleventh century. From that æra, we may date the return of government and manners in a contrary direction, and can trace a succession of causes and events which contributed, some with a nearer and more powerful, others with a more remote and less perceptible influence, to abolish confusion and barbarism, and to introduce order, regularity, and refinement.

In pointing out and explaining these causes and events, it is not necessary to observe the order of time with a chronological accuracy; it is of more importance to keep in view their mutual connection and dependence, and to show how the operation of one event, or one cause, prepared the way for another, and augmented its influence. We have hitherto been contemplating the progress of that darkness which spread over Europe from its first approach, to the period of greatest obscuration; a more pleasant exercise begins here, to observe

Sect. I.

Necessary to point out the causes and events which contribute towards this improvement.

Sect. I. serve the first dawnings of returning light, to mark the various accessions by which it gradually increased and advanced towards the full splendor of day.

<small>The tendency of the Crusades to introduce a change in government and manners.

The more remote causes of these expeditions.</small>

I. The Crusades, or expeditions in order to rescue the Holy Land out of the hands of Infidels, seem to be the first event that rouzed Europe from the lethargy in which it had been long sunk, and that tended to introduce any change in government, or in manners. It is natural to the human mind to view those places which have been distinguished by being the residence of any illustrious personage, or the scene of any great transaction, with some degree of delight and veneration. From this principle flowed the superstitious devotion with which Christians, from the earliest ages of the church, were accustomed to visit that country which the Almighty had selected as the inheritance of his favourite people, and in which the son of God had accomplished the redemption of mankind. As this distant pilgrimage could not be performed without considerable expence, fatigue, and danger, it appeared the more meritorious, and came to be considered as an expiation for almost every crime. An opinion which spread with rapidity over Europe about the close of the tenth and beginning of the eleventh century, and which gained universal credit, wonderfully augmented the number of these credulous pilgrims, and increased the ardour with which they undertook this useless voyage. The thousand years mentioned by

St.

St. John [f] were supposed to be accomplished, and the end of the world to be at hand. A general consternation seized mankind; many relinquished their possessions; and abandoning their friends and families, hurried with precipitation to the Holy Land, where they imagined that Christ would quickly appear to judge the world [g]. While Palestine continued subject to the Caliphs, they had encouraged the resort of pilgrims to Jerusalem; and considered this as a beneficial species of commerce, which brought into their dominions gold and silver, and carried nothing out of them but relicks and consecrated trinkets. But the Turks having conquered Syria about the middle of the eleventh century, pilgrims were exposed to outrages of every kind from these fierce barbarians [h]. This change happening precisely at the juncture when the panic terror which I have mentioned rentioned pilgrimages most frequent, filled Europe with alarm and indignation. Every person who returned from Palestine related the dangers which he had encountered, in visiting the holy city, and described with exaggeration the cruelty and vexations of the Turks.

[f] Revel. xx. 2, 3, 4.

[g] Chronic. Will. Godelli ap. Bouquet Recueil des Historiens de France. tom. x. p. 262. Vita Abbonis, ibid. p. 332. Chronic. S. Pantaleonis ap. Eccard. Corp. Script. medii ævi, vol. I. p. 909. Annalista Saxo, ibid. 576.

[h] Jo. Dan. Schoepflini de sacris Gallorum in orientem expeditionibus, p. 4. Argent. 1726. 4to.

SECT. I. WHEN the minds of men were thus prepared, the
zeal of a fanatical monk, who conceived the idea of
leading all the forces of Chriſtendom againſt the
infidels, and of driving them out of the Holy Land
by violence, was ſufficient to give a beginning to
that wild enterprize. Peter the hermit, for that
was the name of this martial apoſtle, run from
province to province with a crucifix in his hand,
exciting Princes and people to this Holy war, and
wherever he came kindled the ſame enthuſiaſtic
ardour for it with which he himſelf was animated.
The council of Placentia, where upwards of thirty
thouſand perſons were aſſembled, pronounced the
ſcheme to have been ſuggeſted by the immediate
inſpiration of heaven. In the council of Clermont,
ſtill more numerous, as ſoon as the meaſure was
propoſed, all cried out with one voice, " It is the
" will of God." Perſons of all ranks were ſmitten with the contagion; not only the gallant nobles
of that age, with their martial followers, whom
the boldneſs of a romantic enterprize might have
been apt to allure, but men in the more humble
and pacific ſtations of life; eccleſiaſtics of every
order, and even women and children, engaged with
emulation in an undertaking which was deemed
ſacred and meritorious. If we may believe the
concurring teſtimony of contemporary authors, ſix
millions of perſons aſſumed the croſs [1], which was
the badge that diſtinguiſhed ſuch as devoted themſelves to this holy warfare. All Europe, ſays the

[1] Fulcherius Carnotenſis ap. Bongarſii Geſta Dei per Francos, vol. i. 387. edit. Han. 1611.

Princess Anna Comnena, torn up from the foundation, seemed ready to precipitate itself in one united body upon Asia[k]. Nor did the fumes of this enthusiastic zeal evaporate at once: the frenzy was as lasting, as it was extravagant. During two centuries, Europe seems to have had no object but to recover, or keep possession of the Holy Land, and through that period vast armies continued to march thither [N].

The first efforts of valour animated by enthusiasm were irresistible; part of the lesser Asia, all Syria and Palestine were wrested from the infidels; the banner of the cross was displayed on Mount Sion; Constantinople, the capital of the Christian empire in the East, was seized by a body of these adventurers, who had taken arms against the Mahometans, and an Earl of Flanders, and his descendants, kept possession of the Imperial throne during half a century. But though the first impression of the Crusaders was so unexpected that they made their conquests with great ease, they found infinite difficulty in preserving them. Establishments so distant from Europe, surrounded by warlike nations, animated with fanatical zeal scarcely inferior to that of the Crusaders themselves, were perpetually in danger of being overturned. Before the expiration of the thirteenth century, the Christians were driven out of all their Asiatic possessions, in acquiring of which incredible numbers of men had perished,

The success of the Crusades.

A. D. 1191.

[k] Alexias. lib. x. ap. Byz. script. vol. xi. p. 224.
[N] NOTE XIII.

perished, and immense sums of money had been wasted. The only common enterprize in which the European nations ever engaged, and which all undertook with equal ardour, remains a singular monument of human folly.

The beneficial effects of the Crusades on manners.

BUT from these expeditions, extravagant as they were, beneficial consequences followed, which had neither been foreseen nor expected. In their progress towards the Holy Land, the followers of the cross marched through countries better cultivated, and more civilized than their own. Their first rendezvous was commonly in Italy, in which Venice, Genoa, Pisa and other cities had begun to apply themselves to commerce, and had made some advances towards wealth as well as refinement. They embarked there, and landing in Dalmatia, pursued their rout by land to Constantinople. Though the military spirit had been long extinct in the eastern Empire, and a despotism of the worst species had annihilated almost every publick virtue, yet Constantinople, having never felt the destructive rage of the barbarous nations, was the greatest, as well as the most beautiful city in Europe, and the only one in which there remained any image of the ancient elegance in manners and arts. The naval power of the eastern Empire was considerable. Manufactures of the most curious fabrick were carried on in its dominions. Constantinople was the only mart in Europe for the commodities of the East Indies. Although the Saracens and Turks had torn from the Empire many of its richest provinces,

vinces, and had reduced it within very narrow
bounds, yet great wealth flowed into the capital
from thefe various fources, which not only cherifhed fuch a tafte for magnificence, but kept alive
fuch a relifh for the fciences as appears confiderable when compared with what was known in
other parts of Europe. Even in Afia, the Europeans who had affumed the crofs, found the remains of the knowledge and arts which the example and encouragement of the Caliphs had diffufed
through their Empire. Although the attention of
the hiftorians of the Crufades was fixed on other
objects than the ftate of fociety and manners among
the nations which they invaded, although moft of
them had neither tafte nor difcernment enough to
defcribe thefe, they relate, however, fuch fignal
acts of humanity and generofity in the conduct of
Saladin, as well as fome other leaders of the Mahometans, as give us a very high idea of their
manners. It was not poffible for the Crufaders to
travel through fo many countries, and to behold
their various cuftoms and inftitutions, without
acquiring information and improvement. Their
views enlarged; their prejudices wore off; new
ideas crowded into their minds; and they muft have
been fenfible on many occafions of the rufticity of
their own manners when compared with thofe of a
more polifhed people. Thefe impreffions were
not no flight as to be effaced upon their return to
their native countries. A clofe intercourfe fubfifted
between the Eaft and Weft during two centuries;
new armies were continually marching from Europe

Sect. I. rope to Asia, while former adventurers returned home and imported many of the customs to which they had been familiarized by a long residence abroad. Accordingly, we discover, soon after the commencement of the Crusades, greater splendour in the courts of Princes, greater pomp in publick ceremonies, a more refined taste in pleasure and amusements, together with a more romantic spirit of enterprize spreading gradually over Europe; and to these wild expeditions, the effect of superstition or folly, we owe the first gleams of light which tended to dispel barbarity and ignorance.

Their influence on the state of property. But these beneficial consequences of the Crusades took place slowly; their influence upon the state of property, and consequently of power, in the different kingdoms of Europe, was more immediate as well as discernible. The nobles who assumed the cross, and bound themselves to march to the Holy Land, soon perceived that great sums were necessary towards defraying the expence of such a distant expedition, and enabling them to appear with suitable dignity at the head of their vassals. But the genius of the feudal system was averse to the imposition of extraordinary taxes; and subjects in that age were unaccustomed to pay them. No expedient remained for levying the sums requisite, but the sale of their possessions. As men were inflamed with romantic expectations of the splendid conquests which they hoped to make in Asia, and possessed with such zeal for recovering the

Holy

Holy Land as fwallowed up every other paffion, they relinquifhed their ancient inheritances without any reluctance, and for prices far below their value, that they might fally forth as adventurers in queft of new fettlements in unknown countries. The Monarchs of the different kingdoms, none of whom had engaged in the firft Crufade, eagerly feized this opportunity of annexing confiderable territories to their crowns at fmall expence[1]. Befides this, feveral great barons who perifhed in the Holy war, having left no heirs, their fiefs reverted of courfe to their refpective fovereigns; and by thefe acceffions of property as well as power taken from the one fcale and thrown into the other, the regal authority increafed in proportion as that of the Ariftocracy declined. The abfence, too, of many potent vaffals, accuftomed to controul and give law to their fovereigns, afforded them an opportunity of extending their prerogative, and of acquiring a degree of weight in the conftitution which they did not formerly poffefs. To thefe circumftances, we may add, that as all who affumed the crofs were taken under the immediate protection of the church, and its heavieft anathemas were denounced againft fuch as fhould difquiet or annoy thofe who had devoted themfelves to this fervice; the private quarrels and hoftilities which banifhed tranquillity from a feudal kingdom were fufpended or extinguifhed; a more general and fteady adminiftration

---

[1] Willelm. Malmfbur. Guibert. Abbaf. ap. Bongarf. vol. i. 481.

of justice began to be introduced, and some advances were made towards the establishment of regular government in the several kingdoms of Europe ⁿ [O].

Their commercial effects.

THE commercial effects of the Crusades were not less considerable than those which I have already mentioned. The first armies under the standard of the cross, which Peter the hermit and Godfrey of Bouillon led through Germany and Hungary to Constantinople, suffered so much by the length of the march, as well as by the fierceness of the barbarous people who inhabited those countries, that it deterred others from taking the same route; so that rather than encounter so many dangers, they chose to go by sea. Venice, Genoa, and Pisa furnished the transports on which they embarked. The sum which these cities received merely for freight from such numerous armies was immense °. This, however, was but a small part of what they gained by the expeditions to the Holy Land; the Crusaders contracted with them for military stores and provisions; their fleets kept on the coast as the armies advanced by land, and supplying them with whatever was wanting, engrossed all the profits of that lucrative branch of commerce. The success which attended the arms of the Crusaders was productive of advantages

ⁿ Du Cange Glossar. voc. *Cruce signatus*. Guil. Abbas ap. Bongars. vol. i. 180. 482.

[O] NOTE XIV.

° Muratori Antiquit. Italic. medii ævi, vol. ii. 905.

still more permanent. There are charters yet extant, containing grants to the Venetians, Pisans, and Genoese of the most extensive immunities in the several settlements which the Christians made in Asia. All the commodities which they imported or exported are thereby exempted from every imposition; the property of entire suburbs in some of the maritime towns, and of large streets and houses in others, is vested in them; and all questions arising among persons settled within their precincts, or who traded under their protection, are appointed to be tried by their own laws and by judges of their own appointment[o]. When the Crusaders seized Constantinople, and placed one of their own leaders on the Imperial throne, the Italian States were likewise gainers by that event. The Venetians who had planned the enterprize, and took a considerable part in carrying it into execution, did not neglect to secure to themselves the chief advantages redounding from its success. They made themselves masters of part of the ancient Peleponnesus in Greece, together with some of the most fertile islands in the Archipelago. Many valuable branches of the commerce, which formerly centered in Constantinople, were transferred to Venice, Genoa, or Pisa. Thus a succession of events occasioned by the Holy war, opened various sources, from which wealth flowed in such

[o] Muratori Antiquit. Italic. medii ævi, vol. ii. 906, &c.

SECT. I. abundance in these cities [f], as enabled them, in concurrence with another institution which shall be immediately mentioned, to secure their own liberty and independence.

The establishment of communities favourable to government and order.

II. THE institution to which I alluded was the forming of cities into communities, corporations, or bodies politick, and granting them the privilege of municipal jurisdiction, which contributed more, perhaps, than any other cause to introduce regular government, police and arts, and to diffuse them over Europe. The feudal government had degenerated into a system of oppression. The usurpations of the nobles were become unbounded and intolerable: they had reduced the great body of the people into a state of actual servitude: the condition of those dignified with the name of freemen, was often little preferable to that of the other. Nor was such oppression the portion of those alone who dwelt in the country, and were employed in *The ancient state of cities.* cultivating the estate of their master. Cities and villages held of some great lord, on whom they depended for protection, and were no less subject to his arbitrary jurisdiction. The inhabitants were deprived of the natural, and most unalienable rights of humanity. They could not dispose of the effects which their own industry had acquired, either by a latter will, or by any deed executed during

[f] Villehardouin hist. de Constant. sous l'Empereur François, 105, &c.

their life ^{q}. They had no right to appoint guar- Sect. I.
dians for their children, during their minority.
They were not permitted to marry without purchasing the consent of the lord on whom they depended ^{r}. If once they had commenced a law-suit,
they durst not terminate it by an accommodation,
because that would have deprived the lord in
whose court they pleaded, of the perquisites due
to him on passing sentence ^{s}. Services of various
kinds, no less disgraceful than oppressive, were exacted from them without mercy or moderation.
The spirit of industry was checked in some cities
by absurd regulations, and in others by un-
reasonable exactions: nor would the narrow and
oppressive maxims of a military aristocracy have
permitted it ever to rise to any degree of height
or vigour ^{t}.

But as soon as the cities of Italy began to turn The free-
their attention towards commerce, and to conceive first esta-
some idea of the advantages which they might de- blished in
rive from it, they became impatient to shake off Italy.
the yoke of their insolent lords, and to establish
among themselves such a free and equal govern-

^{q} Dacherii Spicileg. tom. xi. 374, 375. edit. in 4to. Ordonances des Rois de France, tom. iii. 204. N°. 2. 6.

^{r} Ordonnances des Rois de France, tom. i. p. 22. tom. iii.
203. N°. 1. Murat. Antiq. Ital. vol. iv. p. 20. Dacher. Spicel.
vol. xi. 325, 341.

^{s} Dacher. Spicel. vol. ix. 182.

^{t} M. l'Abbè Mably observat. sur l'hist de France, tom. ii.
p. 2. 96.

ment as would render property secure, and industry flourishing. The German Emperors, especially those of the Franconian and Suabian lines, as the seat of their government was far distant from Italy, possessed a feeble and imperfect jurisdiction in that country. Their perpetual quarrels either with the Popes or with their own turbulent vassals, diverted their attention from the interior police of Italy, and gave constant employment to their arms. These circumstances encouraged the inhabitants of some of the Italian cities, towards the beginning of the eleventh century, to assume new privileges, to unite together more closely, and to form themselves into bodies politick governed by laws established by common consent [a]. The rights, which many cities acquired by bold or fortunate usurpations, others purchased from the Emperors, who deemed themselves gainers when they received large sums for immunities which they were no longer able to withhold; and some cities obtained them gratuitously from the generosity or facility of the Princes on whom they depended. The great increase of wealth which the Crusades brought into Italy, occasioned a new kind of fermentation and activity in the minds of the people, and excited such a general passion for liberty and independence, that before the conclusion of the last Crusade, all the considerable cities in that country had either purchased or had extorted large immunities from the Emperors [P].

[a] Murat. Antiquit. Ital. vol. iv. p. 5.
[P] NOTE XV.

THIS innovation was not long known in Italy before it made its way into France. Louis the Grofs, in order to create some power that might counterbalance those potent vassals who controuled, or gave law to the crown, first adopted the plan of conferring new privileges on the towns situated within his own domaine. These privileges were called *charters of community*, by which he enfranchised the inhabitants, abolished all marks of servitude, and formed them into corporations or bodies politick, to be governed by a council and magistrates of their own nomination. These magistrates had the right of administering justice within their own precincts, of levying taxes, of embodying and training to arms the militia of the town, which took the field when required by the sovereign, under the command of officers appointed by the community. The great barons, imitated the example of their monarch, and granted like immunities to the towns within their territories. They had wasted such great sums in their expeditions to the Holy Land, that they were eager to lay hold on this new expedient for raising money, by the sale of these charters of liberty. Though the institution of communities was as repugnant to their maxims of policy, as it was adverse to their power, they disregarded remote consequences, in order to obtain present relief. In less than two centuries, servitude was abolished in most of the towns in France, and they became free corporations, instead of dependent villages, without jurisdiction or privileges.

Sect. I. vileges [Q]. Much about the same period, the great cities in Germany began to acquire like immunities, and laid the foundation of their present liberty and independence [R]. The practice spread quickly over Europe, and was adopted in Germany, Spain, England, Scotland, and all the other feudal kingdoms [S].

Its happy effects upon the condition of the Inhabitants;

THE good effects of this new institution were immediately felt, and its influence on government as well as manners was no less extensive than salutary. A great body of the people was released from servitude, and from all the arbitrary and grievous impositions to which that wretched condition had subjected them. Towns, upon acquiring the right of community, became so many little republicks, governed by known and equal laws; and liberty was deemed such an essential and characteristic part in their constitution, that if any slave took refuge in one of them, and resided there during a year without being claimed, he was instantly declared a freeman, and admitted as a member of the community ▾.

Upon the power of the nobility;

As one part of the people owed their liberty to the erection of communities, another was indebted to them for their security. Such had been the state of Europe during several centuries, that self-

[Q] NOTE XVI. [R] NOTE XVII.
[S] NOTE XVIII.
▾ Statut. Humberti Bellojoci Dacher. Spicel. vol. ix. 182, 185. Charta Comit. Forens. ibid. 193.

preservation

preservation obliged every man to court the patron- Sect. I.
age of some powerful baron, and in times of danger
his castle was the place to which all resorted for
safety. But towns surrounded with walls, whose
inhabitants were regularly trained to arms, and
bound by interest, as well by the most solemn engagements, reciprocally to defend each other, afforded a more commodious and secure retreat.
The nobles began to be considered as of less importance, when they ceased to be the sole guardians to whom the people could look up for protection against violence.

IF the nobility suffered some diminution of their Upon the
credit and power by the privileges granted to the the crown;
cities, the crown acquired an increase of both. As
there were no regular troops kept on foot in any
of the feudal kingdoms, the Monarch could bring
no army into the field but what was composed of
soldiers furnished by the crown-vassals, always jealous of the regal authority; nor had he any funds
for carrying on the publick service, but such as they
granted him with a very sparing hand. But when
the members of communities were permitted to
bear arms, and were trained to the use of these,
this in some degree supplied the first defect, and
gave the crown the command of a body of men
independent of its great vassals. The attachment
of the cities to their sovereigns, whom they respected as the first authors of their liberties, and
whom they were obliged to court as the protectors

of

SECT. I. of their immunities against the domineering spirit of the nobles, contributed somewhat towards removing the second evil, as, on many occasions, it procured the crown such supplies of money as added new force to government [a].

Upon the increase of industry.

THE acquisition of liberty made such a happy change in the condition of all the members of communities, as roused them from that stupidity and inaction into which they had been sunk by the wretchedness of their former state. The spirit of industry revived. Commerce became an object of attention, and began to flourish. Population increased. Independence was established; and wealth flowed into cities which had long been the seat of poverty and oppression. Wealth was accompanied by its usual attendants, ostentation and luxury; and though the former was inelegant and cumbersome, and the latter indelicate, they led gradually to greater refinement in manners, and in the habits of life. Together with this improvement in manners, a more regular species of government and police was introduced. As cities grew to be more populous, and the occasions of intercourse among men increased, statutes and regulations multiplied of course, and all became sensible that their common safety depended on observing them with exactness, and on punishing such as violated them, with promptitude and rigour. Laws and subordi-

[a] Ordon. des Rois de France, tom. i. 602, 785. tom. ii. 318. 422.

nation, as well as polished manners, took their rise in cities, and diffused themselves insensibly through the rest of the society.

III. The inhabitants of cities having obtained personal freedom and municipal jurisdiction, soon acquired civil liberty and political power. It was a fundamental principle in the feudal system of policy, that no freeman could be governed or taxed unless by his own consent. In consequence of this, the vassals of every baron were called to his court, in which they established, by mutual consent, such regulations as they deemed most beneficial to their small society, and granted their superior such supplies of money, as were proportional to their abilities, or to his wants. The barons themselves, conformably to the same maxim, were admitted into the supreme assembly of the nation, and concurred with the sovereign in enacting laws, or in imposing taxes. As the superior lord, according to the original plan of feudal policy, retained the direct property of those lands which he granted, in temporary possession, to his vassals, the law, even after fiefs became hereditary, still supposed this original practice to subsist, and a baron continued to be considered as the guardian of all who resided within his territories. The great council of each nation, whether distinguished by the name of a parliament, a diet, the Cortes, or the states general, was composed entirely of such barons, and dignified ecclesiasticks, as held immediately of

the

Sect. I. the crown. Towns, whether situated within the royal domaine, or on the lands of a subject, depended for protection on the lord of whom they held. They had no legal name, no political existence, which could entitle them to be admitted into the legislative assembly, or could give them any authority there. But as soon as they were enfranchised, and formed into Bodies Corporate, they became legal and independent members of the constitution, and acquired all the rights essential to freemen. Amongst these, the most valuable, was the privilege of a decisive voice in enacting laws, and in granting subsidies. It was natural for cities, accustomed to a form of municipal government, according to which no regulation could be established, and no money could be raised without their own consent, to claim this privilege. The wealth, the power and consideration which they acquired on recovering their liberty, added weight to their claim; and favourable events happened, or fortunate conjunctures occurred in the different kingdoms of Europe, which facilitated or forwarded their obtaining possession of this important right. In England, one of the first countries in which the representatives of boroughs were admitted into the great council of the nation, the

A. D. 1265. barons who took arms against Henry III. summoned them to attend parliament in order to add greater popularity to their party, and to strengthen the barrier against the encroachment of regal power. In France, Philip the Fair, a Monarch no less sagacious

cious than enterprizing, confidered them as inftruments which might be employed with equal advantage to extend the royal prerogative, to counterbalance the exorbitant power of the nobles, and to facilitate the impofition of new taxes. With thefe views, he introduced the deputies of fuch towns as were formed into communities into the ftates general of the nation[y]. In the Empire, the wealth and immunities of the Imperial cities placed them on a level with the moft confiderable members of the Germanic body. Confcious of their own power and dignity, they pretended to the privilege of forming a feparate bench in the diet; and made good their pretenfion[z].

But in what way foever the reprefentatives of cities firft gained a place in the legiflature, that event had great influence on the form and genius of government. It tempered the rigour of ariftocratical oppreffion, with a proper mixture of popular liberty: It fecured to the great body of the people, who had formerly no reprefentatives, active and powerful guardians of their rights and privileges: It eftablifhed an intermediate power between the King and nobles, to which each had recourfe alternately, and which at fome times oppofed the ufurpations of the former, on other occafions checked the encroachments of the latter. As foon

[y] Pafquier Recherches de la France, p. 81. edit. Par. 1633.
[z] Pfeffel Abregè de l'hiftoire & droit d'Allemagne, p. 408. 451.

SECT. I. as the reprefentatives of communities gained any degree of credit and influence in the legiflature, the fpirit of laws became different from what it had formerly been; it flowed from new principles; it was directed towards new objects; equality, order, the publick good, and the redrefs of grievances, were phrafes and ideas brought into ufe, and which grew to be familiar in the ftatutes and jurifprudence of the European nations. Almoft all the efforts in favour of liberty in every country of Europe, have been made by this new power in the legiflature. In proportion as it rofe to confideration and influence, the feverity of the ariftocratical fpirit decreafed; and the privileges of the people became gradually more extenfive as the ancient and exorbitant jurifdiction of the nobles was abridged [T].

The people acquire liberty by enfranchifements.

IV. THE inhabitants of towns having been declared free by the charters of communities, that part of the people which refided in the country, and was employed in agriculture, began to recover liberty by enfranchifement. During the rigour of feudal government, as hath been already obferved, the great body of the lower people was reduced to fervitude. They were flaves fixed to the foil which they cultivated, and together with it were transferred from one proprietor to another, by fale, or by conveyance. The fpirit of feudal policy did not favour the enfranchifement of that order of men. It was an eftablifhed maxim, that no vaffal

[T] NOTE XIX.

could legally diminish the value of a fief, to the detriment of the lord from whom he had received it. In consequence of this, manumission by the authority of the immediate master was not valid; and unless it was confirmed by the superior lord of whom he held, slaves of this species did not acquire a complete right to their liberty. Thus it became necessary to ascend through all the gradations of feudal holding to the King, the lord Paramount[*]. A form of procedure so tedious and troublesome, discouraged the practice of manumission. Domestic or personal slaves often obtained liberty from the humanity or beneficence of their masters, to whom they belonged in absolute property. The condition of slaves fixed to the soil, was much more unalterable.

But the freedom and independence which one part of the people had obtained by the institution of communities, inspired the other with the most ardent desire of acquiring the same privileges; and their superiors, sensible of the benefits which they themselves had derived from former concessions, were less unwilling to gratify them by the grant of new immunities. The enfranchisement of slaves became more frequent; and the Monarchs of France, prompted by necessity no less than by their inclination to reduce the power of the nobles, endeavoured to render it general. Louis X. and his brother Philip, issued ordinances, declaring,

[*] Etablissemens de St. Louis, liv. ii. ch. 3 § Ordon. tom. i. 383. not. (a).

" That

SECT. I. "That as all men were by nature free-born, and as their kingdom was called the kingdom of Franks, they determined that it should be so in reality as well as in name; therefore they appointed that enfranchisements should be granted throughout the whole kingdom, upon just and reasonable conditions [b]." These edicts were carried into immediate execution within the royal domaine. The example of their sovereigns, together with the expectation of considerable sums which they might raise by this expedient, led many of the nobles to set their dependents at liberty; and servitude was gradually abolished in almost every province of the kingdom [U]. In Italy, the establishment of republican government in their great cities, the genius and maxims of which were extremely different from those of the feudal policy, together with the ideas of equality, which the progress of commerce had rendered familiar, gradually introduced the practice of enfranchising the ancient *predial* slaves. In some provinces of Germany, the persons who had been subject to this species of bondage, were released; in others, the rigour of their state was mitigated. In England, as the spirit of liberty gained ground, the very name and idea of personal servitude, without any formal interposition of the legislature to prohibit it, was totally banished.

[b] Ordon. tom. i. p. 583, 653.

[U] NOTE XX.

The effects of such a remarkable change in the condition of so great a part of the people, could not fail of being considerable and extensive. The husbandman, master of his own industry, and secure of reaping for himself the fruits of his labour, became the farmer of the same fields where he had formerly been compelled to toil for the benefit of another. The odious names of master and of slave, the most mortifying and depressing of all distinctions to human nature, were abolished. New prospects opened, and new incitements to ingenuity and enterprize presented themselves to those who were emancipated. The expectation of bettering their fortune, as well as that of raising themselves to a more honourable condition, concurred in calling forth their activity and genius; and a numerous class of men, who formerly had no political existence, and were employed merely as instruments of labour, became useful citizens, and contributed towards augmenting the force or riches of the society, which adopted them as members.

V. The various expedients which were employed in order to introduce a more regular, equal, and vigorous administration of justice, contributed greatly towards the improvement of society. What was the particular mode of dispensing justice in the several barbarous nations which over-ran the Roman Empire, and took possession of its different provinces, cannot now be determined with certainty. We may conclude from the form of government established among them, as well as from their

Sect. I. their ideas concerning the nature of society, that the authority of the magistrate was extremely limited, and the independence of individuals proportionally great. History and records, as far as these reach back, justify this conclusion, and represent the ideas and exercise of justice in all the countries of Europe, as little different from those which must take place in a state of nature. To maintain the order and tranquillity of society by the regular execution of known laws; to inflict vengeance on crimes destructive of the peace and safety of individuals, by a prosecution carried on in the name, and by the authority of the community; to consider the punishment of criminals as a public example to deter others from violating the laws; were objects of government little understood in theory, and less regarded in practice. The magistrate could scarce be said to hold the sword of justice; it was left in the hands of private persons. Resentment was almost the sole motive for prosecuting crimes; and to gratify that passion, was the end and rule in punishing them. He who suffered the wrong, was the only person who had a right to pursue the aggressor, and to exact or to remit the punishment. From a system of judicial procedure, so crude and defective as seems to be scarce compatible with the subsistence of civil society, disorder and anarchy flowed. Superstition concurred with this ignorance concerning the nature of government, in obstructing the administration of justice, or in rendering it capricious and unequal. To provide remedies for these evils, so

as to give a more regular courſe to juſtice, was, Sect. I.
during ſeveral centuries, one great object of political wiſdom. The regulations for this purpoſe may be reduced to three general heads: To explain theſe, and to point out the manner in which they operated, is an important article in the hiſtory of ſociety among the nations of Europe.

1. The firſt conſiderable ſtep towards eſtabliſhing an equal adminiſtration of juſtice, was the aboliſhment of the right which individuals claimed of waging war with each other, in their own name, and by their own authority. To repel injuries, and to revenge wrongs, is no leſs natural to man than to cultivate friendſhip; and while ſociety remains in its moſt ſimple ſtate, the former is conſidered as a perſonal right no leſs unalienable than the latter. Nor do men in this ſituation deem that they have a title to redreſs their own wrongs alone; they are touched with the injuries of thoſe with whom they are connected, or in whoſe honour they are intereſted; and are no leſs prompt to avenge them. The ſavage, how imperfectly ſoever he may comprehend the principles of political union, feels warmly the ſentiments of ſocial affection, and the obligations ariſing from the ties of blood. On the appearance of an injury or affront offered to his family or tribe, he kindles into rage, and purſues the authors of it with the keeneſt reſentment. He conſiders it as cowardly to expect redreſs from any arm but his own, and as infamous to give up to another the right of determining what repara-

This effected by aboliſhing the practice of private war.

Original ideas of men concerning juſtice.

tion

Sect. I. tion he should accept, or with what vengeance he should rest satisfied.

These lead to the practice of private war.

THE maxims and practice of all uncivilized nations, with respect to the prosecution and punishment of offenders, particularly those of the ancient Germans, and other Barbarians who invaded the Roman Empire, are perfectly conformable to these ideas [c]. While they retained their native simplicity of manners, and continued to be divided into small tribes or societies, the defects in this imperfect system of criminal jurisprudence (if it merits that name) were less sensibly felt. When they came to settle in the extensive provinces which they had conquered, and to form themselves into great monarchies; when new objects of ambition presenting themselves, increased both the number and the violence of their dissensions, they ought to have adopted new maxims concerning the redress of injuries, and to have regulated by general and equal laws, that which they formerly left to be directed by the caprice of private passion. But fierce and haughty chieftains, accustomed to avenge themselves on such as had injured them, did not think of relinquishing a right which they considered as a privilege of their order, and a mark of their independence. Laws enforced by the authority of Princes and Magistrates who possessed little power, commanded no great degree of reverence. The administration of justice among rude

[c] Tacit. de Mor. German. cap. 21. Vell. Patere. lib. ii. c. 113.

illiterate people, was not so accurate, or decisive, or uniform, as to induce men to submit implicitly to its determinations. Every offended baron buckled on his armour, and sought redress at the head of his vassals. His adversary met him in like hostile array. Neither of them appealed to impotent laws, which could afford them no protection. Neither of them would submit points, in which their passions were warmly interested, to the slow determination of a judicial enquiry. Both trusted to their swords for the decision of the contest. The kindred and dependents of the aggressor, as well as of the defender, were involved in the quarrel. They had not even the liberty of remaining neutral. Such as refused to act in concert with the party to which they belonged, were not only exposed to infamy, but subjected to legal penalties.

The different kingdoms of Europe were torn and afflicted, during several centuries, by intestine wars, excited by private animosities, and carried on with all the rage natural to men of fierce manners, and of violent passions. The estate of every baron was a kind of independent territory, disjoined from those around it, and the hostilities between them were perpetual. The evil became so inveterate and deep-rooted, that the form and laws of private war were ascertained, and regulations concerning it made a part in the system of jurisprudence[d], in the same manner as if this practice

[d] Beaumanoir Coutumes de Beauvoisis, ch. 59, et les notes de Thaumassiere, p. 447.

SECT. I. had been founded in some natural right of humanity, or in the original constitution of civil society.

Various methods employed in order to abolish it.

So great was the disorder, and such the calamities which these perpetual hostilities occasioned, that various efforts were made to wrest from the nobles this pernicious privilege which they claimed. It was the interest of every sovereign to abolish a practice which almost annihilated his authority. Charlemagne prohibited it by an express law, as an invention of the devil to destroy the order and happiness of society[*]; but the reign of one Monarch, however vigorous and active, was too short to extirpate a custom so firmly established. Instead of enforcing this prohibition, his feeble successors durst venture on nothing more than to apply palliatives. They declared it unlawful for any person to commence war, until he had sent a formal defiance to the kindred and dependents of his adversary; they ordained that, after the commission of the trespass or crime which gave rise to a private war, forty days must elapse before the person injured should attack the vassals of his adversary; they enjoined all persons to suspend their private animosities, and to cease from hostilities when the King was engaged in any war against the enemies of the nation. The church co-operated with the civil magistrate, and interposed its authority in order to extirpate a practice so repugnant to the spirit of Christianity. Various councils issued decrees, prohibiting all private wars; and

[*] Capitul. A. D. 801. Edit. Baluz. Vol. i. p. 371.

denounced

denounced the heaviest anathemas against such as should disturb the tranquillity of society, by claiming or exercising that barbarous right. The aid of religion was called in to combat and subdue the ferocity of the times. The Almighty was said to have manifested, by visions and revelations to different persons, his disapprobation of that spirit of revenge, which armed one part of his creatures against the other. Men were required, in the name of God, to sheath their swords, and to remember the sacred ties which united them as Christians, and as members of the same society. But this junction of civil and ecclesiastic authority, though strengthened by every thing most apt to alarm and to overawe the credulous spirit, of those ages, produced no other effect than some temporary suspensions of hostilities, and a cessation from war on certain days and seasons consecrated to the more solemn acts of devotion. The nobles continued to assert this dangerous privilege; they refused to obey some of the laws calculated to annul or circumscribe it; they eluded others; they petitioned; they remonstrated; they struggled for the right of private war as the highest and most honourable distinction of their order. Even so late as the fourteenth century, we find the nobles in several provinces of France contending for their ancient method of terminating their differences by the sword, in preference to that of submitting them to the decision of any judge. The final abolition of this practice in that kingdom, and the other countries in which it prevailed, is not to be ascribed so much to the force of statutes

56 A VIEW OF THE

SECT. I. tutes and decrees, as to the gradual increase of the royal authority, and to the imperceptible progress of juster sentiments concerning government, order, and public security [X].

The prohibition of trial by judicial combat, another improvement in the administration of justice.

2. THE prohibition of the form of trial by judicial combat, was another considerable step towards the introduction of such regular government as secured publick order and private tranquillity. As the right of private war left many of the quarrels among individuals to be decided, like those between nations, by arms; the form of trial by judicial combat, which was established in every country of Europe, banished equity from courts of justice, and rendered chance or force the arbiter of their determinations. In civilized nations, all transactions of any importance are concluded in writing.

Defects in the judicial proceedings of the middle ages.

The exhibition of the deed or instrument is full evidence of the fact, and ascertains with precision what each party has stipulated to perform. But among a rude people, when the arts of reading and writing were such uncommon attainments, that to be master of either, intitled a person to the appellation of a clerk or learned man, scarcely any thing was committed to writing but treaties between Princes, their grants and charters to their subjects, or such transactions between private parties as were of extraordinary consequence, or had an extensive effect. The greater part of affairs in common life and business, were carried on by verbal con-

[X] NOTE XXI.

tracts

tracts or promises. This, in many civil questions, not only made it difficult to bring proof sufficient to establish any claim, but encouraged falsehood and fraud by rendering them extremely easy. Even in criminal cases, where a particular fact must be ascertained, or an accusation be disproved, the nature and effect of legal evidence was little understood by barbarous nations. To define with accuracy that species of evidence which a court had reason to expect; to determine when it ought to insist on positive proof, and when it should be satisfied with a proof from circumstances; to compare the testimony of discordant witnesses; and to fix the degree of credit due to each; were discussions too intricate and subtile for the jurisprudence of ignorant ages. In order to avoid encumbering themselves with these, a more simple form of procedure was introduced into courts as well civil as criminal. In all cases, where the notoriety of the fact did not furnish the clearest and most direct evidence, the person accused, or he against whom an action was brought, was called legally, or offered voluntarily to purge himself by oath; and upon his declaring his innocence, he was instantly acquitted [f]. This absurd practice effectually screened guilt and fraud from detection or punishment, by rendering the temptation to perjury so powerful, that it was not easy to resist it. The pernicious effects of it were sensibly felt; and in order to guard

[f] Leg. Burgund. Tit. 8, & 45. Leg. Aleman. Tit. 89. Leg. Baiwar. Tit. 8. § 5. 2. &c.

SECT. I. against them, the laws ordained, that oaths should be administered with great solemnity, and accompanied with every circumstance which could inspire religious reverence, or superstitious terror [g]. This, however, proved a feeble remedy: these ceremonious rites became familiar, and their impression on the imagination gradually diminished; men who could venture to disregard truth, were not apt to startle at the solemnities of an oath. Their observation of this, put legislators upon devising a new expedient for rendering the purgation by oath more certain and satisfactory. They required the person accused to appear with a certain number of freemen, his neighbours or relations, who corroborated the oath which he took, by swearing that they believed all that he had uttered to be true. These were called *Compurgators*, and their number varied according to the importance of the subject in dispute, or the nature of the crime with which a person was charged [h]. In some cases, the concurrence of no less than three hundred of these auxiliary witnesses was requisite to acquit the person accused [i]. But even this device was found to be ineffectual. It was a point of honour with every man in Europe, during several ages, not to desert the chief on whom he depended, and to stand by those with whom the ties of blood connected him. Whoever then was bold enough to violate

[g] Du Cange Glossar. voc. *Juramentum*, vol. iii. p. 1607. Edit. Benedict. [h] Du Cange, ibid. vol. iii. p. 1599.
[i] Spelman Glossar. voc. *Assath*. Gregor. Turon. Hist. lib. viii. c. 9.

the laws, was sure of devoted adherents, willing to abet, and eager to serve him in whatever manner he required. The formality of calling Compurgators, proved an apparent, not a real security, against falsehood and perjury; and the sentences of courts, while they continued to refer every point in question to the oath of the defendant, became so flagrantly iniquitous as excited universal indignation against this method of procedure [k].

SENSIBLE of these defects, but strangers to the manner of correcting them, or of introducing a more proper form, our ancestors, as an infallible method of discovering truth, and of guarding against deception, appealed to Heaven, and referred every point in dispute to be determined, as they imagined, by the decisions of unerring wisdom and impartial justice. The person accused, in order to prove his innocence, submitted, in some cases, to trial, by plunging his arm in boiling water; by lifting a red-hot iron with his naked hand; by walking bare-foot over burning plough-shares; or by other experiments equally perilous and formidable. On other occasions, he challenged his accuser to fight him in single combat. All these various forms of trial were conducted with many devout ceremonies; the ministers of religion were employed, the Almighty was called upon to interpose for the manifestation of guilt, and for the protection of innocence; and whoever escaped unhurt, or came off victorious,

[k] Leg. Langobard. lib. ii. tit. 55. § 34.

Sect. I. was pronounced to be acquitted by the *Judgment of God*[1].

The introduction of this practice favoured by the superstition of the middle ages.

AMONG all the whimsical and absurd institutions which owe their existence to the weakness of human reason, this, which submitted questions that affected the property, the reputation, and the lives of men, to the determination of chance, or of bodily strength and address, appears to be the most extravagant and preposterous. There were circumstances, however, which led the nations of Europe to consider this equivocal mode of deciding any point in contest, as a direct appeal to heaven, and a certain method of discovering its will. As men are unable to comprehend the manner in which the Almighty carries on the government of the universe, by equal, fixed, and general laws, they are apt to imagine, that in every case which their passions or interest render important in their own eyes, the Supreme Ruler of all ought visibly to display his power, in vindicating innocence and punishing vice. It requires no inconsiderable degree of science and philosophy to correct this popular error. But the sentiments prevalent in Europe during the dark ages, instead of correcting, strengthened it. Religion, for several centuries, consisted chiefly in believing the legendary history of those saints whose names croud and disgrace the Romish calendar. The fabulous tales concerning their miracles, had been declared authentic by the bulls of Popes, and

[1] Murat. Dissertatio de judiciis Dei. Antiquit. Italic. vol. iii. p. 612.

the decrees of councils; they made the great sub- Sect. I.
ject of the instructions which the clergy offered to
the people, and were received by them with implicit credulity and admiration. By these, men
were accustomed to believe that the established
laws of nature might be violated on the most frivolous occasions, and were taught to look rather
for particular and extraordinary acts of power under the divine administration, than to contemplate
the regular progress and execution of a general
plan. One superstition prepared the way for another; and whoever believed that the Supreme Being
had interposed miraculously on those trivial occasions mentioned in legends, could not but expect
his intervention in matters of greater importance,
when solemnly referred to his decision.

WITH this superstitious opinion, the martial *And likewise by their martial spirit.*
spirit of Europe, during the middle ages, concurred
in establishing the mode of trial by judicial combat. To be ready to maintain with his sword
whatever his lips had uttered, was the first maxim
of honour with every gentleman. To assert their
own rights by force of arms, to inflict vengeance
on those who had injured or affronted them, were
the distinction and pride of high-spirited nobles.
The form of trial by combat coinciding with this
maxim, flattered and gratified these passions. Every
man was the guardian of his own honour, and of
his own life; the justice of his cause, as well as his
future reputation, depended on his own courage
and prowess. This mode of decision was considered,

SECT. I. sidered, accordingly, as one of the happiest efforts of wise policy; and as soon as it was introduced, all the forms of trial by fire or water, and other superstitious experiments, fell into disuse, or were employed only in controversies between persons of inferior rank. The trial by combat was authorized over all Europe, and received in every country with equal satisfaction. Not only questions concerning uncertain or contested facts, but general and abstract points in law, were determined by the issue of a combat; and the latter was deemed a method of discovering truth more liberal as well as more satisfactory, than that by examination and argument. Not only might parties, whose minds were exasperated by the eagerness and the hostility of opposition, defy their antagonist, and require him to make good his charge, or to prove his innocence, with his sword; but witnesses, who had no interest in the issue of the question, though called to declare the truth by laws which ought to have afforded them protection, were equally exposed to the danger of a challenge, and equally bound to assert the veracity of their evidence by dint of arms. To complete the absurdities of this military jurisprudence, even the character of a judge was not sacred from its violence. Any one of the parties might interrupt a judge when about to deliver his opinion; might accuse him of iniquity and corruption in the most reproachful terms, and throwing down his gauntlet, might challenge him to defend his integrity in the field; nor could he, without infamy, refuse

to

to accept the defiance, or decline to enter the lifts against such an adversary.

Thus the form of trial by combat, like other abuses, spread gradually, and extended to all persons, and almost to all cases. Ecclesiastics, women, minors, superannuated and infirm persons, who could not with decency or justice be compelled to take arms, and to maintain their own cause, were obliged to produce champions, whom they engaged, by affection or rewards, to fight their battles. The solemnities of a judicial combat were such as were natural in an action, which was considered both as a formal appeal to God, and as the final decision of questions of the highest moment. Every circumstance relating to them, was regulated by the edicts of Princes, and explained in the comments of lawyers, with a minute and even superstitious accuracy. Skill in these laws and rites was the only science of which warlike nobles boasted, or which they were ambitious to attain [a].

By this barbarous custom, the natural course of proceeding, both in civil and criminal questions, was entirely perverted. Force usurped the place of equity in courts of judicature, and justice was banished from her proper mansion. Discernment, learning, integrity, were qualities less necessary to a judge than bodily strength and dexterity in the

[a] See a curious discourse concerning the laws of judicial combat, by Thomas of Woodstock, Duke of Gloucester, uncle to Richard II. in Spelman's Gloffar. voc. *Campus*.

Sect. I. use of arms. Daring courage, and superior vigour or address, were of more moment towards securing the favourable issue of a suit, than the equity of a cause, or the clearness of the evidence. Men, of course, applied themselves to cultivate the talents which they found to be of greatest utility. As strength of body and address in arms were no less requisite in those lists which they were obliged to enter in defence of their private rights, than in the field of battle, where they met the enemies of their country, it became the great object of education, as well as the chief employment in life, to acquire these martial accomplishments. The administration of justice, instead of accustoming men to listen to the voice of equity, or to reverence the decisions of law, added to the ferocity of their manners, and taught them to consider force as the great arbiter of right and wrong.

Various expedients for abolishing this practice. THESE pernicious effects of the trial by combat were so obvious, that they did not altogether escape the view of the unobserving age in which it was introduced. The clergy, from the beginning, remonstrated against it as repugnant to the spirit of Christianity, and subversive of justice and order[a]. But the maxims and passions which favoured it, had taken such hold of the minds of men, that they disregarded admonitions and censures, which, on other occasions, would have struck them with terror. The evil was too great and inveterate to yield to that remedy, and continuing to increase,

[a] Du Cange Glossar. voc. *Duellum*, vol. ii. p. 1675.

the civil power at length found it necessary to interpose. Conscious, however, of their own limited authority, monarchs proceeded with caution, and their first attempts to restrain, or to set any bounds to this practice, were extremely feeble. One of the earliest restrictions of this practice which occurs in the history of Europe, is that of Henry I. of England. It extended no farther than to prohibit the trial by combat in questions concerning property of small value.*. Louis VII. of France imitated his example, and issued an edict to the same effect[†]. St. Louis, whose ideas as a legislator were far superior to those of his age, endeavoured to introduce a more perfect jurisprudence, and to substitute the trial by evidence, in place of that by combat. But his regulations, with respect to this, were confined to his own domains; for the great vassals of the crown possessed such independent authority, and were so fondly attached to the ancient practice, that he durst not venture to extend it to the whole kingdom. Some barons voluntarily adopted his regulations. The spirit of courts of justice became averse to the mode of decision by combat, and discouraged it on every occasion. The nobles, nevertheless, thought it so honourable to depend for the security of their lives and fortunes on their own courage alone, and contended with so much vehemence for the preservation of this favourite privilege of their order, that the suc-

* Brussel Usage des Fiefs. vol. ii. p. 961.
† Ordon. tom. i. p. 16.

Sect. I. cessors of St. Louis, unable to oppose, and afraid of offending such powerful subjects, were obliged not only to tolerate, but to authorize the practice which he had attempted to abolish [1]. In other countries of Europe, efforts equally zealous were employed to maintain the established custom; and similar concessions were extorted from their respective sovereigns. It continued, however, to be an object of policy with every monarch of abilities or vigour, to explode the trial by combat; and various edicts were issued for this purpose. But the observation which was made concerning the right of private war, is equally applicable to the mode of trial under review. No custom, how absurd soever it may be, if it has subsisted long, or derives its force from the manners and prejudices of the age in which it prevails, was ever abolished by the bare promulgation of laws and statutes. The sentiments of the people must change, or some new power sufficient to counteract it must be introduced. Such a change, accordingly, took place in Europe, as science gradually increased, and society advanced towards more perfect order. In proportion as the prerogative of Princes extended, and came to acquire new force, a power, interested in suppressing every practice favourable to the independence of the nobles, was introduced. The struggle, nevertheless, subsisted for several centuries; sometimes the new regulations and ideas seemed to gain ground; sometimes ancient habits recurred; and though, upon the whole, the trial

[1] Ordon. tom. i. p. 328, 390, 435.

by

by combat went more and more into difuse, yet inflances of it occur, as late as the sixteenth century, in the history both of France and of England. In proportion as it declined, the regular administration of justice was restored, the proceedings of courts were directed by known laws, the study of these became an object of attention to judges, and the people of Europe advanced fast towards civility, when this great cause of the ferocity of their manners was removed [Y].

3. By authorizing the right of appeal from the courts of the Barons to those of the King, and subjecting the decisions of the former to the review of the latter, a new step, not less considerable than these which I have already mentioned, was taken towards establishing the regular, consistent, and vigorous administration of justice. Among all the encroachments of the feudal nobles on the prerogative of their Monarchs, their usurping the administration of justice with supreme authority, both in civil and criminal causes, within the precincts of their own estates, was the most singular. In other nations, subjects have contended with their Princes, and have endeavoured to extend their own power and privileges; but in the history of their struggles and pretensions, we discover nothing similar to this right which the feudal barons claimed, and acquired. It must have been something peculiar in their genius and manners that suggested this idea, and prompted

The privilege of appealing from the courts of the barons, another great improvement in the administration of justice.

Origin of the supreme and independent jurisdiction of the nobility.

[Y] NOTE XXII.

them

Sect I. them to infist on such a claim. Among the rude people who conquered the various provinces of the Roman Empire, and established new kingdoms there, the passion of resentment, too impetuous to bear controul, was permitted to remain almost unrestrained by the authority of laws. The person offended, as has been observed, retained not only the right of prosecuting but of punishing his adversary. To him it belonged to inflict such vengeance as satiated his rage, or to accept of such satisfaction as appeased it. But while fierce barbarians continued to be the sole judges in their own cause, their enmities were implacable, and immortal; they set no bounds either to the degree of their vengeance, or to the duration of their resentment. The excesses which this occasioned, proved so destructive of peace and order in society, as forced them to think of some remedy. At first, arbiters interposed, and by persuasion or intreaty prevailed on the party offended to accept of a fine or composition from the aggressor, and to drop all farther prosecution. But as submission to persons who had no legal or magisterial authority was altogether voluntary, it became necessary to establish judges with power sufficient to enforce their own decisions. The leader whom they were accustomed to follow and to obey, whose courage they respected, and in whose integrity they placed confidence, was the person to whom a martial people naturally committed this important prerogative. Every chieftain was the commander of his tribe in war, and their

judge

judge in peace. Every baron led his vassals to
the field, and administered justice to them in his
hall. Their high-spirited dependents would not
have recognized any other authority, or have submitted to any other jurisdiction. But in times of
turbulence and violence, the exercise of this new
function was attended not only with trouble, but
with danger. No person could assume the character of a judge, if he did not possess power sufficient to protect the one party from the violence
of private revenge, and to compel the other to
accept of such reparation as he enjoined. In consideration of the extraordinary efforts which this
office required, judges, besides the fine which they
appointed to be paid as a compensation to the
person or family who had been injured, levied an
additional sum as a recompence for their own
labour; and in all the feudal kingdoms the latter
was as precisely ascertained, and as regularly exacted, as the former.

Thus, by the natural operation of circumstances peculiar to the manners or political state of the feudal nations, separate and territorial jurisdictions came not only to be established in every kingdom, but were established in such a way, that the interest of the barons concurred with their ambition in maintaining and extending them. It was not merely a point of honour with the feudal nobles to dispense justice to their vassals; but from the exercise of that power arose one capital branch of their revenue; and the emoluments of their courts

SECT. I. were frequently the main support of their dignity. It was with infinite zeal that they asserted and defended this high privilege of their order. By this institution, however, every kingdom in Europe was split into as many separate principalities as it contained powerful barons. Their vassals, whether in peace or in war, were hardly sensible of any authority, but that of their superior lord. They felt themselves subject to no other command. They were amenable to no other jurisdiction. The ties which linked together these smaller confederacies became close and firm; the bonds of public union relaxed, or were dissolved. The nobles strained their invention in devising regulations that tended to ascertain and perpetuate this distinction. In order to guard against any appearance of subordination in their courts to those of the crown, they constrained their monarchs to prohibit the royal judges from entering their territories, or from claiming any jurisdiction there; and if, either through mistake, or from the spirit of encroachment, any royal judge ventured to extend his authority to the vassals of a baron, they might plead their right of exemption, and the lord of whom they held could not only rescue them out of his hands, but was intitled to legal reparation for the injury and affront offered to him. The jurisdiction of the royal judges scarcely reached beyond the narrow limits of the King's demesnes. Instead of a regular gradation of courts, all acknowledging the authority of the same general laws, and looking up to these

as

as the guides of their decisions, there were in
every feudal kingdom a thousand independent tribunals, the proceedings of which were directed by
local customs and contradictory forms. The collision of jurisdiction between these numerous
courts often retarded the execution of justice.
The variety and caprice of their modes of procedure must have for ever kept the administration
of it from attaining any degree of uniformity or
perfection.

Expedients employed in order to limit or abolish it.

ALL the monarchs of Europe perceived these encroachments on their jurisdiction, and bore them with impatience. But the usurpations of the nobles were so firmly established, and the danger of endeavouring to overturn them by open force was so manifest, that they were obliged to remain satisfied with attempts to undermine them. Various expedients were employed for this purpose; each of which merit attention, as they mark the progress of law and equity in the several kingdoms of Europe. At first, Princes endeavoured to circumscribe the jurisdiction of the barons, by permitting them to take cognizance only of smaller offences, reserving those of greater moment, under the appellation of *Pleas of the Crown*, and *Royal Causes*, to be tried in the King's courts. This affected only the barons of inferior note; the more powerful nobles scorned such a distinction, and not only claimed unlimited jurisdiction, but obliged their sovereigns to grant them charters, conveying or recognizing this privilege in the most ample form. The attempt, neverthelefs, was productive of fome good confequences, and paved the way for more. It turned the attention of men towards a jurifdiction diftinct from that of the baron whofe vaffals they were; it accuftomed them to the pretenfions of fuperiority which the crown claimed over territorial judges; and taught them, when oppreffed by their own fuperior lord, to look up to their fovereign as their protector. This facilitated the introduction of appeals, by which Princes brought the decifions of the baron's courts under the review of the royal judges. While trial by combat fubfifted in full vigour, no point decided according to that mode, could be brought under the review of another court. It had been referred to the judgment of God; the iffue of battle had declared his will; and it would have been impious to have called in queftion the equity of the divine decifion. But as foon as that barbarous cuftom began to fall into difufe, Princes encouraged the vaffals of the barons to fue for redrefs, by appealing to the royal courts. The progrefs of this practice, however, was flow and gradual. The firft inftances of appeals were on account of *the delay*, or *the refufal of juftice* in the baron's court; and as thefe were countenanced by the ideas of fubordination in the feudal conftitution, the nobles allowed them to be introduced without much oppofition. But when thefe were followed by appeals on account of *the injuftice* or *iniquity of the fentence*, the nobles then began to be fenfible, that if this innovation became general,

general, the shadow of power alone would remain in their hands, and all real authority and jurisdiction would center in those courts which possessed the right of review. They instantly took the alarm, remonstrated against the encroachment, and contended boldly for their ancient privileges. But the monarchs in the different kingdoms of Europe pursued their plan with steadiness and prudence. Though forced to suspend their operations on some occasions, and seemingly to yield when any formidable confederacy of their vassals united against them, they resumed their measures as soon as they observed the nobles to be remiss or feeble, and pushed them with vigour. They appointed the royal courts, which originally were ambulatory, and irregular with respect to their times of meeting, to be held in a fixed place, and at stated seasons. They were solicitous to name judges of more distinguished abilities than such as presided in the courts of the barons. They added dignity to their character, and splendour to their assemblies. They laboured to render their forms regular, and their decrees consistent. Such judicatories became, of course, the objects of public confidence as well as veneration. The people, relinquishing the partial tribunals of their lords, were eager to bring every subject of contest under the more equal and discerning eye of those whom their sovereign had chosen to give judgment in his name. Thus Kings became once more the heads of the community, and the dispensers of

justice

SECT. I. justice to their subjects. The barons, in some kingdoms, ceased to exercise their right of jurisdiction, because it sunk into contempt; in others, it was circumscribed by such regulations as rendered it innocent, or it was entirely abolished by express statutes. Thus the administration of justice taking its rise from one source, and following one direction, held its course in every state with more uniformity, and with greater force [Z].

The regulations of the canon law promote a more perfect administration.

VI. THE forms and maxims of the canon law, which were become universally respectable from their authority in the spiritual courts, contributed not a little towards these improvements in jurisprudence which I have enumerated. If the canon law be considered politically, either as a system framed on purpose to assist the clergy in usurping powers and jurisdiction no less repugnant to the nature of their function, than inconsistent with the order of government; or as the chief instrument in establishing the dominion of the Popes, which shook the throne, and endangered the liberties of every kingdom in Europe, we must pronounce it one of the most formidable engines ever formed against the happiness of civil society. But if we contemplate it merely as a code of laws respecting the rights and property of individuals, and attend only to the civil effects of its decisions

The progress of ecclesiastical usurpation.

concerning these, we must view it in a different, and a much more favourable light. In ages of

[Z] NOTE XXIII.

ignorance

ignorance and credulity, the ministers of religion are the objects of superstitious veneration. When the barbarians who over-ran the Empire first embraced the Christian faith, they found the clergy in possession of considerable power; and they naturally transferred to these new guides the profound submission and reverence which they were accustomed to yield to the priests of that religion which they had forsaken. They deemed their persons to be as sacred as their function; and would have considered it as impious to subject them to the profane jurisdiction of the laity. The clergy were not blind to the advantages which the weakness of mankind afforded them. They established courts, in which every question relating to their own character, their function, or their property, was tried. They pleaded, and obtained an almost total exemption from the authority of civil judges. Upon different pretexts, and by a multiplicity of artifices, they communicated this privilege to so many persons, and extended their jurisdiction to such a variety of cases, that the greater part of those affairs which give rise to contest and litigation, was drawn under the cognizance of the spiritual courts.

But in order to dispose the laity to suffer these usurpations without murmuring or opposition, it was necessary to convince them, that the administration of justice would be rendered more perfect by the establishment of this new jurisdiction.

The plan of ecclesiastical jurisprudence more perfect than that in the civil courts.

This

Sect. I. This was not a difficult undertaking, at the period when the clergy carried on their encroachments with the greatest success. That scanty portion of science which served to guide men in the ages of darkness, was wholly engrossed by the clergy. They alone were accustomed to read, to enquire, and to reason. Whatever knowledge of ancient jurisprudence had been preserved, either by tradition, or in such books as had escaped the destructive rage of barbarians, was possessed only by them. Upon the maxims of that excellent system, they founded a code of laws consonant to the great principles of equity. Being directed by fixed and known rules, the forms of their courts were ascertained, and their decisions became uniform and consistent. Nor did they want authority sufficient to enforce their sentences. Excommunication and other ecclesiastical censures, were punishments more formidable than any that civil judges could inflict in support of their decrees.

The good effects of imitating and adopting it.

It is not surprizing, then, that ecclesiastical jurisprudence should become such an object of admiration and respect; that exemption from civil jurisdiction was courted as a privilege, and conferred as a reward. It is not surprizing, that even to rude people, the maxims of the canon law should appear more equal and just than that ill-digested jurisprudence which directed all proceedings in the civil courts. According to the latter, the differences between contending barons were terminated,

terminated, as in a state of nature, by the sword; according to the former, every matter was subjected to the decision of laws. The one, by permitting judicial combats, left chance and force to be arbiters of right or wrong, of truth or falsehood; the other, passed judgment with respect to these by the maxims of equity, and the testimony of witnesses. Any error or iniquity in a sentence pronounced by a baron to whom feudal jurisdiction belonged, was irremediable, because originally it was subject to the review of no superior tribunal; the ecclesiastical law established a regular gradation of courts, through all which a cause might be carried by appeal, until it was determined by that authority which was held to be supreme in the church. Thus the genius and principles of the canon law prepared men for approving these three great alterations in the feudal jurisprudence which I have mentioned. But it was not with respect to these points alone that the canon law suggested improvements beneficial to society. Many of the regulations, now deemed the barriers of personal security, or the safeguards of private property, are, contrary to the spirit, and repugnant to the maxims of the civil jurisprudence, known in Europe during several centuries, and were borrowed from the rules and practice of the ecclesiastical courts. By observing the wisdom and equity of the decisions in these courts, men began to perceive the necessity either of deserting the martial

tribunals

SECT. I. tribunals of the barons, or of attempting to reform them [AA].

The revival of the Roman law contributes more liberal ideas concerning justice and order.

VII. THE revival of the knowledge and study of the Roman law co-operated with the causes which I have mentioned, in introducing more just and liberal ideas concerning the nature of government, and the administration of justice. Among the calamities which the devastations of the barbarians who broke in upon the Empire brought upon mankind, one of the greatest was their overturning the system of Roman jurisprudence, the noblest monument of the wisdom of that great people, formed to subdue and to govern the world. The laws and regulations of a civilized community, were altogether repugnant to the manners and ideas of these fierce invaders. They had respect to objects, of which a rude people had no conception; and were adapted to a state of society with which they were entirely unacquainted. For this reason, wherever they settled, the Roman jurisprudence soon sunk into oblivion, and lay buried for some centuries under the load of those institutions which the inhabitants of Europe dignified with the name of laws. But towards the middle of the twelfth century, a copy of Justinian's Pandects was accidentally discovered in Italy. By that time, the state of society was so far advanced, and the ideas of men so much en-

The circumstances from which the Roman law fell into oblivion.

[AA] NOTE XXIV.

larged

larged and improved by the occurrences of several centuries, during which they had continued in political union, that they were struck with admiration of a system which their ancestors could not comprehend. Though they had not hitherto attained such a degree of refinement, as to catch from the ancients a relish for true philosophy, or speculative science; though they were still insensible to the beauty and elegance of classical composition; they were sufficiently qualified to judge with respect to the merit of their system of laws, in which all the points most interesting to mankind, and the chief objects of their attention in every age, were settled with discernment, precision and equity. All men of letters studied this new science with eagerness; and within a few years after the discovery of the Pandects, professors of civil law were appointed, who taught it publickly in most countries of Europe.

Sect. I. Circumstances which favoured the revival of it.

The effects of having such a perfect model to study and to imitate were soon manifest. Men, as soon as they were acquainted with fixed and general laws, perceived the advantage of them, and became impatient to ascertain the principles and forms by which judges should regulate their decisions. Such was the ardour with which they carried on an undertaking of so great importance to society, that before the close of the twelfth century, the feudal law was reduced into a regular system; the code of canon law was enlarged and methodized;

The effects of this upon the ideas of men, and the dispensation of justice.

methodized; and the loose uncertain customs of different provinces or kingdoms were collected and arranged with an order and accuracy acquired from the knowledge of Roman jurisprudence. In some countries of Europe the Roman law was adopted as subsidiary to their own municipal law; and all cases to which the latter did not extend, were decided according to the principles of the former. In others, the maxims as well as forms of Roman jurisprudence mingled imperceptibly with the laws of the country, and had a powerful, though less sensible, influence, in improving and perfecting them [BB].

From all these arose a distinction in professions.

THESE various improvements in the system of jurisprudence, and administration of justice, occasioned a change in manners, of great importance, and of extensive effect. They gave rise to a distinction of professions; they obliged men to cultivate different talents, and to aim at different accomplishments, in order to qualify themselves for the various departments and functions which became necessary in society'. Among uncivilized nations, there is but one profession honourable, that of arms. All the ingenuity and vigour of the human mind are exerted in acquiring military skill, or address. The functions of peace are few and simple; and require no particular course of

[BB] NOTE XXV.

' Dr. Ferguson's Essay on the History of Civil Society, part iv. sect. 1.

education

education or of study, as a preparation for discharging them. This was the state of Europe during several centuries. Every gentleman, born a soldier, scorned any other occupation; he was taught no science but that of war; even his exercises and pastimes were feats of martial prowess. Nor did the judicial character, which persons of noble birth were alone intitled to assume, demand any degree of knowledge beyond that which such untutored soldiers possessed. To recollect a few traditionary customs which time had confirmed, and rendered respectable; to mark out the lists of battle with due formality; to observe the issue of the combat; and to pronounce whether it had been conducted according to the laws of arms; included every thing that a baron, who acted as a judge, found it necessary to understand.

But when the forms of legal proceedings were fixed, when the rules of decision were committed to writing, and collected into a body, law became a science, the knowledge of which required a regular course of study, together with long attention to the practice of courts. Martial and illiterate nobles, had neither leisure nor inclination to undertake a task so laborious, as well as so foreign from all the occupations which they deemed entertaining, or suitable to their rank. They gradually relinquished their places in courts of justice, where their ignorance exposed them to contempt. They became weary of attending to the discussion

SECT. I. of cases, which grew too intricate for them to comprehend. Not only the judicial determination of points which were the subject of controversy, but the conduct of all legal business and transactions was committed to persons trained by previous study and application to the knowledge of law. An order of men, to whom their fellow-citizens had daily recourse for advice, and to whom they looked up for decision in their most important concerns, naturally acquired consideration and influence in society. They were advanced to honours which had been considered as the peculiar rewards of military virtue. They were entrusted with offices of the highest dignity, and most extensive power. Thus, another profession than that of arms, came to be introduced among the laity, and was reputed honourable. The functions of civil life were attended to. The talents requisite for discharging them were cultivated. A new road was opened to wealth and eminence. The arts and virtues of peace were placed in their proper rank, and received their due recompence [CC].

The spirit of chivalry introduces more liberal sentiments, and more generous manners.

VIII. WHILE improvements so important with respect to the state of society and the administration of justice, gradually made progress in Europe, sentiments more liberal and generous had begun to animate the nobles. These were inspired by the spirit of Chivalry, which, though considered, commonly, as a wild institution, the effect of

[CC] NOTE XXVI.

caprice,

caprice, and the source of extravagance, arose naturally from the state of society at that period, and had a very serious influence in refining the manners of the European nations. The feudal state was a state of perpetual war, rapine, and anarchy; during which the weak and unarmed were exposed every moment to insults or injuries. The power of the sovereign was too limited to prevent these wrongs, and the administration of justice too feeble to redress them. There was scarcely any protection against violence and oppression, but what the valour and generosity of private persons afforded. The same spirit of enterprize which had prompted so many gentlemen to take arms in defence of the oppressed pilgrims in Palestine, incited others to declare themselves the patrons and avengers of injured innocence at home. When the final reduction of the Holy Land under the dominion of Infidels put an end to these foreign expeditions, the latter was the only employment left for the activity and courage of adventurers. To check the insolence of overgrown oppressors; to succour the distressed; to rescue the helpless from captivity; to protect, or to avenge women, orphans, and ecclesiastics, who could not bear arms in their own defence; to redress wrongs, and to remove grievances; were deemed acts of the highest prowess and merit. Valour, humanity, courtesy, justice, honour, were the characteristic qualities of chivalry. To these were added religion, which mingled itself with every passion and institution during the middle ages,

Sect. I. ages, and by infusing a large proportion of enthusiastic zeal, gave them such force, as carried them to romantic excess. Men were trained to knighthood by a long previous discipline; they were admitted into the order by solemnities no less devout than pompous; every person of noble birth courted that honour; it was deemed a distinction superior to royalty; and monarchs were proud to receive it from the hands of private gentlemen.

Its beneficial effects.

THIS singular institution, in which valour, gallantry, and religion, were so strangely blended, was wonderfully adapted to the taste and genius of martial nobles; and its effects were soon visible in their manners. War was carried on with less ferocity, when humanity came to be deemed the ornament of knighthood no less than courage. More gentle and polished manners were introduced, when courtesy was recommended as the most amiable of knightly virtues. Violence and oppression decreased, when it was reckoned meritorious to check and to punish them. A scrupulous adherence to truth, with the most religious attention to fulfil every engagement, became the distinguishing characteristic of a gentleman, because chivalry was regarded as the school of honour, and inculcated the most delicate sensibility with respect to that point. The admiration of these qualities, together with the high distinctions and prerogatives conferred on knighthood in every part of Europe, inspired persons of noble birth on

some

some occasions with a species of military fanaticism, and led them to extravagant enterprizes. But they imprinted deeply in their minds the principles of generosity and honour. These were strengthened by every thing that can affect the senses, or touch the heart. The wild exploits of those romantic knights who sallied forth in quest of adventures, are well known, and have been treated with proper ridicule. The political and permanent effects of the spirit of chivalry have been less observed. Perhaps, the humanity which accompanies all the operations of war, the refinements of gallantry, and the point of honour, the three chief circumstances which distinguish modern from ancient manners, may be ascribed in a great measure to this whimsical institution, seemingly of little benefit to mankind. The sentiments which chivalry inspired, had a wonderful influence on manners and conduct during the twelfth, thirteenth, fourteenth, and fifteenth centuries. They were so deeply rooted, that they continued to operate after the vigour and reputation of the institution itself began to decline. Some considerable transactions, recorded in the following history, resemble the adventurous exploits of chivalry, rather than the well regulated operations of sound policy. Some of the most eminent personages, whose characters will be delineated, were strongly tinctured with this romantic spirit. Francis I. was ambitious to distinguish himself by all the qualities of an accomplished knight, and endeavoured

Sect. I. deavoured to imitate the enterprizing genius of chivalry in war, as well as its pomp and courtesy during peace. The fame which he acquired by these splendid actions, so far dazzled his more temperate rival, that he departed on some occasions from his usual prudence and moderation, and emulated Francis in deeds of prowess, or of gallantry [DD].

The progress of science has great influence on the manners and character of men.

IX. The progress of science, and the cultivation of literature, had considerable effect in changing the manners of the European nations, and introducing that civility and refinement by which they are now distinguished. At the time when their Empire was overturned, the Romans, though they had lost that correct taste which has rendered the productions of their ancestors the standards of excellence, and models for imitation to succeeding ages, still preserved their love of letters, and cultivated the arts with great ardour. But rude barbarians were so far from being struck with any admiration of these unknown accomplishments, that they despised them. They were not arrived at that state of society, in which those faculties of the human mind, that have beauty and elegance for their objects, begin to unfold themselves. They were strangers to all those wants and desires which are the parents of ingenious invention; and as they did not comprehend either the merit or utility of the Roman arts, they destroyed the mo-

Ignorance of the middle ages.

[DD] NOTE XXVII.

numents

numents of them, with industry not inferior to that with which their posterity have since studied to preserve, or to recover them. The convulsions occasioned by their settlement in the Empire; the frequent as well as violent revolutions in every kingdom which they established; together with the interior defects in the form of government which they introduced, banished security and leisure; prevented the growth of taste, or the culture of science; and kept Europe, during several centuries, in that state of ignorance which has been already described. But the events and institutions which I have enumerated, produced great alterations in society. As soon as their operation, in restoring liberty and independence to one part of the community, began to be felt; as soon as they began to communicate to all the members of society some taste of the advantages arising from commerce, from public order, and from personal security, the human mind became conscious of powers which it did not formerly perceive, and fond of occupations or pursuits of which it was formerly incapable. Towards the beginning of the twelfth century, we discern the first symptoms of its awakening from that lethargy in which it had been long sunk, and observe it turning with curiosity and attention towards new objects.

THE first literary efforts, however, of the European nations in the middle ages, were extremely ill-directed. Among nations, as well as individuals, the powers of imagination attain some degree

Sect. I. of vigour before the intellectual faculties are much exercised in speculative or abstract disquisition. Men are poets before they are philosophers. They feel with sensibility, and describe with force, when they have made but little progress in investigation or reasoning. The age of Homer and of Hesiod long preceded that of Thales, or of Socrates. But, unhappily for literature, our ancestors deviating from this course which nature points out, plunged at once into the depths of abstruse and metaphysical inquiry. They had been converted to the Christian faith, soon after they settled in their new conquests. But they did not receive it pure. The presumption of men had added to the simple and instructive doctrines of Christianity, the theories of a vain philosophy, that attempted to penetrate into mysteries, and to decide questions which the limited faculties of the human mind are unable to comprehend, or to resolve. These over-curious speculations were incorporated with the system of religion, and came to be considered as the most essential part of it. As soon, then, as curiosity prompted men to inquire and to reason, these were the subjects which first presented themselves, and engaged their attention. The scholastic theology, with its infinite train of bold disquisitions, and subtile distinctions concerning points which are not the object of human reason, was the first production of the spirit of enquiry after it began to resume some degree of activity and vigour in Europe. It was not this circumstance alone that gave

such

respect to them were written in that language. To have treated of any important subject in a modern language, would have been deemed a degradation of it. This confined science within a very narrow circle. The learned alone were admitted into the temple of knowledge; the gate was shut against all others, who were allowed to remain involved in their former darkness and ignorance.

But though science was thus prevented, during several ages, from diffusing itself through society, and its influence was so much circumscribed; the progress which it made may be mentioned, nevertheless, among the great causes which contributed to introduce a change of manners into Europe. That ardent, though ill-judged spirit of enquiry which I have described, occasioned a fermentation of mind which put ingenuity and invention in motion, and gave them vigour. It led men to a new employment of their faculties, which they found to be agreeable as well as interesting. It accustomed them to exercises and occupations which tended to soften their manners, and to give them some relish for those gentle virtues, which are peculiar to nations among whom science hath been cultivated with success [EE].

X. The progress of commerce had considerable influence in polishing the manners of the European nations, and in leading them to order, equal laws,

[EE] NOTE XXVIII.

and

Sect. I. and humanity. The wants of men, in the original and most simple state of society, are so few, and their desires so limited, that they rest contented with the natural productions of their climate and soil, or with what they can add to these by their own rude industry. They have no superfluities to dispose of, and few necessities that demand a supply. Every little community subsisting on its own domestick stock, and satisfied with it, is either unacquainted with the states around it, or at variance with them. Society and manners must be considerably improved, and many provisions must be made for public order and personal security, before a liberal intercourse can take place between different nations. We find, accordingly, that the first effect of the settlement of the barbarians in the Empire, was to divide those nations which the Roman power had united. Europe was broken into many separate communities. The intercourse between these divided states, ceased almost totally during several centuries. Navigation was dangerous in seas infested by pirates; nor could strangers trust to a friendly reception in the ports of uncivilized nations. Even between distant parts of the same kingdom, the communication was rare and difficult. The lawless rapine of banditti, together with the avowed exactions of the nobles, scarcely less formidable and oppressive, rendered a journey of any length a perilous enterprize. Fixed to the spot in which they resided, the greater part of the inhabitants of Europe lost, in a great measure, the knowledge of remote regions, and were

Low state of commerce in the middle ages.

unacquainted

STATE OF EUROPE, 93

unacquainted with their names, their situations, Sect. I.
their climates, and their commodities [FF].

VARIOUS causes, however, contributed to revive Causes of its
the spirit of commerce, and to renew, in some de- revival.
gree, the intercourse between different nations.
The Italians, by their connection with Constantinople and other cities of the Greek empire, had
preserved in their own country some relish for the
precious commodities and curious manufactures
of the East. They communicated some knowledge of these to the countries contiguous to Italy.
But this commerce was extremely limited, nor was
the intercourse which it occasioned between different nations considerable. The Crusades, by leading multitudes from every corner of Europe into
Asia, opened a more extensive communication between the East and West, which subsisted for two
centuries; and though the object of these expeditions was conquest and not commerce; though
the issue of them proved as unfortunate, as the
motives for undertaking them were wild and enthusiastic, their commercial effects, as hath been
shewn, were both beneficial and permanent. During the continuance of the Crusades, the great cities
in Italy, and in other countries of Europe, acquired
liberty, and together with it such privileges as rendered them respectable and independent communities. Thus, in every state there was formed a
new order of citizens, to whom commerce presented itself as their proper object, and opened to

[FF] NOTE XXIX.

them

Sect. I. them a certain path to wealth and dignity. Soon after the close of the Holy war, the mariner's compass was invented, which, by rendering navigation more secure as well as more adventrous, facilitated the communication between remote nations, and brought them nearer to each other.

First among the Italians. THE Italian States, during the same period, established a regular commerce with the East in the ports of Egypt, and drew from thence all the rich products of the Indies. They introduced into their own territories manufactures of various kinds, and carried them on with great ingenuity and vigour. They attempted new arts; and transplanted from warmer climates, to which they had been hitherto deemed peculiar, several natural productions which now furnish the materials of a lucrative and extended commerce. All these commodities, whether imported from Asia, or produced by their own skill, they disposed of to great advantage among the other people of Europe, who began to acquire some taste of elegance unknown to their ancestors, or despised by them. During the twelfth and thirteenth centuries, the commerce of Europe was almost entirely in the hands of the Italians, more commonly known in those ages by the name of Lombards. Companies or societies of Lombard merchants settled in every different kingdom. They were taken under the immediate protection of the several governments. They enjoyed extensive privileges and immunities. The operation of the ancient barbarous laws concerning strangers,

ſtrangers, was ſuſpended with reſpect to them. They became the carriers, the manufacturers, and the bankers of all Europe.

WHILE the Italians, in the ſouth of Europe, cultivated trade with ſuch induſtry and ſucceſs, the commercial ſpirit awakened in the North towards the middle of the thirteenth century. As the nations around the Baltick were, at that time, extremely barbarous, and infeſted that ſea with their piracies, this obliged the cities of Lubeck and Hamburgh, ſoon after they began to open ſome trade with theſe people, to enter into a league of mutual defence. They derived ſuch advantages from this union, that other towns acceded to their confederacy, and, in a ſhort time, eighty of the moſt conſiderable cities ſcattered through thoſe vaſt countries which ſtretch from the bottom of the Baltick to Cologne on the Rhine, joined in the famous Hanſeatick league, which became ſo formidable, that its alliance was courted, and its enmity was dreaded by the greateſt monarchs. The members of this powerful aſſociation formed the firſt ſyſtematick plan of commerce known in the middle ages, and conducted it by common laws enacted in their general aſſemblies. They ſupplied the reſt of Europe with naval ſtores, and pitched on different towns, the moſt eminent of which was Bruges in Flanders, where they eſtabliſhed ſtaples in which their commerce was regularly carried on. Thither the Lombards brought the productions of

Then by means of the Hanſeatick.

Sect. I. India, together with the manufactures of Italy, and exchanged them for the more bulky, but not less useful commodities of the North. The Hanseatick merchants disposed of the cargoes which they received from the Lombards, in the ports of the Baltick, or carried them up the great rivers into the interior parts of Germany.

Commerce makes progress in the Netherlands;

This regular intercourse opened between the nations in the North and South of Europe, made them sensible of their mutual wants, and created such new and vast demands for commodities of every kind, that it excited among the inhabitants of the Netherlands a more vigorous spirit in carrying on the two great manufactures of wool and flax, which seem to have been considerable in that country as far back as the age of Charlemagne. As Bruges became the center of communication between the Lombard and Hanseatick merchants, the Flemings traded with both in that city to such extent as well as advantage, as spread among them a general habit of industry, which long rendered Flanders and the adjacent provinces the most opulent, the most populous, and best cultivated countries in Europe.

And in England.

Struck with the flourishing state of these provinces, of which he discerned the true cause, Edward III. of England endeavoured to excite a spirit of industry among his own subjects, who, blind to the advantages of their situation, and ignorant

of

of the source from which opulence was destined to flow into their country, totally neglected commerce, and did not even attempt those manufactures, the materials of which they furnished to foreigners. By alluring Flemish artisans to settle in his dominions, as well as by many wise laws for the encouragement and regulation of trade, Edward gave a beginning to the woollen manufactures of England, and first turned the active and enterprizing genius of his people towards those arts which have raised the English to the highest rank among commercial nations.

THIS increase of commerce, and of intercourse between nations, how inconsiderable soever it may appear in respect of their rapid and extensive progress during the last and present age, seems vast, when we compare it with the state of both in Europe previous to the twelfth century. It did not fail of producing great effects. Commerce tends to wear off those prejudices which maintain distinction and animosity between nations. It softens and polishes the manners of men. It unites them by one of the strongest of all ties, the desire of supplying their mutual wants. It disposes them to peace, by establishing in every state an order of citizens bound by their interest to be the guardians of publick tranquillity. As soon as the commercial spirit begins to acquire vigour, and to gain an ascendant in any society, we discover a new genius in its policy, its alliances, its wars, and its negociations.

SECT. I. Conspicuous proofs of this occur in the history of the Italian States, of the Hanseatick league, and the cities of the Netherlands during the period under review. In proportion as commerce made its way into the different countries of Europe, they successively turned their attention to those objects, and adopted those manners, which occupy and distinguish polished nations [GG].

[GG] NOTE XXX.

A VIEW
OF THE
PROGRESS OF SOCIETY
IN
EUROPE,
FROM THE
SUBVERSION OF THE ROMAN EMPIRE,
TO THE
BEGINNING OF THE SIXTEENTH CENTURY.

SECTION II.

View of the Progress of Society in Europe, with respect to the command of the national force requisite in foreign operations.

SUCH are the events and institutions, which by their powerful operation contributed, gradually, to introduce more regular government and more polished manners into the various nations of Europe. When we survey the state of society, or the character of individuals, at the opening of the fifteenth

Sect. II. State of society greatly improved at the beginning of the fifteenth century.

Sect. II. fifteenth century, and then turn back to view the condition of both at the time when the barbarous tribes which overturned the Roman power completed their settlement in their new conquests, the progress which mankind had made towards order and refinement will appear immense.

Still defective with respect to the command of the national force.

GOVERNMENT, however, was still far from having attained that state, in which extensive monarchies act with united vigour, or carry on great undertakings with perseverance and success. Small tribes or communities, even in their rudest state, may operate in concert, and exert their utmost force. They are excited to act not by the distant objects, and subtile speculations, which interest or affect men in polished societies, but by their present feelings. The insults of an enemy kindle resentment; the success of a rival tribe awakens emulation: these passions communicate from breast to breast, and all the members of the community, with united ardour, rush into the field in order to gratify their revenge, or to acquire distinction. But in widely extended states, such as the great kingdoms of Europe at the beginning of the fifteenth century, where there is little intercourse between the distant members of the community, and where every great enterprize requires previous concert and long preparation, nothing can rouse and call forth their united strength, but the absolute command of a Despot, or the powerful influence of regular policy. Of the former the vast

Empires

STATE OF EUROPE.

Empires in the East are an example; the irresistible mandate of the Sovereign reaches the most remote provinces of his dominions, and compels whatever number of his subjects he is pleased to summon, to follow his standard. The kingdoms of Europe, in the present age, are an instance of the latter; the Prince, by the less violent, but no less effectual operation of laws and a well regulated government, is enabled to avail himself of the whole force of his state, and to employ it in enterprizes which require strenuous and persevering efforts.

But, at the opening of the fifteenth century, the political constitution in all the kingdoms of Europe was very different from either of these states of government. The several monarchs, though they had somewhat enlarged the boundaries of prerogative by successful encroachments on the immunities and privileges of the nobility, were possessed of an authority extremely limited. The laws and interior police of kingdoms, though much improved by the various events and regulations which I have enumerated, were still feeble and imperfect. In every country, a numerous body of nobles, still formidable notwithstanding the various expedients employed to depress them, watched all the motions of their sovereign with a jealous attention, which set bounds to his ambition, and either prevented his forming schemes of

The power of Monarchs very limited.

Sect. II. extensive enterprize, or thwarted the execution of them.

Their revenues small.

THE ordinary revenues of every Prince were so extremely small as to be inadequate to any great undertaking. He depended for extraordinary supplies on the good will of his subjects, who granted them often with a reluctant and always with a sparing hand.

Their armies unfit for conquest.

As the revenues of Princes were inconsiderable, the armies which they could bring into the field were unfit for long and effectual service. Instead of being able to employ troops trained to skill in arms, and to military subordination, by regular discipline, Monarchs were obliged to depend on such forces as their vassals conducted to their standard in consequence of their military tenures. These, as they were bound to remain under arms only for a short time, could not march far from their usual place of residence, and being more attached to the lord of whom they held, than to the Sovereign whom they served, were often as much disposed to counteract as to forward his schemes. Nor were they, even if they had been more subject to the command of the monarch, proper instruments to carry into execution any great and arduous enterprize. The strength of an army formed either for conquest or defence lies in infantry. To the stability and discipline of their legions, consisting chiefly of infantry, the

Romans

Romans during the times of the republick were indebted for all their victories; and when their descendants, forgetting the institutions which had led them to universal dominion, so far altered their military system as to place their principal confidence in a numerous cavalry, the undisciplined impetuosity of the barbarous nations who fought mostly on foot, was sufficient, as I have already observed, to overcome them. These nations soon after they settled in their new conquests, uninstructed by the fatal error of the Romans, relinquished the customs of their ancestors, and converted the chief force of their armies into cavalry. Among the Romans this change was occasioned by the effeminacy of their troops, who could not endure the fatigues of service, which their more virtuous and hardy ancestors sustained with ease. Among the people who established the new monarchies into which Europe was divided, this innovation in military discipline seems to have flowed from the pride of the nobles, who scorning to mingle with persons of inferior rank, aimed at being distinguished from them in the field as well as during peace. The institution of chivalry, and the frequency of tournaments, in which knights, in complete armour, entered the lists on horseback, with extraordinary splendour, displaying amazing address, and force, and valour, brought cavalry into still greater esteem. The fondness for that service increased to such a degree, that, during the thirteenth and fourteenth centuries, the armies

SECT. II. of Europe were composed almost entirely of cavalry. No gentleman would appear in the field but on horseback. To serve in any other manner he would have deemed derogatory to his rank. The cavalry, by way of distinction, was called, *The battle*, and on it alone depended the fate of every action. The infantry, collected from the dregs and refuse of the people, ill armed and worse disciplined, was of no account.

They are incapable of forming any general or extensive plan of operation.

As these circumstances rendered the operations of particular kingdoms less considerable and less vigorous, so they long kept the Princes of Europe from giving such attention to the schemes and transactions of their neighbours, as led them to form any regular system of publick security. They prevented them from uniting in confederacy, or from acting with concert, in order to establish such a distribution and balance of power, as should hinder any state from rising to a superiority, which might endanger the general liberty and independence. During several centuries, the nations of Europe appear to have considered themselves as separate societies, scarcely connected together by any common interest, and little concerned in each others affairs or operations. An extensive commerce did not afford them an opportunity of observing and penetrating into the schemes of every different state. They had not ambassadors residing constantly in every court to watch and give early intelligence of all its motions. The expectation of

STATE OF EUROPE.

of remote advantages, or the prospect of distant and contingent evils, were not sufficient to excite nations to take arms. They only, who were within the sphere of immediate danger, and unavoidably exposed to injury or insult, thought themselves interested in any contest, or bound to take precautions for their own safety.

WHOEVER records the transactions of any of the more considerable European states during the two last centuries, must write the history of Europe. Its various kingdoms, throughout that period, have been formed into one great system, so closely united, that each holding a determinate station, the operations of one are so felt by all, as to influence their counsels and regulate their measures. But previous to the fifteenth century, unless when vicinity of territory rendered the occasions of discord frequent and unavoidable, or when national emulation fomented or embittered the spirit of hostility, the affairs of different countries are seldom interwoven. In each kingdom of Europe great events and revolutions happened, which the other powers beheld with almost the same indifference as if they had been uninterested spectators, to whom the effect of these transactions could never extend.

They were little connected with each other.

DURING the violent struggles between France and England, and notwithstanding the alarming progress which was made towards rendering one

A confirmation of this from the affairs of France.

Prince

Sect. II. Prince the master of both these kingdoms, hardly one measure which can be considered as the result of a sagacious and prudent policy, was formed in order to guard against an event so fatal to Europe. The Dukes of Burgundy and Bretagne, whom their situation would not permit to remain neutral, engaged, it is true, in the contest; but they more frequently took the part to which their passions prompted them, than that which a just discernment of the danger which threatened themselves and the tranquillity of Europe should have pointed out. The other Princes, seemingly unaffected by the alternate successes of the contending parties, left them to decide the quarrel, or interposed only by feeble and ineffectual negociations.

From those of Spain.

Notwithstanding the perpetual hostilities in which the various kingdoms of Spain were engaged during several centuries, and the successive occurrences which visibly tended to unite that part of the continent into one great monarchy, the Princes of Europe scarcely took a single step, which discovers that they gave any attention to that important event. They permitted a power to arise imperceptibly, and to acquire strength there, which soon became formidable to all its neighbours.

From those of Germany.

Amidst the violent convulsions with which the spirit of domination in the See of Rome, and the turbulent ambition of the German nobles, agitated the Empire, neither the authority of the Popes, seconded by all their artifices and intrigues, nor the

the solicitations of the Emperors, could induce any of the powerful monarchs in Europe to engage in their quarrel, or to avail themselves of many favourable opportunities of interposing with effect and advantage.

THIS amazing inactivity, during transactions so interesting, is not to be imputed to any incapacity of discerning their political consequences. The power of judging with sagacity, and of acting with vigour, is the portion of men in every age. The Monarchs who reigned in the different kingdoms of Europe during several centuries were not blind to their particular interest, negligent of the publick safety, or strangers to the method of securing both. If they did not adopt that salutary system, which teaches modern politicians to take the alarm at the prospect of distant dangers, which prompts them to check the first encroachments of any formidable power, and which renders each state the guardian, in some degree, of the rights and independence of all its neighbours, this was owing entirely to such imperfections and disorders in the civil government of each country, as made it impossible for sovereigns to act suitably to those ideas which the posture of affairs, and their own observation, must have suggested.

BUT during the course of the fifteenth century, various events happened, which, by giving Princes more entire command of the force in their respective dominions, rendered their operations more vigorous

Sect. II

tions more powerful and extensive.

vigorous and extensive. In consequence of this, the affairs of different kingdoms becoming more frequently as well as more intimately connected, they were gradually accustomed to act in concert and confederacy, and were insensibly prepared for forming a system of policy, in order to establish or to preserve such a balance of power as was most consistent with the general security. It was during the reign of Charles the fifth, that the ideas, on which this system is founded, first came to be fully understood. It was then, that the maxims by which it has been uniformly maintained since that æra were universally adopted. On this account, a view of the causes and events which contributed to establish a plan of policy more salutary and extensive than any that has taken place in the conduct of human affairs, is not only a necessary introduction to the following work, but is a capital object in the history of Europe.

The first of these was the depriving the English of their territories on the continent.

THE first event, that occasioned any considerable alteration in the arrangement of affairs in Europe, was the annexation of the extensive territories, which England possessed on the continent, to the crown of France. While the English were masters of several of the most fertile and opulent provinces in France, and a great part of its most martial inhabitants was bound to follow their standard, an English monarch considered himself rather as the rival, than as the vassal of the sovereign of whom he held. The Kings of France, circumscribed

scribed and thwarted in their schemes and opera-
tions by an adversary no less jealous than formidable, durst not venture upon any enterprize of importance or of difficulty. The English were always at hand, ready to oppose them. They disputed even their right to their crown, and being able to penetrate, with ease, into the heart of the kingdom, could arm against them those very hands which ought to have been employed in their defence. Timid counsels, and feeble efforts were natural to monarchs in such a situation. France, dismembered and over-awed, could not attain its proper station in the system of Europe. But the death of Henry V. of England, happily for France, and not unfortunately for his own country, delivered the French from the calamity of having a foreign master seated on their throne. The weakness of a long minority, the dissensions in the English court, together with the unsteady and languid conduct which these occasioned, afforded the French a favourable opportunity of recovering the territories which they had lost. The native valour of the French nobility heightened to an enthusiastick confidence, by a supposed interposition of heaven in their behalf; conducted in the field by skilful leaders; and directed in the cabinet by a prudent monarch; was exerted with such vigour and success, during this favourable juncture, as not only wrested from the English their new conquests, but stript them of their ancient possessions in France, and reduced them within

the

SECT. II. the narrow precincts of Calais, and its petty territory.

The effect of this on increasing the power of the French monarchy.

As soon as so many considerable provinces were re-united to their dominions, the Kings of France, conscious of this acquisition of strength, began to form bolder schemes of interior policy, as well as of foreign operations. They immediately became formidable to their neighbours, who began to fix their attention on their measures and motions, the importance of which they fully perceived. From this æra, France, possessed of the advantages which it derives from the situation and contiguity of its territories, as well as from the number and valour of its people, rose to new influence in Europe, and was the first power in a condition to give alarm to the jealousy or fears of the states around it.

On the state of the military force in the nation.

Nor was France indebted for this increase of importance merely to the re-union of the provinces which had been torn from it. A circumstance attended the recovery of these, which, though less considerable, and less observed, contributed not a little to give additional vigour and decision to all the efforts of that monarchy. During the obstinate struggles between France and England, all the defects of the military system under the feudal government were sensibly felt. A war of long continuance languished, when carried on by troops bound and accustomed to keep the field only for

a few

a few weeks. Armies, compofed chiefly of heavy
armed cavalry, were unfit either for the attack or
the defence of the many towns and caftles, which
it became neceffary to guard or to reduce. In order
to obtain fuch permanent and effective force,
as became requifite during thefe lengthened contefts,
the Kings of France took into their pay confiderable
bands of mercenary foldiers, levied fometimes
among their own fubjects, and fometimes in
foreign countries. But as the feudal policy provided
no fufficient fund for fuch extraordinary fervice,
thefe adventurers were difmiffed at the clofe
of every campaign, or upon any profpect of accommodation;
and having been little accuftomed
to the reftraints of difcipline, they frequently turned
their arms againft the country which they had been
hired to defend, and defolated it with no lefs cruelty
than its foreign enemies.

A BODY of troops kept conftantly on foot, and
regularly trained to military fubordination, would
have fupplied what was wanting in the feudal conftitution,
and have furnifhed Princes with the
means of executing enterprizes, to which they were
then unequal. Such an eftablifhment, however,
was fo repugnant to the genius of feudal policy,
and fo incompatible with the privileges and pretenfions
of the nobility, that during feveral centuries
no monarch was either fo bold, or fo powerful,
as to venture on any ftep towards introducing
it. At laft, Charles VII. availing himfelf of the
reputation which he had acquired by his fucceffes

againft

Sect. II. against the English, and taking advantage of the impressions of terror which such a formidable enemy had left upon the minds of his subjects, executed that which his predecessors durst not attempt. Under pretence of keeping always on foot a force sufficient to defend the kingdom against any sud-
A. D. 1445. den invasion of the English, he, at the time when he disbanded his other troops, retained under arms a body of nine thousand cavalry, and of sixteen thousand infantry. He appropriated funds for the regular payment of these; he stationed them in different places of the kingdom, according to his pleasure; and appointed the officers, who commanded and disciplined them. The prime nobility courted this service, in which they were taught to depend on their sovereign, to execute his orders, and to look up to him as the judge and rewarder of their merit. The feudal militia, composed of the vassals whom the nobles could call out to follow their standard, as it was in no degree comparable to a body of soldiers regularly trained to war, sunk gradually in reputation. The strength of armies came to be estimated only by the number of disciplined men which they contained. In less than a century, the nobles and their military tenants, though sometimes summoned to the field, according to ancient form, were considered as an incumbrance upon the troops with which they acted; and were viewed with contempt by soldiers accustomed to the vigorous and steady operations of regular service.

Thus

THUS the regulations of Charles the seventh, by establishing the first standing army known in Europe, occasioned an important revolution in its affairs and policy. By depriving the nobles of that direction of the military force of the state, which had raised them to such high authority and importance, a deep wound was given to the feudal aristocracy, in that part where its power seemed to be most complete.

Sect. II.
The effects of this.

FRANCE, by forming this body of regular troops, at a time when there was scarcely a squadron or company kept in constant pay in any other part of Europe, acquired such advantages, either for attack or defence, over its neighbours, that self-preservation made it necessary for them to imitate its example. Mercenary troops were introduced into all the considerable kingdoms on the continent. They gradually became the only military force that was employed or trusted. It has long been the chief object of policy to increase and to support them. It has long been the great aim of Princes and ministers to discredit and to annihilate all other means of national activity or defence.

As the Kings of France got the start of other powers in establishing a military force in their dominions, which enabled them to carry on foreign operations with more vigour, and to greater extent, so they were the first who effectually broke the feudal aristocracy, and humbled the great vas-

The monarchs of France encouraged to extend their prerogative.

VOL. I. I sals

Sect. II. sals of the crown, who by their exorbitant power had long circumscribed the royal prerogative within very narrow limits, and had rendered all the efforts of the monarchs of Europe inconsiderable. Many things concurred to undermine, gradually, the power of the feudal aristocracy in France. The wealth and property of the nobility were greatly impaired during the long wars which the kingdom was obliged to maintain with the English. The extraordinary zeal with which they exerted themselves in defence of their country against its ancient enemies, exhausted the fortunes of some great families. As almost every province in the kingdom was, in its turn, the seat of war, the lands of others were exposed to the depredations of the enemy, were ravaged by the mercenary troops which their sovereigns hired occasionally, but could not pay, or were desolated with rage still more destructive by the peasants, in their different insurrections. At the same time, the necessities of government having forced their Kings upon the desperate expedient of making great and sudden alterations in the current coin of the kingdom, the fines, quit-rents, and other payments fixed by ancient custom, sunk much in value, and the revenues of a fief were reduced far below the sum which it had once yielded. During their contests with the English, in which a generous nobility courted every station where danger appeared, or honour could be gained, many families of note became extinct, and their fiefs were reunited to the crown. Other fiefs, in a long course of years, fell to female heirs,

heirs, and were divided among them; were diminished by profuse donations to the church, or were broken and split by the succession of remote collateral heirs [1].

ENCOURAGED by these manifest symptoms of decline in that body which he wished to depress, Charles VII. during the first interval of peace with England, made several efforts towards establishing the regal prerogative on the ruins of the aristocracy. But his obligations to the nobles were so many, as well as recent, and their services in recovering the kingdom so splendid, as made it necessary for him to proceed with moderation and caution. Such, however, was the authority which the crown had acquired by the progress of its arms against the English, and so much was the power of the nobility diminished, that, without any opposition, he soon made innovations of great consequence in the constitution. He not only established that formidable body of regular troops, which has been mentioned, but he was the first monarch of France who, by his royal edict, without the concurrence of the States-general of the kingdom, levied an extraordinary subsidy on his people. He prevailed likewise with his subjects, to render several taxes perpetual, which had formerly been imposed occasionally, and exacted during a short time. By means of all these, he acquired such an increase of power, and extended

Sect. II.

The progress of the royal power under Charles VII.

A. D. 1440.

[1] Boulainvilliers Histoire de Gouvernement de France, Lettre xii.

SECT. II. his prerogative so far beyond its ancient limits, that, from being the most dependent Prince who had ever sat upon the throne of France, he came to possess, during the latter years of his reign, a degree of authority which none of his predecessors had enjoyed for several ages[1].

Under Louis XI.

THAT plan of humbling the nobility which Charles formed, his son Louis XI. carried on with a bolder spirit, and with greater success. Louis was formed by nature to be a tyrant; and at whatever period he had been called to ascend the throne, his reign must have abounded with schemes to oppress his people, and to render his own power absolute. Subtle, unfeeling, cruel; a stranger to every principle of integrity, and regardless of decency, he scorned all the restraints which a sense of honour, or the desire of fame, impose even upon ambitious men. Sagacious, at the same time, to discern his true interest, and influenced by that alone, he was capable of pursuing it with a persevering industry, and of adhering to it with a systematic spirit, from which no object could divert, and no danger could deter him.

His measures for humbling the nobility;

THE maxims of his administration were as profound as they were fatal to the privileges of the nobility. He filled all the departments of government with new men, and often with persons whom

[1] Histoire de France par Velly & Villaret, tom. xv. 331, &c. 389. tom. xvi. 324. Variations de la Monarchie Françoise, tom. iii. 162.

he called from the lowest as well as most despised
functions in life, and raised at pleasure to stations
of great power or trust. These were his only con-
fidents, whom he consulted in forming his plans,
and to whom he committed the execution of them:
While the nobles, accustomed to be the companions, the favourites, and the ministers of their
sovereigns, were treated with such studied and
mortifying neglect, that if they would not submit
to follow a court, in which they appeared without
any shadow of their ancient power, they were
obliged to retire to their castles, where they remained unemployed and forgotten. Not satisfied
with having rendered the nobles of less consideration, by taking out of their hands the sole direction of affairs, Louis added insult to neglect; and
by violating their most valuable privileges, endeavoured to degrade the order, and to reduce the
members of it to the same level with other subjects. Persons of the highest rank among them,
if so bold as to oppose his schemes, or so unfortunate as to awaken the jealousy of his capricious
temper, were prosecuted with rigour, from which
all who belonged to the order of nobility had
hitherto been exempt; they were tried by judges
who had no right to take cognizance of their
actions; and were subjected to torture, or condemned to an infamous death, without regard to
their birth or condition. The people, accustomed
to see the blood of the most illustrious personages
shed by the hands of the common executioner, to
behold them shut up in dungeons, and carried
about

SECT. II. about in cages of iron, began to view the nobility with less reverence than formerly, and looked up with terror to the royal authority, which seemed to have humbled or annihilated every other power in the kingdom.

And of dividing them.

AT the same time, Louis, being afraid that opposition might rouze the nobles, whom the rigour of his government had intimidated, or that self-preservation might at last teach them to unite, dexterously scattered among them the seeds of discord; and industriously fomented those ancient animosities between the great families, which the spirit of jealousy and emulation, natural to the feudal government, had originally kindled and still kept alive. To accomplish this, all the arts of intrigue, all the mysteries and refinements of his fraudulent policy were employed, and with such success, that at a juncture which required the most strenuous efforts, as well as the most perfect union, the nobles never acted, except during one short sally of resentment at the beginning of his reign, either with vigour or with concert.

He adds to the number of standing forces.

As he stripped the nobility of their privileges, he added to the power and prerogative of the crown. In order to have at command such a body of soldiers as might be sufficient to crush any force that his disaffected subjects could draw together, he not only kept on foot the regular troops which his father had raised, but took into his pay six thousand Swiss, at that time the best disciplined and

and most formidable infantry in Europe [a]. From the jealousy natural to tyrants, he confided in these foreign mercenaries, as the most devoted instruments of oppression, and the most faithful guardians of the power which he had acquired. That they might be ready to act on the shortest warning, he, during the latter years of his reign, kept a considerable body of them encamped in one place [b].

GREAT funds were requisite, not only to defray the expence of this additional establishment, but to supply the sums employed in the various enterprizes which the restless activity of his genius prompted him to undertake. But the prerogative that his father had assumed of levying taxes without the concurrence of the states-general, which he was careful not only to retain but to extend, enabled him to provide in some measure for the increasing charges of government.

He augments the revenues of the crown.

WHAT his prerogative, enlarged as it was, could not furnish, his address procured. He was the first monarch in Europe who discovered the method of managing those great assemblies, in which the feudal policy had vested the power of granting subsidies and of imposing taxes. He first taught other Princes the fatal art of beginning their attack on publick liberty, by corrupting the source from which it should flow. By exerting all

His address in managing the assembly of states.

[a] Mem. de Comines, tom. i. 367. Dan. Hist. de la Milice Francoise, tom. i. 182. [b] Mem. de Com. tom. i. 381.

Sect. II. his power and address in influencing the election of representatives, by bribing or overawing the members, and by various changes which he artfully made in the form of their deliberations, Louis acquired such entire direction of these assemblies, that, from being the vigilant guardians of the privileges and property of the people, he rendered them tamely subservient, in promoting the most odious measures of his reign [x]. As no power remained to set bounds to his exactions, he not only continued all the taxes imposed by his father, but made immense additions to them, which amounted to a sum that appeared astonishing to his contemporaries [y].[*]

He enlarges the bounds of the French monarchy.

Nor was it the power alone or wealth of the crown that Louis increased; he extended its territories by acquisitions of various kinds. He got possession of Roussillon by purchase; Provence was conveyed to him by the will of Charles de Anjou; and upon the death of Charles the Bold, he seized with a strong hand Burgundy and Artois, which had belonged to that Prince. Thus, during the course of a single reign, France was formed into one compact kingdom, and the steady unrelenting policy of Louis XI. not only subdued

---

[x] Mem. de Comin. tom. i. 156. Chron. Scandal. ibid. tom. ii. p. 71.   [y] Mem. de Com. tom. i. 334.

[*] Charles VII. levied taxes to the amount of 1,800,000 francs; Louis XI. raised 4,700,000. The former had in pay 9000 cavalry and 16,000 infantry. The latter augmented the cavalry to 15,000, and the infantry to 25,000. Mem. de Comines, L. 384.

the haughty spirit of the feudal nobles, but esta- **Sect. II.**
blished a species of government, scarcely less absolute, or less terrible, than eastern despotism.

But fatal as his administration was to the liber- *By all these*
ties of his subjects, the authority which he ac- *government*
quired, the resources of which he became master, *rendered*
and his freedom from restraint both in concerting *and enter-*
his plans and in executing them, rendered his *prising.*
reign active and enterprizing. Louis negociated
in all the courts of Europe; he observed the
motions of all his neighbours; he engaged, either
as principal, or as an auxiliary, in every great
transaction; his resolutions were prompt; his operations vigorous; and upon every emergence he
could call forth into action the whole force of his
kingdom. From the æra of his reign, instead of
the feeble efforts of monarchs fettered and circumscribed by a jealous nobility, the Kings of France,
more masters at home, have exerted themselves
more abroad, have formed more extensive schemes
of foreign conquests, and have carried on war with
a spirit and vigour long unknown in Europe.

The example which Louis set was too inviting *Steps taken*
not to be imitated by other Princes. Henry VII. *tending the*
as soon as he was seated on the throne of England, *the crown*
formed the plan of enlarging his own prerogative, *in England.*
by breaking the power of the nobility. The circumstances under which he undertook to execute
it, were less favourable than those under which
Charles VII. had made the same attempt; and
the

Sect. II. the spirit with which he conducted it, was very different from that of Louis XI. Charles, by the success of his arms against the English, by the merit of having expelled them out of so many provinces, had established himself so firmly in the confidence of his people, as encouraged him to make bold encroachments on the ancient constitution. The daring genius of Louis broke through every barrier, and endeavoured to overturn or to remove every obstacle that stood in his way. But Henry held the sceptre by a disputed title; a popular faction was ready every moment to take arms against him; and after long civil wars, during which the nobility had often displayed their power in creating and deposing Kings, he felt that the regal authority had been so much relaxed, and that he entered into possession of a prerogative so much abridged, as made it necessary to carry on his measures deliberately, and without any violent exertion. He endeavoured to undermine that formidable structure, which he durst not attack with open force. His schemes, though cautious and slow in their operation, were well concerted, and productive in the end of great effects. By his laws, permitting the barons to break the entails of their estates, and to expose them to sale; by his regulations to prevent the nobility from keeping in their service those numerous bands of retainers, which rendered them formidable, and turbulent; by encouraging population, agriculture and commerce; by securing to his subjects, during a long reign, the enjoyment of the blessings which

which flow from the arts of peace; by accuf- Sect. II.
toming them to an adminiftration of government,
under which the laws were executed with fteadi-
nefs and vigour; he made imperceptibly fuch
alterations in the Englifh conftitution, that he
tranfmitted to his fucceffor authority fo extenfive,
as rendered him one of the moft abfolute Monarchs in Europe, and capable of the greateft and
moft vigorous efforts.

In Spain, the union of all its crowns by the *And in Spain.*
marriage of Ferdinand and Ifabella; the glory that
they acquired by the conqueft of Granada, which
brought the odious dominion of the Moors to a
period; the command of the great armies which
it had been neceffary to keep long on foot, in
order to accomplifh this; the wifdom and fteadi-
nefs of their adminiftration; and the addrefs with
which they availed themfelves of every incident
to humble the nobility, and to extend their own
prerogative, confpired in raifing thefe monarchs
to fuch eminence and authority, as none of their
predeceffors had ever enjoyed. Though feveral
caufes, which fhall be explained in another place,
prevented their attaining the fame extenfive powers
with the Kings of France and England, and preferved the feudal conftitution in Spain longer
entire, their great abilities fupplied the defects of
their prerogative, and improved with fuch dexterity all the advantages which they poffeffed, that
Ferdinand carried on his foreign operations, which

were

were very extensive, with extraordinary vigour and effect.

Events happened, which called the several monarchs to exert the new powers which they had acquired.

WHILE these Princes were thus enlarging the boundaries of prerogative, and taking such steps towards rendering their kingdoms capable of acting with union and with force, events occurred, which called them forth to exert the new powers which they had acquired. These engaged them in such a series of enterprizes and negociations, that the affairs of all the considerable nations in Europe came to be insensibly interwoven with each other; and a great political system was gradually formed, which grew to be an object of universal attention.

The first of these events was the marriage of the heiress of the house of Burgundy.

THE first event which merits notice, on account of its influence in producing this change in the state of Europe, was the marriage of the daughter of Charles the Bold, the sole heiress of the house of Burgundy. For some years before her father's death, she had been considered as the apparent successor to his territories, and Charles had made proposals of marrying her to several different Princes, with a view of alluring them, by that offer, to favour the schemes which his restless ambition was continually forming.

The importance of this to the state of Europe.

THIS rendered the alliance with her an object of general attention; and all the advantages of acquiring possession of her territories, the most opulent at that time and best cultivated of any on this

this side of the Alps, were perfectly understood. As soon, then, as the untimely death of Charles opened the succession, the eyes of all the Princes in Europe were turned towards Mary, and they felt themselves deeply interested in the choice which she was about to make of the person, on whom she would bestow that rich inheritance.

SECT. II.

A. D. 1477.
January 5.

LOUIS XI. from whose kingdom several of the provinces which she possessed had been dismembered, and whose dominions stretched along the frontier of her territories, had every inducement to court her alliance. He had, likewise, a good title to expect the favourable reception of any reasonable proposition he should make, with respect to the disposal of a Princess, who was the vassal of his crown, and descended from the royal blood of France. There were only two propositions, however, which he could make with propriety. The one was the marriage of the Dauphin, the other that of the Count of Angouleme, a Prince of the blood, with the heirefs of Burgundy. By the former, he would have annexed all her territories to his crown, and have rendered France at once the most respectable monarchy in Europe. But the great disparity of age between the two parties, Mary being twenty, and the Dauphin only eight years old; the avowed resolution of the Flemings, not to chuse a master possessed of such power as might enable him to form schemes dangerous to their liberties; together with their dread of falling under the odious and oppressive government

Views of Louis XI. with respect to it.

SECT. II. ment of Louis, were obstacles in the way of executing this plan, which it was vain to think of surmounting. By the latter, the accomplishment of which might have been attained with ease, Mary having discovered some inclination to a match with the Count of Angouleme [a], Louis would have prevented the dominions of the house of Burgundy from being conveyed to a rival power, and in return for such a splendid establishment for the Count of Angouleme, he must have obtained, or would have extorted from him concessions highly beneficial to the crown of France. But Louis had been accustomed so long to the intricacies of a crooked and insidious policy, that he could not be satisfied with what was obvious and simple; and was so fond of artifice and refinement, that he came to consider these as his ultimate object, not as the means only of conducting affairs. From this principle, no less than from his unwillingness to aggrandize any of his own subjects, or from his desire of oppressing the house of Burgundy, which he hated, he neglected the course which a Prince less able and artful would have taken, and followed one more suited to his own genius.

The singular course which he followed.

He proposed to render himself, by force of arms, master of those provinces which Mary held of the crown of France, and even to push his conquests into her other territories, while he amused her with insisting continually on the impracticable match with the Dauphin. In prosecuting this plan,

[a] Mem. de Comines, i. 358.

plan, he displayed wonderful talents and industry, SECT. II. and exhibited such scenes of treachery, falsehood and cruelty, as are amazing even in the history of Louis XI. Immediately upon the death of Charles, he put his troops in motion, and advanced towards the Netherlands. He corrupted the leading men in the provinces of Burgundy and Artois, and seduced them to desert their sovereign. He got admission into some of the frontier towns by bribing the governors; the gates of others were opened to him in consequence of his intrigues with the inhabitants. He negociated with Mary; and, in order to render her odious to her subjects, he betrayed to them her most important secrets. He carried on a private correspondence with the two ministers whom she chiefly trusted, and then communicated the letters which he had received from them to the States of Flanders, who, enraged at their perfidy, brought them immediately to trial, tortured them with extreme cruelty, and, unmoved by the tears and intreaties of their sovereign, who knew and approved of all that the ministers had done, they beheaded them in her presence [a].

WHILE Louis, by this conduct, unworthy of a great monarch, was securing the possession of Burgundy, Artois, and the towns on the Somme, the States of Flanders carried on a negociation with the Emperor Frederick III. and concluded a treaty of marriage between their sovereign and his

The effect of this, the marriage of Maximilian with the heiress of Burgundy. A. D. 1477.

[a] Mem. de Comines, liv. v. ch. 15. p. 309, &c.

Sect. II. son Maximilian, Archduke of Auſtria. The illuſtrious birth of that Prince, as well as the high dignity of which he had the proſpect, rendered the alliance honourable for Mary, while, from the diſtance of his hereditary territories, and the ſcantineſs of his revenues, his power was ſo inconſiderable as did not excite the jealouſy or fear of the Flemings.

The influence of that on the ſtate of Europe.

Thus Louis, by the caprice of his temper, and the exceſs of his refinements, put the houſe of Auſtria in poſſeſſion of this noble inheritance. By this acquiſition, the foundation of the future grandeur of Charles V. was laid; and he became maſter of thoſe territories, which enabled him to carry on his moſt formidable and deciſive operations againſt France. Thus, too, the ſame monarch who firſt united the interior force of France, and eſtabliſhed it on ſuch a footing as to render it formidable to the reſt of Europe, contributed, far contrary to his intention, to raiſe up a rival power, which, during two centuries, has thwarted the meaſures, oppoſed the arms, and checked the progreſs of his ſucceſſors.

The next conſiderable event was the invaſion of Italy by Charles VIII. A. D. 1494

The next event of conſequence in the fifteenth century, was the expedition of Charles VIII. into Italy. This occaſioned revolutions no leſs memorable; produced alterations, which were more immediately perceived, both in the military and political ſyſtem; rouzed the ſtates of Europe to bolder efforts; and blended their affairs and intereſts

interests more closely together. The mild admi- Sect. II.
nistration of Charles, a weak but generous Prince, The motives
seems to have revived the spirit and genius of of this.
the French nation, which the rigid despotism of
Louis XI. his father had depressed, and almost
extinguished. The ardour for military service,
natural to the French nobility, returned, and their
young monarch was impatient to distinguish his
reign by some splendid enterprize. While he was
uncertain towards what quarter he should turn his
arms, the solicitations and intrigues of an Italian
politician, no less infamous on account of his
crimes, than eminent for his abilities, determined
his choice. Ludovico Sforza, having formed the
design of deposing his nephew the duke of Milan,
and of placing himself on the ducal throne, was
so much afraid of a combination of the Italian
powers to thwart this measure, and to support the
injured Prince, with whom most of them were
connected by blood or alliance, that he saw the
necessity of securing the aid of some able protector. The King of France was the person to
whom he applied; and without disclosing to him
his own intentions, he laboured to prevail with
him to march into Italy, at the head of a powerful
army, in order to seize the crown of Naples, to
which he had pretensions as heir of the house of
Anjou. The right to that kingdom, claimed by
the Angevin family, had been conveyed to Louis
XI. by Charles of Anjou, count of Maine and
Provence. But that sagacious monarch, though
he took immediate possession of those territories of

Vol. I. K which

Sect. II. which Charles was really master, totally disregarded his ideal title to a kingdom, over which another Prince reigned in tranquillity; and uniformly declined involving himself in the labyrinth of Italian politicks. His son, more adventurous, or more inconsiderate, embarked eagerly in this enterprize; and contemning all the remonstrances of his most experienced counsellors, prepared to carry it on with the utmost vigour.

His resources for this enterprize. The power which Charles possessed was so great, that he reckoned himself equal to this arduous undertaking. His father had transmitted to him such an ample prerogative, as gave him the entire command of his kingdom. He himself had added considerably to the extent of his dominions, by his prudent marriage with the heiress of Bretagne, which rendered him master of that province, the last of the great fiefs that remained to be annexed to the crown. He soon assembled forces which he thought sufficient; and so impatient was he to enter on his career as a conqueror, that sacrificing what was real, for what was chimerical, he restored Roussillon to Ferdinand, and gave up part of his father's acquisitions in Artois to Maximilian, with a view of inducing these Princes not to molest France, while he was carrying on his operations in Italy.

His preparations for it. But so different were the efforts of the States of Europe in the fifteenth century, from those which

which we shall behold in the course of this history, that the army, with which Charles undertook this great enterprize, did not exceed twenty thousand men. The train of artillery, however, the ammunition, and warlike stores of every kind provided for its use, were so considerable as to bear some resemblance to the immense apparatus of modern war [b].

WHEN the French entered Italy, they met with nothing able to resist them. The Italian powers having remained, during a long period, undisturbed by the invasion of any foreign enemy, had formed a system with respect to their affairs, both in peace and war, peculiar to themselves. In order to adjust the interests, and balance the power of the different states into which Italy was divided, they were engaged in perpetual and endless negociations with each other, which they conducted with all the subtlety of a refining and deceitful policy. Their contests in the field, when they had recourse to arms, were decided in mock battles, by innocent and bloodless victories. Upon the first appearance of the danger which now impended, they had recourse to the arts which they had studied, and employed their utmost skill in intrigue in order to avert it. But this proving ineffectual, their effeminate mercenaries, the only military force that remained in the country, being fit only for the parade of service, were terrified

[b] Mezeray Hist. tom. ii. 777.

Sect. II. at the aspect of real war, and shrunk at its approach. The impetuosity of the French valour appeared to them irresistible. Florence, Pisa, and Rome opened their gates as the French army advanced. The prospect of this dreadful invasion struck one King of Naples with such panic terror, that he died (if we may believe historians) of the fright. Another abdicated his throne from the same pusilanimous spirit. A third fled out of his dominions, as soon as the enemy appeared on the Neapolitan frontiers. Charles, after marching thither from the bottom of the Alps, with as much rapidity, and almost as little opposition, as if he had been on a progress through his own dominions, took quiet possession of the throne of Naples, and intimidated or gave law to every power in Italy.

Its effects, particularly in giving rise to the system concerning a balance of power.

Such was the conclusion of this expedition, which must be considered as the first great exertion of those new powers which the Princes of Europe had acquired, and now began to exercise. Its effects were no less considerable than its success had been astonishing. The Italians, unable to resist the impression of the enemy which broke in upon them, permitted him to hold on his course undisturbed. They quickly perceived that no single power, which they could rouse to action, was an equal match for a monarch, who ruled over such extensive territories, and was at the head of such a martial people; but that a confederacy

deracy might accomplish what the separate members of it durst not attempt. To this expedient,
the only one that remained to deliver or to preserve them from the yoke, they had recourse.
While Charles inconsiderately wasted his time at
Naples in festivals and triumphs on account of
his past successes, or was fondly dreaming of future conquests in the East, to the empire of which
he now aspired, they formed against him a powerful combination of almost all the Italian states,
supported by the Emperor Maximilian, and Ferdinand King of Aragon. The union of so many
powers, who suspended or forgot all their particular animosities, that they might act with concert against an enemy who had become formidable
to them all, awakened Charles from his thought-
less security. He saw now no prospect of safety
but in returning to France. An army of thirty
thousand men, assembled by the allies, was ready
to obstruct his march; and though the French,
with a daring courage, which more than counterbalanced their inferiority in number, broke through
that great body, and gained a victory, which
opened to their monarch a safe passage into his
own territories, he was stripped of all his conquests in Italy in as short a time as it had taken
to acquire them; and the political system in that
country resumed the same appearance as before his
invasion.

The sudden and decisive effect of this confederacy, seems to have instructed the Princes and
statesmen

SECT. II.

This becomes the great object of policy, first in Italy, and then in Europe.

statesmen of Italy as much as the irruption of the French had disconcerted and alarmed them. They had extended, on this occasion, to the affairs of Europe, the maxims of that political science which had hitherto been applied only to regulate the operations of the petty states in their own country. They had discovered the method of preventing any monarch from rising to such a degree of power, as was inconsistent with the general liberty; and had manifested the importance of attending to that great secret in modern policy, the preservation of a proper distribution of power among all the members of the system into which the states of Europe are formed. During all the wars of which Italy thenceforth became the theatre, and amidst the hostile operations which the imprudence of Louis XII. and the ambition of Ferdinand of Aragon, carried on in that country, with little interruption, from the close of the fifteenth century to that period at which the subsequent history commences, the maintaining a proper balance of power between the contending parties, became the great object of attention to the statesmen of Italy. Nor was the idea confined to them. Self-preservation taught other powers to adopt it. It grew to be fashionable and universal. From this æra we can trace the progress of that intercourse between nations, which has linked the powers of Europe so closely together; and can discern the operations of that provident policy, which, during peace, guards against remote and contingent dangers; which,

in

in war, hath prevented rapid and destructive conquests.

This was not the only effect of the operations which the great powers of Europe carried on in Italy. They contributed to render such a change, as the French had begun to make in the state of their troops, general; and obliged all the Princes, who appeared on this new theatre of action, to establish the military force of their kingdoms on the same footing with that of France. When the seat of war came to be remote from the countries which maintained the contest, the service of the feudal vassals ceased to be of any use; and the necessity of employing troops regularly trained to arms, and kept in constant pay, came at once to be evident. When Charles marched into Italy, his cavalry was entirely composed of those companies of Gendarmes, embodied by Charles VII. and continued by Louis XI. his infantry consisted partly of Swifs, hired of the Cantons, and partly of Gascons, armed and disciplined after the Swiss model. To these Louis XII. added a body of Germans, well known in the wars of Italy by the name of the Black Bands. But neither of these monarchs made any account of the feudal militia, or ever had recourse to that military force which they might have commanded, in virtue of the ancient institutions in their kingdom. Maximilian and Ferdinand, as soon as they began to act in Italy, employed the same instruments, and trusted the execution

SECT. II. execution of their plans entirely to mercenary troops.

Tenth the Europeans the superior importance of infantry in war.

THIS innovation in the military system was quickly followed by another, which the custom of employing Swifs in the Italian wars, was the occasion of introducing. The arms and discipline of the Swifs, were different from those of other European nations. During their long and violent struggles in defence of their liberties against the house of Austria, whose armies, like those of other considerable Princes, consisted chiefly of heavy armed cavalry, the Swifs found that their poverty, and the small number of gentlemen residing in their country, at that time barren and uncultivated, put it out of their power to bring into the field any body of horse capable of facing the enemy. Necessity compelled them to place all their confidence in infantry; and in order to render it capable of withstanding the shock of cavalry, they gave the soldiers breast-plates and helmets as defensive armour; together with long spears, halberts, and heavy swords, as weapons of offence. They formed them into large battalions, ranged in deep and close array, so that they could present on every side a formidable front to the enemy^c. The men at arms could make no impression on the solid strength of such a body. It repulsed the Austrians in all their attempts to conquer Swisserland. It broke the Burgundian Gendarmerie, which was scarcely inferior to that of France, either in number or reputation:

^c Machiavel Art of War, b. ii. chap. ii. p. 451.

putation: And when firſt called to act in Italy, it bore down by its irreſiſtible force every enemy that attempted to oppoſe it. Theſe repeated proofs of the deciſive effect of infantry, exhibited on ſuch conſpicuous occaſions, reſtored that ſervice to reputation, and gradually re-eſtabliſhed the opinion, which had been long exploded, of its ſuperior importance in the operations of war. But the glory which the Swiſs had acquired, having inſpired them with ſuch high ideas of their own proweſs and conſequence as rendered them mutinous and inſolent, the Princes who employed them became weary of depending on the caprice of foreign mercenaries, and began to turn their attention towards the improvement of their national infantry.

THE German powers having the command of men, whom nature has endowed with that ſteady courage and perſevering ſtrength which forms them to be ſoldiers, ſoon modelled their troops in ſuch a manner, that they vied with the Swiſs both in diſcipline and valour.

National infantry eſtabliſhed in Germany.

THE French monarchs, though more ſlowly, and with greater difficulty, accuſtomed the impetuous ſpirit of their people to ſubordination and diſcipline; and were at ſuch pains to render their national infantry reſpectable, that as early as the reign of Louis XII. ſeveral gentlemen of high rank had ſo far abandoned their ancient ideas, as to condeſcend to enter into that ſervice [d].

In France.

[d] Brantome, tom. x. p. 18. Mem. de Fleuranges, 143.

Sect. II.
In Spain.

The Spaniards, whose situation made it difficult to employ any other than their national troops in the southern parts of Italy, which was the chief scene of their operations in that country, not only adopted the Swiss discipline, but improved upon it, by mingling a proper number of soldiers, armed with heavy muskets, in their battalions; and thus formed that famous body of infantry, which, during a century and a half, was the admiration and terror of all Europe. The Italian states gradually diminished the number of their cavalry, and, in imitation of their more powerful neighbours, brought the strength of their armies to consist in foot soldiers. From this period, the nations of Europe have carried on war with forces more adapted to every species of service, more capable of acting in every country, and better fitted both for making conquests, and for preserving them.

The Italian wars occasion an increase of the publick revenue in Europe.

As their efforts in Italy led the people of Europe to these improvements in the art of war, they gave them likewise the first idea of the expence which accompanies great and continued operations, and accustomed them to the burden of those impositions, which are necessary for supporting them. While the feudal policy subsisted in full vigour, while armies were composed of military vassals called forth to attack some neighbouring power, and to perform, in a short campaign, the services which they owed to their sovereign, the expence of war was extremely moderate. A small subsidy enabled a Prince to begin and to finish his greatest operations.

operations. But when Italy became the theatre on which the powers of Europe contended for superiority, the preparations requisite for such a distant expedition, the pay of armies kept constantly on foot, their subsistance in a foreign country, the sieges to be undertaken, and the towns to be defended, swelled the charges of war immensely, and, by creating demands unknown in less active times, multiplied taxes in every kingdom. The progress of ambition, however, was so rapid, and Princes extended their operations so fast, that it was impossible at first to establish funds proportional to the increase of expence which these occasioned. When Charles VIII. invaded Naples, the sums requisite for carrying on that enterprize so far exceeded those which France had been accustomed to contribute, that before he reached the frontiers of Italy, his treasury was exhausted, and the domestic resources, of which his extensive prerogative gave him the command, were at an end. As he durst not venture to lay any new imposition on his people, oppressed already with the weight of unusual burdens; the only expedient that remained was, to borrow of the Genoese as much money as might enable him to continue his march. But he could not obtain the sum that was requisite, without consenting to pay annually the exorbitant interest of forty-two livres for every hundred that he received[e]. We may observe the same disproportion between the efforts and revenues of other

[e] Mem. de Comines, lib. vii. c. 5. p. 440.

Sect. II. Princes, his contemporaries. From this period, taxes went on increasing; and during the reign of Charles V. such sums were levied in every state, as would have appeared prodigious at the close of the fifteenth century, and gradually prepared the way for the more exorbitant exactions of modern times.

The league of Cambray another important occurrence.

THE last transaction, previous to the reign of Charles V. that merits attention on account of its influence upon the state of Europe, is the league of Cambray. To humble the republick of Venice, and to divide its territories, was the object of all the powers who united in this confederacy. The civil constitution of Venice, established on a firm basis, had suffered no considerable alteration for several centuries; during which, the senate conducted its affairs by maxims of policy no less prudent than vigorous, and adhered to these with an uniform consistent spirit, which gave that commonwealth great advantage over other states, whose views and measures changed as often as the form of their government, or the persons who administered it. By these unintermitted exertions of wisdom and valour, the Venetians enlarged the dominions of their commonwealth, until it became the most considerable power in Italy. While their extensive commerce, the useful and curious manufactures which they carried on, together with their monopoly of the precious commodities of the East, rendered Venice the most opulent state in Europe.

Their

Their power was the object of terror to their Italian neighbours. Their wealth was viewed with envy by the greatest monarchs, who could not vie with their private citizens in the magnificence of their buildings, in the richness of their dress and furniture, or in splendor and elegance of living [f]. Julius II. whose ambition was superior, and his abilities equal, to those of any Pontiff who ever sat on the Papal throne, formed the idea of this league against the Venetians, and endeavoured, by applying to these passions which I have mentioned, to persuade other Princes to join in it. By working upon the fears of the Italian powers, and upon the avarice of the monarchs beyond the Alps, he induced them, in concurrence with other causes, which it is not my province to explain, to form against these haughty republicans one of the most extensive confederacies Europe had ever beheld.

The Emperor, the King of France, the King of Aragon, the Pope, were principals in the league of Cambray, to which almost all the Princes of Italy acceded, the least considerable of them hoping for some share in the spoils of a state, which they already deemed to be devoted to destruction. The Venetians might have diverted this storm, or have broken its force; but with a presumptuous rashness, to which there is nothing similar in the course of their history, they waited its approach. The impetuous valour of the French, rendered

[f] Heliani oratio apud Goldastum in polit. Imperial. p. 930.

ineffectual

Sect. II. ineffectual all their precautions for the safety of the republick; and the fatal battle of Ghiarradadda entirely ruined the army, on which they relied for defence. Julius seized all the towns which they held in the ecclesiastical territories. Ferdinand re-annexed the towns of which they had got possession on the coast of Calabria, to his Neapolitan dominions. Maximilian, at the head of a powerful army, advanced towards Venice on the one side. The French pushed their conquests on the other. The Venetians, surrounded by so many enemies, and left without one ally, sunk from the height of presumption to the depths of despair; abandoned all their territories on the continent; and shut themselves up in their capital, as their last refuge, and the only place which they hoped to preserve.

Division arises among them. This rapid success, however, proved fatal to the confederacy. The members of it, united while they were engaged in seizing their prey, began to feel their ancient jealousy and animosities revive, as soon as they had a prospect of dividing it. When the Venetians observed these symptoms of alienation and distrust, a ray of hope broke in upon them; the spirit natural to their councils returned; they resumed such wisdom and firmness, as made some atonement for their former imprudence and dejection; they recovered part of the territory which they had lost; they appeased the Pope and Ferdinand by well-timed concessions in their favour; and at length dissolved the confederacy,

which

which had brought their commonwealth to the brink of ruin.

Julius, elated with beholding the effects of a league which he himself had planned, and imagining that nothing was too ardous for him to undertake, conceived the idea of expelling every foreign power out of Italy, and bent all the force of his mind towards executing a scheme so well suited to his vast and enterprizing genius. He directed his first attack against the French, who, on many accounts, were more odious to the Italians, than any of the foreigners who had acquired dominion in their country. By his activity and address, he prevailed on most of the powers, who had joined in the league of Cambray, to turn their arms against the King of France, their former ally; and engaged Henry VIII. who had lately ascended the throne of England, to favour their operations by invading France. Louis XII. resisted all the efforts of this formidable and unexpected confederacy, with undaunted fortitude. Hostilities were carried on, during several campaigns, in Italy, on the frontiers of Spain, and in Picardy, with alternate success. Exhausted, at length, by the variety as well as extent of his operations; unable to withstand a confederacy which brought against him superior force, conducted with wisdom, and acting with perseverance; Louis found it necessary to conclude separate treaties of peace with

his

Sect. II his enemies; and the war terminated with the loss of every thing which the French had acquired in Italy, except the castle of Milan, and a few inconsiderable towns in that dutchy.

By this the intercourse among the European nations increases.

THE various negociations carried on during this busy period, and the different combinations formed among powers hitherto little connected with each other, greatly increased that intercourse between the nations of Europe, which I have mentioned as one effect of the events in the fifteenth century. While the greatness of the objects at which they aimed, the distant expeditions which they undertook, as well as the length and obstinacy of the contests in which they engaged, obliged them to exert themselves with a vigour and perseverance unknown in the preceding ages.

They are prepared for the transactions of the sixteenth century.

THOSE active scenes which the following History will exhibit, and the variety and importance of those transactions which distinguish the period to which it extends, are not to be ascribed solely to the ambition, to the abilities, or to the rivalship of Charles V. and of Francis I. The kingdoms of Europe had arrived at such a degree of improvement in the internal administration of government, and Princes had acquired such command of the national force which was to be exerted in foreign wars, that they were in a condition to enlarge the sphere of their operations, and to increase

increase the vigour of their efforts. Their contests in Italy, which led them first to try the extent of the power that they had acquired, gave rise to so many opposite claims and pretensions, excited such a spirit of discord and rivalship between nations, and laid the foundation of so many quarrels, as could not fail of producing extraordinary convulsions in Europe; and the sixteenth century opened with the certain prospect of its abounding in great and interesting events.

A VIEW

OF THE

PROGRESS OF SOCIETY

IN

EUROPE,

FROM THE

SUBVERSION OF THE ROMAN EMPIRE,

TO THE

BEGINNING OF THE SIXTEENTH CENTURY.

SECTION III.

View of the political Constitution of the principal States in Europe, at the Commencement of the sixteenth Century.

SECT III.
A considerable variety in the constitution of the different nations of Europe.

HAVING thus enumerated the principal causes and events, the influence of which extended to all the states in Europe, and contributed either to improve their internal government and police, or to enlarge the sphere of their activity, and to augment their national force; nothing remains, in order to prepare my readers for entering

ing with full information upon perusing the History of the Reign of Charles V. but to give some view of the particular constitution and form of civil government, in each of the nations which acted any considerable part during that period. While these institutions and occurrences, which I have mentioned, formed the people of Europe to resemble each other, and conducted them from barbarism to refinement, in the same path, and with almost equal steps, there were other circumstances which occasioned a difference in their political establishments, and gave rise to those peculiar modes of government, which have produced such variety in the character and genius of nations.

It is no less necessary to become acquainted with the latter, than to have contemplated the former. The view which I have exhibited of the causes and events, whose influence was universal, will enable my readers to account for the surprising resemblance among the nations of Europe in their interior police, and foreign operations. But, without a distinct knowledge of the peculiar form and genius of their civil government, a great part of their transactions must appear altogether mysterious and inexplicable. The historians of particular States, as they seldom extended their views farther than to the amusement or instruction of their fellow-citizens, by whom they might presume that all domestick customs and institutions were perfectly understood, have often neglected to descend

SECT. III. descend into such details with respect to these, as are sufficient to convey to foreigners full light and information concerning the occurrences which they relate. But a history, which comprehends the transactions of so many different countries, would be extremely imperfect, without a previous survey of their respective constitutions and political state. It is from his knowledge of these, that the reader must draw those principles, which will enable him to judge with discernment, and to decide with certainty concerning the conduct of nations.

A MINUTE detail, however, of the peculiar forms and regulations in every country, would lead to deductions of immeasurable length. To sketch out the great lines which distinguish and characterize each government, is all that the nature of my present work will admit of, and all that is necessary to illustrate the events which it records.

The State of Italy.

AT the opening of the sixteenth century, the political face of Italy was extremely different from that of any other part of Europe. Instead of those extensive monarchies, which occupied the rest of the continent, that delightful country was parcelled out among many small states, each of which possessed sovereign and independent jurisdiction. The only monarchy in Italy was that of Naples. The dominion of the Popes was of a peculiar species, to which there is nothing similar either in ancient or modern times. In Venice and Florence,

Florence, a republican form of government was established. Milan was subject to sovereigns, who had assumed no higher title than that of Dukes.

The Pope was the first of these powers in dignity, and not the least considerable by the extent of his territories. In the primitive church, the jurisdiction of bishops was equal and co-ordinate. They derived, perhaps, some degree of consideration from the dignity of the See in which they presided. They possessed, however, no real authority or pre-eminence, but what they acquired by superior abilities, or superior sanctity. As Rome had so long been the seat of Empire, and capital of the world, its bishops were on that account entitled to respect; they received it; but during several ages they claimed and received nothing more. From these humble beginnings, they advanced with such an adventurous and well-directed ambition, that they established a spiritual dominion over the minds and sentiments of men, to which all Europe submitted with implicit obedience. Their claim of universal jurisdiction, as heads of the church, and their pretensions to infallibility in their decisions, as successors of St. Peter, are as chimerical, as they are repugnant to the genius of the Christian religion. But on these foundations, the superstition and credulity of mankind enabled them to erect an amazing superstructure. In all ecclesiastical controversies, their decisions were received as the infallible oracles of truth. Nor was the plenitude of their power confined

Sect. III. fined to these alone; they dethroned monarchs; disposed of crowns; absolved subjects from the obedience due to their sovereigns; and laid kingdoms under interdicts. There was not a state in Europe which had not been disquieted by their ambition. There was not a throne which they had not shaken; nor a Prince, who did not tremble at their power.

The territories of the Popes inadequate to support their spiritual jurisdiction.

Nothing was wanting to render this Empire absolute, and to establish it on the ruins of all civil authority, but that the Popes should have possessed such a degree of temporal power, as was sufficient to second and enforce their spiritual decrees. Happily for mankind, while their spiritual jurisdiction was most extensive, and at its greatest height, their temporal property was extremely limited. They were powerful Pontiffs, formidable at a distance; but they were petty Princes, without any considerable domestick force. They had early endeavoured, indeed, to acquire territory by arts, similar to those which they had employed in extending their jurisdiction. Under pretence of a donation from Constantine, and of another from Charlemagne or his father Pepin, they attempted to take possession of some towns adjacent to Rome. But these donations were fictitious, and availed them little. The benefactions, for which they were indebted to the credulity of the Norman adventurers, who conquered Naples, and to the superstition of the countess Matilda,

were

were real, and added ample domains to the Holy See.

But the power of the Popes did not increase in proportion to the extent of territory which they had acquired. In the dominions annexed to the Holy See, as well as in those subject to other Princes in Italy, the sovereign of a state was far from having the command of the force which it contained. During the turbulence and confusion of the middle ages, the powerful nobility or leaders of popular factions in Italy, had seized the government of different towns; and after strengthening their fortifications, and taking a body of mercenaries into pay, they aspired at independence. The territory which the church had gained, was filled with petty tyrants of this kind, who left the Pope hardly the shadow of dominion.

As these usurpations almost annihilated the Papal power in the greater part of the towns subject to the church, the Roman barons frequently disputed the authority of the Popes, even in Rome itself. In the twelfth century, an opinion began to be propagated, "That as the function of ecclesiastics was purely spiritual, they ought to possess no property, and to claim no temporal jurisdiction; but, according to the laudable example of their predecessors in the primitive church, should subsist wholly upon their tithes, or upon the voluntary oblations of the people [*]." This doctrine being

[*] Otto Frisingensis de Gestis Frider. Imp. lib. ii. cap. 20.

addressed

SECT. III. addressed to men, who had beheld the scandalous manner in which the avarice and ambition of the clergy had prompted them to contend for wealth, and to exercise power, they listened to it with fond attention. The Roman barons, who had felt most sensibly the rigour of ecclesiastical oppression, adopted these sentiments with such ardour, that they set themselves instantly to shake off the yoke.

A.D. 1143. They endeavoured to restore some image of their ancient liberty, by reviving the institution of the Roman senate, in which they vested supreme authority; committing the executive power sometimes to one chief senator, sometimes to two, and sometimes to a magistrate dignified with the name of *The Patrician*. The Popes exerted themselves with vigour, in order to check this fatal encroachment on their jurisdiction. One of them, finding all his endeavours ineffectual, was so much mortified, that extreme grief cut short his days. Another, having ventured to attack the senators at the head of some armed men, was mortally wounded in the fray [b]. During a considerable period, the power of the Popes, before which the greatest monarchs in Europe trembled, was circumscribed within such narrow limits in their own capital, that they durst hardly exert any act of authority without the permission and concurrence of the senate.

[b] Otto Frising. Chron. lib. vii. cap. 27, 31. Id. de Gest. Frid. lib. i. c. 27. Muratori Annali d' Italia, vol. ix. 398, 404.

ENCROACHMENTS were made upon the Papal authority, not only by the usurpations of the Roman nobility, but by the mutinous spirit of the people. During seventy years of the fourteenth century, the Popes fixed their residence in Avignon. The inhabitants of Rome, accustomed to consider themselves as the descendants of the people who had conquered the world, and had given laws to it, were too high-spirited to submit with patience to the delegated authority of those persons, to whom the Popes committed the government of the city. On many occasions, they opposed the execution of the Papal mandates, and on the slightest appearance of innovation or oppression, they were ready to take arms in defence of their own immunities. Towards the middle of the fourteenth century, being instigated by Nicolas Rienzo, a man of low birth and a seditious spirit, but of popular eloquence and an enterprizing ambition, they drove all the nobility out of the city, established a democratical form of government, elected Rienzo Tribune of the people, and invested him with extensive authority. But though the frantick proceedings of the Tribune soon overturned this new system; though the government of Rome was reinstated in its ancient form; yet every fresh attack contributed to weaken the papal jurisdiction; and the turbulence of the people concurred with the spirit of independence among the nobility, to circumscribe it within very

narrow

SECT. III. narrow bounds [c]. Gregory VII. and other domineering Pontiffs, accomplished those great things which rendered them so formidable to the Emperors with whom they contended, not by the force of their arms, or by the extent of their power, but by the dread of their spiritual censures, and by the effect of their intrigues, which excited rivals, and called forth enemies against every Prince, whom they wished to depress or to destroy.

Alexander VI. and Julius II. render the Popes considerable Princes.

MANY attempts were made by the Popes, not only to humble these usurpers, who lorded it over the cities in the ecclesiastical state, but to break the turbulent spirit of the Roman people. These were long unsuccessful. At last Alexander VI. with a policy no less artful than flagitious, subdued and extirpated most of the great Roman barons, and rendered the Popes masters of their own dominions. The enterprising ambition of Julius II. added conquests of no inconsiderable value to the patrimony of St. Peter. Thus the Popes, by degrees, became powerful temporal Princes. Their territories, in the age of Charles V. were of greater extent than at present; their country seems to have been better cultivated, and more populous; and as they drew large contributions from every part of Europe, their revenues

[c] Historie Fiorentine de Giov. Villani, lib. xii. c. 89. 104. ap. Murat. Script. Rerum. Ital. vol. xiii. Vita de Cola di Rienzo, ap. Murat. Antiq. Ital. vol. iii. p. 399, &c. Hist. de Nic. Rienzy, par M. de Boispreaux, p. 91, &c.

far

far exceeded those of the neighbouring powers, and rendered them capable of more sudden and vigorous efforts.

THE genius of the papal government, however, was better adapted to the exercise of spiritual dominion, than of temporal power. With respect to the former, all its maxims were steady and invariable. Every new Pontiff adopted the plan of his predecessor. By education and habit, Ecclesiastics were so formed, that the character of the individual was sunk in that of the profession; and the passions of the man were sacrificed to the interest and honour of the order. The hands which held the reins of administration might change; but the spirit which conducted them was always the same. While the measures of other governments fluctuated, and the objects at which they aimed varied, the church kept one end in view; and to this unrelaxing constancy of pursuit, it was indebted for its success in the boldest attempts ever made by human ambition.

Defects in the nature of ecclesiastical dominion.

BUT in their civil administration, the Popes followed no such uniform or consistent plan. There, as in other governments, the character, the passions, and the interests of the person who had the supreme direction of affairs, occasioned a variation both in objects and measures. As few Prelates reached the summit of ecclesiastical dignity, until they were far advanced in life, a change of masters was

Sect. III. was more frequent in the Papal dominions than in other states, and the political system was, of course, less stable and permanent. Every Pope was eager to make the most of the short period, during which he had the prospect of enjoying power, in order to aggrandize his own family, and to attain his private ends; and it was often the first business of his successor to undo all that he had done, and to overturn what he had established.

As Ecclesiasticks were trained to pacifick arts, and early initiated in the mysteries of that policy, by which the court of Rome extended or supported its spiritual dominion, the Popes were apt to conduct their temporal affairs with the same spirit; and in all their measures were more ready to employ the refinements of intrigue, than the force of arms. It was in the Papal court that address and subtlety in negociation first became a science; and during the sixteenth century, Rome was considered as the school in which it might be best acquired.

As the decorum of their ecclesiastical character prevented the Popes from placing themselves at the head of their armies, or taking the command, in person, of the military force in their dominions, they were afraid to arm their subjects; and in all their operations, whether offensive or defensive, they trusted entirely to mercenary troops.

As

As their power and dominions could not defcend to their pofterity, the Popes were lefs folicitous than other Princes to form or to encourage fchemes of publick utility and improvement. Their tenure was only for a fhort life; prefent advantage was all that they attended to; to fqueeze and to amafs, not to meliorate, was their object. They erected, perhaps, fome work of oftentation, to remain as a monument of their Pontificate; they found it neceffary, at fome times, to eftablifh ufeful inftitutions, in order to footh and filence the turbulent populace of Rome; but plans of general benefit to their fubjects, and framed with a view to futurity, were rarely objects of attention in the Papal policy. The patrimony of St. Peter was worfe governed than any part of Europe; and though a generous Pontiff might fufpend for a little, or counter-act the effects of thofe vices which are peculiar to the adminiftration of ecclefiafticks; the difeafe not only remained incurable, but has gone on increafing from age to age; and the decline of the ftate has kept pace with its progrefs.

ONE circumftance, farther, concerning the Papal government, is fo fingular, as to merit attention. As the fpiritual fupremacy and temporal power was united in one perfon, and uniformly aided each other in their operations, they became fo blended together, that it was difficult to feparate them, even in imagination. The potentates, who found it neceffary to oppofe the meafures which the Popes

The Popes derive fome advantages from the union of their fpiritual and temporal authority.

SECT. III. Popes pursued as temporal Princes, could not divest themselves of the reverence which they imagined to be due to them as heads of the church, and vicars of Jesus Christ. It was with reluctance that they could be brought to a rupture with them; they were averse to push their operations against them to extremity; they listened eagerly to the first overtures of accommodation, and were willing to procure it almost upon any terms. Their consciousness of this, encouraged the enterprizing Pontiffs, who filled the Papal throne about the beginning of the sixteenth century, to engage in schemes seemingly the most extravagant. They trusted, that if their temporal power was not sufficient to carry them through with success, the respect paid to their spiritual dignity would enable them to extricate themselves with facility and with honour [c].

But

---

[c] The manner in which Louis XII. of France undertook and carried on war against Julius II. remarkably illustrates this observation. Louis solemnly consulted the clergy of France, whether it was lawful to take arms against a Pope, who had wantonly kindled war in Europe, and whom neither the faith of treaties, nor gratitude for favours received, nor the decorum of his character, could restrain from the most violent actions, to which the lust of power prompts ambitious Princes. Though his clergy authorised the war, yet Anne of Bretagne, his Queen, entertained scruples with regard to the lawfulness of it. The King himself, from some superstition of the same kind, carried it on faintly; and, upon every fresh advantage, renewed his propositions of peace. Mezeray, Hist. de France, fol. edit. 1685. tom. i. 852. I shall produce another proof of this reverence for the Papal character still more striking. Guicciardini, the most sagacious, perhaps, of all modern historians, and

the

STATE OF EUROPE.

But when Popes came to take part more frequently in the contests among Princes, and to engage as principals or auxiliaries in every war kindled in Europe, this veneration for their sacred character began to abate; and striking instances will occur in the following history of its being almost totally extinct.

Of all the Italian powers, the republick of Venice, next to the Pope, was most connected with the rest of Europe. The rise of that commonwealth, during the inroads of the Huns in the fifth century; the singular situation of its capital in the small isles of the Adriatick gulf; and the more singular form of its civil constitution, are generally known. If we view the Venetian government as calculated for the order of nobles alone, its institutions are so excellent; the deliberative, legislative and executive powers are so admirably distributed and adjusted, that it must be regarded as a perfect model of political wisdom. But if we consider it as formed for a numerous body of people subject to its jurisdiction, it will appear a rigid and partial aristocracy, which lodges all power in the hands of a few members of the community, while it degrades and oppresses the rest.

Sect. III.

Constitution of the republick of Venice, with its rise and progress.

the boldest in painting the vices and ambition of the Popes, represents the death of Migliau, a Spanish officer, who was killed during the siege of Naples, as a punishment inflicted on him by heaven, on account of his having opposed the setting of Clement VII. at liberty. Guic. Historia d'Italia, Genev. 1645. vol. ii. lib. 18. p. 467.

SECT. III.

Defects in its government, particularly with respect to its military organization.

THE spirit of government, in a commonwealth of this species, was, of course, timid and jealous. The Venetian nobles distrusted their own subjects, and were afraid of allowing them the use of arms. They encouraged among them the arts of industry and commerce; they employed them in manufactures and in navigation; but never admitted them into the troops which the state kept in its pay. The military force of the republick consisted entirely of foreign mercenaries. The command of these was never trusted to noble Venetians, lest they should acquire such influence over the army, as might endanger the publick liberty; or become accustomed to the exercise of such power, as would make them unwilling to return to the condition of private citizens. A soldier of fortune was placed at the head of the armies of the commonwealth; and to obtain that honour, was the great object of the Italian *Condottieri*, or leaders of bands, who, in the fifteenth and sixteenth centuries, made a trade of war, and raised and hired out soldiers to different states. But the same suspicious policy, which induced them to employ these adventurers, prevented their placing entire confidence in them. Two noblemen, appointed by the senate, accompanied their army when it took the field, with the appellation of *Proveditori*, and like the field-deputies of the Dutch republick in latter times, observed all the motions of the general, and checked and controuled him in all his operations.

A COMMONWEALTH, with such civil and military institutions, was not formed to make conquests. While its subjects were disarmed, and its nobles excluded from military command, it carried on its warlike enterprizes with great disadvantage. This ought to have taught the Venetians to make self-preservation, and the enjoyment of domestick security, the objects of their policy. But republicks are apt to be seduced by the spirit of ambition, as well as Princes. When the Venetians so far forgot the interior defects in their government, as to aim at extensive conquests, the fatal blow, which they received in the war excited by the league of Cambray, convinced them of the imprudence and danger of making violent efforts, in opposition to the genius and tendency of their constitution.

IT is not, however, by its military, but by its naval and commercial power, that the importance of the Venetian commonwealth must be estimated. In the latter, the real force and nerves of the state consisted. The jealousy of government did not extend to this department. Nothing was apprehended from this quarter, that could prove formidable to liberty. The senate encouraged the nobles to trade, and to serve on board the fleet. They became merchants and admirals. They increased the wealth of their country by their industry. They added to its dominions, by the valour with which they conducted its naval armaments.

Sect. III.

The extent of its commerce.

The Venetian commerce was an inexhaustible source of opulence. All the nations in Europe depended upon them, not only for the commodities of the East, but for various manufactures fabricated by them alone, or finished with a dexterity and elegance unknown in other countries. From this extensive commerce, the state derived such immense supplies, as concealed these vices in its constitution which I have mentioned; and enabled it to keep on foot such armies, as were not only an over-match for the force which any of its neighbours could bring into the field, but were sufficient to contend, for some time, with the powerful monarchs beyond the Alps. During its struggles with the Princes united against it by the league of Cambray, the republick levied sums which, even in the present age, would be deemed considerable; and while the King of France paid the exorbitant interest which I have mentioned for the money advanced to him, and the Emperor eager to borrow, but destitute of credit, was known by the name of *Maximilian the Money-less*, the Venetians raised whatever sums they pleased, at the moderate premium of five in the hundred [*].

The constitution of Florence.

The constitution of Florence was perfectly the reverse of that of Venice. It partook as much of the democratical turbulence and licentiousness, as

[*] Hist. de la ligue faite a Cambray par M. l'Abbé du Bos. lib. v. Sandi Storia Civil Veneziana, lib. viii. c. 16. p. 891, &c.

the other of aristocratical rigour. Florence, however, was a commercial, not a military democracy. The nature of its institutions were favourable to commerce, and the genius of the people was turned towards it. The vast wealth which the family of Medici had acquired by trade; together with the magnificence, the generosity, and the virtue of the first Cosmo, gave him such an ascendant over the affections as well as the councils of his countrymen, that though the forms of popular government were preserved, though the various departments of administration were filled by magistrates distinguished by the ancient names, and elected in the usual manner, he was in reality the head of the commonwealth, and in the station of a private citizen he possessed supreme authority. Cosmo transmitted a considerable degree of this power to his descendants; and during the greater part of the fifteenth century, the political state of Florence was extremely singular. The appearance of republican government subsisted, the people were passionately attached to it, and on some occasions contended warmly for their privileges, and yet they permitted a single family to assume a direction of their affairs, almost as absolute as if it had been formally invested with sovereign power. The jealousy of the Medici concurred with the commercial spirit of the Florentines, in putting the military force of the republick upon the same footing with that of the other Italian states. The troops, which the Florentines employed in their wars,

Sect. III. wars, consisted almost entirely of mercenary soldiers, furnished by the *Condottieri*, or leaders of bands, whom they took into their pay.

The constitution of the kingdom of Naples.

In the kingdom of Naples, to which the sovereignty of the island of Sicily was annexed, the feudal government was established in the same form, and with the same defects, as in the other nations of Europe. The frequent and violent revolutions which happened in that monarchy, had considerably increased these defects, and rendered them more intolerable. The succession to the crown of Naples had been so often interrupted or altered, and so many Princes of foreign blood had taken possession of the throne, that the Neapolitan nobility had lost, in a great measure, that attachment to the family of their sovereigns, as well as that reverence for their persons, which, in other feudal kingdoms, contributed to set some bounds to the encroachments of the barons upon the royal prerogative and power. At the same time, the different pretenders to the crown, being obliged to court the barons who adhered to them, and on whose support they depended for the success of their claims, they augmented their privileges by liberal concessions, and connived at their boldest usurpations. Even when seated on the throne, it was dangerous for a Prince, who held his sceptre by a disputed title, to venture on any step towards extending his own power, or circumscribing that of the nobles.

FROM all thefe caufes, the kingdom of Naples Sect. III. was the moft turbulent of any in Europe, and the authority of its Monarchs the leaft extenfive. Though Ferdinand I. who began his reign in the year one thoufand four hundred and fixty-eight, attempted to break the power of the ariftocracy; though his fon Alfonfo, that he might crufh it at once by cutting off the leaders of greateft reputation and influence among the Neapolitan barons, ventured to commit one of the moft perfidious and cruel actions recorded in hiftory; the order of A.D. 1437. nobles was neverthelefs more exafperated than humbled by their meafures[f]. The refentment which thefe outrages excited was fo violent, and the power of the malecontent nobles was ftill fo formidable, that to thefe may be afcribed, in a great degree, the eafe and rapidity with which Charles VIII. conquered the kingdom of Naples[g].

THE event that gave rife to the violent contefts State of the difpute concerning the fucceffion to the crown of Naples cerning the right of fucand Sicily, which brought fo many calamities ceffion to upon thefe kingdoms, happened in the thirteenth the crown. century. Upon the death of the Emperor Frederick II. Manfred his natural fon afpiring to the Neapolitan throne, murdered his brother the Em- A.D. 1254. peror Conrad (if we may believe contemporary hiftorians) and by that crime obtained poffeffion of it[h]. The Popes, from their implacable enmity

---

[f] Giannone, book xxviii. chap. 2. vol. ii. p. 410, &c.
[g] Giannone, ibid. p. 414.
[h] Struv. corp. hift. Germ. i. 481. Giannone, book xviii. ch. 5.

SECT. III. to the house of Swabia, not only refused to recognize Manfred's title, but endeavoured to excite against him some rival capable of wresting the sceptre out of his hand. Charles Count of Anjou, the brother of St. Louis King of France, undertook this; and he received from the Popes, the investiture of the kingdom of Naples and Sicily as a fief held of the Holy See. The Count of Anjou's efforts were crowned with success; Manfred fell in battle; and he took possession of the vacant throne. But soon after, Charles sullied the glory which he had acquired, by the injustice and cruelty with which he put to death, by the hands of the executioner, Conradin, the last Prince of the house of Swabia, and the rightful heir of the Neapolitan crown. That gallant young Prince asserted his title, to the last, with a courage, worthy of a better fate. On the scaffold, he declared Peter, at that time Prince, and soon after King of Aragon, who had married Manfred's only daughter, his heir; and throwing his glove among the people, he entreated that it might be carried to Peter as the symbol by which he conveyed all his rights to him [1]. The desire of avenging the insult offered to royalty by the death of Conradin concurred with ambition, in prompting Peter to take arms in support of the title, which he had acquired. From that period, during almost two centuries, the houses of Aragon and Anjou contended for the crown of Naples. Amidst a succession of revolutions more rapid, as well as of

[1] Giannone, book xix. ch. 4. § 2.

crimes

crimes more atrocious, than what occur in the history of almost any other kingdom, Monarchs sometimes of the Aragonese line, and sometimes of the Angevin, were seated on the throne. At length the Princes of the house of Aragon obtained such firm possession of this long-disputed inheritance, that they transmitted it quietly to a bastard branch of their family [k].

THE race of the Angevin Kings, however, was not extinct; nor had they relinquished their title to the Neapolitan crown. The Count of Maine and Provence, the heir of this family, conveyed all his rights and pretensions to Louis XI. and to his successors. Charles VIII, as I have already related, crossed the Alps at the head of a powerful army, in order to prosecute his claim with a degree of vigour far superior to that, which the Princes from whom he derived it, had been capable of exerting. The rapid progress of his arms in Italy, as well as the short time during which he enjoyed the fruits of his success, are well known. Frederick, the heir of the illegitimate branch of the Aragonese family, soon recovered the throne of which Charles had dispossessed him. Louis XII. and Ferdinand of Aragon united against this Prince, whom both, though for different reasons, considered as an usurper, and agreed to divide his dominions between them. Frederick, unable to resist the combined Monarchs, each of whom was far his superior in power, resigned his sceptre.

[k] Giannone, book xxvi. ch. 2.

Sect. III. Louis and Ferdinand, though they had concurred in making the conquest, differed about the division of it; and from allies became enemies. But Gonsalvo de Cordova, partly by the exertion of such military talents as gave him a just title to the appellation of the *Great Captain*, which the Spanish historians have bestowed upon him; and partly by such shameless and frequent violations of the most solemn engagements, as leave an indelible stain on his memory; stripped the French of all that they possessed in the Neapolitan dominions, and secured the peaceable possession of them to his master. These, together with his other kingdoms, Ferdinand transmitted to his grandson Charles V, whose right to possess them, if not altogether uncontravertible, seems, at least, to be as well founded as that, which the Kings of France set in opposition to it [1].

State of the dutchy of Milan, and the right of succession to it.

There is nothing in the political constitution, or interior government of the dutchy of Milan, so remarkable, as to require a particular explanation. But as the right of succession to that fertile province was the cause or the pretext of almost all the wars carried on in Italy during the reign of Charles V, it is necessary to trace these disputes to their source, and to inquire into the pretensions of the various competitors.

[1] Droits des Rois de France au Royaume de Sicile. Mem. de Comin. Edit. de Fresnoy, tom. iv. part ii. p. 5.

During

DURING the long and fierce contests excited in Italy by the violence of the Guelf and Ghibelline factions, the family of Visconti rose to great eminence among their fellow-citizens of Milan. As the Visconti had adhered uniformly to the Ghibelline or Imperial interest, they, by way of recompence, received, from one Emperor, the dignity of perpetual vicars of the Empire in Italy * : they were created by another, Dukes of Milan, and together with that title, the possession of the city and its territories was bestowed upon them as an hereditary fief *. John King of France, among other expedients for raising money, which the calamities of his reign obliged him to employ, condescended to give one of his daughters in marriage to John Galeazzo Visconti the first Duke of Milan, from whom he had received considerable sums. Valentine Visconti one of the children of this marriage married her cousin, Louis Duke of Orleans, the only brother of Charles VI. In their marriage contract, which the Pope confirmed, it was stipulated that, upon failure of heirs-male in the family of Visconti, the dutchy of Milan should descend to the posterity of Valentine and the Duke of Orleans. That event took place. In the year one thousand four hundred and forty-seven, Philip Maria the last Prince of the ducal family of Visconti died. Various competitors pretended to the succession. Charles Duke of Orleans

* Petrarch epist. ap. Strav. corp. i. 625.
* Leibnit cod. jur. gent. diplom. vol. i. 257.

pleaded

Sect. III. pleaded his right to it, founded on the marriage-contract of his mother Valentine Visconti. Alfonso King of Naples claimed it in consequence of a will made by Philip Maria in his favour. The Emperor contended that, upon the extinction of male issue in the family of Visconti, the fief returned to the superior Lord, and ought to be re-annexed to the Empire. The people of Milan, smitten with that love of liberty which prevailed among the Italian States, declared against the dominion of any master, and established a republican form of government.

But during the struggle among so many competitors, the prize for which they contended was seized by one from whom none of them apprehended any danger. Francis Sforza, the natural son of Jacomuzzo Sforza, whom his courage and abilities had elevated from the rank of a peasant to be one of the most eminent and powerful of the Italian *Condottieri*, having succeeded his father in the command of the adventurers who followed his standard, had married a natural daughter of the last Duke of Milan. Upon this shadow of a title Francis founded his pretensions to the dutchy, which he supported with such talents and valour as placed him at last on the ducal throne. The virtues as well as abilities with which he governed, inducing his subjects to forget the defects in his title, he transmitted his dominions quietly to his son; from whom they descended to his grandson. He was murdered by his grand uncle Ludovico, surnamed

surnamed the Moor, who took poffeffion of the
dutchy; and his right to it was confirmed by the
inveftiture of the Emperor Maximilian in the year
one thousand four hundred and ninety-four [a].

Louis XI. who took pleafure in depreffing the
Princes of the blood, and who admired the political abilities of Francis Sforza, would not permit
the Duke of Orleans to take any ftep in profecution of his right to the dutchy of Milan. Ludovico the Moor kept up fuch a clofe connection
with Charles VIII. that, during the greater part of
his reign, the claim of the family of Orleans continued to lie dormant. But when the crown of
France devolved to Louis XII. Duke of Orleans,
he inftantly afferted the rights of his family with
the ardour which it was natural to expect. Ludovico Sforza, incapable of contending with fuch
a rival, was ftripped of all his dominions in the
fpace of a few days. The King, clad in the ducal
robes, entered Milan in triumph; and foon after,
Ludovico having been betrayed by the Swifs in
his pay, was fent a prifoner into France, and fhut
up in the caftle of Loches, where he lay unpitied
during the remainder of his days. In confequence
of one of the fingular revolutions which occur fo
frequently in the hiftory of the Milanefe, his fon
Maximilian Sforza was placed on the ducal throne,
of which he kept poffeffion during the reign of

[a] Ripalm. hift. Mediol. lib. vi. 654. ap. Struv. corp. i. 930.
Du Mont Corps Diplom. tom. iii. p ii. 333. ibid.

Sect. III. Louis XII. But his successor Francis I. was too
A.D. 1515. high-spirited and enterprizing tamely to relinquish
his title. As soon as he was seated upon the
throne, he prepared to invade the Milanese; and
his right of succession to it, appears from this
detail, to have been more natural and more just
than that of any other competitor.

It is unnecessary to enter into any detail with
respect to the form of government in Genoa,
Parma, Modena, and the other inferior States of
Italy. Their names, indeed, will often occur in
the following history. But the power of these
States themselves was so inconsiderable, that their
fate depended little upon their own efforts; and
the frequent revolutions which they underwent,
were brought about by the operations of the
Princes who attacked or defended them, rather than
by any thing peculiar in their internal constitution.

The constitution and government of Spain. Of the great kingdoms on this side of the Alps,
Spain is one of the most considerable; and as it
was the hereditary domain of Charles V, as well
as the chief source of his power and wealth, a
distinct knowledge of its political constitution is
of capital importance towards understanding the
transactions of his reign.

Conquered by the Vandals. The Vandals and Goths, who overturned the
Roman power in Spain, established a form of
government in that country, and brought in customs and laws, perfectly similar to those which
were

were introduced into the rest of Europe, by the other victorious tribes which acquired settlements there. For some time, society advanced, among the new inhabitants of Spain, by the same steps, and seemed to hold the same course, as in other European nations. To this progress, a sudden stop was put by the invasion of the Saracens or Moors. The Goths could not withstand the efforts of their enthusiastick valour, which subdued Spain, with the same impetuous rapidity that distinguishes all the operations of their arms. The conquerors introduced into the country in which they settled the Mahometan religion, the Arabick language, the manners of the East, together with that taste for the arts, and that love of elegance and splendour, which the Caliphs had begun to cultivate among their subjects.

SECT. III.

A. D. 712. and by the Moors.

Such Gothick nobles, as disdained to submit to the Moorish yoke, fled for refuge to the inaccessible mountains of Asturias. There they comforted themselves with enjoying the exercise of the Christian religion, and with maintaining the authority of their ancient laws. Being joined by many of the boldest and most warlike among their countrymen, they sallied out upon the adjacent settlements of the Moors, in small parties; but venturing only upon short excursions at first, they were satisfied with plunder and revenge, without thinking of conquest. By degrees, their strength increased, their views enlarged, a regular government was established among them, and they began

The Christians gradually recover dominion in Spain.

to

Sect. III. to aim at extending their territories. While they pushed on their attacks with the unremitting ardour excited by zeal for religion, by the desire of vengeance, and by the hope of rescuing their country from oppression; while they conducted their operations with the courage natural to men who had no other occupation but war, and who were strangers to all the arts which corrupt or enfeeble the mind, the Moors gradually lost many of the advantages, to which they had been indebted for their first success. They threw off all dependence on the Caliphs [*]; they neglected to preserve a close connection with their contrymen in Africa; their Empire in Spain was split into many small kingdoms; the arts which they cultivated, together with the luxury to which these gave rise, relaxed, in some measure, the force of their military institutions, and abated the vigour of their warlike spirit. The Moors, however, continued still to be a gallant people, and possessed great resources. According to the magnificent stile of the Spanish historians, eight centuries of almost uninterrupted war elapsed, and three thousand seven hundred battles were fought before

1492. the last of the Moorish kingdoms in Spain submitted to the Christian arms.

The union of its various kingdoms. As the Christians made their conquests upon the Mahometans at various periods, and under different leaders, each formed the territory which he had wrested from the common enemy, into an

[*] Jos. Sim. Assemanni Hisor. Ital. Scriptores. vol. iii. p. 135.

independent

independent State. Spain was divided into as many separate kingdoms, as it contained provinces, and in each city of note, a petty Monarch established his throne, and assumed all the ensigns of royalty. In a series of years, however, by the usual events of intermarriages, or legal succession, or conquest, all these inferior principalities were annexed to the more powerful kingdoms of Castile and of Aragon. At length, by the fortunate marriage of Ferdinand and Isabella, the former the hereditary Monarch of Aragon, and the latter raised to the throne of Castile by the affection of her subjects, all the Spanish crowns were united, and descended in the same line.

Sect. III.

1481.

From this period, the political constitution of Spain began to assume a regular and uniform appearance; the genius of government may be delineated, and the progress of its laws and manners may be traced with certainty. Notwithstanding the singular revolution which the invasion of the Moors occasioned in Spain, and the peculiarity of its fate, in being so long subjected to the Mahometan yoke, the customs introduced by the Vandals and Goths had taken such deep root, and were so thoroughly incorporated with the frame of its government, that in every province which the Christians recovered from the Moors, we find the condition of individuals, as well as the political constitution, nearly the same as in other nations of Europe. Lands were held by the same tenure; justice was dispensed in the same form; the same

Their ancient customs and laws survived amidst all their revolutions.

privileges

Sect. III.
which renders their state in some degree similar to that of other nations of Europe.

privileges were claimed by the nobility; and the same power exercised by the Cortes, or general assembly of the kingdom. Several circumstances contributed to secure this permanence of the feudal institutions in Spain, notwithstanding the conquest of the Moors, which seemed to have overturned them. Such of the Spaniards, as preserved their independence, adhered to their ancient customs, not only from attachment to them, but out of antipathy to the Moors, to whose ideas concerning property and government these customs were totally repugnant. Even among the Christians, who submitted to the Moorish conquerors, and consented to become their subjects, ancient customs were not entirely abolished. They were permitted to retain their religion; their laws concerning private property; their forms of administering justice; and their mode of levying taxes. The followers of Mahomet are the only enthusiasts, who have united the spirit of toleration with zeal for making proselytes, and who, at the same time that they took arms to propagate the doctrine of their prophet, permitted such as would not embrace it, to adhere to their own tenets, and to practise their own rites. To this peculiarity in the genius of the Mahometan religion, as well as to the desire which the Moors had of reconciling the Christians to their yoke, it was owing that the ancient manners and laws in Spain survived the violent shock of a conquest, and were permitted to subsist, notwithstanding the introduction of a new religion

and

and a new form of government into that country. It is obvious from all these particulars, that the Christians must have found it extremely easy to re-establish manners and government on their ancient foundations, in those provinces of Spain, which they wrested successively from the Moors. A considerable part of the people retained such a fondness for the customs, and such a reverence for the laws of their ancestors, that they wished to see them completely restored with full authority, and were not only willing but eager to resume the former, and to recognize the authority of the latter.

But though the feudal form of government, with all the institutions that characterize it, was thus preserved entire in Castile and Aragon, as well as in all the kingdoms which depended on these crowns, there were certain peculiarities in their political constitutions which distinguish them from those of any other country in Europe. The regal prerogative, extremely limited in every feudal kingdom, was circumscribed, in Spain, within such narrow bounds, as reduced the power of the sovereign almost to nothing. The privileges of the nobility were vast in proportion, and extended so far, as to border on absolute independence. The immunities of the cities were great, they possessed considerable influence in the Cortes or supreme assemblies of the nations, and they aspired at obtaining more. Such a state of society, in which the political machine was so ill adjusted,

Sect. III. and the several members of the legislature so improperly balanced, produced interior disorders in the kingdoms of Spain, which rose beyond the pitch of turbulence and anarchy, usual under the feudal government. The whole tenor of the Spanish history confirms the truth of this observation; and when the mutinous spirit, to which the genius of their policy gave birth and vigour, was no longer restrained and overawed by the immediate dread of the Moorish arms, it broke out into more frequent insurrections against the government of their Princes, as well as more outrageous insults on their dignity, than occur in the annals of any other country. These were accompanied at some times with more liberal sentiments concerning the rights of the people, at other times with more elevated notions concerning the privileges of the nobles, than were common in other nations.

Instances of this.

A. D. 1462.

In the principality of Catalonia, which was annexed to the kingdom of Aragon, the impatience of the people to obtain the redress of their grievances having prompted them to take arms against their sovereign John II, they, by a solemn deed, recalled the oath of allegiance which they had sworn to him, declared him and his posterity to be unworthy of the throne [p], and endeavoured to establish a republican form of government, in order to secure the perpetual enjoyment of that liberty,

[p] Zurita Anales de Arag. tom. iv. 113. 115. &c.

liberty, after which they aspired [q]. Nearly about the same period, the indignation of the Castilian nobility against the weak and flagitious administration of Henry IV, having led them to combine against him, they arrogated, as one of the privileges belonging to their order, the right of trying and of passing sentence on their sovereign. That the exercise of this power might be as publick and solemn, as the pretension to it was bold, they summoned all the nobility of their party to meet at Avila; a spacious theatre was erected in a plain without the walls of the town, an image representing the King, was seated on a throne, clad in royal robes, with a crown on its head, a sceptre in its hand, and the sword of justice by its side. The accusation against the King was read, and the sentence of deposition was pronounced, in presence of a numerous assembly. At the close of the first article of the charge, the archbishop of Toledo advanced, and tore the crown from the head of the image; at the close of the second, the Conde de Placentia snatched the sword of justice from its side; at the close of the third, the Conde de Benevente wrested the sceptre from its hand; at the close of the last, Don Diego Lopes de Stuniga tumbled it headlong from the throne. At the same instant, Don Alfonso, Henry's brother, was proclaimed King of Castile and Leon in his stead [r].

A.D. 1465.

[q] Ferreras hist. d'Espagne, tom. vii. p. 92. P. Orleans revol. d'Espagne, tom. iii. p. 155. L. Marinæus Siculus de reb. Hispan. apud Schotti Script. Hispan. vol. 429.
[r] Marian. hist. lib. xxiii. c. 9.

SECT. III. THE most daring leaders of faction would not have ventured on these measures, nor have conducted them with such publick ceremony, if the sentiments of the people concerning the royal dignity, had not been so formed by the laws and policy, to which they were accustomed both in Castile and Aragon, as prepared them to approve of such extraordinary proceedings, or to acquiesce in them.

The constitution and government of Aragon.

IN Aragon, the form of government was monarchical, but the genius and maxims of it were purely republican. The Kings, who were long elective, retained only the shadow of power; the real exercise of it was in the Cortes or parliament of the kingdom. This supreme assembly was composed of four different *arms* or members. The nobility of the first rank. The Equestrian order, or nobility of the second class. The representatives of the cities and towns, whose right to a place in the Cortes, if we may give credit to the historians of Aragon, was coeval with the constitution. The ecclesiastical order, composed of the dignitaries of the church, together with the representatives of the inferior clergy [r]. No law could pass in this assembly without the assent of every single member who had a right to vote [s]. Without the permission of the Cortes, no tax could be imposed; no war could be declared; no peace concluded; no money could be coined; nor any alteration be

[r] Forma de celebrar Cortes en Aragon, por Geron. Martel.
[s] Martel. ibid. p. 2.

made

made in the current specie[s]. The power of reviewing the proceedings of all inferior courts, the privilege of inspecting every department of administration, and the right of redressing all grievances, belonged to the Cortes. Nor did those who conceived themselves to be aggrieved, address the Cortes in the humble tone of supplicants, and petition for redress; they demanded it as the birthright of freemen, and required the guardians of their liberty to decide with respect to the points which they laid before them[x]. This sovereign court was held, during several centuries, every year; but, in consequence of a regulation introduced about the beginning of the fourteenth century, it was convoked from that period only once in two years. After it was assembled, the King had no right to prorogue or dissolve it without its own consent; and the session continued forty days[y].

Not satisfied with having erected these barriers against the encroachments of the royal prerogative, nor willing to rely for the preservation of their liberties on the vigilance and authority of an assembly, similar to the diets, states-general, and parliaments, in which the other feudal nations placed so much confidence, the Aragonese had recourse to an institution peculiar to themselves, and elected a *Justiza* or supreme judge. This magis-

Office and Jurisdiction of the Justiza.

[s] Hier. Blanca comment. rer. Aragon. ap. Schot. Script. Hispan. vol. iii. p. 750.
[x] Martel. Forma de celebr. p. 2.
[y] Hier. Blanca comment. 763.

SECT. III. trate, whose office bore some resemblance to that of the Ephori in ancient Sparta, acted as the guardian of the people, and the comptroller of the Prince. The person of the Justiza was sacred, and his power and jurisdiction almost unbounded. He was the supreme interpreter of the laws. Not only inferior judges, but the Kings themselves were bound to consult him in every doubtful case, and to receive his responses with implicit deference[*]. An appeal lay to him from the royal judges, as well as from those appointed by the barons within their respective territories. Even when no appeal was made to him, he could interpose by his own authority, prohibit the ordinary judge to proceed, take immediate cognizance of the cause himself, and remove the party accused to the *Manifestation* or prison of the state, to which no person had access but by his permission. His power was exerted with no less vigour and effect in superintending the administration of government, than in regulating the course of justice. It was the prerogative of the Justiza to inspect the conduct of the King. He had a title to review all the royal proclamations and patents, and to declare whether or not they were agreeable to law, and ought to be carried into execution. He, by his sole authority, could exclude any of the King's ministers from the conduct of affairs, and call them to answer for

[*] Blanca has preserved two responses of the Justiza to James II. who reigned towards the close of the thirteenth century, Blanca 748.

their mal-adminiſtration. He himſelf was accountable to the Cortes alone, for the manner in which
he diſcharged the duties of this high office, and
performed functions of the greateſt importance that
could be committed to a ſubject [HH]*.

It is evident from a bare enumeration of the privileges of the Aragoneſe Cortes, as well as of the rights belonging to the Juſtiza, that a very ſmall portion of power remained in the hands of the King. The Aragoneſe ſeem to have been ſolicitous that their Monarchs ſhould know and feel this ſtate of impotence, to which they were reduced. Even in ſwearing allegiance to their ſovereign, an act which ought, naturally, to be accompanied with profeſſions of ſubmiſſion and reſpect, they deviſed an oath, in ſuch a form, as to remind him of his dependence on his ſubjects. "We,' ſaid the Juſtiza to the King in name of his high-ſpirited barons, " who are each of us as good, and who are altogether more powerful than you, promiſe obedience to your government, if you maintain our rights and liberties; but if not, not." Conformably to this oath, they eſtabliſhed it as a fundamental article in their conſtitution, that if the King ſhould violate their rights and privileges, it was lawful for the people to diſclaim him as their ſovereign, and to elect another, even though a heathen, in his place¹. The attachment of the

marginal note: The regal power circumſcribed within narrow limits.

[HH] NOTE XXXI.
* Hier. Blanca Comment. p. 747—755.
¹ Hier. Blanca Comment. 720.

Sect. III Aragonese to this singular constitution of government, was extreme, and their respect for it approached to superstitious veneration [II]. In the preamble to one of their laws, they declare, that such was the barrenness of their country, and the poverty of the inhabitants, that, if it were not on account of the liberties by which they were distinguished from other nations, the people would abandon it, and go in quest of a settlement to some more fruitful region [b].

Constitution and government of Castile.

In Castile, there were not such peculiarities in the form of government, as to establish any remarkable distinction between it and that of the other European nations. The executive part of government was committed to the King, but with a prerogative extremely limited. The legislative authority resided in the Cortes, which was composed of the nobility, the dignified ecclesiasticks, and the representatives of the cities. The assembly of the Cortes in Castile was very ancient, and seems to have been coeval with the constitution. The members of the three different orders, who had a right of suffrage, met in one place, and deliberated as one collective body; the decisions of which were regulated by the sentiments of the majority. The right of imposing taxes, of enacting laws, and of redressing grievances belonged to this assembly; and in order to secure the assent of the King to such statutes and regulations as were deem-

[II] NOTE XXXII.
[b] Hier. Blanca Com. p. 754.

ed falutary or beneficial to the kingdom, it was Sect. III.
ufual in the Cortes, to take no ftep towards granting money, until all bufinefs relative to the publick welfare was concluded. The reprefentatives of cities feem to have obtained a feat very early in the Cortes of Caftile, and foon acquired fuch influence and credit, as were very uncommon, at a period when the fplendor and pre-eminence of the nobility had eclipfed or annihilated all other orders of men. The number of members from cities, bore fuch a proportion to that of the whole collective body, as rendered them extremely refpectable in the Cortes [KK]. The degree of confideration, which they poffeffed in the ftate, may be eftimated by one event. Upon the death of John I. A.D. 1390. a council of regency was appointed to govern the kingdom during the minority of his fon. It was compofed of an equal number of noblemen, and of deputies chofen by the cities; the latter were admitted to the fame rank, and invefted with the fame powers, as prelates and grandees of the firft order[c]. But though the members of communities in Caftile were elevated above the condition wherein they were placed in other kingdoms of Europe; though they had attained to fuch political importance, that even the proud and jealous fpirit of the feudal ariftocracy could not exclude them from a confiderable fhare in government; yet the nobles, notwithftanding thefe acquifitions of the commons, continued to affert the privileges of

[KK] NOTE XXXII.
[c] Marian. hift. lib. xviii. c. 15.

their

Sect. III. their order, in opposition to the crown, in a tone extremely high. There was not any body of nobility in Europe more distinguished for independence of spirit, haughtiness of deportment, and bold pretensions, than that of Castile. The history of that monarchy affords the most striking examples of the vigilance with which they observed, and of the vigour with which they opposed every scheme of their Kings, that tended to encroach on their jurisdiction, to diminish their dignity, or to abridge their power. Even in their ordinary intercourse with their Monarchs, they preserved such a consciousness of their rank, that the nobles of the first order claimed it as a privilege to be covered in the royal presence, and approached their sovereigns rather as equals than as subjects.

The constitution of the subordinate monarchies, which depended on the crowns of Castile and Aragon, nearly resembled that of the kingdom to which they were annexed. In all of them, the dignity and independence of the nobles were great; the immunities and power of the cities were considerable.

Various causes of the limited authority of the Spanish Monarchs. An attentive observation of the singular situation of Spain, as well as the various events which occured there, from the invasion of the Moors to the union of its kingdoms under Ferdinand and Isabella, will discover the causes, to which all the peculiarities in its political constitution, that I have pointed out, ought to be ascribed.

As

As the provinces of Spain were wrested from the Mahometans gradually and with difficulty, the nobles, who followed the standard of any eminent leader in these wars, conquered not for him alone, but for themselves. They claimed a share in the lands which their valour had torn from the enemy, and their prosperity and power increased, in proportion as the territory of the Prince extended.

During their perpetual wars with the Moors, the Monarchs of Spain depended so much on their nobles, that it became necessary to conciliate their good-will by successive grants of new honours and privileges. By the time that any Prince could establish his dominion in a conquered province, the greater part of the property was parcelled out by him among his barons, with such jurisdiction and immunities, as raised them almost to sovereign power.

At the same time, the kingdoms erected in so many different corners of Spain, were extremely inconsiderable. The petty Monarch was but little elevated above his nobles. They, feeling themselves to be almost his equals, acted as such. The Kings of such limited domains could neither command much respect, nor possess great power; and noblemen, so nearly on the same level, could not look up to them with that reverence, with which the sovereigns of the great monarchies in Europe were viewed by their subjects [LL].

[LL] NOTE XXXIV.

These

SECT. III. THESE circumstances concurred in exalting the nobility, and in depressing the royal authority; there were other causes which raised the cities in Spain to consideration and power.

As the open country, during the wars with the Moors, was perpetually exposed to the excursions of the enemy, with whom no peace or truce was so permanent as to prove any lasting security, self-preservation obliged persons of all ranks to fix their residence in places of strength. The castles of the barons, which, in other countries, afforded a commodious retreat from the depredations of banditti, or from the transient violence of any interior commotion, were unable to resist an enemy whose operations were conducted with regular and persevering vigour. Cities, in which great numbers united for their mutual defence, were the only places in which people could fix their residence with any prospect of safety. To this was owing the rapid growth of those cities in Spain of which the Christians recovered possession. All who fled from the Moorish yoke resorted to them, as to an asylum; and there, the greater part of those, who took the field against the Mahometans, established their families.

EACH of these cities, during a longer or shorter course of years, was the capital of a little state, and enjoyed all the advantages, which accelerate the increase of inhabitants in every place that is the seat of government.

THE number of cities in Spain, at the beginning of the fifteenth century, was considerable, and they were peopled far beyond the proportion which was common in other parts of Europe, except in Italy and the Low-Countries. The Moors had introduced manufactures into these cities, while under their dominion. The Christians, who, by intermixture with them, had learned their arts, continued to cultivate these. The trade of several of the Spanish towns appears to have been considerable; and the spirit of commerce continued to preserve the number of their inhabitants, as the sense of danger had first induced them to crowd together.

As the Spanish cities were populous, many of the inhabitants were of a rank superior to those who resided in towns in other countries of Europe. That cause, which contributed chiefly to their population, affected equally persons of every condition, who flocked thither promiscuously, in order to find shelter, or in hopes of making a stand there against the enemy, with greater advantage than in any other station. The persons elected as their representatives in the Cortes by the cities, or promoted to offices of trust and dignity in the government of the community, were often, as will appear from transactions which I shall hereafter relate, of such considerable rank in the kingdom, as reflected lustre on their constituents, and on the stations wherein they were placed.

SECT. III. As it was impossible to carry on a continual war against the Moors, without some other military force, than that which the barons were obliged to bring into the field, in consequence of the feudal tenures, it became necessary to have some troops, particularly a body of light cavalry, in constant pay. It was one of the privileges of the nobles, that their lands were exempt from the burden of taxes. The charge of supporting the troops requisite for the publick safety, fell wholly upon the cities; and their Kings, being obliged frequently to apply to them for aid, found it necessary to gain their favour by concessions, which extended their immunities, and added to their wealth and power.

When the influence of all these circumstances, peculiar to Spain, is added to the general and common causes, which contributed to aggrandize cities in other countries of Europe, this will fully account for the extensive privileges which they acquired, as well as for the extraordinary consideration to which they attained, in all the Spanish kingdoms [MM].

Measures of different Princes in order to extend their power. By these exorbitant privileges of the nobility, and this unusual power of the cities in Spain, the royal prerogative was hemmed in on every side, and reduced within very narrow bounds. Sensible of this, and impatient of such restraint, different Monarchs endeavoured, at various junctures, to enlarge their own jurisdiction, and to circumscribe

[MM] NOTE XXXV.

that of their subjects. Their power, however, or their abilities were so unequal to the undertaking, that their efforts were attended with little success. But when Ferdinand and Isabella found themselves at the head of all the united kingdoms of Spain, and delivered from the danger and interruption of domestick wars, they were not only in a condition to resume, but were able to prosecute with advantage, the schemes of extending the prerogative, which their ancestors had attempted in vain. Ferdinand's profound sagacity in concerting his measures, his persevering industry in conducting them, and his uncommon address in carrying them into execution, fitted him admirably for an undertaking which required all these talents.

Particularly of Ferdinand and Isabella.

As the overgrown power, and high pretensions of the nobility were what the Monarchs of Spain felt most sensibly, and bore with the greatest impatience, the great object of Ferdinand's policy was to reduce these within more moderate bounds. Under various pretexts, sometimes by violence, more frequently in consequence of decrees obtained in the courts of law, he wrested from the barons a great part of the lands, which had been granted to them by the inconsiderate bounty of former Monarchs, particularly during the feeble and profuse reign of his predecessor Henry IV. He did not give the entire conduct of affairs to persons of noble birth, who were accustomed to occupy every department of importance in peace or in war, as if it had been a privilege peculiar to their

Ferdinand's different schemes for abridging the privileges and power of the nobility.

Sect. III. their order, to be employed as the sole counsellors and ministers of the crown. He often transacted business of great consequence without their intervention, and committed many offices of power and trust to new men, devoted to his interest [a]. He introduced a degree of state and dignity into his court, which being unknown in Spain, while it remained split into many small kingdoms, taught the nobles to approach their sovereign with more ceremony, and gradually rendered him the object of greater deference and respect.

Particularly by annexing the grand-masterships of the three orders to the crown. THE annexing the masterships of the three military orders of St. Jago, Calatrava, and Alcantara, to the crown, was another expedient, by which Ferdinand greatly augmented the revenue and power of the Kings of Spain. These orders were instituted in imitation of those of the Knights Templars and of St. John of Jerusalem, on purpose to wage perpetual war with the Mahometans, and to protect the pilgrims who visited Compostella, or other places of eminent sanctity in Spain. The zeal and superstition of the ages, in which they were founded, prompted persons of every rank to bestow such liberal donations on these holy warriors, that, in a short time, they engrossed a considerable share in the property and wealth of the kingdom. The masterships of these orders came to be stations of the greatest power and opulence to which a Spanish nobleman could be advanced. These high dignities were in the disposal

[a] Zurita anales de Arag. tom. vi. p. 22.

of the Knights of the Order, and placed the per- SECT. III.
sons on whom they conferred them almost on a
level with their sovereign [NN]. Ferdinand, unwilling that the nobility, whom he considered as
already too formidable, should derive such additional credit and influence from possessing the
government of these wealthy fraternities, was solicitous to wrest it out of their hands, and to vest
it in the crown. His measures for accomplishing A. D. 1476,
this, were wisely planned, and executed with and 1493.
vigour [e]. By address, by promises, and by threats,
he prevailed on the Knights of each Order to
place Isabella and him at the head of it. Innocent VIII. and Alexander VI. gave this election
the sanction of papal authority [f]; and subsequent
Pontiffs rendered the annexation of these masterships to the crown perpetual.

WHILE Ferdinand, by this measure, diminished And by cir-
the power and influence of the nobility, and added cumscribing
new lustre or authority to the crown, he was tion of the
taking other important steps with a view to the nobility.
same object. The sovereign jurisdiction which the
feudal barons exercised within their own territories,
was the pride and distinction of their order. To
have invaded openly a privilege which they prized
so highly, and in defence of which they would

[NN] NOTE XXXVI.
[e] Marian. hist. lib. xxv. c. 5.
[f] Zurita anales tom. v. p. 22. Ælii. Anton. Nebrissensis
rerum a Ferdinand & Elizabe gestarum decades. ii. apud
Schot. script. Hispan. i. 860.

VOL. I.   O   have

Sect. III. have run so eagerly to arms, was a measure too daring for a Prince of Ferdinand's cautious temper. He took advantage, however, of an opportunity which the state of his kingdoms and the spirit of his people presented him, in order to undermine what he durst not assault. The incessant depredations of the Moors, the want of discipline among the troops which were employed to oppose them, the frequent civil wars between the crown and the nobility, as well as the undiscerning rage with which the barons carried on their private wars with each other, filled all the provinces of Spain with disorder. Rapine, outrage, and murder, became so common, as not only to interrupt commerce, but in a great measure to suspend all intercourse between one place and another. That security and protection which men expect from entering into civil society, ceased almost totally. Interior order and police, while the feudal institutions remained in vigour, were so little objects of attention, and the administration of justice was so extremely feeble, that it would have been vain to have expected relief from the established laws or the ordinary judges. But the evil became so intolerable, and the inhabitants of cities, who were the chief sufferers, grew so impatient of this anarchy, that self-preservation forced them to have recourse to an extraordinary remedy. About the middle of the thirteenth century, the cities in the kingdom of Aragon, and after their example those in Castile, formed themselves into an association,

ciation, diftinguifhed by the name of the *Holy Brotherhood.* They exacted a certain contribution from each of the aſſociated towns; they levied a confiderable body of troops, in order to protect travellers, and to purfue criminals; they appointed judges, who opened their courts in various parts of the kingdom. Whoever was guilty of murder, robbery, or of any act that violated the publick peace, and was feized by the troops of the *Brotherhood,* was carried before their own judges, who, without paying any regard to the exclufive and fovereign jurifdiction which the lord of the place might claim, tried and condemned the criminals. By means of this, the prompt and impartial adminiftration of juftice was reftored; and together with it, internal tranquillity and order began to return. The nobles alone murmured at this falutary inftitution. They complained of it as an encroachment on one of their moft valuable privileges. They remonftrated againſt it in an high tone; and, on fome occaſions, refufed to grant any aid to the crown, unlefs it were abolifhed. Ferdinand, however, was fenfible not only of the good effects of the Holy Brotherhood with refpect to the police of his kingdoms, but perceived its tendency to abridge, and at length to annihilate the territorial jurifdiction of the nobility. He countenanced the inftitution on every occaſion. He fupported it with the whole force of royal authority; and befides the expedients employed by him in common with the other monarchs of Europe,

Sect. III. rope, he availed himself of this institution, which was peculiar to his kingdom, in order to limit and abolish that independent jurisdiction of the nobility, which was no less inconsistent with the authority of the Prince, than with the order of society [OO].

Notwithstanding all these, the government of Spain still extremely free.

But though Ferdinand by these measures considerably enlarged the boundaries of prerogative, and acquired a degree of influence and power far beyond what any of his predecessors had enjoyed, yet the limitations of the royal authority, and the barriers against its encroachments, continued to be many and strong. The spirit of liberty was vigorous among the people of Spain; the spirit of independence was high among the nobility; and though the love of glory, peculiar to the Spaniards in every period of their history, prompted them to support Ferdinand with zeal in his foreign operations, and to afford him such aid as enabled him not only to undertake but to execute great enterprizes; he reigned over his subjects with a jurisdiction less extensive than that of any of the great monarchs in Europe. It will appear from many passages in the following history, that, during a considerable part of the reign of his successor Charles V. the prerogative of the Spanish crown was equally circumscribed.

Constitution and government of France.

The ancient government and laws in France so nearly resembled those of the other feudal king-

[OO] NOTE XXXVII.

doms,

doms, that such a detail with respect to them as was necessary, in order to convey some idea of the nature and effects of the peculiar institutions which took place in Spain, would be superfluous. In the view which I have exhibited of the means by which the French monarchs acquired such full command of the national force of their kingdom, as enabled them to engage in extensive schemes of foreign operation, I have already pointed out the great steps by which they advanced towards a more ample possession of political power, and a more uncontrouled exercise of their royal prerogative. All that now remains is to take notice of such particulars in the constitution of France, as serve either to distinguish it from that of other countries, or tend to throw any light on the transactions of that period to which the following history extends.

UNDER the French monarchs of the first race, the royal prerogative was very inconsiderable. The General Assemblies of the nation, which met annually at stated seasons, extended their authority to every department of government. The power of electing Kings, of enacting laws, of redressing grievances, of passing judgment in the last resort, with respect to every person and to every cause, and of conferring donations on the Prince, resided in this great convention of the nation. Under the second race of Kings, notwithstanding the power and splendour which the conquests of Charlemagne added to the crown, the general

Power of the General Assemblies under the first race of Kings.

Under the second.

assemblies

Sect. III. assemblies of the nations continued to possess extensive authority. The right of determining which of the royal family should be placed on the throne, was vested in them. The Princes elevated to that dignity by their suffrage were accustomed regularly to call and to consult them with respect to every affair of importance to the state, and without their consent no law was passed, and no new tax was levied.

Under the third.

But, by the time that Hugh Capet, the father of the third race of Kings, took possession of the throne of France, such changes had happened in the political state of the kingdom, as considerably affected the power and jurisdiction of the general assembly of the nation. The royal authority in the hands of the degenerate posterity of Charlemagne, had dwindled into insignificance and contempt. Every considerable proprietor of land had formed his territory into a barony, almost independent of the sovereign. The dukes or governors of provinces, the counts or governors of towns and small districts, and the great officers of the crown, had rendered these dignities, originally granted only during pleasure or for life, hereditary in their families. Each of these had usurped all the rights which hitherto had been deemed the distinctions of royalty, particularly the privileges of dispensing justice within their own domains, of coining money, and of waging war. Every district was governed by local customs, acknowledged a distinct lord, and pursued a separate interest. The formality of doing homage to their sovereign, was

almost

almost the only act of subjection which haughty barons would perform, and that bound them no farther than they were willing to acknowledge its obligation [PP].

In a kingdom broken into so many independent baronies, hardly any common principle of union remained; and the general assembly in its deliberations could scarce consider the nation as forming one body, or establish common regulations to be of equal force in every part. Within the immediate domains of the crown the King might publish laws, and they were obeyed, because there he was acknowledged as the only lord. But if he had aimed at rendering these general, that would have alarmed the barons as an encroachment upon the independence of their jurisdiction. The barons, with no less care, avoided the enacting of general laws, because the execution of them must have been vested in the King, and would have enlarged that paramount power, which was the object of their jealousy. Thus, under the descendants of Hugh Capet, the States General (for that was the name by which the supreme assembly of the French nation came then to be distinguished) lost their legislative authority, or at least entirely relinquished the exercise of it. From that period, the jurisdiction of the States General extended no farther than to the imposition of new taxes, the determination of questions with respect to the right of succession

[PP] NOTE XXXVIII.

Sect. III to the crown, the settling of the regency when the preceding monarch had not fixed it by his will, and the presenting remonstrances enumerating the grievances of which the nation wished to obtain redress.

As, during several centuries, the monarchs of Europe seldom demanded extraordinary subsidies of their subjects, and the other events which required the interposition of the States, rarely occurred, their meetings in France were not frequent. They were summoned occasionally by their Kings, when compelled by their wants or by their fears to have recourse to their aid; but they did not, like the Diet in Germany, the Cortes in Spain, or the Parliament in England, form an essential member of the constitution, the regular exertion of whose powers was requisite to give vigour and order to government.

The crown begins to assume the legislative authority.

When the States of France ceased to exercise legislative authority, the Kings began to assume it. They ventured at first on acts of legislation with great reserve; and after taking every precaution that could prevent their subjects from being alarmed at the exercise of a new power. They did not at once issue their ordinances in a tone of authority and command. They treated with their subjects; they pointed out what was best; and allured them to comply with it. By degrees, however, as the prerogative of the crown extended, and as the supreme jurisdiction of the royal courts came to be established,

established, the Kings of France assumed more Sect. III.
openly the stile and authority of law-givers; and
before the beginning of the fifteenth century,
the complete legislative power was vested in
them [QQ].

HAVING secured this important acquisition, the *and the*
steps that led to the right of imposing taxes were ren- *power of*
levying
dered few and easy. The people, accustomed to see *taxes.*
their sovereigns, by their sole authority, issue ordinances which regulated points of the greatest consequence with respect to the property of their subjects,
were not alarmed when they were required, by the
royal edicts, to contribute certain sums towards supplying the exigencies of government, and carrying
forward the measures of the nation. When Charles
VII. and Louis XI. first ventured to exercise this
new power, in the manner which I have already
described, the gradual increase of the royal authority had so imperceptibly prepared the minds of
the people of France for this innovation, that it
excited no commotion in the kingdom, and seems
scarcely to have given rise to any murmur or
complaint.

WHEN the Kings of France had thus engrossed *Govern-*
every power which can be exerted in government; *France be-*
when the right of making laws, of levying money, *purely mo-*
of keeping an army of mercenaries in constant *narchical.*
pay, of declaring war and of concluding peace

[QQ] NOTE XXXIX.
centered

SECT. III. centered in the crown, the constitution of the kingdom, which, under the first race of Kings, was nearly democratical, which, under the second race, became an aristocracy, terminated, under the third race, in a pure monarchy. Every thing that tended to preserve the appearance, or revive the memory of the ancient mixed government, seems from that period to have been industriously avoided. During the long and active reign of Francis I. the variety as well as extent of whose operations obliged him to lay many heavy impositions on his subjects, the States General of France were not once assembled, nor were the people once allowed to exert the power of taxing themselves, which, according to the original ideas of feudal government, was a right essential to every freeman.

The exercise of prerogative restrained by the privileges of the nobility;

Two things, however, remained, which moderated the exercise of the regal prerogative, and restrained it within such bounds as preserved the constitution of France from degenerating into mere despotism. The rights and privileges claimed by the nobility, must be considered as one barrier against the absolute dominion of the crown. Though the nobles of France had lost that political power which was vested in their order as a body, they still retained the personal rights and pre-eminence which they derived from their rank. They preserved a consciousness of elevation above other classes of citizens; an exemption from burdens to which they were subject; a contempt of the occupations in which they were engaged; the

privilege

privilege of assuming ensigns that indicated their dignity; a right to be treated with a certain degree of deference during peace; and a claim to various distinctions when in the field. Many of these pretensions were not founded on the words of statutes, or derived from positive laws; they were defined and ascertained by the maxims of honour, a title more delicate, but no less sacred. These rights, established and protected by a principle equally vigilant in guarding, and intrepid in defending them, are to the Sovereign himself objects of respect and veneration. Wherever they stand in its way, the royal prerogative is bounded. The violence of a Despot may exterminate such an order of men; but as long as it subsists, and its ideas of personal distinction remain entire, the power of the Prince has limits [x].

As in France, the body of nobility was very numerous, and the individuals of which it was composed retained an high sense of their own pre-eminence, to this we may ascribe, in a great measure, the mode of exercising the royal prerogative which peculiarly distinguishes the government of that kingdom. An intermediate order was placed between the Monarch and his other subjects, and in every act of authority it became necessary to attend to its privileges, and not only to guard against any real violation of these, but to avoid any suspicion of its being possible that they might be violated.

[x] De l'Esprit des Loix, liv. ii. c. 4. Dr. Ferguson's Essay on the Hist. of Civil Society, part i. sec. 10.

Thus

Sect. III.

Thus a species of government was established in France, unknown in the ancient world, that of a monarchy, in which the power of the sovereign, though unconfined by any legal or constitutional restraint, has certain bounds set to it by the ideas which one class of his subjects entertain concerning their own dignity.

And by the jurisdiction of the parliaments, particularly that of Paris.

The jurisdiction of the Parliaments in France, particularly that of Paris, was the other barrier which served to confine the exercise of the royal prerogative within certain limits. The parliament of Paris was originally the court of the Kings of France, to which they committed the supreme administration of justice within their own domains, as well as the power of deciding with respect to all cases brought before it by appeals from the courts of the barons. When, in consequence of events and regulations which have been mentioned formerly, the time and place of its meeting were fixed, when not only the form of its procedure, but the principles on which it decided, were rendered regular and consistent, when every cause of importance was finally determined there, and when the people became accustomed to resort thither as to the supreme temple of justice, the parliament of Paris rose to high estimation in the kingdom, its members acquired dignity, and its decrees were submitted to with deference. Nor was this the only source of the power and influence which the parliament obtained. The Kings of France, when they first began to assume the legislative power, in order

order to reconcile the minds of their people to this new exertion of prerogative, produced their edicts and ordinances in the parliament of Paris, that they might be approved of and regiſtered there, before they were publiſhed and declared to be of authority in the kingdom. During the intervals between the meetings of the States General of the kingdom, or under thoſe reigns when the States General were not aſſembled, the Monarchs of France were accuſtomed to conſult the parliament of Paris with reſpect to the moſt arduous affairs of government, and frequently regulated their conduct by its advice, in declaring war, in concluding peace, and in other tranſactions of publick concern. Thus there was erected in the kingdom a tribunal which became the great depoſitory of the laws, and by the uniform tenor of its decrees, it eſtabliſhed principles of juſtice and forms of proceeding which were conſidered as ſo ſacred, that even the ſovereign power of the Monarch durſt not venture to diſregard or to violate them. The members of this illuſtrious body, though they neither poſſeſs legiſlative authority, nor can be conſidered as the repreſentatives of the people, have availed themſelves of the reputation and influence which they had acquired among their countrymen, in order to make a ſtand to the utmoſt of their ability againſt every unprecedented and exorbitant exertion of the prerogative. In every period of the French hiſtory, they have merited the praiſe of being the virtuous

tuous but feeble guardians of the rights and privileges of the nation [RR].

Constitution and government of the German Empire.

THE kingdom of France extends to the confines of the German Empire, from which Charles V. derived his title of highest dignity. In explaining the political constitution of this vast and complex body at the beginning of the sixteenth century, I shall avoid entering into such a detail as would involve my readers in that inextricable labyrinth, which is formed by the multiplicity of its tribunals, the number of its members, their interfering rights, and by the endless discussions or refinements of the publick lawyers of Germany with respect to all these.

Its state under Charlemagne and his descendants.

THE Empire of Charlemagne was a structure erected in so short a time that it could not be permanent. Under his immediate successor it began to totter; and it soon fell to pieces. The crown of Germany was separated for ever from that of France, and the descendants of Charlemagne established two great monarchies so situated as to give rise to a perpetual rivalship and enmity between them. But the Princes of the race of Charlemagne who were placed on the Imperial throne, were not altogether so degenerate, as those of the same family who reigned in France. In the hands of the former the royal authority retained some vigour, and the nobles of Germany, though pos-

[RR] NOTE XL.

sessed

STATE OF EUROPE.

feſſed of extenſive privileges as well as ample ter- Sect. III.
ritories, did not ſo early attain independence.
The great offices of the crown continued to be at
the diſpoſal of the ſovereign, and during a long
period, fiefs remained in their original ſtate, without becoming hereditary and perpetual in the
families to which they had been granted.

At length the German branch of the family of Other famiCharlemagne became extinct, and his feeble de- ed to the
ſcendants who reigned in France had ſunk into Imperial
ſuch contempt, that the Germans, without looking
towards them, exerciſed the right inherent in a
free people; and in a general aſſembly of the A.D. 911.
nation elected Conrad Count of Franconia Emperor. After him Henry of Saxony, and his deſcendants the three Othos, were placed, in ſucceſſion, on the Imperial throne, by the ſuffrages
of their countrymen. The extenſive territories of
the Saxon Emperors, their eminent abilities and
enterprizing genius, not only added new vigour to
the Imperial dignity, but raiſed it to higher power
and pre-eminence. Otho the Great marched at A.D. 972,
the head of a numerous army into Italy, and after
the example of Charlemagne, gave law to that
country. Every power there recognized his authority. He created Popes and depoſed them by
his ſovereign mandate. He annexed the kingdom
of Italy to the German Empire. Elated with his
ſucceſs, he aſſumed the title of Cæſar Auguſtus [b].
A Prince born in the heart of Germany pretended

[b] Annaliſta Saxo, &c. ap. Struv. Corp. vol. i. p. 246.

to

208   A VIEW OF THE

SECT. II. to be the successor of the Emperors of ancient Rome, and claimed a right to the same power and prerogative.

The German nobility acquire independent and sovereign authority.

BUT while the Emperors, by means of these new titles, and new dominions, gradually acquired additional authority and splendour, the nobility of Germany went on at the same time extending their privileges and jurisdiction. The situation of affairs was favourable to their attempts. The vigour which Charlemagne had given to government quickly relaxed. The inability of some of his successors was such, as would have encouraged vassals less enterprizing than the nobles of that age, to have claimed new rights and to have assumed new powers. The civil wars in which other Emperors were engaged, obliged them to pay perpetual court to their subjects on whose support they depended, and not only to connive at their usurpations, but to permit and even to authorize them. Fiefs gradually became hereditary. They were transmitted not only in the direct, but in the collateral line. The investiture of them was demanded not only by male but by female heirs. Every baron began to exercise sovereign jurisdiction within his own domains; and the Dukes and Counts of Germany took wide steps towards rendering their territories distinct and independent States¹. The Saxon Emperors observed their progress, and were aware of its tendency.

The German ecclesiasticks raised to the same power.

¹ Pfeffel. Abregé. p. 120, 152. Lib. Feudor. tit. 1.

dency. But as they could not hope to humble Sect. III.
vassals already grown too potent, unless they had
turned their whole force as well as attention to
that enterprize, and as they were extremely intent
on their expeditions into Italy, which they could
not undertake without the concurrence of their
nobles, they were solicitous not to alarm them by
any direct attack on their privileges and jurisdictions. They aimed, however, at undermining
their power, and inconsiderately bestowed additional territories, and accumulated new honours
on the clergy, in hopes that this order might serve
as a counterpoise to that of the nobility in any
future struggle [k].

The unhappy effects of this fatal error in policy *The fatal effects of aggrandizing the clergy.* A. D. 1024.
were quickly felt. Under the Emperors of the
Franconian and Swabian lines, whom the Germans by their voluntary election placed on the
Imperial throne, a new face of things appeared,
and a scene was exhibited in Germany, which
astonished all Christendom at that time, and which
in the present age appears almost incredible. The
Popes, hitherto dependent on the Emperors, and
indebted for their power as well as dignity to their
beneficence and protection, began to claim a superior jurisdiction; and in virtue of authority
which they pretended to derive from heaven, tried,
condemned, excommunicated and deposed their
former masters. Nor is this to be considered

[k] Pfeffel. Abregé. p. 154.

Vol. I.   P   merely

Sect. III. merely as a frantick sally of passion in a pontiff intoxicated with high ideas concerning the extent of priestly domination, and the plenitude of papal power. Gregory VII. was able as well as daring. His presumption and violence were accompanied with political discernment and sagacity. He had observed that the Princes and nobles of Germany, had acquired such considerable territories and such extensive jurisdiction as rendered them not only formidable to the Emperors, but disposed them to favour any attempt to circumscribe their power. He foresaw that the ecclesiasticks of Germany, raised almost to a level with its Princes, were ready to support any person who would stand forth as the protector of their privileges and independence. With both of these Gregory negociated, and had secured many devoted adherents among them, before he ventured to enter the lists against the head of the Empire.

The contests between the Popes and Emperors, and the consequences of these.

He began his rupture with Henry IV. upon a pretext that was popular and plausible. He complained of the venality and corruption with which the Emperor had granted the investiture of benefices to ecclesiasticks. He contended that this right belonged to him as head of the church; he required Henry to confine himself within the bounds of his civil jurisdiction, and to abstain for the future from such sacrilegious encroachments on his spiritual dominion. All the censures of the church were denounced against Henry, because he he refused to relinquish those powers which his predecessors had uniformly exercised. The most considerable of the German Princes and ecclesiasticks were excited to take arms against him. His mother, his wife, his sons were wrought upon to disregard all the ties of blood as well as of duty, and to join the party of his enemies [k]. Such were the successful arts with which the court of Rome inflamed the superstitious zeal, and conducted the factious spirit of the Germans and Italians, that an Emperor, distinguished not only for many virtues, but possessed of considerable talents, was at length obliged to appear as a supplicant at the gate of the castle in which the Pope resided, and to stand there, three days, bare-footed, in the depth of winter, imploring a pardon, which at length he obtained with difficulty [SS].

A.D. 1077.

This act of humiliation degraded the Imperial dignity. Nor was the depression only momentary. The contest between Gregory and Henry gave rise to the two great factions of the Guelfs and Ghibellines; the former of which supporting the pretensions of the Popes, and the latter defending the rights of the Emperor, kept Germany and Italy in perpetual agitation during three centuries. A regular system for humbling the Emperors and circumscribing their power was formed, and adhered to uniformly throughout that period. The Popes, the free States in Italy, the nobility and

The Imperial authority gradually declines.

[k] Annal. German. ap. Struv. i. p. 325.
[SS] NOTE XLI.

SECT. III. ecclesiasticks of Germany, were all interested in its success; and notwithstanding the return of some short intervals of vigour, under the administration of a few able Emperors, the Imperial
A.D. 1256. authority continued to decline. During the anarchy of the long interregnum subsequent to the death of William of Holland, it dwindled down
A.D. 1273. to nothing. Rodulph of Hapsburgh, the founder of the house of Austria, and who first opened the way to its future grandeur, was at length elected Emperor, not that he might re-establish and extend the Imperial authority, but because his territories and influence were so inconsiderable as to excite no jealousy in the German Princes, who were willing to preserve the forms of a constitution, the power and vigour of which they had destroyed. Several of his successors were placed on the Imperial throne from the same motive; and almost every remaining prerogative was wrested out of the hands of feeble Princes unable to exercise or to defend them.

A total change in the political constitution of the Empire.

DURING this period of turbulence and confusion the constitution of the Germanick body underwent a total change. The ancient names of courts and magistrates, together with the original forms and appearance of policy, were preserved; but such new privileges and jurisdiction were assumed, and so many various rights established, that the same species of government no longer subsisted. The Princes, the great nobility, the dignified ecclesiasticks, the free cities had taken advantage of

STATE OF EUROPE.

the interregnum, which I have mentioned, to establish or to extend their usurpations. They claimed and exercised the right of governing their respective territories with full sovereignty. They acknowledged no superior with respect to any point, relative to the interior administration and police of their domains. They enacted laws, imposed taxes, coined money, declared war, concluded peace, and exerted every prerogative peculiar to independent States. The ideas of order and political union which had formed the various provinces of Germany into one body were entirely lost; and the society must have dissolved, if the forms of feudal subordination had not preserved such an appearance of connection or dependence among the various members of the community, as preserved it from falling to pieces.

Sect. III.

This bond of union, however, was extremely feeble; and no principle remained in the German constitution of sufficient force to maintain publick order, and hardly to ascertain personal security. From the accession of Rodulph of Hapsburgh, to the reign of Maximilian, the immediate predecessor of Charles V. the Empire felt every calamity which a state must endure when the authority of government is so much relaxed as to have lost all vigour. The causes of dissension among that vast number of members which composed the Germanick body, were infinite and unavoidable. These gave rise to perpetual private wars, carried on with all the violence of resentment when un-

Expedients for putting an end to this state of anarchy.

restrained

SECT. III. restrained by superior authority. Rapine, outrage, exactions, became universal. Commerce was interrupted; industry suspended; and every part of Germany resembled a country which an enemy had plundered and laid desolate [l]. The variety of expedients employed with a view to restore order and tranquillity, prove that the grievances occasioned by this state of anarchy had grown intolerable. Arbiters were appointed to terminate the differences among the several states. The cities united in a league, the object of which was to check the rapine and extortions of the nobility. The nobility formed confederacies, on pupose to maintain tranquillity among their own order. Germany was divided into several Circles, in each of which a provincial and partial jurisdiction was established, to supply the place of a publick and common tribunal [m].

Particularly by the institution of the Imperial Chamber.

BUT all these remedies were so fruitless, that they served only to demonstrate the violence of that anarchy which prevailed, and the inefficacy of the means employed to correct it. At length Maximilian re-established publick order in the Empire, by instituting the Imperial chamber, a tribunal composed of judges named partly by the Emperor, partly by the several States, and vested with authority to decide finally concerning all differences among the members of the Germanick

A. D. 1495.

[l] See above, page 53 and note xxi. Datt. de pace publica Imper. p. 15, no. 53. p. 28, no. 26. p. 35, no. 11.
[m] Datt. passim. Strav. Corp. Hist. i. 510, &c.

body,

body. A few years after, by giving a new form to the Aulick council, which takes cognizance of all feudal causes, and such as belong to the Emperor's immediate jurisdiction, he restored some degree of vigour to the Imperial authority.

Sect. III.
A.D. 1512.

But notwithstanding the salutary effects of these regulations and improvements, the political constitution of the German Empire, at the commencement of the period of which I propose to write the history, was of a species so peculiar, as not to resemble perfectly any form of government known either in the ancient or modern world. It was a complex body, formed by the association of several States, each of which possessed sovereign and independent jurisdiction within its own territories. Of all the members which composed this united body, the Emperor was the head. In his name, all decrees and regulations with respect to points of common concern, were issued; and to him the power of carrying them into execution was committed. But this appearance of monarchical power in the Emperor was more than counterbalanced by the influence of the Princes and States of the Empire in every act of administration. No law extending to the whole body could pass, no resolution that affected the general interest could be taken, without the approbation of the Diet of the Empire. In this assembly, every sovereign Prince and State of the Germanick body had a right to be present, to deliberate, and to vote. The decrees

At the beginning of the sixteenth century, the Empire an association of sovereign states.

Sect. III. or *Recesses* of the Diet were the laws of the Empire, which the Emperor was bound to ratify and enforce.

Peculiarities in the nature of this association. Under this aspect the constitution of the Empire appears a regular confederacy, similar to the Achæan league in ancient Greece, or to that of the United Provinces and of the Swiss Cantons in modern times. But if viewed in another light, striking peculiarities in its political state, present themselves. The Germanick body was not formed by the union of members altogether distinct and independent. All the Princes and States joined in this association, were originally subject to the Emperors, and acknowledged them as sovereigns. Besides this, they originally held their lands as Imperial fiefs, and in consequence of this tenure owed the Emperors all those services which feudal vassals are bound to perform to their liege lord. But though this political subjection was entirely at an end, and the influence of the feudal relation much diminished, the ancient forms and institutions introduced when the Emperors governed Germany with authority, not inferior to that which the other monarchs of Europe possessed, still remained. Thus an opposition was established between the genius of the government, and the forms of administration in the German Empire. The former considered the Emperor only as the head of a confederacy, the members of which, by their voluntary choice, have raised him to that dignity; the latter seemed to imply, that he is really

really invested with sovereign power. By this cir- SECT. III.
cumstance, such principles of hostility and discord The defects
were interwoven in the frame of the Germanick in the con-
body, as affected each of its members, rendering the Empire.
their interior union incomplete, and their external
efforts feeble and irregular. The effects of this
vice or disorder inherent in the constitution of the
Empire are so considerable, that, without attending to them, it is impossible to comprehend many
transactions in the reign of Charles V. or to form
just ideas concerning the genius of the German
government.

THE Emperors of Germany, at the beginning Arising
of the sixteenth century, were distinguished by the mited power
most pompous titles, and by such ensigns of dig- perors.
nity as intimated their authority to be superior to
that of all other monarchs. The greatest Princes
of the Empire attended and served them on some
occasions, as the officers of their houshold. They
exercised prerogatives which no other sovereign
ever claimed. They retained pretensions to all
the extensive powers which their predecessors had
enjoyed in any former age. But at the same time,
instead of possessing that ample domain which had
belonged to the ancient Emperors of Germany,
and which stretched from Basil to Cologne, along
both banks of the Rhine [a], they were stript of all
territorial property, and had not a single city, a
single castle, a single foot of land, that pertained
to them as heads of the Empire. As their demain

[a] Pfeffel. Abregé, &c. p. 241.

was

SECT. III. was alienated, their stated revenues were reduced almost to nothing; and the extraordinary aids which on a few occasions they obtained, were granted sparingly, and paid with reluctance. The Princes and States of the Empire, though they seemed to recognize the Imperial authority, were subjects only in name, each of them possessing a compleat municipal jurisdiction within the precincts of his own territories.

From the nature of their titles and pretensions.

FROM this ill-compacted frame of government, effects that were unavoidable resulted. The Emperors, dazzled with the splendour of their titles, and the exterior signs of vast authority, were apt to imagine themselves to be the real sovereigns of Germany, and were led to aim continually at recovering the exercise of those powers and prerogatives which the forms of the constitution seemed to vest in them, and which their predecessors, Charlemagne and the Othos, had actually enjoyed. The Princes and States, aware of the nature as well as extent of their pretensions, were perpetually on their guard, in order to watch all the motions of the Imperial court, and to circumscribe its power within limits still more narrow. The Emperors, in support of their claims, appealed to ancient forms and institutions, which the States held to be obsolete. The States founded their rights on recent practice and modern privileges, which the Emperors considered as usurpations.

THIS

THIS jealousy of the Imperial authority, toge-ther with the opposition between it and the rights of the States, increased considerably from the time that the Emperors were elected, not by the collective body of German nobles, but by a few Princes of chief dignity. During a long period, all the members of the Germanick body assembled, and made choice of the person whom they appointed to be their head. But amidst the violence and anarchy which prevailed for several centuries in the Empire, seven Princes who possessed the most extensive territories, and who had obtained a hereditary title to the great offices of the State, acquired the exclusive privilege of nominating the Emperor. This right was confirmed to them by the Golden Bull; the mode of exercising it was ascertained, and they were dignified with the appellation of *Electors*. The nobility and free-cities being thus stripped of a privilege which they had once enjoyed, were less connected with a Prince, towards whose elevation they had not contributed by their suffrages, and came to be more apprehensive of his authority. The Electors, by their extensive power, and the distinguishing privileges which they possessed, became formidable to the Emperors, with whom they were placed almost on a level in several acts of jurisdiction. Thus the introduction of the Electoral college into the Empire, and the authority which it acquired, instead of diminishing, contributed to strengthen the principles of hostility and discord in the Germanick constitution.

SECT. III. *From the manner in which they were elected.*

THESE

Sect. III.

From the different forms of government established in the States which composed the Germanick body.

THESE were further augmented by the various and repugnant forms of civil policy in the several States which composed the Germanick body. It is no easy matter to render the union of independent States perfect and entire, even when the genius and forms of their respective governments happen to be altogether similar. But in the German Empire, which was a confederacy of Princes, of Ecclesiasticks, and of free-cities, it was impossible that they could incorporate thoroughly. The free-cities were small republicks, in which the maxims and spirit peculiar to that species of government prevailed. The Princes and nobles, to whom supreme jurisdiction belonged, possessed a sort of monarchical power within their own territories, and the forms of their interior administration nearly resembled those of the great feudal kingdoms. The interests, the ideas, the objects of States so differently constituted, cannot be the same. Nor could their common deliberations be carried on with the same spirit, while the love of liberty and attention to commerce were the reigning principles in the cities; while the desire of power, and ardour for military glory, were the governing passions of the Princes and nobility.

From the opposition between the secular and ecclesiastical members.

THE secular and ecclesiastical members of the Empire were as little fitted for union as the free-cities and the nobility. Vast territories were annexed to several of the German bishopricks and abbeys, and the dignified ecclesiasticks held some of the highest

highest offices in the Empire by hereditary right. Sect. III.
The younger sons of noblemen of the second order,
who had devoted themselves to the church, were
commonly promoted to these stations of eminence
and power; and it was no small mortification to the
Princes and great nobility, to see persons raised
from an inferior rank to the same level with themselves, or even exalted to superior dignity. The
education of these churchmen, the genius of their
profession, and their connection with the court of
Rome, rendered their character as well as interest
different from those of the other members of the
Germanick body, with whom they were called to
act in concert. Thus another source of jealousy
and variance was opened, which ought not to be
overlooked when we are searching into the nature
of the German constitution.

To all these causes of dissention may be added *From the unequal distribution of wealth and power among the members.*
one more, arising from the unequal distribution of
power and wealth among the States of the Empire.
The Electors, and other nobles of the highest rank,
not only possessed sovereign jurisdiction, but governed such extensive, populous, and rich countries, as rendered them great Princes. Many of
the other members, though they enjoyed all the
rights of sovereignty, ruled over such petty domains, that their real power bore no proportion to
this high prerogative. A well-compacted and vigorous confederacy could not be formed of such
dissimilar states. The weaker were jealous, timid,
and unable either to assert or to defend their just
privileges.

SECT. III. privileges. The more powerful were apt to assume and to become oppressive. The Electors and Emperors endeavoured by turns to extend their own authority, by encroaching on the rights of these feeble members of the Germanick body; and they, over-awed or corrupted, tamely gave up their privileges, or meanly favoured the designs formed against them [TT].

All these render the Germanick body incapable of acting with union and vigour.

AFTER contemplating all these principles of disunion and opposition in the constitution of the German Empire, it will be easy to account for the want of concord and uniformity, conspicuous in its councils and proceedings. That slow, dilatory, distrustful and irresolute spirit, which characterizes all its deliberations, will appear natural in a body, the junction of whose members was so incompleat, the different parts of which were held together by such feeble ties, and set at variance by such powerful motives. But the Empire of Germany, nevertheless, comprehended countries of such vast extent, and was inhabited by such a martial and hardy race of men, that when the abilities of an Emperor, or zeal for any common cause, could rouze this unwieldly body to put forth its strength, it acted with irresistible force. In the following history we shall find, that as the measures on which Charles V. was most intent, were often thwarted or rendered abortive by the spirit of jealousy and and division peculiar to the Germanick constitution;

[TT] NOTE XLII.

tion; so it was by the influence which he acquired over the Princes of the Empire, and by engaging them to co-operate with him, that he was enabled to make some of the greatest efforts which distinguish his reign.

<small>Sect. III.</small>

The Turkish history is so blended, during the reign of Charles V. with that of the great nations in Europe, and the Ottoman Porte interposed so often, and with such decisive influence in the wars and negociations of the Christian Princes, that some previous account of the state of government in that great Empire, is no less necessary for the information of my readers, than these views of the constitution of other kingdoms which I have already exhibited to them.

<small>View of the Turkish government.</small>

It has been the fate of the more southern and fertile parts of Asia, at different periods, to be conquered by that warlike and hardy race of men, who inhabit the vast country known to the ancients by the name of Scythia, and among the moderns by that of Tartary. One tribe of these people, called Turks or Turcomans, extended its conquests, under various leaders, and during several centuries, from the shore of the Caspian to the Streights of the Dardanelles. Towards the middle of the fifteenth century, these formidable conquerors took Constantinople by storm, and established the seat of their government in that Imperial city. Greece, Moldavia, Walachia, and the other provinces of the ancient kingdoms of Thrace and Macedonia, to-

<small>Its origin.</small>

gether

Sect. III. gether with part of Hungary, were subjected to their power.

Its despotic genius.

But though the seat of the Turkish government was fixed in Europe, and the Sultans obtained possession of such extensive dominions in that quarter of the globe, the genius of their policy was purely Asiatick; and may be properly termed a despotism, in contradistinction to those monarchical and republican forms of government which we have been hitherto contemplating. The supreme power was vested in Sultans of the Ottoman race, that blood being deemed so sacred, that no other was thought worthy of the throne. From this elevation, these sovereigns could look down, and behold all their subjects reduced to the same level before them. The maxims of Turkish policy admit not any of those institutions, which, in other countries, limit the exercise, or moderate the rigour of monarchical power: no great court with constitutional and permanent jurisdiction to interpose both in the enactment and execution of laws: no body of hereditary nobles, whose sense of their own pre-eminence, whose consciousness of what is due to their rank and character, whose jealousy of their privileges circumscribe the authority of the Prince, and serve not only as a barrier against the excesses of his caprice, but stand as an intermediate order between him and the people. Under the Turkish government, the political condition of every subject is equal. To be employed in the service of the Sultan, is the only circumstance that confers distinction.

STATE OF EUROPE.

tion. Even this diſtinction is annexed ſo cloſely to the ſtations in which perſons ſerve, that it is ſcarcely communicated to thoſe who are placed in them. The higheſt dignity in the Empire does not give any rank or pre-eminence to the family of him who enjoys it. As every man, before he is raiſed to any ſtation of authority, muſt go through the preparatory diſcipline of a long and ſervile obedience °, the moment he is deprived of power, he and his poſterity return to the ſame condition with other ſubjects, and ſink back into obſcurity. It is the diſtinguiſhing and odious characteriſtick of the Eaſtern deſpotiſm, that it annihilates all other ranks of men, in order to exalt the monarch; that it leaves nothing to the former, while it gives every every thing to the latter; that it endeavours to fix in the minds of thoſe who are ſubject to it, the idea of no relation between men, but that of a maſter and of a ſlave, the former deſtined to command and to puniſh, the latter formed to tremble and to obey [UU].

Power of the Sultan limited by religion;

BUT as there are circumſtances which frequently obſtruct or defeat the ſalutary effects of the beſt-regulated governments, there are others which contribute to mitigate the evils of the moſt vicious forms of policy. There can, indeed, be no conſtitutional reſtraints upon the will of a Prince in a deſpotic government; but there may be ſuch as

° State of the Turkiſh Empire by Rycaut, p. 25.
[UU] NOTE XLIII.

SECT. III. are accidental. Absolute as the Turkish Sultans are, they feel themselves circumscribed both by religion, the principle on which their authority is founded [f], and by the army, the instrument which they must employ in order to maintain it. Whereever religion interposes, the will of the Sovereign must submit to its decrees. When the Koran hath prescribed any religious rite, hath enjoined any moral duty; or hath confirmed, by its sanction, any political maxim, the command of the Sultan cannot overturn that which an higher authority hath established. The chief restriction, however, on the will of the Sultans, is imposed by the mili-

and by the military. tary power. An armed force must surround the throne of every Despot, to maintain his authority, and to execute his commands. As the Turks extended their empire over nations, which they did not exterminate, but reduce to subjection, they found it necessary to render their military establish-

Origin of the Janisaries, A. D. 1361. ment numerous and formidable. Amurath, their third Sultan, in order to form a body of devoted troops, that might serve as the immediate guards of his person and dignity, appointed his officers to seize annually, as the Imperial property, the fifth part of the youth taken in war. These, after being instructed in the Mahometan religion, inured to obedience by severe discipline, and trained to warlike exercises, were formed into a body distinguished by the name of *Janizaries*, or new soldiers. Every sentiment which enthusiasm can inspire, every mark of distinction that the favour of the Prince

[f] Rycaut, p. 8.

could

could confer, were employed in order to animate this body with martial ardour, and with a consciousness of its own pre-eminence [q]. The Janizaries soon became the chief strength and pride of the Ottoman armies; and by their number as well as reputation, were distinguished above all the troops, whose duty it was to attend on the person of the Sultans [XX].

Thus, as the supreme power in every society is possessed by those who have arms in their hands, this formidable body of soldiers, destined to be the instruments of enlarging the Sultan's authority, acquired, at the same time, the means of controuling it. The Janizaries in Constantinople, like the Prætorian bands in ancient Rome, quickly perceived all the advantages which they derived from being stationed in the capital; from their union under one standard; and from being masters of the person of the Prince. The Sultans became no less sensible of their influence and importance. The *Capiculy*, or soldiery of the Port, was the only power in the Empire that a Sultan or his Visier had reason to dread. To preserve the fidelity and attachment of the Janizaries, was the great art of government, and the principal object of attention in the policy of the Ottoman court. Under a monarch, whose abilities and vigour of mind fit him for command, they are obsequious instruments; execute whatever he enjoins; and render his power

Their vast influence in the Turkish government.

[q] Prince Cantemir's History of the Othman Empire, p. 87.
[XX] NOTE XLIV.

irresistible.

SECT. III. irresistible. Under feeble Princes, or such as are unfortunate, they become turbulent and mutinous; assume the tone of masters; degrade and exalt Sultans at pleasure; and teach those to tremble, on whose nod, at other times, life or death depend.

Progress of the Turks towards dominion.

From Mahomet II. who took Constantinople, to Solyman, who began his reign a few months after Charles V. was placed on the Imperial throne of Germany, a succession of illustrious Princes ruled over the Turkish Empire. By their great abilities, they kept their subjects of every order, military as well as civil, submissive to government; and had the absolute command of whatever force their vast Empire was able to exert. Solyman, in particular, who is known to the Christians chiefly as a conqueror, but is celebrated in the Turkish annals as the great law-giver who established order and police in their Empire, governed during his long reign with no less authority that wisdom. He divided his dominions into several districts; he appointed the number of soldiers which each should furnish; he appropriated a certain proportion of the lands in every province for their maintenance; he regulated, with a minute accuracy, every thing relative to their discipline, their arms, and the nature of their service. He put the finances of the Empire into an orderly train of administration; and though the taxes in the Turkish dominions, as well as in the other despotic monarchies of the East, are far from being considerable, he supplied that defect by an attentive and severe œconomy.

Nor

STATE OF EUROPE.

Nor was it only under such Sultans as Solyman, whose talents were no less adapted to preserve interior order than to conduct the operations of war, that the Turkish Empire engaged with advantage in its contests with the Christian states. The long succession of able Princes, which I have mentioned, had given such vigour and firmness to the Ottoman government, that it seems to have attained, during the sixteenth century, the highest degree of perfection of which its constitution was capable. Whereas the great monarchies in Christendom were still far from that state, which could enable them to act with a full exertion of their force. Besides this, the Turkish troops in that age possessed every advantage which arises from superiority in military discipline. At the time when Solyman began his reign, the Janizaries had been embodied near a century and a half, and during that long period, the severity of their military discipline had in no degree relaxed. The soldiers drawn from the provinces of the Empire, had been kept almost continually under arms, in the various wars which the Sultans had carried on with hardly any interval of peace. Against troops thus trained and accustomed to service, the forces of the Christian powers took the field with great disadvantage. The most intelligent as well as impartial authors of the sixteenth century, acknowledge and lament the superior attainments of the Turks in the military art [YY]. The success which uniformly attended their arms in all their

Sect. III. Advantages which they possessed over the Christian powers in the sixteenth century.

[YY] NOTE XLV.

wars,

SECT. III. wars, demonstrates the justness of this observation. The Christian armies did not acquire that superiority over the Turks, which they now possess, until the long establishment of standing forces had improved military discipline among the former; and until various causes and events, which it is not my province to explain, had corrupted or abolished their ancient warlike institutions among the latter.

PROOFS

AND

ILLUSTRATIONS.

PROOFS

AND

ILLUSTRATIONS.

NOTE I. Sect. I. p. 3. [A].

THE consternation of the Britons, when invaded by the Picts and Caledonians after the Roman legions were called out of the island, may give some idea of the degree of debasement to which the human mind was reduced by long servitude under the Romans. In their supplicatory letter to Aetius, which they call the *groans of Britain*, " We know not (say they) which way to turn us. The barbarians drive us to the sea; and the sea forces us back on the barbarians; between which we have only the choice of two deaths, either to be swallowed up by the waves, or to be butchered by the sword." Histor. Gildæ. ap. Gale. Hist. Britan. Script. p. 6.—— One can scarce believe this dastardly race to be the descendants of that gallant people, who repulsed Cæsar, and defended their liberty so long against the Roman arms.

PROOFS AND ILLUSTRATIONS.

NOTE II. Sect. I. p. 4. [B].

The barbarous nations were not only illiterate, but regarded literature with contempt. They found the inhabitants of all the provinces of the Empire funk in effeminacy, and averfe to war. Such a character was the object of fcorn to an high-fpirited and gallant race of men. "When we would brand an enemy," fays Liutprandus, "with the moft difgraceful and contumelious appellation, we call him a Roman; hoc folo, id eft *Romani* nomine, quicquid ignobilitatis, quicquid timiditatis, quicquid avaritiæ, quicquid luxuriæ, quicquid mendacii, immo quicquid vitiorum eft comprehendentes." Liutprandi Legatio apud Murat. Scriptor. Italic. vol. ii. pars 1. p. 481. This degeneracy of manners, illiterate barbarians imputed to their love of learning. Even after they fettled in the countries which they had conquered, they would not permit their children to be inftructed in any fcience; "for, (faid they) inftruction in the fciences tends to corrupt, enervate, and deprefs the mind; and he who has been accuftomed to tremble under the rod of a pedagogue, will never look on a fword or fpear with an undaunted eye." Procop. de bello Gothor. lib. i. p. 4. ap. Scrip. Byz. edit. Venet. vol. i. A confiderable number of years elapfed, before nations fo rude, and fo unwilling to learn, could produce hiftorians capable of recording their tranfactions, or of defcribing their manners and inftitutions. By that time, all memory of their ancient con-

dition was loft, and no monument remained to
guide their firft writers to any certain knowledge
of it. If one expects to receive any fatisfactory
account of the manners and laws of the Goths,
Lombards, or Franks, during their refidence in
thofe countries where they were originally feated,
from Jornandes, Paulus Warnefridus, or Gregory
of Tours, the earlieft and moft authentick hiftorians of thefe people, he will be miferably difap-
pointed. Whatever imperfect knowledge has been
conveyed to us of their ancient ftate, we owe not
to their own writers, but to the Greek and Roman
hiftorians.

NOTE III. Sect. I. p. 6. [C].

A CIRCUMSTANCE related by Prifcus in his hiftory of the embaffy to Attila, King of the Huns,
gives a ftriking view of the enthufiaftick paffion
for war, which prevailed among the barbarous
nations. When the entertainment to which that
fierce conqueror admitted the Roman ambaffadors
was ended, two Scythians advanced towards Attila, and recited a poem in which they celebrated
his victories, and military virtues. All the Huns
fixed their eyes with attention on the bards.
Some feemed to be delighted with the verfes;
others, remembering their own battles and exploits,
exulted with joy; while thofe who were become
feeble through age, burft out into tears, bewail-
ing the decay of their vigour, and the ftate of
inactivity in which they were now obliged to
remain.

PROOFS AND ILLUSTRATIONS.

NOTE V. Sect. I. p. 13. [E].

PROCOPIUS, the hiftorian, declines, from a principle of benevolence, to give any particular detail of the cruelties of the Goths; " Left, fays he, I fhould tranfmit a monument and example of inhumanity to fucceeding ages." Proc. de bello Goth. lib. iii. cap. 10. ap. Byz. Script. vol. i. 126. But as the change, which I have pointed out as a confequence of the fettlement of the barbarous nations in the countries formerly fubject to the Roman Empire, could not have taken place, if the greater part of the ancient inhabitants had not been extirpated, an event of fuch importance and influence merits a more particular illuftration. This will juftify me for exhibiting fome part of that melancholy fpectacle, over which humanity prompted Procopius to draw a veil. I fhall not, however, difguft my readers by a long detail; but reft fatisfied with collecting fome inftances of the devaftations made by two of the many nations, which fettled in the Empire. The Vandals were the firft of the barbarians who invaded Spain. It was one of the richeft and moft populous of the Roman Provinces; the inhabitants had been diftinguifhed for courage, and had defended their liberty againft the arms of Rome, with greater obftinacy, and during a longer courfe of years, than any nation in Europe. But fo entirely were they enervated by their fubjection to the Romans, that the Vandals who entered the kingdom A. D. 409. compleated the conqueft of it with fuch rapidity,

that

that in the year 411, thefe barbarians divided it among them by cafting lots. The defolation occafioned by their invafion is thus defcribed by Idatius an eye-witnefs. "The barbarians wafted every thing with hoftile cruelty. The peftilence was no lefs deftructive. A dreadful famine raged, to fuch a degree, that the living were conftrained to feed on the dead bodies of their fellow-citizens; and all thefe terrible plagues defolated at once the unhappy kingdoms." Idatii Chron. ap. Biblioth. Patrum. vol. vii. p. 1233. edit. Lugd. 1677. The Goths having attacked the Vandals in their new fettlements, a fierce war enfued; the country was plundered by both parties; the cities which efcaped at firft, were laid in afhes, and the inhabitants expofed to fuffer every thing that the wanton cruelty of barbarians could inflict. Idatius defcribes thefe, ibid. p. 1235. b. 1236. c. f. A fimilar account of their devaftations is given by Ifidorus Hifpalenfis, and the contemporary writers. Ifid. Chron. ap. Grot. hift. Goth. 732. From Spain the Vandals paffed over to Africa, A. D. 428. Africa was, next to Egypt, the moft fertile of the Roman provinces. It was one of the granaries of the Empire, and is called by an ancient writer, the foul of the commonwealth. Though the army with which the Vandals invaded it, did not exceed 30,000 fighting men, they became abfolute mafters of the province in lefs than two years. A contemporary author gives a dreadful account of the havock which they made: "They found a province well cultivated, and enjoying plenty, the

beauty

beauty of the whole earth. They carried their deftructive arms into every corner of it; they difpeopled it by their devaftations; exterminating every thing with fire and fword. They did not even fpare the vines, and fruit trees, that thofe, to whom caves and inacceffible mountains had afforded a retreat, might find no nourifhment of any kind. Their hoftile rage could not be fatiated, and there was no place exempted from the effects of it. They tortured their prifoners with the moft exquifite cruelty, that they might force from them a difcovery of their hidden treafures. The more they difcovered, the more they expected, and the more implacable they became. Neither the infirmities of age nor of fex; neither the dignity of nobility, nor the fanctity of the facerdotal office, could mitigate their fury; but the more illuftrious their prifoners were, the more barbaroufly they infulted them. The publick buildings which refifted the violence of the flames, they levelled with the ground. They left many cities without an inhabitant. When they approached any fortified place, which their undifciplined army could not reduce, they gathered together a multitude of prifoners, and putting them to the fword, left their bodies unburied, that the ftench of the carcaffes might oblige the garrifon to abandon it." Victor Vitenfis de perfecutione Africana. ap. Bibl. Patrum. vol. viii. p. 666. St. Auguftin an African, and a contemporary author, gives a fimilar defcription of their cruelties, opera v. x. p. 372. edit. 1616.—About an hundred

years

years after the settlement of the Vandals in Africa, Belisarius attacked and dispossessed them. Procopius, a contemporary historian, describes the devastation which that war occasioned. "Africa, says he, was so entirely dispeopled, that one might travel several days in it without meeting one man; and it is no exaggeration to say, that in the course of the war five millions of persons perished." Proc. hist. Arcana cap. 18. ap. Byz. Script. vol. i. 315.——I have dwelt longer upon the calamities of this province, because they are described not only by contemporary authors, but by eye-witnesses. The present state of Africa confirms their testimony. Many of the most flourishing and populous cities with which it was filled, were so entirely ruined, that no vestiges remain to point out where they were situated. That fertile territory which sustained the Roman Empire lies in a great measure uncultivated; and that province, which Victor in his barbarous Latin called *Speciositas totius terræ florentis*, is now the retreat of pirates and banditti.

WHILE the Vandals laid waste one part of the Empire, the Huns desolated the rest of it. Of all the barbarous tribes they were the fiercest and most formidable. Ammianus Marcellinus, a contemporary author, and one of the best of the later historians, gives an account of their policy and manners. They nearly resemble those of the Scythians described by the ancients, and of the Tartars

known

known to the moderns. In some parts of their character, and in several of their customs, they resemble the savages in North America. Their passion for war and action was extreme. "As in polished societies (says Ammianus) ease and tranquillity are courted, they delight in war and dangers. He who falls in battle is reckoned happy. They who die of old age or of disease are deemed infamous. They boast, with the utmost exultation, of the number of enemies whom they have slain, and as the most glorious of all ornaments, they fasten the scalps of those who have fallen by their hand to the trappings of their horses." Ammian. Marc. lib. xxxi. p. 477. edit. Gronov. Ludg. 1693.——Their incursions into the Empire began in the fourth century; and the Romans, though no strangers, by that time, to the effects of barbarous rage, were astonished at the cruelty of their devastations. Thrace, Pannonia, and Illyricum were the countries which they first laid desolate. As they had no thoughts of settling in Europe, their inroads were frequent, and Procopius computes that in each of these, at a medium, two hundred thousand persons perished or were carried off as slaves. Procop. hist. Arcan. ap. Byz. script. vol. i. 316. Thrace, the best cultivated province in that quarter of the Empire, was converted into a desert, and when Priscus accompanied the ambassadors sent to Attila, there were no inhabitants in some of the cities, but a few miserable people who had taken shelter among the

ruins of the churches; and the fields were covered with the bones of those who had fallen by the sword. Priscus ap. Byz. Script. vol. i. 34. Attila became King of the Huns, A. D. 434. He is one of the greatest and most enterprizing conquerors mentioned in history. He extended his Empire over all the vast countries, comprehended under the general names of Scythia and Germany in the ancient division of the world. While he was carrying on his wars against the barbarous nations, he kept the Roman Empire under perpetual apprehensions, and extorted vast subsidies from the timid and effeminate monarchs who governed it. In the year 451, he entered Gaul, at the head of an army composed of all the various nations which he had subdued. It was more numerous than any with which the barbarians had hitherto invaded the Empire. The devastations which he committed were horrible; not only the open country, but the most flourishing cities were desolated. The extent and cruelty of his devastations are described by Salvianus de Gubernat. Dei. edit. Baluz. Par. 1669. p. 139, &c. and by Idatius ubi supra p. 1235. Aetius put a stop to his progress in that country by the famous battle of Chalons, in which (if we may believe the historians of that age) three hundred thousand persons perished. Idat. ibid. Jornandes de rebus Geticis ap. Grot. hist. Gothor. p. 671. Amst. 1665. But next year he resolved to attack the center of the Empire, and marching into Italy, wasted it with
rage,

rage, inflamed by the sense of his late disgrace. What Italy suffered by the Huns exceeded all the calamities which the preceding incursions of the barbarians had brought upon it. Conringius has collected several passages from the ancient historians, which prove that the devastations committed by the Vandals and Huns in the countries situated on the banks of the Rhine, were no less cruel and fatal to the human race. Exercitatio de urbibus Germaniæ. Opera, vol. i. 489. But it is endless, it is shocking to follow these destroyers of mankind through so many scenes of horror, and to contemplate the havock which they made of the human species.

But the state in which Italy appears to have been, during several ages, after the barbarous nations settled in it, is the most decisive proof of the cruelty as well as extent of their devastations. Whenever any country is thinly inhabited, trees and shrubs spring up in the uncultivated fields, and spreading by degrees form large forests; by the overflowing of rivers, and the stagnating of waters, other parts of it are converted into lakes and marshes. Ancient Italy, the seat of the Roman elegance and luxury, was cultivated to the highest pitch. But so effectually did the devastations of the barbarians destroy all the effects of their industry and cultivation, that in the eighth century Italy appears to have been covered with forests and marshes of vast extent. Muratori enters into a long detail concerning the situation and limits of these; and proves by the most authentick evidence, that great tracts of territory, in all the different provinces of Italy, were either over-run with wood, or laid under water. Nor did these occupy parts of the country naturally barren or of little value, but were spread over districts, which ancient writers represent as extremely fertile, and which at present are highly cultivated. Muratori antiquitates Italicæ medii ævi, differt. xxi. v. ii. p. 149, 153, &c. A strong proof of this occurs in a description of the city of Modena, by an author of the tenth century. Murat. script. Rerum Italic. vol. ii. pars ii. p. 691. The state of desolation in other countries of Europe seems to have been the same. In many of the most early charters now extant, the lands granted to monasteries or to private persons, are distinguished into such as are cultivated or inhabited, and such as were *eremi*, desolate. In many instances, lands are granted to persons because they had taken them from the desert, *ab eremo*, and had cultivated and planted them with inhabitants. This appears from a charter of Charlemagne, published by Eckhart de rebus Franciæ Orientalis, vol. ii. p. 864, and from many charters of his successors quoted by Du Cange voc. *Eremus*.

MURATORI adds, that during the eighth and ninth centuries, Italy was greatly infested by wolves and other wild beasts; another mark of its being destitute of inhabitants. Murat. Antiq. vol. ii. p. 163. Thus Italy, the pride of the ancient

world

world for its fertility and cultivation, was reduced to the state of a country newly peopled, and rendered habitable.

I AM sensible, not only that some of these descriptions of the devastations which I have quoted, may be exaggerated, but that the barbarous tribes proceeded in different manners, in making their new settlements. Some of them seemed to be bent on exterminating the ancient inhabitants; others were more disposed to incorporate with them. It is not my province either to enquire into the causes which occasioned this variety in the conduct of the conquerors, or to describe the state of those countries where the ancient inhabitants were treated most mildly. The facts which I have produced are sufficient to prove that the destruction of the human species, occasioned by the hostile invasions of the northern nations, and their subsequent settlements, was much greater than the generality of writers seem to imagine.

NOTE VI. SECT. I. p. 14. [F].

I HAVE observed, Note II. that our only certain information concerning the ancient state of the barbarous nations must be derived from the Greek and Roman writers. Happily an account of the institutions and customs of one people, to which those of all the rest seem to have been in a great measure similar, has been transmitted to us by two authors, the most capable, perhaps, that ever wrote,

PROOFS AND ILLUSTRATIONS.

wrote, of observing them with profound discernment, and of describing them with propriety and force. The reader must perceive that I have Cæsar and Tacitus in my eye. The former gives a short account of the ancient Germans in a few chapters of the sixth book of his commentaries: The latter wrote a treatise expressly on that subject. These are the most precious and instructive monuments of antiquity to the present inhabitants of Europe. From them we learn,

1. THAT the state of Society among the ancient Germans was of the rudest and most simple form. They subsisted entirely by hunting or by pasturage. Cæf. lib. vi. c. 21. They neglected agriculture, and lived chiefly on milk, cheese, and flesh. Ibid. c. 22. Tacitus agrees with him in most of these points; de morib. Germ. c. 14, 15, 23. The Goths were equally negligent of agriculture. Prisc. Rhet. ap. Byz. Script. v. i. p. 31. B. Society was in the same state among the Huns, who disdained to cultivate the earth, or to touch a plough. Amm. Marcel. lib. xxxi. p. 475. The same manners took place among the Alans; ibid. p. 477. While society remains in this simple state, men by uniting together scarcely relinquish any portion of their natural independence. Accordingly we are informed, 2. That the authority of civil government was extremely limited among the Germans. During times of peace they had no common or fixed magistrate, but the chief men

of

of every district dispensed justice, and accommodated differences. Cæf. ibid. c. 23. Their Kings had not absolute or unbounded power; their authority confisted rather in the privilege of advising, than in the power of commanding. Matters of small consequence were determined by the chief men; affairs of importance by the whole community. Tacit. c. 7, 11. The Huns, in like manner, deliberated in common concerning every business of moment to the society; and were not subject to the rigour of regal authority. Amm. Marcel. lib. xxxi. p. 474. 3. Every individual among the ancient Germans was left at liberty to chuse whether he would take part in any military enterprize which was proposed; there seems to have been no obligation to engage in it imposed on him by publick authority. " When any of the chief men proposes any expedition, such as approve of the cause and of the leader rise up, and declare their intention of following him; those who do not fulfil this engagement, are considered as deserters and traitors, and are looked upon as infamous." Cæf. ibid. c. 23. Tacitus plainly points at the same custom, though in terms more obscure. Tacit. c. 11. 4. As every individual was so independent, and master in so great a degree of his own actions, it became, of consequence, the great object of every person among the Germans who aimed at being a leader, to gain adherents, and attach them to his person and interest. These adherents Cæsar calls *Ambacti* and *Clientes*, i. e.

i. e. retainers or clients; Tacitus, *Comites*, or companions. The chief distinction and power of the leaders, consisted in being attended by a numerous band of chosen youth. This was their pride as well as ornament during peace, and their defence in war. The leaders gained or preserved the favour of these retainers by presents of armour, and of horses, or by the profuse, though inelegant hospitality, with which they entertained them. Tacit. c. 14, 15. 5. Another consequence of the personal liberty and independence which the Germans retained, even after they united in society, was their circumscribing the criminal jurisdiction of the magistrate within very narrow limits, and their not only claiming but exercising almost all the rights of private resentment and revenge. Their magistrates had not the power either of imprisoning, or of inflicting any corporal punishment on a free man. Tacit. c. 7. Every person was obliged to avenge the wrongs which his parents or friends had sustained. Their enmities were hereditary, but not irreconcilable. Even murder was compensated by paying a certain number of cattle. Tac. c. 21. A part of the fine went to the King, or state, a part to the person who had been injured, or to his kindred. Ibid. c. 12.

These particulars concerning the institutions and manners of the Germans, though well known to every person conversant in ancient literature, I have thought proper to arrange in this order, and

to

PROOFS AND ILLUSTRATIONS.

to lay before such of my readers as may be less acquainted with these facts, both because they confirm the account which I have given of the state of the barbarous nations, and because they tend to illustrate all the observations that I shall have occasion to make concerning the various changes in their government and customs. The laws and customs introduced by the barbarous nations into their new settlements, are the best commentary on the writings of Cæsar and Tacitus; and their observations are the best key to a perfect knowledge of these laws and customs.

One circumstance with respect to the testimonies of Cæsar and Tacitus concerning the Germans, merits attention. Cæsar wrote his brief account of their manners more than an hundred years before Tacitus composed his treatise De moribus Germanorum. An hundred years make a considerable period in the progress of national manners, especially if, during that time, those people who are rude and unpolished have had much communication with more civilized states. This was the case with the Germans. Their intercourse with the Romans began when Cæsar crossed the Rhine, and increased prodigiously during the interval between that event and the time when Tacitus flourished. Besides this, there was a considerable difference between the state of society among the different tribes of Germans. The Suiones were so much improved, that they began to be corrupted. Tac. cap. 44. The Fenni were so barbarous, that it is
wonderful

PROOFS AND ILLUSTRATIONS.

wonderful how they were able to subsist. Ibid. cap. 46. Whoever undertakes to describe the manners of the Germans, or to found any political theory upon the state of society among them, ought carefully to attend to both these circumstances.

BEFORE I quit this subject, it may not be improper to observe, that though successive alterations in their institutions, together with the gradual progress of refinement, have made an entire change in the manners of the various people who conquered the Roman Empire, there is still one race of men nearly in the same political situation with that in which they were when they first settled in their new conquests: I mean the various tribes and nations of Savages in North America. It cannot then be considered either as a digression, or as an improper indulgence of curiosity, to enquire, whether this similarity in their political state has occasioned any resemblance between their character and manners. If the likeness turns out to be striking, it is a stronger proof that a just account has been given of the ancient inhabitants of Europe, than the testimony even of Cæsar or of Tacitus.

1. The Americans subsist chiefly by hunting and fishing. Some tribes neglect agriculture entirely. Among those who cultivate some small spot near their huts, that, together with all works of labour, is performed by the women. P. Charlevoix Journal Historique d'un Voyage de L'Amerique 4°.

Par.

PROOFS AND ILLUSTRATIONS.

Par. 1744. p. 334. In such a state of society, the common wants of men being few, and their mutual dependence upon each other small, their union is extremely imperfect and feeble, and they continue to enjoy their natural liberty almost unimpaired. It is the first idea of an American, that every man is born free and independent, and that no power on earth hath any right to diminish or circumscribe his natural liberty. There is hardly any appearance of subordination either in civil or domestic government. Every one does what he pleases. A father and mother with their children, live like persons whom chance has brought together, and whom no common bond unites. Their manner of educating their children is suitable to this principle. They never chastise or punish them, even during their infancy. As they advance in years, they allow them to be entirely masters of their own actions, and responsible to no body. Id. p. 272, 273.——— 2. The power of their civil magistrates is extremely limited. Among most of their tribes, the Sachem, or chief is elective. A council of old men is chosen to assist him, without whose advice he determines no affair of importance. The Sachems neither possess nor claim any great degree of authority. They propose and intreat rather than command. The obedience of their people is altogether voluntary. Id. p. 266, 268.——— 3. The savages of America engage in any military enterprize, not from constraint, but choice. When war is resolved, a chief arises, and offers himself to be the leader. They who are willing (for they compel no person) stand up one after another, and sing their war song. But if after this, any of these should refuse to follow the leader, to whom they have engaged, his life would be in danger, and he would be considered as the most infamous of all men. Id. p. 217, 218. ——4. Such as engage to follow any leader, expect to be treated by him with great attention and respect; and he is obliged to make them presents of considerable value. Id. p. 218.——5. Among the Americans, the magistrate has scarce any criminal jurisdiction. Id. 272. Upon receiving any injury, the person or family offended, may inflict what punishment they please on the person who was the author of it. Id. p. 274. Their resentment and desire of vengeance are excessive and implacable. Time can neither extinguish or abate it. It is the chief inheritance parents leave to their children; it is transmitted from generation to generation, until an occasion be found of satisfying it. Id. p. 309. Sometimes, however, the offended party is appeased. A compensation is paid for a murder that has been committed. The relations of the deceased receive it; and it consists most commonly of a captive taken in war, who being substituted in place of the person who was murdered, assumes his name, and is adopted into his family. Id. p. 274. The resemblance holds in many other particulars. It is sufficient for my purpose to have pointed out the similarity of those great features which distinguish and characterize both people. Bochart, and other philologists of the last century, who, with more erudition

than

than science, endeavoured to trace the migrations of various nations, and who were apt, upon the flighteft appearance of refemblance, to find an affinity between nations far removed from each other, and to conclude that they were defcended from the fame anceftors, would hardly have failed, on viewing fuch an amazing fimilarity, to pronounce with confidence, "That the Germans and Americans muft be the fame people." But a philofopher will fatisfy himfelf with obferving, "That the characters of nations depend on the ftate of fociety in which they live, and on the political inftitutions eftablifhed among them; and that the human mind, whenever it is placed in the fame fituation, will, in ages the moft diftant, and in countries the moft remote, affume the fame form, and be diftinguifhed by the fame manners."

I have pufhed the comparifon between the Germans and Americans no farther than was neceffary for the illuftration of my fubject. I do not pretend that the ftate of fociety in the two countries was perfectly fimilar. Many of the German tribes were more civilized than the Americans. Some of them were not unacquainted with agriculture; almoft all of them had flocks of tame cattle, and depended for the chief part of their fubfiftence upon thefe. Moft of the American tribes fubfift by hunting, and are in a ruder and more fimple ftate than the ancient Germans. The refemblance, however, between their condition, is greater perhaps than any that hiftory affords an

opportunity

opportunity of observing between two races of uncivilized nations, and this has produced a surprizing similarity of manners.

NOTE VII. SECT. I. p. 14. [G].

THE booty gained by an army belonged to the army. The King himself had no part of it but what he acquired by lot. A remarkable instance of this occurs in the history of the Franks. The army of Clovis, the founder of the French monarchy, having plundered a church, carried off, among other sacred utensils, a vase of extraordinary size and beauty. The bishop sent deputies to Clovis, beseeching him to restore the vase, that it might be again employed in the sacred services to which it had been consecrated. Clovis desired the the deputies to follow him to Soissons, as their booty was to be divided in that place, and promised, that if the lot should give him the disposal of the vase, he would grant what the bishop desired. When he came to Soissons, and all the booty was placed in one great heap in the middle of the army, Clovis intreated, that before making the division, they would give him that vase over and above his share. All appeared willing to gratify the King, and to comply with his request, when a fierce and haughty soldier lifted up his battle-axe, and striking the vase with the utmost violence, cried out with a loud voice, " You shall receive nothing here but that to which the lot gives you a right." Gregor. Turon, Histor. Francorum. lib. ii. c. 27. p. 70. Par. 1610.

PROOFS AND ILLUSTRATIONS.

NOTE VIII. Sect. I. p. 18. [H].

The history of the establishment and progress of the feudal system, is an interesting object to all the nations of Europe. In some countries, their jurisprudence and laws are still in a great measure feudal. In others, many forms and practices established by custom, or founded on statutes, took their rise from the feudal law, and cannot be understood without attending to the ideas peculiar to it. Several authors of the highest reputation for genius and erudition, have endeavoured to illustrate this subject, but they have left many parts of it obscure. I shall endeavour to trace, with precision, the progress and variation of ideas concerning property in land among the barbarous nations; and shall attempt to point out the causes which introduced these changes, as well as the effects which followed upon them. Property in land seems to have gone through four successive changes among the people who settled in the various provinces of the Roman Empire.

I. While the barbarous nations remained in their original countries, they had no fixed property in land, and no certain limits to their possessions. After feeding their flocks in one district, they removed with them, their wives and families, to another; and abandoned that likewise in a short time. They were not, in consequence of this imperfect species of property, brought under any positive or formal obligation to serve the community; all their
services

256   PROOFS AND ILLUSTRATIONS.

services were purely voluntary. Every individual was at liberty to chuse how far he would contribute towards carrying on any military enterprize. If he followed a leader in any expedition, it was from attachment, not from a sense of obligation. The clearest proof of this has been produced in Note VI. While property continued in this state, we can discover nothing that bears any resemblance to a feudal tenure, or to the subordination and military service which the feudal system introduced.

II. Upon settling in the countries which they had subdued, the victorious troops divided the conquered lands. That portion which fell to every soldier, he seized as a recompence due to his valour, as a settlement acquired by his own sword. He took possession of it as a freeman in full property. He enjoyed it during his own life, and could dispose of it at pleasure, or transmit it as an inheritance to his children. Thus property in land became fixed. It was at the same time *allodial*, i. e. the possessor had the entire right of property and dominion; he held of no sovereign or superior lord, to whom he was bound to do homage, and perform service. But as these new proprietors were in some danger (as has been observed in the text) of being disturbed by the remainder of the ancient inhabitants, and in still greater danger of being attacked by successive colonies of barbarians as fierce and rapacious as themselves, they saw the necessity of coming under

obligations

PROOFS AND ILLUSTRATIONS.

obligations to defend the community, more explicit than those to which they had been subject in their original habitations. On this account, immediately upon their fixing in their new settlements, every freeman became bound to take arms in defence of the community, and if he refused or neglected so to do, was liable to a considerable penalty. I do not mean that any contract of this kind was formally concluded, or mutually ratified by any legal solemnity. It was established by tacit consent, like the other compacts which hold society together; and their mutual security and preservation made it the interest of all to recognize its authority, and to enforce the observation of it. We can trace back this new obligation on the proprietors of land to a very early period in the history of the Franks. Chilperic, who began his reign A. D. 562, exacted a fine, *bannos jussit exigi*, from certain persons who had refused to accompany him in an expedition. Gregor. Turon. lib. v. c. 26. p. 211. Childibert, who began his reign A. D. 576, proceeded in the same manner against others who had been guilty of a like crime. Id. lib. vii. c. 42. p. 342. Charlemagne ordained, that every freeman who possessed five mansi, i. e. sixty acres of land, *in property*, should march in person against the enemy. Capitul. A. D. 807. Louis le Debonnaire, A. D. 815, granted lands to certain Spaniards who fled from the Saracens, and allowed them to settle in his territories, on condition that they should serve in the army *like other free men.* Capitul. vol. i. p. 500. By land possessed *in property*, which is mentioned in the law of Charlemagne, we are to understand, according to the stile of that age, allodial land; *alodes* and *proprietas*, *alodum* and *proprium* being words perfectly synonimous. Du Cange voce Alodis. The clearest proof of the distinction between allodial and beneficiary possession, is contained in two charters published by Muratori, by which it appears that a person might possess one part of his estate as allodial, which he could dispose of at pleasure, the other as a beneficium, of which he had only the usufruct, the property returning to the superior Lord on his demise. Antiq. Ital. medii ævi, vol. i. p. 559, 565. The same distinction is pointed out in a Capitulare of Charlemagne, A. D. 812. edit. Baluz. vol. i. p. 491. In the curious testament of count Everard, who married a daughter of Louis le Debonnaire, by which he disposes of his vast estate among his children, he distinguishes between what he possessed *proprietate*, and what he held *beneficio*, and it appears that the greater part was allodial. A. D. 837. Aub. Miræi Opera Diplomatica Lovan. 1723. Vol. p. 19.

In the same manner *Liber homo* is commonly opposed to *Vassus* or *Vassallus*; the former denotes an allodial proprietor, the latter one who held of a superior. These *free* men were under an obligation to serve the state; and this duty was considered

sidered as so sacred, that free men were prohibited from entering into holy orders unless they had obtained the consent of the sovereign. The reason given for this in the statute is remarkable, " For we are informed that some do so, not so much out of devotion, as in order to avoid that military service which they are bound to perform. Capitul. lib. i. § 114. If upon being summoned into the field, any free man refused to obey, a full *Herebannum*, i. e. a fine of sixty crowns, was to be exacted from him according to the law of the Franks." Capit. Car. magn. ap. Leg. Longob. lib. i. tit. 14. § 13. p. 539. This expression, according to the law of the Franks, seems to imply that both the obligation to serve, and the penalty on those who disregarded it, were coëval with the laws made by the Franks at their first settlement in Gaul. This fine was levied with such rigour, " That if any person convicted of this crime was insolvent; he was reduced to servitude, and continued in that state until such time as his labour should amount to the value of the *berebannum*." Ibid. The Emperor Lotharius rendered the penalty still more severe; and if any person possessing such an extent of property as made it incumbent on him to take the field in person refused to obey the summons, all his goods were declared to be forfeited, and he himself might be punished with banishment. Murat. Script. Ital. vol. i. pars ii. p. 153.

S 2　　　　III. PROPERTY

PROOFS AND ILLUSTRATIONS.

III. PROPERTY in land having thus become fixed and subject to military service, another change was introduced, though slowly, and step by step. We learn from Tacitus, that the chief men among the Germans endeavoured to attach to their persons and interests certain adherents, whom he calls *Comites.* These fought under their standard, and followed them in all their enterprizes. The same custom continued among them in their new settlements, and those attached or devoted followers were called *fideles, antrustiones, homines in truste Dominica, leudes.* Tacitus informs us, that the rank of a Comes was deemed honourable, De morib. Germ. c. 13. The composition, which is the standard by which we must judge of the rank and condition of persons in the middle ages, paid for the murder of one *in truste Dominica*, was triple to that paid for the murder of a freeman. Leg. Salicor. Tit. 44. § 1. & 2. While the Germans remained in their own country they courted the favour of these Comites by presents of arms and horses, and by hospitality. See Note VI. As long as they had no fixed property in land, these were the only gifts that they could bestow, and the only reward which their followers desired. But upon their settling in the countries which they conquered, and when the value of property came to be understood among them, instead of these slight presents, the Kings and chieftains bestowed a more substantial recompence in land on their adherents. These grants were called *beneficia,* because

cause they were gratuitous donations; and *honores*, because they were regarded as marks of diſtinction. What were the ſervices originally exacted in return for theſe *beneficia* cannot be determined with abſolute preciſion; becauſe there are no records ſo ancient. When allodial poſſeſſions were firſt rendered feudal, they were not, at once, ſubjected to all the feudal ſervices. The tranſition here, as in all other changes of importance, was gradual. As the great object of a feudal vaſſal was to obtain protection, when allodial proprietors firſt conſented to become vaſſals of any powerful leader, they continued to retain as much of their ancient independence as was conſiſtent with that new relation. The homage which they did to the ſuperior of whom they choſe to hold, was called *homagium planum*, and bound them to nothing more than fidelity, but without any obligation either of military ſervice, or attendance in the courts of their ſuperior. Of this *homagium planum* ſome traces, though obſcure, may ſtill be diſcovered. Bruſſel, tom. i. p. 97. Among the ancient writs publiſhed by D. D. De Vic & Vaiſette hiſt. de Langued. are a great many which they call homagia. They ſeem to be an intermediate ſtep between the homagium planum mentioned by Bruſſel, and the engagement to perform complete feudal ſervice. The one party promiſes protection, and grants certain caſtles or lands, the other engages to defend the perſon of the granter, and to aſſiſt him likewiſe in defending his property as often as he ſhall
be

be summoned to do so. But these engagements are accompanied with none of the feudal formalities, and no mention is made of any of the other feudal services. They appear rather to be a mutual contract between equals, than the engagement of a vassal to perform services to a superior Lord. Preuves de l'hist. de Lang. tom. ii. 173. & passim. As soon as men were accustomed to these, the other feudal services were gradually introduced. M. de Montesquieu considers these *beneficia* as fiefs, which originally subjected those who held them to military service. L'espr. des Loix, l. xxx. c. 3. & 16. M. L'abbé de Mably contends that such as held these were at first subjected to no other service than what was incumbent on every free man. Observations sur l'histoire de France I. 356. But upon comparing their proofs and reasonings and conjectures, it seems to be evident, that as every free man, in consequence of his allodial property, was bound to serve the community under a severe penalty, no good reason can be assigned for conferring these beneficia, if they did not subject such as received them, to some new obligation. Why should a King have stripped himself of his domain, if he had not expected, that, by parcelling it out, he might acquire a right to services to which he had formerly no title? We may then warrantably conclude, " That as allodial property subjected those who possessed it to serve the community, so *beneficia* subjected such as held them, to personal service and fidelity

to

to him from whom they received these lands. These beneficia were granted originally only during pleasure. No circumstance relating to the customs of the middle ages is better ascertained than this; and innumerable proofs of it might be added to these produced in L'esprit des Loix, l. xxx. c. 16. and by Du Cange voc. *beneficium & feudum*.

IV. But the possession of benefices did not continue long in this state. A precarious tenure during pleasure, was not sufficient to satisfy those who held it, and to attach them to their superior Lord, they soon obtained the confirmation of their benefices during life. Feudor. lib. tit. i. Du Cange produces several quotations from ancient charters and chronicles in proof of this; Gloss. voc. *Beneficium*. After this it was easy to obtain or extort charters rendering beneficia hereditary, first in the direct line, then in the collateral, and at last in the female line. Leg. Longob. lib. iii. tit. 8. Du Cange, voc. *Beneficium*.

It is no easy matter to fix the precise time when each of these changes took place. M. l'Ab. Mably conjectures with some probability, that Charles Martel first introduced the practice of granting beneficia for life: Observat. tom. i. p. 103, 160; and that Louis le Debonnaire was among the first who rendered them hereditary, is evident from the authorities to which he refers; Id. 429. Mabillon however has published a placitum of Louis le Debonnaire, A. D. 860. by which it appears, that he still continued to grant some beneficia only during life. De re' Diplomatica, lib. vi. p. 353. In the year 889, Odo King of France granted lands to Ricabodo fideli suo jure beneficiario & fructuario during his own life; and if he should die, and a son were born to him, that right was to continue during the life of his son. Mabillon ut supra, p. 556. This was an intermediate step between fiefs merely during life, and fiefs hereditary to perpetuity. While beneficia continued under their first form, and were held only during pleasure, he who granted them not only exercised the *Dominium* or prerogative of superior Lord, but he retained the property, giving his vassal only the *ufufruct*. But under the latter form, when they became hereditary, although feudal lawyers continued to define a beneficium agreeably to its original nature, the property was in effect taken out of the hands of the superior Lords, and lodged in those of the vassal. As soon as the reciprocal advantages of the feudal mode of tenure came to be understood by superiors as well as vassals, that species of holding became so agreeable to both, that not only lands, but casual rents, such as the profits of a toll, the fare paid at ferries, &c. the salaries or perquisites of offices, and even pensions themselves, were granted and held as fiefs; and military service was promised and exacted on account of these. Morice Mem. pour servir de preuves a l'hist. de Bretagne, tom. ii. 78. 690. Brussel, tom. i. p. 41. How absurd soever it may seem to grant or to hold such precarious

rious and casual property as a fief, there are instances of feudal tenures still more singular. The profits arising from the masses said at an altar, were properly an ecclesiastical revenue, belonging to the clergy of the church or monastery which performed that duty, but these were sometimes seized by the powerful barons. In order to ascertain their right to them, they held them as fiefs of the church, and parcelled them out in the same manner as other property to their sub-vassals. Bouquet. recueil des hist. vol. x. 238. 480. The same spirit of encroachment which rendered fiefs hereditary, led the nobles to extort from their sovereigns hereditary grants of offices. Many of the great offices of the crown became hereditary in most of the kingdoms in Europe; and so conscious were monarchs of this spirit of usurpation among the nobility, and so solicitous to guard against it, that, on some occasions, they obliged the persons whom they promoted to any office of dignity, to grant an obligation that neither they, nor their heirs, should claim it as belonging to them by hereditary right. A remarkable instance of this is produced, Mem. de l'Acad. des Inscript. tom. xxx. p 595. Another occurs in the Thesaur. anecdot. published by Martene & Durand, vol. i. p. 873.—This revolution in property occasioned a change corresponding to it in political government; the great vassals of the crown, as they acquired such extensive possessions, usurped a proportional degree of power, depressed the jurisdiction of the crown, and trampled on

the

the privileges of the people. It is on account of this connection, that the tracing the progress of feudal property becomes an object of attention in history; for upon discovering in what state property was at any particular period, we may determine with precision what was the degree of power possessed by the King or by the nobility at that juncture.

ONE circumstance more, with respect to the changes which property underwent, deserves attention. I have shewn, that when the various tribes of barbarians divided their conquests in the fifth and sixth centuries, the property which they acquired was allodial; but in several parts of Europe, property had become almost entirely feudal by the beginning of the tenth century. The former species of property seems to be so much better and more desirable than the latter; that such a change appears surprizing, especially when we are informed that allodial property was frequently converted into feudal, by a voluntary deed of the possessor. The motives which determined them to a choice so repugnant to the ideas of modern times concerning property, have been investigated and explained by M. de Montesquieu with his usual discernment and accuracy, lib. xxxi. c. 8. The most considerable is that of which we have an hint in Lambertus Ardensis, an ancient writer quoted by Du Cange, voce *Alodis*. In those times of anarchy and disorder which became general in Europe

after

after the death of Charlemagne, when there was scarcely any union among the different members of the community, and individuals were exposed, single and undefended by government, to rapine and oppression, it became necessary for every man to have a powerful protector, under whose banner he might range himself, and obtain security against enemies whom he could not singly oppose. For this reason he relinquished his allodial independence, and subjected himself to the feudal services, that he might find safety under the patronage of some respectable superior. In some parts of Europe, this change from allodial to feudal property became so general, that he who possessed land had no longer any liberty of choice left. He was obliged to recognize some liege Lord, and to hold of him. Thus Beaumanoir informs us, that in the counties of Clermont and Beauvois, if the Lord or Count discovered any lands within his jurisdiction, for which no service was performed, and which paid to him no tax or customs, he might instantly seize it as his own; for, says he, according to our custom no man can hold allodial property. Couft. ch. 24. p. 123. Upon the same principle is founded a maxim, which has at length become general in the law of France, *Nulle terre fans Seigneur*. In other provinces of France, allodial property seems to have remained longer unalienated, and to have been more highly valued. A vast number of charters containing grants, or sales, or exchanges of allodial lands in the province of Languedoc are published Hift. gener. de Langued.

par

par D. D. De Vic & Vaisette, tom. ii. During the ninth, tenth, and great part of the eleventh century, the property in that province seems to have been entirely allodial; and scarcely any mention of feudal tenures occurs in the deeds of that country. The state of property, during these centuries, seems to have been perfectly similar in Catalonia, and the country of Roussillon, as appears from the original charters published in the appendix to Petr. de la Marca's treatise de Marca sive limite Hispanico. Allodial property seems to have continued in the Low Countries, to a period still later. During the eleventh, twelfth, and thirteenth centuries, this species of property appears to have been of confiderable extent. Miræi opera Diplom. vol. i. 34, 74, 75. 83, 817, 296, 842, 847, 578. Some vestiges of allodial property appear there as late as the fourteenth century. Ibid. 218. Several facts which prove that allodial property subsisted in different parts of Europe long after the introduction of feudal tenures, and which tend to illustrate the distinction between these two different species of possession, are produced by M. Houard. Anciennes Loix des François, conservées dans les Coutumes Angloises, vol. i. p. 192, &c. The notions of men with respect to property, vary according to the diversity of their understandings, and the caprice of their passions. At the same time that some persons were fond of relinquishing allodial property, in order to hold it by feudal tenure, others seem to have been solicitous to convert their fiefs into allodial property. An instance of this

PROOFS AND ILLUSTRATIONS.

occurs in a charter of Louis le Debonnaire, published by Eckhard, Commentarii de rebus Franciæ Orientalis, vol. ii. 885. Another occurs in the year 1299. Reliquiæ MSS. omnis ævi, by Ludwig, vol. i. p. 209. and even one as late as the year 1337. ibid. vol. vii. p. 40. The same thing took place in the Low-Countries. Miræi oper. 1. 52.

In tracing these various revolutions of property, I have hitherto chiefly confined myself to what happened in France, because the ancient monuments of that nation have either been more carefully preserved, or have been more clearly illustrated than those of any people in Europe.

In Italy, the same revolutions happened in property, and succeeded each other in the same order. There is some ground, however, for conjecturing that allodial property continued longer in estimation among the Italians, than among the French. It appears, that many of the charters granted by the Emperors in the ninth century, conveyed an allodial right to land. Murat. antiq. med. ævi. v. i. p. 575, &c. But in the eleventh century, we find some examples of persons who resigned their allodial property, and received it back as a feudal tenure. Id. p. 610, &c. Muratori observes, that the word *feudum*, which came to be substituted in place of *beneficium*, does not occur in any authentick charter previous to the eleventh century. Id. 594. A charter of King Robert of France, A. D. 1008, is the earliest deed in which I have met with
the

the word *feudum*. Bouquet recueil des hiſtoriens de Gaule & de la France, tom. x. p. 593. b. This word occurs indeed in an edict, A. D. 790, publiſhed by Bruſſel, vol. i. p. 77. But the authenticity of that deed has been called in queſtion, and perhaps the frequent uſe of the word *feudum* in it, is an additional reaſon for doing ſo. The account which I have given of the nature both of allodial and feudal poſſeſſions receives ſome confirmation from the etymology of the words themſelves. *Alode* or *allodium* is compounded of the German particle *an* and *lot*, *i. e.* land obtained by lot. Wachteri Gloſſar. Germanicum, voc. *Allodium*, p. 35. It appears from the authorities produced by him and by Du Cange, voc. *fors*, that the northern nations divided the lands which they had conquered in this manner. Feodum is compounded of *od* poſſeſſion or eſtate, and *feo* wages, pay; intimating that it was ſtipendiary and granted as a recompence for ſervice. Wachterus ibid. voc. *feodum*, p. 441.

THE progreſs of the feudal ſyſtem among the Germans was perfectly ſimilar to that which we have traced in France. But as the Emperors of Germany, eſpecially after the Imperial crown paſſed from the deſcendants of Charlemagne to the houſe of Saxony, were far ſuperior to the contemporary Monarchs of France, in abilities, the Imperial vaſſals did not aſpire ſo early to independence, nor did they ſo ſoon obtain the privilege of poſſeſſing their benefices by hereditary right.

right. According to the compilers of the Libri Feudorum, Conrad II. or the Salic, was the first Emperor, who rendered fiefs hereditary. Lib. i. tit. 1. Conrad began his reign A. D. 1024. Ludovicus Pius, under whose reign, grants of hereditary fiefs were frequent in France, succeeded his father, A. D. 814. Not only was this innovation so much later in being introduced among the vassals of the German Emperors, but even after Conrad had established it, the law continued favourable to the ancient practice, and unless the charter of the vassal bore expressly that the fief descended to his heirs, it was presumed to be granted only during life. Lib. feud. ibid. Even after the alteration made by Conrad, it was not uncommon in Germany to grant fiefs only for life; a charter of this kind occurs as late as the year 1376. Charta ap. Boehmer. Princip. Jur. feud. p. 361. The transmission of fiefs to collateral and female heirs, took place very slowly among the Germans. There is extant a charter, A. D. 1201. conveying the right of succession to females, but it is granted as an extraordinary mark of favour, and in reward of uncommon services. Boehmer. ibid. p. 365. In Germany, as well as in France and Italy, a considerable part of the lands continued to be allodial long after the feudal mode of tenure was introduced. It appears from the Codex Diplomaticus Monasterii Buch, that a great part of the lands in the marquisate of Misnia was still allodial as late as the thirteenth century. N° 31, 36, 37, 46, &c. ap. Scriptores hist. German.

man. cura Schoetgenii & Kreyfigii. Altenb. 1755. vol. ii. 183, &c. Allodial property seems to have been common in another district of the same province, during the same period. Reliquiæ Diplomaticæ Sanctimonial. Beutiz. Nº 17, 36, 58. ibid. 374, &c.

NOTE IX. SECT. I. p. 19. [I].

As I shall, in another note, have occasion to represent the condition of that part of the people who dwelt in cities, I will confine myself in this to consider the state of the inhabitants of the country. The persons employed in cultivating the ground during the ages under review may be divided into three classes: I. *Servi* or slaves. This seems to have been the most numerous class, and consisted either of captives taken in war, or of persons the property in whom was acquired in some one of the various methods enumerated by Du Cange, voc. *servus*, v. 6. p. 447. The wretched condition of this numerous race of men will appear from several circumstances. 1. Their masters had absolute dominion over their persons. They had the power of punishing their slaves capitally, without the intervention of any judge. This dangerous right they possessed not only in the more early periods, when their manners were fierce, but it continued as late as the twelfth century. Joach. Potgiesserus de statu servorum. Lemgov. 1736. 4to. lib. ii. cap. 1. § 4, 10, 13, 24. Even after this jurisdiction of masters came to be restrained, the life of a slave was deemed to be be of so little value, that a very slight compensation attoned for taking it away. Idem, lib. iii. c. 6. If masters had power over the lives of their slaves, it is evident that almost no bounds would be set to the rigour of the punishments which they might inflict upon them. The Codes of ancient laws prescribed punishments for the crimes of slaves different from those which were inflicted on free men. The latter paid only a fine or compensation, the former were subjected to corporal punishments. The cruelty of these was in many instances excessive. Slaves might be put to the rack on very slight occasions. The laws with respect to these points are to be found in Potgiesserus, lib. iii. cap. 7. 2. If the dominion of masters over the lives and persons of their slaves was thus extensive, it was no less so over their actions and property. They were not originally permitted to marry. Male and female slaves were allowed and even encouraged to cohabit together. But this union was not considered as a marriage, it was called *contubernium*, not *nuptiæ* or *matrimonium*. Potgiess. lib. ii. c. 2. § 1. This notion was so much established, that during several centuries after the barbarous nations embraced the Christian religion, slaves who lived as husband and wife, were not joined together by any religious ceremony, and did not receive the nuptial benediction from a priest. Ibid. § 10, 11. When this conjunction between slaves came to be considered as a lawful marriage, they were not permitted to marry without the consent of their master, and such as ventured to do so without obtaining that, were punished with great severity, and sometimes were put to death. Potgieff. ibid. § 12, &c. Gregor. Turon. histor. lib. v. c. 3. When the manners of the European nations became more gentle, and their ideas more liberal, slaves who married without their master's consent, were subjected only to a fine. Potgieff. ibid. § 20. Du Cange Gloss. voc. *Forismaritagium*. 3. All the children of slaves were in the same condition with their parents, and became the property of the master. Du Cange Gloss. voc. *servus*, vol. vi. 450. Murat. antiq. Ital. vol. i. 766. 4. Slaves were so entirely the property of their masters, that they could sell them at pleasure. While domestick slavery continued, the property in a slave was sold in the same manner with that which a person had in any other moveable. Afterwards slaves became *adscripti* glebæ, and were conveyed by sale, together with the farm or estate to which they belonged. Potgiesserus has collected the laws and charters which illustrate this well-known circumstance in the condition of slaves. Lib. ii. c. 4. 5. Slaves had a title to nothing but subsistence and clothes from their master; all the profits of their labour accrued to him. If a master, from indulgence, gave his slaves any *peculium* or fixed allowance for their subsistence, they had no right of property in what they saved out of that. All that they accumulated belonged to their master. Potgieff. lib. ii. c. 10. Murat. antiq. Ital. vol. 768. Du Cange, voc. *servus*, vol. vi. p. 451. Conformably

formably to the fame principle, all the effects of flaves belonged to their master at their death, and they could not difpofe of them by teftament. Potgieff. lib. ii. c. 11. 6. Slaves were diftinguifhed from free men by a peculiar drefs. Among all the barbarous nations, long hair was a mark of dignity and of freedom, flaves were for that reafon obliged to fhave their heads; and by this diftinction, how indifferent foever it may be in its own nature, they were reminded every moment of the inferiority of their condition. Potgieff. lib. iii. c. 4. For the fame reafon it was enacted in the laws of almoft all the nations of Europe, that no flave fhould be admitted to give evidence againft a free man in a court of juftice. Du Cange, voc. *fervus*, vol. vi. p. 451, Potgieff. lib. iii. c. 3.

2, *Villani.* They were likewife *adfcripti glebæ* or *villæ*, from which they derived their name, and were transferable along with it. Du Cange, voc. *villanus*, But in this they differed from flaves, that they paid a fixed rent to their mafter for the land which they cultivated, and after paying that, all the fruits of their labour and induftry belonged to themfelves in property. This diftinction is marked by Piere de Fontaine's Confeil. Vie de St. Louis par Joinville, p. 119. edit. de Du Cange. Several cafes decided agreeably to this principle are mentioned by Murat. Ibid. p. 773.

3. The laft clafs of perfons employed in agriculture were free men. Thefe are diftinguifhed by

PROOFS AND ILLUSTRATIONS.

by various names among the writers of the middle ages, *Arimanni, conditionales, originarii, tributales, &c.* These seem to have been persons who possessed some small allodial property of their own, and besides that, cultivated some farm belonging to their more wealthy neighbours, for which they paid a fixed rent; and bound themselves likewise to perform several small services *in prato vel in messe, in aratura vel in vinea,* such as ploughing a certain quantity of their landlord's ground, assisting him in harvest and vintage work, &c. The clearest proof of this may be found in Muratori, v. i. p. 712. and in Du Cange under the respective words abovementioned. I have not been able to discover whether these *arimanni*, &c. were removeable at pleasure, or held their farms by lease for a certain number of years. The former, if we may judge from the genius and maxims of the age, seems to be most probable. These persons, however, were considered as free men in the most honourable sense of the word; they enjoyed all the privileges of that condition, and were even called to serve in war; an honour to which no slave was admitted. Murat. Antiq. vol. i. p. 743. vol. ii. p. 446. This account of the condition of these three different classes of persons, will enable the reader to apprehend the full force of an argument which I shall produce in confirmation of what I have said in the text concerning the wretched state of the people during the middle ages. Notwithstanding the immense difference between the first of these classes and the third, such was the

spirit

spirit of tyranny which prevailed among the great proprietors of land, and so various their opportunities of oppressing those who were settled on their estates, and of rendering their condition intolerable, that many free men, in despair, renounced their liberty, and voluntarily surrendered themselves as slaves to their powerful masters. This they did, in order that their masters might become more immediately interested to afford them protection, together with the means of subsisting themselves and their families. The forms of such a surrender, or *obnoxiatio*, as it was then called, are preserved by Marculfus, lib. ii. c. 28; and by the anonymous author published by M. Bignon, together with the collection of *formulæ* compiled by Marculfus, c. 16. In both, the reason given for the *obnoxiatio*, is the wretched and indigent condition of the person who gives up his liberty. It was still more common for free men to surrender their liberty to bishops or abbots, that they might partake of the security which the vassals and slaves of churches and monasteries enjoyed, in consequence of the superstitious veneration paid to the saint under whose immediate protection they were supposed to be taken. Du Cange, voc. *oblatus*, vol. iv. p. 1286. That condition must have been miserable indeed, which could induce a free man voluntarily to renounce his liberty, and to give up himself as a slave to the disposal of another. The number of slaves in all the nations of Europe was prodigious. The greater part of the inferior clafs of people in France were reduced to this ftate, at the commencement of the third race of Kings. L'efpr. des Loix, liv. xxx. c. 11. The fame was the cafe in England. Brady Pref. to Gen. Hift. Many curious facts with refpect to the ancient ftate of *villains* or flaves in England, are publifhed in Obfervations on the ftatutes, chiefly the more ancient, 2d edit. p. 244.

NOTE X. SECT. I. p. 22. [K].

INNUMERABLE proofs of this might be produced. Many charters granted by perfons of the higheft rank are preferved, from which it appears that they could not fubfcribe their name. It was ufual for perfons who could not write, to make the fign of the crofs in confirmation of a charter. Several of thefe remain, where Kings and perfons of great eminence affix *fignum crucis manu propria pro ignoratione literarum*. Du Cange, voc. Crux, vol. iii. p. 1191. From this is derived the phrafe of figning inftead of fubfcribing a paper. In the ninth century, Herbaud Comes Palatii, though fupreme judge of the Empire by virtue of his office, could not fubfcribe his name. Nouveau Traité de Diplomatique par deux Benedictins, 4to. tom. ii. p. 422. So late as the fourteenth century, Du Guefclin, conftable of France, the greateft man in the ftate, and one of the greateft men of his age, could neither read nor write. St. Palaye Memoires fur l'ancienne Chevalerie, t. ii. p. 82.

p. 82. Nor was this ignorance confined to laymen; the greater part of the clergy was not many degrees superior to them in science. Many dignified ecclesiasticks could not subscribe the canons of those councils, in which they sat as members. Nouv. Traité de Diplom. tom. ii. p. 424. One of the questions appointed by the canons to be put to persons who were candidates for orders was this, " Whether they could read the gospels and epistles, and explain the sense of them, at least literally?" Regino Prumiensis ap. Bruck. Hist. Philos. v. iii. p. 631. Alfred the Great complained, that from the Humber to the Thames there was not a priest who understood the liturgy in his mother-tongue, or who could translate the easiest piece of Latin; and that from the Thames to the sea, the ecclesiasticks were still more ignorant. Asserus de rebus gestis Alfredi, ap. Camdeni. Anglica, &c. p. 25. The ignorance of the clergy is quaintly described by an author of the dark ages. " Potius dediti gulæ quam Glossæ; potius colligunt libras quam legunt libros; libentius intuentur Martham quam Marcum; malunt legere in Salmone quam in Solomone. Alanus de art. Predicat. ap. Lebeuf. Dissert. tom. ii. p. 21. To the obvious causes of such universal ignorance, arising from the state of government and manners, from the seventh to the eleventh century, we may add the scarcity of books during that period, and the difficulty of rendering them more common. The Romans wrote their books either on parchment

ment or on paper made of the Egyptian papyrus. The latter being the cheapest, was of course the most commonly used. But after the Saracens conquered Egypt in the seventh century, the communication between that country and the people settled in Italy or in other parts of Europe, was almost entirely broken off, and the papyrus was no longer in use among them. They were obliged, on that account, to write all their books upon parchment, and as the price of that was high, books became extremely rare and of great value. We may judge of the scarcity of the materials for writing them from one circumstance. There still remain several manuscripts of the eighth, ninth, and following centuries, wrote on parchment, from which some former writing had been erased, in order to substitute a new composition in its place. In this manner, it is probable, that several works of the ancients perished. A book of Livy or of Tacitus might be erased, to make room for the legendary tale of a saint, or the superstitious prayers of a missal. Murat. Antiq. Ital. v. iii. p. 833. P. de Montfaucon affirms, that the greater part of the manuscripts on parchment which he has seen, those of an ancient date excepted, are written on parchment from which some former treatise had been erased. Mem. de l'Acad. des inscript. tom. ix. p. 325. As the want of materials for writing, is one reason why so many of the works of the ancients have perished, it accounts likewise for the small number of manuscripts of
any

any kind, previous to the eleventh century, when they began to multiply from a cause which shall be mentioned. Hist. Liter. de France, tom. vi. p. 6. Many circumstances prove the scarcity of books during these ages. Private persons seldom possessed any books whatever. Even monasteries of considerable note had only one missal. Murat. Antiq. v. ix. p. 789. Lupus, abbot of Ferrieres, in a letter to the Pope, A. D. 855, beseeches him to lend him a copy of Cicero de Oratore & Quintilian's Institutions, "for," says he, "although we have parts of those books, there is no complete copy of them in all France. Murat. Ant. v. iii. p. 835. The price of books became so high, that persons of a moderate fortune could not afford to purchase them. The countess of Anjou paid for a copy of the Homilies of Haimon, bishop of Halberstadt, two hundred sheep, five quarters of wheat, and the same quantity of rye and millet. Histoire Literaire de France par des Religieux Benedictins, tom. vii. p. 3. Even so late as the year 1471, when Louis XI. borrowed the works of Rasis, the Arabian physician, from the faculty of medicine in Paris, he not only deposited in pledge a considerable quantity of plate, but was obliged to procure a nobleman to join with him as surety in a deed, binding himself under a great forfeiture to restore it. Gabr. Naudè Addit. à l'histoire de Louys XI. par Comines, edit. de Fresnoy, tom. iv. p. 281. Many curious circumstances with respect to the extravagant price of books in the middle

ages,

ages, are collected by that industrious compiler, to whom I refer such of my readers as deem this small branch of literary history an object of curiosity. When any person made a present of a book to a church or a monastery, in which were the only libraries during these ages, it was deemed a donative of such value, that he offered it on the altar *pro remedio animæ suæ*, in order to obtain the forgiveness of his sins. Murat. vol. iii. p. 836. Hist. Liter. de France, tom. vi. p. 6. Nouv. Trait. du Diplomat. par deux Benedictins, 4to. tom. i. p. 481. In the eleventh century, the art of making paper in the manner now become universal, was invented; by means of that not only the number of manuscripts increased, but the study of the sciences was wonderfully facilitated. Murat. ib. p. 871. The invention of the art of making paper, and the invention of the art of printing, are two considerable events in literary history. It is remarkable that the former preceded the first dawning of letters and improvement in knowledge towards the close of the eleventh century; the latter ushered in the light which spread over Europe at the æra of the Reformation.

NOTE XI. Sect. I. p. 23. [L].

All the religious maxims and practices of the dark ages are a proof of this. I shall produce one remarkable testimony in confirmation of it, from an author canonized by the church of Rome, St. Eloy or Egidius, bishop of Noyon, in the seventh century.

century. "He is a good Christian who comes frequently to church; who presents the oblation which is offered to God upon the altar; who doth not taste of the fruits of his own industry until he has consecrated a part of them to God; who, when the holy festivals shall approach, lives chastely even with his own wife during several days, that with a safe conscience he may draw near to the altar of God; and who, in the last place, can repeat the Creed and the Lord's Prayer. Redeem then your souls from destruction while you have the means in your power; offer presents and tythes to churchmen; come more frequently to church; humbly implore the patronage of the saints; for if you observe these things, you may come with security in the day of retribution to the tribunal of the eternal Judge, and say, "Give to us, O Lord, for we have given unto thee." Dacherii Specilegium Vet. Script. v. ii. p. 94. The learned and judicious translator of Dr. Mosheim's Ecclesiastical History, from one of whose additional notes I have borrowed this passage, subjoins a very proper reflection; "We see here a large and ample description of a good Christian, in which there is not the least mention of the love of God, resignation to his will, obedience to his laws, or of justice, benevolence, and charity towards men." Mosh. Ecclef. Hist. v. i. p. 324.

NOTE XII. Sect. I. p. 23. [M].

It is no inconsiderable misfortune to the church of Rome, whose doctrine of infallibility renders all such

such institutions and ceremonies as have been once universally received, immutable and everlasting, that she must continue to observe in enlightened times, those rights which were introduced during the ages of darkness and credulity. What delighted and edified the latter, must disgust and shock the former. Many of these rites appear manifestly to have been introduced by a superstition of the lowest and most illiberal species. Many of them were borrowed, with little variation, from the religious ceremonies established among the ancient Heathens. Some were so ridiculous, that if every age did not furnish instances of the fascinating influence of superstition, as well as of the whimsical forms which it assumes, it must appear incredible that they should ever be received or tolerated. In several churches of France, they celebrated a festival in commemoration of the Virgin Mary's flight into Egypt. It was called the feast of the Ass. A young girl richly dressed, with a child in her arms, was set upon an ass superbly caparisoned. The ass was led to the altar in solemn procession. High Mass was said with great pomp. The ass was taught to kneel at proper places; a hymn no less childish than impious was sung in his praise: And when the ceremony was ended, the priest, instead of the usual words with which he dismissed the people, brayed three times like an ass; and the people, instead of their usual response, We bless the Lord, brayed three times in the same manner. Du Cange, voc. Festum. v. iii. p. 424. This ridiculous

diculous ceremony was not, like the festival of fools, and some other pageants of those ages, a mere farcical entertainment exhibited in a church, and mingled, as was then the custom, with an imitation of some religious rites; it was an act of devotion, performed by the ministers of religion, and by the authority of the church. However, as this practice did not prevail universally in the Catholick church, its absurdity contributed at last to abolish it.

NOTE XIII. SECT. I. p. 29. [N].

As there is no event in the history of mankind more singular than that of the Crusades, every circumstance that tends to explain or to give any rational account of this extraordinary frenzy of the human mind is interesting. I have asserted in the text, that the minds of men were prepared gradually for the amazing effort which they made in consequence of the exhortations of Peter the hermit, by several occurrences previous to his time. A more particular detail of this curious and obscure part of history, may perhaps appear to some of my readers to be of importance. That the end of the world was expected about the close of the tenth and beginning of the eleventh century; and that this occasioned a general alarm, is evident from the authors to whom I refer in the text. This belief was so universal and so strong, that it mingled itself with their civil transactions. Many charters, in the latter part of the tenth century, begin in

this

this manner: "Apropinquante mundi termino," &c. As the end of the world is now at hand, and by various calamities and judgments the signs of its approach are now manifest. Hist. de Langued. par D. D. de Vic Vaisette, tom. ii. Preuves. p. 86, 89, 90, 117, 158, &c. One effect of this opinion was, that a great number of pilgrims resorted to Jerusalem, with a resolution to die there, or to wait the coming of the Lord; Kings, Earls, Marquisses, Bishops, and even a great number of women, besides persons of inferior rank, flocked to the Holy Land. Glaber. Rodulph. Hist. chez Bouquet Recueil, tom. x. p. 50, 52. Another historian mentions a vast cavalcade of pilgrims who accompanied the count of Angouleme to Jerusalem in the year 1026. Chronic. Ademari, ibid. p. 162. These pilgrims filled Europe with lamentable accounts of the state of Christians in the Holy Land. Willerm. Tyr. Hist. ap. Gest. Dei per Franc. vol. ii. p. 636. Guibert. Abbat. Hist. ibid. vol. i. p. 476. Besides this, it was usual for many of the Christian inhabitants of Jerusalem, as well as of other cities in the East, to travel as mendicants through Europe; and by describing the wretched condition of the professors of the Christian faith under the dominion of Infidels, to extort charity, and to excite zealous persons to make some attempt in order to deliver them from oppression. Baldrici Archiepiscopi Histor. ap. Gesta Dei, &c. vol. i. p. 86. In the year 986, Gerbert, archbishop of Ravenna, afterwards Pope Silvester II. addressed a letter to all Christians

PROOFS AND ILLUSTRATIONS:

Christians in the name of the church of Jerusalem. It is eloquent and pathetic, and contains a formal exhortation to take arms against the Pagan oppressors, in order to rescue the holy city from their yoke. Gerberti Epistolæ ap. Bouquet, Recueil, tom. x. p. 426. In consequence of this spirited call, some subjects of the republick of Pisa equipped a fleet, and invaded the territories of the Mahometans in Syria. Murat. Script. Rer. Italic. vol. iii. p. 400. The alarm was taken in the East, and an opinion prevailed, A. D. 1010, that all the forces of Christendom were to unite, in order to drive the Mahometans out of Palestine. Chron. Ademari ap. Bouquet, tom. x. p. 152. It is evident from all these particulars, that the ideas which led the Crusaders to undertake their wild enterprize were gradually formed; so that the universal concourse to the standard of the cross when erected by Urban II. will appear less surprising.

If the various circumstances which I have enumerated in this note, as well as in the history, are sufficient to account for the ardour with which such vast numbers engaged in such a dangerous undertaking, the extensive privileges and immunities granted to those who assumed the cross, serve to account for the long continuance of this spirit in Europe. 1. They were exempted from prosecutions on account of debt during the time of their being engaged in this holy service. Du Cange, voc. *Crucis privilegium*, v. ii. p. 1194.—2. They were exempted from paying interest for the money which they had borrowed.

borrowed. Ibid.—3. They were exempted either entirely, or at least during a certain time, from the payment of taxes. Ibid. Ordonances des Rois de France, tom. i. p. 33.—4. They might alienate their lands without the consent of the superior lord of whom they held. Ib.—5. Their persons and effects were taken under the protection of St. Peter, and the anathemas of the church were denounced against all who should molest them, or carry on any quarrel or hostility against them, during their absence, on account of the holy war. Du Cange, Ib. Guibertus Abbas ap. Bongarſ. i. p. 480, 482.— 6. They enjoyed all the privileges of Ecclesiasticks, and were not bound to plead in any civil court, but were declared subject to the spiritual jurisdiction alone. Du Cange, Ib. Ordon. des Rois, tom. i. p. 34, 174.—7. They obtained a plenary remission of all their sins, and the gates of heaven were set open to them, without requiring any proof of their penitence, but their engaging in this expedition, and thus gratifying their favourite passion, the love of war. Guibert. Abbas, p. 480. When we behold the civil and ecclesiastical powers vying with each other, and straining their invention in order to devise expedients for encouraging and adding strength to the spirit of superstition, can we be surprised that it should become so general as to render it infamous, and a mark of cowardice to decline engaging in the holy war? Willierm Tyrienſis ap. Bongarſ. vol. ii. p. 641. The histories of the Crusades written by modern authors, who are

apt

PROOFS AND ILLUSTRATIONS.

apt to substitute the ideas and maxims of their own age in the place of those which influenced the persons whose actions they attempt to relate, convey a very imperfect notion of the spirit at that time predominant in Europe. The original historians, who were animated themselves with the same passions which possessed their contemporaries, exhibit to us a more striking picture of the times and manners which they describe. The enthusiastic rapture with which they account for the effects of the Pope's discourse in the council of Clermont; the exultation with which they mention the numbers who devoted themselves to this holy warfare; the confidence with which they rely on the divine protection; the extasy of joy with which they describe their taking possession of the holy city, will enable us to conceive in some degree the extravagance of that zeal which agitated the minds of men with such violence, and will suggest as many singular reflections to a philosopher, as any occurrence in the history of mankind.—It is unnecessary to select the particular passages in the several historians which confirm this observation. But lest these authors may be suspected of adorning their narrative with any exaggerated description, I shall appeal to one of the leaders who conducted the enterprize. There is extant a letter from Stephen, the earl of Chartres and Blois, to Adela his wife, in which he gives her an account of the progress of the Crusaders. He describes the Crusaders as the chosen army of Christ, as the servants and foldiers of God, as men who marched under the immediate protection of the Almighty, being conducted by his hand to victory and conquest. He speaks of the Turks as accursed, sacrilegious, and devoted by heaven to destruction; and when he mentions the soldiers in the Christian army who had died, or were killed, he is confident that their souls were admitted directly into the joys of Paradise. Dacherii Specilegium, vol. iv. p. 257.

THE expence of conducting numerous bodies of men from Europe to Asia, must have been excessive, and the difficulty of raising the necessary sums must have been proportionally great, during ages when the publick revenues in every nation of Europe were extremely small. Some account is preserved of the expedients employed by Humbert II. Dauphin of Vienne, in order to levy the money requisite towards equipping him for the Crusade, A. D. 1346. These I shall mention, as they tend to shew the considerable influence which the Crusades had, both on the state of property and of civil government. 1. He exposed to sale part of his domains; and as the price was destined for such a sacred service, he obtained the consent of the French King, of whom these lands were held, ratifying the alienation. Hist. de Dauphiné, tom. i. p. 332. 335.—2. He issued a proclamation, in which he promised to grant new privileges to the nobles, as well as new immunities to the cities and towns, in his territories, in consideration of

certain

certain fums which they were inftantly to pay on that account. Ibid. tom. ii. p. 512. Many of the charters of community, which I fhall mention in another note, were obtained in this manner.— 3. He exacted a contribution towards defraying the charges of the expedition from all his fubjects, whether ecclefiafticks or laymen, who did not accompany him in perfon to the Eaft. Ibid. tom. i. p. 335.—4. He appropriated a confiderable part of his ufual revenues for the fupport of the troops to be employed in this fervice. Ibid. tom. ii. p. 518.—5. He exacted confiderable fums not only of the Jews fettled in his dominions, but alfo of the Lombards and other bankers who had fixed their refidence there. Ibid. tom. i. p. 338. tom. ii. 528. Notwithftanding the variety of thefe refources, the Dauphin was involved in fuch expence by this expedition, that on his return he was obliged to make new demands on his fubjects, and to pillage the Jews by frefh exactions. Ibid. tom. i. p. 344, 347. When the count de Foix engaged in the firft Crufade, he raifed the money neceffary for defraying the expences of that expedition, by alienating part of his territories. Hift. de Langued. par D. D. de Vic & Vaifette, tom. ii. p. 287. In like manner Baldwin, count of Hainaut, mortgaged or fold part of his dominions to the bifhop of Liege. A. D. 1096. Du Mont Corps Diplomatique, tom. i. p. 59. At a later period, Baldwin Count of Namur fold part of his eftate to a monaftery, when he intended to affume the crofs. A. D. 1139. Miræi Oper. i. 313.

NOTE

PROOFS AND ILLUSTRATIONS.

NOTE XIV. Sect. I. p. 34. [O].

The usual method of forming an opinion concerning the comparative state of manners in two different nations, is by attending to the facts which historians relate concerning each of them. Various passages might be selected from the Byzantin historians, describing the splendor and magnificence of the Greek Empire. P. de Montfaucon has produced from the writings of St. Chrysostom a very full account of the elegance and luxury of the Greeks in his age. That father in his sermons enters into such details concerning the manners and customs of his contemporaries, as appear strange in discourses from the pulpit. P. de Montfaucon has collected these descriptions, and ranged them under different heads. The court of the more early Greek Emperors seems to have resembled those of Eastern monarchs, both in magnificence and in corruption of manners. The Emperors in the eleventh century, though inferior in power, did not yield to them in ostentation and splendor. Memoires de l'Acad. des Inscript. tom. xx. p. 197.——But we may decide concerning the comparative state of manners in the Eastern Empire, and among the nations in the west of Europe by another method, which, if not more certain, is at least more striking. As Constantinople was the place of rendezvous for all the armies of the crusaders, this brought together the people of the east and west as to one great interview. There are extant several contemporary

temporary authors, both among the Greeks and Latins, who were witnesses of this singular congress of people, formerly strangers, in a great measure, to each other. They describe with simplicity and candour, the impression which that new spectacle made upon their own minds. This may be considered as the most lively and just picture of the real character and manners of each people. When the Greeks speak of the Franks, they describe them as barbarians, fierce, illiterate, impetuous and savage. They assume a tone of superiority, as a more polished people, acquainted with the arts both of government and of elegance, of which the other were ignorant. It is thus Anna Comnena describes the manners of the Latins, Alexias, p. 224. 231. 237. ap. Byz. Script. vol. xi. She always treats them with contempt as a rude people, the very mention of whose names was sufficient to contaminate the beauty and elegance of history, p. 229. Nicetas Choniatas inveighs against them with still more violence, and gives an account of their ferocity and devastations, in terms not unlike those which preceding historians had employed in describing the incursions of the Goths and Vandals. Nicet. Chon. ap. Byz. Script. vol. iii. p. 302, &c. But, on the other hand, the Latin historians were struck with astonishment at the magnificence, wealth, and elegance which they discovered in the Eastern Empire. " O what a vast city is Constantinople (exclaims Fulcherius Carnotensis, when he first

beheld

beheld it) and how beautiful! How many monasteries are there in it, and how many palaces built with wonderful art! How many manufactures are there in the city amazing to behold! It would be astonishing to relate how it abounds with all good things, with gold, silver, and stuffs of various kinds; for every hour ships arrive in its port laden with all things necessary for the use of man." Fulcher. ap. Bongars. vol. i. p. 386. Willermus Archbishop of Tyre, the most intelligent historian of the crusades, takes frequent occasion to describe the elegance and splendour of the court of Constantinople, and adds, that what they observed there exceeded any idea which they could have formed of it, nostrarum enim rerum modum & dignitatem excedunt, Willerm. Tyr. ap. Bong. vol. ii. p. 657. 664. Benjamin the Jew, of Tudela in Navarre, who began his travels A. D. 1173, appears to have been equally astonished at the magnificence of that city, and gives a description of its splendour, in terms of high admiration. Benj. Tudel. chez les Voyages faits en 12, 13, &c. siecles par Bergeron, p. 10. &c. Guntherus, a French monk who wrote a history of the conquest of Constantinople by the crusaders in the thirteenth century, speaks of the magnificence of that city in the same tone of admiration, " Structuram autem Ædificiorum in corpore civitatis, in ecclesiis videlicet, & turribus, & in domibus magnatorum, vix ullus vel describere potest, vel credere describenti, nisi qui ea oculata fide cognoverit."

cognoverit." Hist. Constantinop. ap. Canisii Lectiones Antiquas. fol. Antw. 1725. vol. iv. p. 14. Geoffrey de Villehardouin, a nobleman of high rank, and accustomed to all the magnificence then known in the west, describes, in similar terms, the astonishment and admiration of such of his fellow-soldiers who beheld Constantinople for the first time: " They could not have believed, says he, that there was a city so beautiful and rich in the whole world. When they viewed its high walls, its lofty towers, its rich palaces, its superb churches, all appeared so great that they could have formed no conception of this sovereign city, unless they had seen it with their own eyes." Histoire de la Conquete de Constant. p. 49. From these undisguised representations of their own feelings, it is evident, that to the Greeks, the Latins appeared to be a race of rude, unpolished barbarians; whereas the latter, how much soever they might contemn the unwarlike character of the former, could not help regarding them as far superior to themselves in elegance and arts.—That the state of government and manners was much more improved in Italy than in the other countries of Europe is evident not only from the facts recorded in history, but it appears that the more intelligent leaders of the crusaders were struck with the difference. Jacobus de Vitriaco, a French historian of the holy war, makes an elaborate panegyrick on the character and manners of the Italians. He views them as a more polished people,

people, and particularly celebrates them for their love of liberty, and civil wisdom; " in consiliis circumspecti, in re sua publica procuranda diligentes & studiosi; sibi in posterum providentes; aliis subjici renuentes; ante omnia libertatem sibi defendentes; sub uno quem eligunt capitaneo, communitati suæ jura & instituta dictantes, & similiter observantes." Histor. Hierosol. ap. Gesta Dei per Francos, vol. ii. p. 1085.

NOTE XV. Sect. I. p. 38. [P].

The different steps taken by the cities of Italy in order to extend their power and dominion are remarkable. As soon as their liberties were established, and they began to feel their own importance, they endeavoured to render themselves masters of the territory round their walls. Under the Romans, when cities enjoyed municipal privileges and jurisdiction, the circumjacent lands belonged to each town, and were the property of the community. But as it was not the genius of the feudal policy to encourage cities, or to shew any regard for their possessions and immunities, these lands had been seized, and shared among the conquerors. The barons to whom they were granted, erected their castles almost at the gates of the city, and exercised their jurisdiction there. Under pretence of recovering their ancient property, many of the cities in Italy attacked these troublesome neighbours, and dispossessing them, annexed their territories to the communities, and

made

made thereby a confiderable addition to their power. Several inftances of this occur in the eleventh, and beginning of the twelfth centuries. Murat. antiq. Ital. vol. iv. p. 159, &c. Their ambition increafing together with their power, the cities afterwards attacked feveral barons fituated at a greater diftance from them, and obliged thefe to engage that they fhould become members of their community; that they fhould take the oath of fidelity to their magiftrates; that they fhould fubject their lands to all burdens and taxes impofed by common confent; that they fhould defend the community againft all its enemies; and that they fhould refide within the city during a certain fpecified time in each year. Murat. ibid. 163. This fubjection of the nobility to the municipal government eftablifhed in cities, became almoft univerfal, and was often extremely grievous to perfons accuftomed to confider themfelves as independent. Otto Frifingenfis thus defcribes the ftate of Italy under Frederick I. " The cities fo much affect liberty, and are fo folicitous to avoid the infolence of power, that almoft all of them have thrown off every other authority, and are governed by their own magiftrates. Infomuch that all that country is now filled with free cities, each of which have compelled their bifhops to refide within their walls, and there is fcarcely any nobleman, how great foever his power may be, who is not fubject to the laws and government of fome city. De Geftis Frider. I. Imp. lib. ii. c. 13. p. 453. In another place he obferves of
the

the Marquis of Montferrat that he was almost the only Italian baron, who had preserved his independence, and had not become subject to the laws of any city. See also Muratori Antichita Estensi, vol. i. p. 411, 412. That state into which some of the nobles were compelled to enter, others embraced from choice. They observed that high degree of security as well as of credit and estimation which the growing wealth and dominion of the great communities procured to all the members of them. They were desirous to partake of these, and to put themselves under such powerful protection. With this view they voluntarily became citizens of the towns to which their lands were most contiguous, and abandoning their ancient castles, took up their residence in the cities at least during part of the year. Several deeds are still extant, by which some of the most illustrious families in Italy are associated as citizens of different cities. Murat. ib. p. 165, &c. A charter by which Atto de Macerata is admitted as a citizen of Osimo, A. D. 1198. in the Marcha di Ancona is still extant. In this he stipulates, that he will acknowledge himself to be a burgess of that community; that he will to the utmost of his power promote its honour and welfare; that he will obey its magistrates; that he will enter into no league with its enemies; that he will reside in the town during two months in every year, or for a longer time if required by the magistrates. The community on the other hand take him, his family and friends, under their protection, and

engage

engage to defend him against every enemy. Fr.
Ant. Zacharias Anecdota medii ævi. Aug. Taurin.
1755. fol. p. 66. This privilege was deemed so
important, that not only laymen, but ecclesiasticks
of the highest rank, condescended to be adopted
as members of the great communities, in hopes
of enjoying the safety and dignity which that conferred. Murat. ib. 179. Before the institution
of communities, persons of noble birth had no
other residence but their castles. They kept their
petty courts there; and the cities were deserted,
having hardly any inhabitants but slaves or persons
of low condition. But in consequence of the
practice which I have mentioned, cities not only
became more populous, but were filled with inhabitants of better rank, and a custom which still
subsists in Italy was then introduced, that all
families of distinction reside more constantly in
the great towns, than is usual in other parts of
Europe. As cities acquired new consideration and
dignity by the accession of such citizens, they
became more solicitous to preserve their liberty
and independence. The Emperors, as sovereigns,
had anciently a palace in almost every great city
of Italy; when they visited that country they
were accustomed to reside in these, and the troops
which accompanied them were quartered in the
houses of the citizens. This the citizens deemed
both ignominious and dangerous. They could
not help considering it as receiving a master and
an enemy within their walls. They laboured therefore to get free of this subjection. Some cities
prevailed

prevailed on the Emperors to engage that they should never enter their gates, but take up their refidence without the walls: Chart. Hen. IV. Murat. ib. p. 24. Others obtained the Imperial licence to pull down the palace fituated within their liberties, on condition that they built another in the fuburbs for the reception of the Emperor. Chart. Hen. IV. Murat. ib. p. 25. Thefe various encroachments of the Italian cities alarmed the Emperors, and put them on fchemes for re-eftablifhing the Imperial jurifdiction over them on its ancient footing. Frederick Barbaroffa engaged in this enterprize with great ardour. The free cities of Italy joined together in a general league, and ftood on their defence; and after a long conteft, carried on with alternate fuccefs, a folemn treaty of peace was concluded at Conftance, A. D. 1183. by which all the privileges and immunities granted by former Emperors to the principal cities in Italy were confirmed and ratified. Murat. differt. XLVIII. This treaty of Conftance was confidered as fuch an important article in the jurifprudence of the middle ages, that it is ufually publifhed together with the Libri Feudorum at the end of the Corpus Juris Civilis. The treaty fecured privileges of great importance to the confederate cities, and though it referved a confiderable degree of authority and jurifdiction to the Empire, yet the cities perfevered with fuch vigour in their efforts in order to extend their immunities, and the conjunctures in which they made them were fo favourable, that, before the conclufion

of

of the thirteenth century, moſt of the great cities
in Italy had ſhaken off all marks of ſubjection to
the Empire, and were become independent ſovereign republicks. It is not requiſite that I ſhould
trace the various ſteps by which they advanced to
this high degree of power ſo fatal to the Empire,
and ſo beneficial to the cauſe of liberty in Italy.
Muratori with his uſual induſtry has collected
many original papers which illuſtrate this curious
and little known part of hiſtory. Murat. Antiq.
Ital. Diſſert. L. See alſo Jo. Bapt. Villanovæ hiſt.
Laudis Pompeii ſive Lodi in Græv. Theſ. Antiquit. Ital. vol. iii. p. 838.

NOTE XVI. Sect. I. p. 40. [Q].

Long before the inſtitution of communities in
France, charters of immunity or Franchiſe were
granted to ſome towns and villages by the Lords
on whom they depended. But theſe are very different from ſuch as became common in the twelfth
and thirteenth centuries. They did not erect theſe
towns into corporations; they did not eſtabliſh a
municipal government; they did not grant them
the privilege of bearing arms. They contained
nothing more than a manumiſſion of the inhabitants from the yoke of ſervitude; an exemption
from certain ſervices which were oppreſſive and
ignominious; and the eſtabliſhment of a fixed
tax or rent which they were to pay to their Lord
in place of impoſitions which he could formerly
lay upon them at pleaſure. Two charters of this
kind

kind to two villages in the county of Rouſillon, one A. D. 974. the other A. D. 1025, are ſtill extant. Petr. de Marca *Marca*, ſive limes Hiſpanicus. app. p. 909. 1038. Such conceſſions, it is probable, were not unknown in other parts of Europe, and may be conſidered as a ſtep towards the more extenſive privileges conferred by Louis the Groſs on the towns within his domains. The communities in France never aſpired to the ſame independence with thoſe in Italy. They acquired new privileges and immunities, but the right of ſovereignty remained entire to the King or baron within whoſe territories the reſpective cities were ſituated, and from whom they received the charter of their freedom. A great number of theſe charters granted both by the Kings of France, and by their great vaſſals, are publiſhed by M. D'Achery in his Specilegium, and many are found in the collection of the Ordonances des Rois de France. Theſe convey a very ſtriking repreſentation of the wretched condition of cities previous to the inſtitution of communities, when they were ſubject to the judges appointed by the ſuperior Lords of whom they held, and had ſcarcely any other law but their will. Each conceſſion in theſe charters muſt be conſidered as a grant of ſome new privilege which the people did not formerly enjoy, and each regulation as a method of redreſſing ſome grievance under which they formerly laboured. The charters of communities contain likewiſe the firſt expedients employed for the introduction of
equal

PROOFS AND ILLUSTRATIONS.

equal laws, and regular government. On both thefe accounts they merit particular attention, and therefore, inftead of referring my readers to the many bulky volumes in which they are fcattered, I fhall give them a view of fome of the moft important articles in thefe charters, ranged under two general heads. I. Such as refpect perfonal fafety. II. Such as refpect the fecurity of property.

1. DURING that ftate of turbulence and diforder which the corruption of the feudal government introduced into Europe, perfonal fafety was the chief object of every individual; and as the great military barons alone were able to give fufficient protection to their vaffals, this was one great fource of their power and authority. But, by the inftitution of communities, effectual provifion was made for the fafety of individuals independent of the nobles. For, 1. the fundamental article in every charter was, that all the members of it bound themfelves by oath to affift, defend, and ftand by each other againft all aggreffors, and that they fhould not fuffer any perfon to injure, diftrefs, or moleft, any of their fellow-citizens. D'Acher. Spicel. x. 642. xi. 341, &c.—2. Whoever refided in any town which was made free, was obliged under a fevere penalty to accede to the community, and to take part in the mutual defence of its members. D'Acher. Spic. xi. 344. —3. The communities had the privilege of carrying arms; of making war on their private enemies;

mies; and of executing by military force any sentence which their magistrates pronounced. D'Ach. Spicel. x. 643, 644. xi. 343.—4. The practice of making satisfaction by a pecuniary compensation for murder, assault, or other acts of violence, most inconsistent with the order of society, and the safety of individuals, was abolished; and such as committed these crimes were punished capitally, or with rigour adequate to their guilt. D'Ach. xi. 362. Miræi opera Diplomatica, i. 292. —5. No member of a community was bound to justify or defend himself by battle, or combat, but if he was charged with any crime, he could be convicted only by the evidence of witnesses, and the regular course of legal proceedings. Miræus, ibid. D'Ach. xi. 375, 349. Ordon. tom. iii. 265.—6. If any man suspected himself to be in danger from the malice or enmity of another, upon his making oath to that effect before a magistrate, the person suspected was bound under a severe penalty to give security for his peaceable behaviour. D'Ach. xi. 346. This is the same species of security which is still known in Scotland under the name of *Lawburrows*. In France it was first introduced among the inhabitants of communities, and having been found to contribute considerably towards personal safety, it was extended to all the other members of the society. Establissemens de St. Louis, liv. i. cap. 28. ap. Du Cange vie de St. Louis, p. 15.

PROOFS AND ILLUSTRATIONS.

II. THE provisions in the charters of communities concerning the security of property, are not less considerable than those respecting personal safety. By the ancient law of France, no person could be arrested or confined in prison on account of any private debt. Ordon. des Rois de France, tom. i. p. 72, 80. If any person was arrested upon any pretext, but his having been guilty of a capital crime, it was lawful to rescue him out of the hands of the officers who had seized him. Ordon. iii. p. 17. Freedom from arrest on account of debt, seems likewise to have been enjoyed in other countries. Gudenus Sylloge Diplom. 473. In society, while it remained in its rudest and most simple form, debt seems to have been considered as an obligation merely personal. Men had made some progress towards refinement, before creditors acquired a right of seizing the property of their debtors in order to recover payment. The expedients for this pupose were all introduced originally in communities, and we can trace the gradual progress of them. 1. The simplest and most obvious species of security was, that the person who sold any commodity should receive a pledge from him who bought it, which he restored upon receiving payment. Of this custom there are vestiges in several charters of community. D'Ach. ix. 185. xi. 377.—2. When no pledge was given, and the debtor became refractory or insolvent, the creditor was allowed to seize his effects with a strong hand, and by his private authority; the citizens of Paris are warranted by the royal mandate, " ut ubicumque, et quocumque modo poterunt, tantum capiant, unde pecuniam fibi debitam integrè & plenariè habeant, & inde fibi invicem adjutores exiftant." Ordon, &c. tom. i. p. 6. This rude practice, fuitable only to the violence of a ftate of nature, was tolerated longer than one can conceive to be poffible in any fociety where laws and order were at all known. The ordonance authorizing it was iffued, A. D. 1134; and that which corrects the law, and prohibits creditors from feizing the effects of their debtors, unlefs by a warrant from a magiftrate, and under his infpection, was not publifhed until the year 1351. Ordon. tom. ii. 438. It is probable, however, that men were taught, by obferving the diforders which the former mode of proceeding occafioned, to correct it in practice long before a remedy was provided by a law to that effect. Every difcerning reader will apply this obfervation to many other cuftoms and practices which I have mentioned. New cuftoms are not always to be afcribed to the laws which authorize them. Thefe ftatutes only give a legal fanction to fuch things as the experience of mankind has previoufly found to be proper and beneficial.—3. As foon as the interpofition of the magiftrate became requifite, regular provifion was made for attaching or diftraining the moveable effects of a debtor; and if his moveables were not fufficient to difcharge the debt, his immoveable property, or eftate in land, was liable to the fame diftrefs, and was fold for the benefit of his creditor. D'Ach. ix. p. 184, 185.

PROOFS AND ILLUSTRATIONS.

185. xi. p. 348. 380. As this regulation afforded the most compleat security to the creditor, it was considered as so severe, that humanity pointed out several limitations in the execution of it. Creditors were prohibited from seizing the wearing apparel of their debtors, their beds, the door of their house, their instruments of husbandry, &c. D'Ach. ix. 184. xi. 377. Upon the same principles, when the power of distraining effects became more general, the horse and arms of a gentleman could not be seized. D'Ach. ix. 185. As hunting was the favourite amusement of martial nobles, the Emperor Lodovicus Pius prohibited the seizing of a hawk on account of any composition or debt. Capitul. lib. iv. § 21. But if the debtor had no other moveables, even these privileged articles might be seized.—4. In order to render the security of property compleat within a community, every person who was admitted a member of it, was obliged to buy or build a house, or to purchase lands, within its precincts, or at least to bring into the town a considerable portion of his moveables *per quæ justitiari possit, si quid forte in eum querela evenerit.* D'Ach. xi. 326. Ordon. i. 367. Libertates S. Georgii de Esperanchia. Hist. de Dauphine, tom. i. p. 26.—5. That security might be as perfect as possible, in some towns, the members of the community seem to have been bound for each other. D'Ach. x. 644.—6. All questions with respect to property were tried within the community, by magistrates and judges which the citizens elected or appointed. Their decisions were

more equal and fixed than the sentences which depended on the capricious and arbitrary will of a baron, who thought himself superior to all laws. D'Ach. x. 644, 646. xi. 344. & passim. Ordon. iii. 204.—7. No member of a community could be burdened by any arbitrary tax; for the superior lord who granted the charter of community, accepted of a fixed census or duty in lieu of all demands. Ordon. t. iii. 204. Libertates de Calma. Hift. de Dauphine, tom. i. p. 19. Libert. St. Georgii de Efperanchia, ibid. p. 26. Nor could the members of a community be diftreffed by an unequal impofition of the fum to be levied on the community. Regulations are inferted in the charters of some communities concerning the method of determining the quota of any tax to be levied on each inhabitant. D'Ach. xi. 350, 365. St. Louis published an ordonance concerning this matter, which extended to all the communities. Ordon. t. i. 186. These regulations are extremely favourable to liberty, as they veft the power of proportioning the taxes in a certain number of citizens chofen out of each parifh, who were bound by folemn oath to decide according to juftice.—That the more perfect fecurity of property was one great object of those who inftituted communities, we learn, not only from the nature of the thing, but from the exprefs words of feveral charters, of which I fhall only mention that granted by Alienor, Queen of England and Dutchefs of Guienne, to the community of Poitiers, " ut fua propria melius defendere poffint, & magis integrè cuftodire." Du Cange voc.

voc. *Communia*, v. ii. p. 863.—Such are some of the capital regulations established in communities during the twelfth and thirteenth centuries. These may be considered as the first rudiments of law and order, and contributed greatly to introduce regular government among all the members of society. As soon as communities were instituted, high sentiments of liberty began to appear. When Humbert, lord of Beaujeu, upon granting a charter of community to the town of Belleville, exacted of the inhabitants an oath of fidelity to himself and successors, they stipulated, on their part, that he should swear to maintain their franchises and liberties; and for their greater security, they obliged him to bring twenty gentlemen to take the same oath, and to be bound together with him. D'Ach. ix. 183. In the same manner the lord of Moirens in Dauphiné produced a certain number of persons as his sureties for the observation of the articles contained in the charter of community to that town. These were bound to surrender themselves prisoners to the inhabitants of Moirens, if their liege lord should violate any of their franchises, and they promised to remain in custody until he should grant them redress.' Hist. de Dauphiné, tom. i. p. 17. If the mayor or chief magistrate of a town did any injury to a citizen, he was obliged to give security for his appearance in judgment in the same manner as a private person; and if cast, was liable to the same penalty. D'Ach. ix. 183. These are ideas of equality uncommon in the feudal times. Communities were so favourable

able to freedom, that they were distinguished by the name of *Libertates.* Du Cange, v. ii. p. 863. They were at first extremely odious to the nobles, who foresaw what a check they must prove to their power and domination. Guibert Abbot of Nogent calls them execrable inventions, by which, contrary to law and justice, slaves withdrew themselves from that obedience which they owed to their masters. Du Cange, ib. 862. The zeal with which some of the nobles and powerful ecclesiasticks opposed the establishment of communities, and endeavoured to circumscribe their privileges, was extraordinary. A striking instance of this occurs in the contests between the archbishop of Reims, and the inhabitants of that community. It was the chief business of every archbishop, during a considerable time, to abridge the rights and jurisdiction of the community; and the great object of the citizens, especially when the see was vacant, to maintain, to recover, and to extend their own jurisdiction. Histoire civile & politique de la ville de Reims par M. Anquetil. tom. i. p. 287, &c.

THE observations which I have made concerning the state of cities, and the condition of their inhabitants, are confirmed by innumerable passages in the historians and laws of the middle ages. It is not improbable, however, that some cities of the first order were in a better state, and enjoyed a superior degree of liberty. Under the Roman government, the municipal government established in cities was extremely favourable to liberty. The

jurisdiction

jurifdiction of the fenate in each corporation, and the privileges of the citizens, were both extenfive. There is reafon to believe, that fome of the greater cities which efcaped the deftructive rage of the barbarous nations, ftill retained their ancient form of government, at leaft in a great meafure. They were governed by a council of citizens, and by magiftrates whom they themfelves elected. Very ftrong prefumptions in favour of this opinion, are produced by M. l'Abbé De Bos. Hift. Crit. de la Mon. Franc. tom. i. p. 18, &c. tom. ii. p. 524. edit. 1742. It appears from fome of the charters of community to cities, granted in the twelfth and thirteenth centuries, that thefe only confirm the privileges poffeffed by the inhabitants previous to the eftablifhment of the community. D'Acher. Specileg. vol. xi. p. 345. Other cities claimed their privileges as having poffeffed them without interruption from the times of the Romans. Hift. Crit. de la Mon. Franc. tom. ii. p. 333. But the number of cities which enjoyed fuch immunities was fo fmall, as in no degree to diminifh the force of my conclufions in the text.

NOTE XVII. Sect. I. p. 40. [R].

HAVING given a full account of the eftablifhment as well as effects of communities in Italy and France, it will be neceffary to enquire with fome attention into the progrefs of cities and of municipal government in Germany. The ancient Germans had no cities. Even in their hamlets or villages

lages they did not build their houses contiguous to each other. Tac. de Mor. Germ. cap. 16. They considered it as a badge of servitude to be obliged to dwell in a city surrounded with walls. When one of their tribes had shaken off the Roman yoke, their countrymen required of them, as an evidence of their having recovered liberty, to demolish the walls of a town which the Romans had built in their country. Even the fiercest animals, said they, lose their spirit and courage when they are confined. Tac. Histor. lib. iv. c. 64. The Romans built several cities of note on the banks of the Rhine. But in all the vast countries from that river to the coasts of the Baltick, there was hardly one city previous to the ninth century of the Christian æra. Conringius Exercitatio de Urbibus Germaniæ Oper. vol. i. § 25, 27, 31, &c. Heineccius differs from Conringius with respect to this. But even after allowing to his arguments and authorities their utmost force, they prove only that there were a few places in those extensive regions on which some historians have bestowed the name of towns. Elem. Jur. German. lib. i. § 102. Under Charlemagne, and the Emperors of his family, as the political state of Germany began to improve, several cities were founded, and men became accustomed to associate and to live together in one place. Charlemagne founded two archbishopricks and nine bishopricks in the most considerable towns of Germany. Aub. Miræi Opera Diplomatica, vol. i. p. 16. His successors increased the number of these; and as bishops fixed their residence

dence in thefe cities, and performed religious functions there, that induced many people to fettle in them. Conring. ibid. § 48. But Henry, firnamed the Fowler, who began his reign A. D. 920, muft be confidered as the great founder of cities in Germany. The Empire was at that time infefted by the incurfions of the Hungarians and other barbarous people. In order to oppofe them, Henry encouraged his fubjects to fettle in cities which he furrounded with walls and towers. He enjoined or perfuaded a certain proportion of the nobility to fix their refidence in the towns, and thus rendered the condition of citizens more honourable than it had been formerly. Wittikindus Annal. lib. i. ap. Conring. § 82. From this period the number of cities continued to increafe, and they became more populous and more wealthy. But cities were ftill deftitute of municipal liberty or jurifdiction. Such of them as were fituated in the Imperial demefnes, were fubject to the Emperors. Their *Comites*, *Miffi*, and other judges prefided in them, and difpenfed juftice. Towns fituated on the eftate of a baron, were part of his fief, and he or his officers exerçifed a fimilar jurifdiction in them. Conring. ibid. § 73, 74. Heinec. Elem. Jur. Germ. lib. i. § 104. The Germans borrowed the inftitution of communities from the Italians. Knipfchildius Tractatus Politico. Hiftor. Jurid. de Civitatum Imperialium Juribus, vol. i. lib. i. cap. 5. N°. 23. Frederick Barbaroffa was the firft Emperor who, from the fame political confideration

PROOFS AND ILLUSTRATIONS.

tion that influenced Lewis the Grofs, multiplied communities in order to abridge the power of the nobles. Pfeffel Abregè de l'Hiftoire & du Droit Publique d'Allemagne, 4to. p. 297. From the reign of Henry the Fowler, to the time when the German cities acquired full poffeffion of their immunities, various circumftances contributed to their increafe. The eftablifhment of bifhopricks (already mentioned) and the building of cathedrals, naturally induced many people to fettle there. It became the cuftom to hold councils and courts of judicature of every kind, ecclefiaftical as well as civil, in cities. In the eleventh century, many flaves were enfranchifed, the greater part of which fettled in cities. Several mines were difcovered and wrought in different provinces, which drew together fuch a concourfe of people, as gave rife to feveral cities. Conring. § 105. The cities began in the thirteenth century to form leagues for their mutual defence, and for repreffing the diforders occafioned by the private wars among the barons, as well as by their exactions. This rendered the condition of the inhabitants of cities more fecure than that of any order of men, and allured many to become members of their communities. Conring. § 94. There were inhabitants of three different ranks in the towns of Germany. The nobles, or familiæ, the citizens, or liberi, and the artifans, who were flaves, or homines proprii. Knipfchild. lib. ii. cap. 29. N°. 13. Henry V. who began his reign A. D. 1106, infranchifed the flaves who were artifans or inhabitants in feveral

towns,

towns, and gave them the rank of citizens, or *liberi*. Pfeffel, p. 254. Knipfch. lib. ii. c. 29. N°. 113, 119. Though the cities in Germany did not acquire liberty fo early as thofe in France, they extended their privileges much farther. All the Imperial and free cities, the number of which is confiderable, acquired the full right of being *immediate*; by which term, in the German jurifprudence, we are to underftand, that they are fubject to the Empire alone, and poffefs within their own precincts all the rights of compleat and independent fovereignty. The various privileges of the Imperial cities, the great guardians of the Germanic liberties, are enumerated by Knipfchild, lib. ii. The moft important articles are generally known, and it would be improper to enter into any difquifition concerning minute particulars.

NOTE XVIII. Sect. I. p. 40. [S].

THE Spanifh hiftorians are almoft entirely filent concerning the origin and progrefs of communities in that kingdom; fo that I cannot fix with any degree of certainty the time and manner of their firft introduction there. It appears, however, from Mariana, vol. ii. p. 221, fol. Hagæ 1736, that in the year 1350, eighteen cities had obtained a feat in the Cortes of Caftile. From the account which fhall be given of their conftitution and pretenfions, Sect. III. of this volume, it is evident that their privileges and form of government were the fame with thofe of the other feudal corporations; and this, as well as the perfect fimiliarity of political inſtitutions and tranſactions in all the feudal kingdoms, may lead us to conclude, that communities were introduced there in the ſame manner, and probably about the ſame time, as in the other nations of Europe. In Aragon, as I ſhall have occaſion to obſerve in a ſubſequent note, cities ſeem early to have acquired extenſive immunities, together with a ſhare in the legiſlature. In the year 1118, the citizens of Saragoſſa had not only attained political liberty, but they were declared to be of equal rank with the nobles of the ſecond claſs; and many other immunities, unknown to perſons in their rank of life in other parts of Europe, were conferred upon them. Zurita Anales de Aragon, tom. i. p. 44. In England, the eſtabliſhment of communities or corporations was poſterior to the Conqueſt. The practice was borrowed from France, and the privileges granted by the crown were perfectly ſimilar to thoſe which I have enumerated. But as this part of hiſtory is well known to moſt of my readers, I ſhall, without entering into any critical or minute diſcuſſion, refer them to authors who have fully illuſtrated this intereſting point in the Engliſh hiſtory. Brady's Treatiſe of Boroughs. Madox Firma Burgi, chap. i. ſect. ix. Hume's Hiſtory of England, vol. i. append. i. and ii. It is not improbable that ſome of the towns in England were formed into corporations under the Saxon Kings, and that the charters granted by the Kings of the Norman race were not charters of enfranchiſement from a ſtate of ſlavery, but a confirmation

tion of privileges which they already enjoyed. See Lord Lyttelton's History of Henry II. vol. ii. p. 317. The English cities, however, were very inconsiderable in the twelfth century. A clear proof of this occurs in the history to which I last referred. Fitzstephen, a contemporary author, gives a description of the city of London in the reign of Henry II. and the terms in which he speaks of its trade, its wealth, and the splendour of its inhabitants, would suggest no inadequate idea of its state at present, when it is the greatest and most opulent city of Europe. But all ideas of grandeur and magnificence are merely comparative. It appears from a contemporary author, Peter of Blois, archdeacon of London, who had good opportunity of being well informed, that this city, of which Fitzstephen gives such a pompous account, contained no more than forty thousand inhabitants. Ibid. 315, 316. The other cities were small in proportion, and in no condition to extort any extensive privileges. That the constitution of the boroughs in Scotland, in many circumstances, resembled that of the towns in France and England, is manifest from the Leges Burgorum annexed to the Regiam Majestatem.

NOTE XIX. Sect. I. p. 46. [T].

Soon after the introduction of the third estate into the national council, the spirit of liberty which that excited in France began to produce conspicuous effects. In several provinces of France, the

the nobility and communities formed affociations, whereby they bound themfelves to defend their rights and privileges againft the formidable and arbitrary proceedings of the King. The Count de Boulainvilliers has preferved a copy of one of thefe affociations, dated in the year 1314, twelve years after the admiffion of the deputies from towns into the States General. Hiftoire de l'ancien gouvernement de la France, tom. ii. p. 94. The vigour with which the people afferted and prepared to maintain their rights, obliged their fovereigns to refpect them. Six years after this affociation, Philip the Long iffued a writ of fummons to the community of Narbonne, in the following terms: " Philip, by the Grace, &c. to our wellbeloved, &c. As we defire with all our heart, and above all other things, to govern our kingdom and people in peace and tranquillity, by the help of God; and to reform our faid kingdom in fo far as it ftands in need thereof, for the publick good, and for the benefit of our fubjects, who in times paft have been aggrieved and oppreffed in diverfe manners by the malice of fundry perfons, as we have learned by common report, as well as by the information of good men worthy of credit, and we having determined in our council which we have called to meet in our good city, &c. to give redrefs to the utmoft of our power, by all ways and means poffible, according to reafon and juftice, and willing that this fhould be done with folemnity and deliberation by the advice of the

prelates,

prelates, barons, and good towns of our realm, and particularly of you, and that it should be transacted agreeably to the will of God, and for the good of our people, therefore we command," &c. Mably, Observat. ii. App. p. 386. I shall allow these to be only the formal words of a publick and legal stile, but the ideas are singular, and much more liberal and enlarged than one could expect in that age. A popular monarch of Great Britain could hardly address himself to parliament, in terms more favourable to publick liberty. There occurs in the History of France a striking instance of the progress which the principles of liberty had made in that kingdom, and of the influence which the deputies of towns had acquired in the States General. During the calamities in which the war with England, and the captivity of King John, had involved France, the States General made a bold effort to extend their own privileges and jurisdiction. The regulations established by the States held A. D. 1355, concerning the mode of levying taxes, the administration of which they vested not in the crown, but in commissioners appointed by the States; concerning the coining of money; concerning the redress of the grievance of purveyance; concerning the regular administration of justice; are much more suitable to the genius of a republican government than that of a feudal monarchy. This curious statute is published, Ordon. t. iii. p. 19. Such as have not an opportunity to consult that large

large collection will find an abridgment of it, in Hist. de France par Villaret, tom. ix. p. 130. or in Histoire de Boulainv. tom. ii. 213. The French historians represent the bishop of Laon, and Marcel Provost of the merchants of Paris, who had the chief direction of this assembly, as seditious tribunes, violent, interested, ambitious, and aiming at innovations subversive of the constitution and government of their country. That may have been the case, but these men possessed the confidence of the people; and the measures which they proposed as the most popular and acceptable, plainly prove that the spirit of liberty had spread wonderfully, and that the ideas which then prevailed in France concerning government were extremely liberal. The States General held at Paris A. D. 1355, consisted of about eight hundred members, and above one half of these were deputies from towns. M. Secousse Pref. a Ordon. tom. iii. p. 48. It appears that in all the different assemblies of the States, held during the reign of John, the representatives of towns had great influence, and in every respect the third State was considered as co-ordinate and equal to either of the other two. Ibid. passim. These spirited efforts were made in France long before the House of Commons in England acquired any considerable influence in the legislature. As the feudal system was carried to its utmost height in France sooner than in England, so it began to decline sooner in the former than in the latter kingdom. In England,

land, almost all attempts to establish or to extend the liberty of the people have been succesful; in France they have proved unfortunate. What were the accidental events, or political causes which occasioned this difference, it is not my present business to enquire.

NOTE XX. Sect. I. p. 48. [U].

In a former Note, N° VIII. I have enquired into the condition of that part of the people which was employed in agriculture, and have represented the various hardships and calamities of their situation. When charters of liberty and manumission were granted to such persons, they contained four concessions corresponding to the four capital grievances to which men in a state of servitude are subject. 1. The right of disposing of their persons by sale or grant was relinquished. 2. Power was given to them of conveying their property and effects by will or any other legal deed. Or if they happened to die intestate, it was provided that their property should go to their lawful heirs in the same manner as the property of other persons. 3. The services and taxes which they owed to their superior or liege Lord, which were formerly arbitrary and imposed at pleasure, are precisely ascertained. 4. They are allowed the privilege of marrying whatever person they chose, as formerly they could contract no marriage without their Lord's permission, and with no person but one of his slaves. All these particulars,

particulars are found united in the charter granted
Habitatoribus Montis-Britonis. A. D. 1376. Hist.
de Dauphiné, tom. i. p. 81. Many circumstances
concurred with those which I have mentioned in
the text in procuring them deliverance from that
wretched state. The gentle spirit of the Christian
religion, together with the doctrines which it
teaches, concerning the original equality of mankind, as well as the impartial eye with which the
Almighty regards men of every condition, and
admits them to a participation of his benefits, are
inconsistent with servitude. But in this, as in
many other instances, considerations of interest,
and the maxims of false policy led men to a conduct inconsistent with their principles. They were
so sensible, however, of the inconsistency, that to
set their fellow Christians at liberty from servitude
was deemed an act of piety highly meritorious and
acceptable to heaven. The humane spirit of the
Christian religion struggled with the maxims and
manners of the world, and contributed more than
any other circumstance to introduce the practice
of manumission. When Pope Gregory the Great,
who flourished toward the end of the sixth century, granted liberty to some of his slaves, he
gives this reason for it, " Cum redemptor noster,
totius conditor naturæ, ad hoc propitiatus humaham carnem voluerit assumere, ut divinitatis suæ
gratia, dirempto (quo tenebamur captivi) vinculo,
pristinæ nos restitueret libertati; salubriter agitur,
si homines, quos ab initio liberos natura protulit,
& jus gentium jugo substituit servitutis, in ea,
qua

qui nati fuerant, manumittentis beneficio libertate reddantur." Gregor. Magn. ap. Potgieff. lib. iv. c. i. § 3. Several laws or charters founded on reasons similar to this, are produced by the same author. Accordingly a great part of the charters of manumission previous to the reign of Louis X. are granted pro amore dei, pro remedio animæ, & pro mercede animæ. Murat. Antiq. Ital. vol. i. p. 849, 850. Du Cange, voc. *manumissio*. The formality of manumission was executed in a church, as a religious solemnity. The person to be set free was led round the great altar with a torch in his hand, he took hold of the horns of the altar, and there the solemn words conferring liberty were pronounced. Du Cange, Ib. vol. iv. p. 467. I shall transcribe a part of a charter of manumission granted A. D. 1056; both as it contains a full account of the ceremonies used in this form of manumission, and as a specimen of the imperfect knowledge of the Latin tongue in that barbarous age. It is granted by Willa the widow of Hugo the Duke and Marquis, in favour of Clariza one of her slaves. " Et ideo nos Domine Wille inclite comecisse—libera et absolvo te Cleriza filia Uberto —pro timore omnipotentis dei, & remedio luminarie anime bone memorie quondam supra scripto Domini Ugo gloriosissimo, ut quando illum Dominus de hac vita migrare, jusserit, pars iniqua non abeat potestatem ullam, sed anguelos Domini nostri Jesu Christi colocare dignitur illum inter sanctos dilectos suos; & beatus Petrus princips apostolorum, qui habed potestatem omnium animarum

marum ligandi et abfolvendi, ut ipfi abfolvat
animæ ejus de peccatis fui, & aperiad illum janua
paradifi ; pro eadem vero rationi, in mano mite te
Benzo prefbiter, ut vadat tecum in ecclefia fancti
Bartholomæi apoftoli ; traad te tribus vicibus circa
altare ipfius ecclefiæ cum cæreo apprehenfum in
manibus tuis & manibus fuis ; deinde exite ambulate in via quadrubio, ubi quatuor vie fe devi-
duntur. Statimq; pro remedio luminarie anime
bone memorie quondam fupra fcripto Domini Ugo,
et ipfi prefbiter Benzo fecit omnia, & dixit, Ecce
quatuor vie, ite et ambulate in quacunq; partem
tibi placuerit, tam fic fupra fcripta Cleriza, qua
nofque tui heredes, qui ab ac hora in antea nati,
vel procreati fuerit utriufq; fexus, &c." Murat.
ib. p. 853. Many other charters might have been
felected, which, in point of grammar or ftyle, are
in no wife fuperior to this. Manumiffion was
frequently granted on death-bed or by latter-will.
As the minds of men are at that time awakened
to fentiments of humanity and piety, thefe deeds
proceeded from religious motives, and are granted
pro redemptione animæ, in order to obtain accep-
tance with God. Du Cange ubi fupra, p. 470.
& voc. *fervus,* vol. vi. p. 451. Another method
of obtaining liberty was by entering into holy
orders, or taking the vow in a monaftery. This
was permitted for fome time ; but fo many flaves
efcaped, by this means, out of the hands of their
mafters, that the practice was afterwards reftrained,
and at laft prohibited by the laws of almoft all
the nations of Europe. Murat. ib. p. 842. Conformably

formably to the same principles, Princes, on the birth of a son, or upon any other agreeable event, appointed a certain number of slaves to be enfranchised, as a testimony of their gratitude to God for that benefit. Marculfi Form. lib. i. cap. 39. There are several forms of manumission published by Marculfus, and all of them are founded on religious considerations, in order to procure the favour of God, or to obtain the forgiveness of their sins. Lib. ii. c. 23, 33, 34. edit. Baluz. The same observation holds with respect to the other collections of Formulæ annexed to Marculfus. As sentiments of religion induced some to grant liberty to their fellow-Christians who groaned under the yoke of servitude; so mistaken ideas concerning devotion led others to relinquish their liberty. When a person conceived an extraordinary respect for the saint who was the patron of any church or monastery in which he was accustomed to attend religious worship, it was not unusual among men possessed with an excess of superstitious reverence, to give up themselves and their posterity to be the slaves of the saint. Mabillon. de re Diplomat. lib. vi. 632. The *oblati* or voluntary slaves of churches or monasteries were very numerous, and may be divided into three different classes. The first were such as put themselves and effects under the protection of a particular church or monastery, binding themselves to defend its privileges and property against every aggressor. These were prompted to do so, not merely by devotion, but in order to obtain that security which arose from the protection of the church. They were rather vassals than slaves, and sometimes persons of noble birth found it prudent to secure the protection of the church in this manner. Persons of the second class bound themselves to pay an annual tax or quit-rent out of their estates to a church or monastery. Besides this, they sometimes engaged to perform certain services. They were called *censuales*. The last class consisted of such as actually renounced their liberty, and became slaves in the strict and proper sense of the word. These were called *ministeriales*, and enslaved their bodies, as some of the charters bear, that they might procure the liberty of their souls. Potgiesserus de statu servorum, lib. i. cap. i. § 6, 7. How zealous the clergy were to encourage the opinions which led to this practice will appear from a clause in a charter by which one gives up himself as a slave to a monastery, " Cum sit omni carnali ingenuitate generosius extremum quodcumq; Dei servitium, scilicet quod terrena nobilitas multos plerumq; vitiorum servos facit, servitus vero Christi nobiles virtutibus reddit, nemo autem sani capitis virtutibus vitia comparaverit, claret pro certo eum esse generosiorem, qui se Dei servitio præbuerit proniorem. Quod ego Ragnaldus intelligens, &c." Another author says, " Eligens magis esse servus Dei quam libertus sæculi, firmiter credens & sciens, quod servire Deo, regnare est, summaque ingenuitas sit in qua

servitus

servitus comparabatur Christi, &c." Du Cange, voc. *oblatus*, vol. iv. p. 1286, 1287. It does not appear, that the enfranchisement of slaves was a frequent practice while the feudal system preserved its vigour. On the contrary, there were laws which set bounds to this practice as detrimental to society. Potgiess. lib. iv. c. 2. § 6. The inferior order of men owed the recovery of their liberty to the decline of that aristocratical policy, which lodged the most extensive power in the hands of a few members of the society, and depressed all the rest. When Louis X. issued his ordonance, several slaves had been so long accustomed to servitude, and their minds were so much debased by that unhappy situation, that they refused to accept of the liberty which was offered them. D'Ach. Spicel. v. xi. p. 387. Long after the reign of Louis X. several of the French nobility continued to assert their ancient dominion over their slaves. It appears from an ordonance of the famous Bertrand de Guesclin Constable of France, that the custom of enfranchising them was considered as a pernicious innovation. Morice Mem. pour servir des preuves à l'hist. de Bret. tom. ii. p. 100. In some instances, when the prædial slaves were declared to be freemen, they were still bound to perform certain services to their ancient masters; and were kept in a state different from other subjects, being restricted either from purchasing land, or becoming members of a community within the precincts of the manor to which they formerly belonged. Martene & Durand. Thefaur. Anecdot. vol. i. p. 914. This, however, feems not to have been common.—There is no general law for the manumiffion of flaves in the Statute-book of England fimilar to that which has been quoted from the Ordonnances of the Kings of France. Though the genius of the Englifh conftitution feems early to have favoured perfonal liberty, perfonal fervitude, neverthelefs, continued long in England in fome particular places. In the year 1514, we find a charter of Henry VIII. enfranchifing two flaves belonging to one of his manors. Rym. Fœder. vol. xiii. p. 470. As late as the year 1574, there is a commiffion from Queen Elizabeth with refpect to the manumiffion of certain bondmen belonging to her. Rymer. in Obfervat. on the ftatutes, &c. p. 251.

NOTE XXI. SECT. I. p. 56. [X].

THERE is no cuftom in the middle ages more fingular than that of private war. It is a right of fo great importance, and prevailed fo univerfally, that the regulations concerning it make a confiderable figure in the fyftem of laws during the middle ages. M. de Montefquieu, who has unravelled fo many intricate points in feudal jurifprudence, and thrown light on fo many cuftoms formerly obfcure and unintelligible, was not led by his fubject to confider this. I fhall therefore give a more minute account of the cuftoms and regulations which directed a practice fo contrary

to

to the present ideas of civilized nations concerning government and order. 1. Among the ancient Germans, as well as other nations in a similar state of society, the right of avenging injuries was a private and personal right, exercised by force of arms, without any reference to an umpire, or any appeal to a magistrate for decision. The clearest proofs of this were produced Note VI. 2. This practice subsisted among the barbarous nations after their settlement in the provinces of the Empire which they conquered; and as the causes of dissention among them multiplied, their family feuds and private wars became more frequent. Proofs of this occur in their early historians. Greg. Turon. hist. lib. vii. c. 2. lib. viii. c. 18. lib. x. c. 27. and likewise in the codes of their laws. It was not only allowable for the relations to avenge the injuries of their family, but it was incumbent on them. Thus by the laws of the Angli and Werini, ad quemcunque hereditas terræ pervenerit, ad illum vestis bellica id est lorica & ultio proximi, & solatio leudis, debet pertinere, tit. vi. § 5. ap. Lindenbr. Leg. Salic. tit. 63. Leg. Longob. lib. ii. tit. 14. § 10.—— 3. None but gentlemen, or persons of noble birth, had the right of private war. All disputes among slaves, villani, the inhabitants of towns, and freemen of inferior condition, were decided in the courts of justice. All disputes between gentlemen and persons of inferior rank were terminated in the same manner. The right of private war supposed nobility of birth, and equality of rank in the

the contending parties. Beaumanoir Couftumes de Beauv. ch. lix. p. 300. Ordon. des Rois de France, tom. ii. 395. § xvii. 508. § xv, &c. The dignified ecclefiafticks likewife claimed and exercifed the right of private war; but as it was not altogether decent for them to profecute quarrels in perfon, *advocati* or *vidames* were chofen by the feveral monafteries and bifhopricks. Thefe were commonly men of high rank and reputation, who became the protectors of the churches and convents by whom they were elected; efpoufed their quarrels, and fought their battles; armis omnia quæ erant ecclefiæ viriliter defendebant, et vigilanter protegebant. Bruffel Ufage des Fiefs, tom. i. p. 144. Du Cange, voc. *advocatus*. On many occafions, the martial ideas to which ecclefiafticks of noble birth were accuftomed, made them forget the pacifick fpirit of their profeffion, and led them into the field in perfon at the head of their vaffals, "flamma, ferro, cæde, poffeffiones ecclefiarum prælati defendebant." Guido Abbas ap. Du Cange. Ib. p. 179.—4. It was not every injury or trefpafs that gave a gentleman a title to make war upon his adverfary. Atrocious acts of violence, infults and affronts publickly committed, were legal and permitted motives for taking arms againft the authors of them. Such crimes as are now punifhed capitally in civilized nations, at that time juftified private hoftilities. Beauman. ch. lix. Du Cange Differt. xxix. fur Joinville, p. 331. But though the avenging of injuries was the only motive that could legally authorife a private war,

yet

PROOFS AND ILLUSTRATIONS.

yet disputes concerning civil property often gave rise to hostilities, and were terminated by the sword. Du Cange Differt. p. 332.—5. All persons present when any quarrel arose, or any act of violence was committed, were included in the war which it occasioned, for it was supposed to be impossible for any man in such a situation to remain neutral, without taking side with one or other of the contending parties. Beauman. p. 300. —6. All the kindred of the two principals in the war were included in it, and obliged to espouse the quarrel of the chieftain with whom they were connected. Du Cange, ib. 332. This was founded on the maxim of the ancient Germans, " suscipere tam inimicitias seu patris, seu propinqui, quam amicitias, necesse est;" a maxim natural to all rude and simple nations, among which the form of society, and political union, strengthens such a sentiment. The method of ascertaining the degree of affinity which obliged a person to take part in the quarrel of a kinsman was curious. While the church prohibited the marriage of persons within the seventh degree of affinity, the vengeance of private war extended as far as this absurd prohibition, and all who had such a remote connection with any of the principals were involved in the calamities of war. But when the church relaxed somewhat of its rigour, and did not extend its prohibition of marrying beyond the fourth degree of affinity, the same restriction took place in the conduct of private war. Beauman. 303. Du Cange Differt. 333.—7. A private war
could

could not be carried on between two full brothers, because both have the same common kindred, and consequently neither have any persons bound to stand by him against the other, in the contest; but two brothers of the half blood might wage war, because each of them has a distinct kindred. Beauman. p. 299.—8. The vassals of each principal in any private war were involved in the contest, because by the feudal maxims they were bound to take arms in defence of the chieftain of whom they held, and to assist him in every quarrel. As soon, therefore, as the feudal tenures were introduced, and this artificial connection was established between vassals and the baron of whom they held, vassals came to be considered as in the same state with relations. Beauman. 303.—9. Private wars were very frequent for several centuries. Nothing contributed more to increase those disorders in government, and that ferocity of manners which reduced the nations of Europe to that wretched state which distinguished the period of history which I am reviewing. Nothing was such an obstacle to the introduction of a regular administration of justice. Nothing could more effectually discourage industry, or retard the progress and cultivation of the arts of peace. Private wars were carried on with all the destructive rage, which is to be dreaded from violent resentment when armed with force, and authorised by law. It appears from the laws prohibiting or restraining the exercise of private hostilities, that the invasion of the most barbarous enemy could not be more

desolating

desolating to a country, or more fatal to its inhabitants, than those intestine wars. Ordon. t. i. p. 701. tom. ii. 395, 408, 507, &c. The contemporary historians describe the excesses committed in prosecution of these quarrels in such terms as excite astonishment and horror. I shall mention only one passage from the history of the Holy War, by Guibert Abbot of Nogent: " Erat eo tempore maximis ad invicem hostilitatibus, totius Francorum regni facta turbatio; crebra ubiq; latrocinia, viarum obsessio; audiebantur passim, immo fiebant incendia infinita; nullis præter sola & indomita cupiditate existentibus causis extruebantur prælia; & ut brevi totum claudam; quicquid obtutibus cupidorum subjacebat, nusquam attendendo cujus esset, prædæ patebat." Gesta Dei per Francos, vol. i. p. 482.

Having thus collected the chief regulations which custom had established concerning the right and exercise of private war, I shall enumerate in chronological order the various expedients employed to abolish or restrain this fatal custom. 1. The first expedient employed by the civil magistrate in order to set some bounds to the violence of private revenge, was the fixing by law the fine or composition to be paid for each different crime. The injured person was originally the sole judge concerning the nature of the wrong which he had suffered, the degree of vengeance which he should exact, as well as the species of atonement or reparation with which he should rest satisfied. Resentment sentiment became of course as implacable as it was fierce. It was often a point of honour not to forgive, nor to be reconciled. This made it necessary to fix those compositions which make so great a figure in the laws of barbarous nations. The nature of crimes and offences was estimated by the magistrate, and the sum due to the person offended was ascertained with a minute, and often a whimsical accuracy. Rotharis, the legislator of the Lombards, who reigned about the middle of the seventh century, discovers his intention both in ascertaining the composition to be paid by the offender, and in increasing its value; it is, says he, that the enmity may be extinguished, the prosecution may cease, and peace may be restored. Leg. Langob. lib. i. tit. 7. § 10.—2. About the beginning of the ninth century, Charlemagne struck at the root of the evil, and enacted, " That when any person had been guilty of a crime, or had committed an outrage, he should immediately submit to the penance which the church imposed, and offer to pay the composition which the law prescribed; and if the injured person or his kindred should refuse to accept of this, and presume to avenge themselves by force of arms, their lands and properties should be forfeited." Capitul. A. D. 802. edit. Baluz. vol. i. 371.—3. But in this, as well as in other regulations, the genius of Charlemagne advanced before the spirit of his age. The ideas of his contemporaries concerning regular government were too imperfect, and their manners were too fierce to submit to this law. Private wars, with all the calamities which they occasioned, became more frequent than ever after the death of that great monarch. His successors were unable to restrain them. The church found it necessary to interpose. The most early of these interpositions now extant, is towards the end of the tenth century. In the year 990, several bishops in the south of France assembled, and published various regulations, in order to set some bounds to the violence and frequency of private wars; if any person within their dioceses should venture to transgress, they ordained that he should be excluded from all Christian privileges during his life, and be denied Christian burial after his death. Du Mont Corps Diplomatique, tom. i. p. 41. These, however, were only partial remedies; and therefore a council was held at Limoges, A. D. 994. The bodies of the saints, according to the custom of those ages, were carried thither; and by these sacred relicks men were exhorted to lay down their arms, to extinguish their animosities, and to swear that they would not for the future violate the publick peace by their private hostilities. Bouquet Recueil des Histor. vol. x. p. 49, 147. Several other councils issued decrees to the same effect. Du Cange Dissert. 343.—4. But the authority of councils, how venerable soever in those ages, was not sufficient to abolish a custom which flattered the pride of the nobles, and gratified their favourite passions. The evil grew so intolerable, that it became

came neceſſary to employ ſupernatural means for ſuppreſſing it. A biſhop of Aquitaine, A. D. 1032, pretended that an angel had appeared to him, and brought him a writing from heaven, enjoining men to ceaſe from their hoſtilities, and to be reconciled to each other. It was during a ſeaſon of public calamity that he publiſhed this revelation. The minds of men were diſpoſed to receive pious impreſſions; and willing to perform any thing in order to avert the wrath of heaven. A general peace and ceſſation from hoſtilities took place, and continued for ſeven years; and a reſolution was formed, that no man ſhould in times to come attack or moleſt his adverſaries during the ſeaſons ſet apart for celebrating the great feſtivals of the church, or from the evening of Thurſday in each week to the morning of Monday in the week enſuing, the intervening days being conſidered as particularly holy, our Lord's Paſſion having happened on one of theſe days, and his Reſurrection on another. A change in the diſpoſitions of men ſo ſudden, and which produced a reſolution ſo unexpected, was conſidered as miraculous; and the reſpite from hoſtilities which followed upon it, was called *The Truce of God*. Glaber. Rodulphus Hiſtor. lib. v. ap. Bouquet. vol. x. p. 59. This, from being a regulation or concert in one kingdom, became a general law in Chriſtendom, and was confirmed by the authority of the Pope, and the violaters were ſubjected to the penalty of excommunication. Corpus Jur. Canon. Decretal. lib. i. tit. 34. c. 1. Du Cange Gloſſar. voc. *Treuga*.

An act of the council of Toulujes in Rouffillon, A. D. 1041, containing all the ftipulations required by the truce of God, is publifhed by Dom de Vic & Dom Vaifette Hift. de Languedoc, tom. ii. Preuves, p. 206. A ceffation from hoftilities during three complete days in every week, allowed fuch a confiderable fpace for the paffions of the antagonifts to cool, and for the people to enjoy a refpite from the calamities of war, as well as to take meafures for their own fecurity, that, if this truce of God had been exactly obferved, it muft have gone far towards putting an end to private wars. This, however, feems not to have been the cafe; the nobles, difregarding the truce, profecuted their quarrels without interruption as formerly. Qua nimirum tempeftate, univerfæ provinciæ adeo devaftationis continuæ importunitate inquietantur, ut ne ipfa, pro obfervatione divinæ pacis, profeffa facramenta cuftodiantur. Abbas Ufpergenfis apud Datt de pace imperii publica, p. 13. N°. 35. The violent fpirit of the nobility could not be reftrained by any engagements. The complaints of this were frequent; and bifhops, in order to compel them to renew their vows and promifes of ceafing from their private wars, were obliged to enjoin their clergy to fufpend the performance of divine fervice, and the exercife of any religious function within the parifhes of fuch as were refractory and obftinate. Hift. de Langued. par D. D. de Vic & Vaifette, tom. ii. Preuves, p. 118.—5. The people, eager to obtain relief from their fufferings, called in a fecond time a pretended revelation to their aid. Towards the end of the twelfth century, a carpenter in Guienne gave out, that Jesus Christ, together with the blessed Virgin, had appeared to him, and having commanded him to exhort mankind to peace, had given him, as a proof of his mission, an image of the Virgin holding her son in her arms, with this inscription, *Lamb of God, who takest away the sins of the world, give us peace.* This low fanatick addressed himself to an ignorant age, prone to credit what was marvellous. He was received as an inspired messenger of God. Many prelates and barons assembled at Puy, and took an oath, not only to make peace with all their own enemies, but to attack such as refused to lay down their arms, and to be reconciled to their enemies. They formed an association for this purpose, and assumed the honourable name of *the Brotherhood of God.* Robertus de Monte Michaele ap. M. de Lauriere Pref. tom. i. Ordon. p. 29. But the influence of this superstitious terror or devotion was not of long continuance.—6. The civil magistrate was obliged to exert his authority in order to check a custom which threatened the dissolution of government. Philip Augustus, as some imagine, or St. Louis, as is more probable, published an ordonance, A. D. 1245, prohibiting any person to commence hostilities against the friends and vassals of his adversary, until forty days after the commission of the crime or offence which gave rise to the quarrel; declaring, that if any man presumed to transgress this statute, he should be considered as guilty of a breach of the publick

peace,

peace, and be tried and punished by the judge ordinary as a traitor. Ordon. tom. i. p. 56. This was called *the Royal Truce*, and afforded time for the violence of resentment to subside, as well as leisure for the good offices of such as were willing to compose the difference. The happy effects of this regulation seem to have been considerable, if we may judge from the solicitude of succeeding monarchs to enforce it.—7. In order to restrain the exercise of private war still farther, Philip the Fair, towards the close of the same century, A. D. 1296, published an ordonance commanding all private hostilities to cease, while he was engaged in war against the enemies of the state. Ordon. tom. i. p. 328, 390. This regulation, which seems to be almost essential to the existence and preservation of society, was often renewed by his successors, and being enforced by the regal authority, proved a considerable check to the destructive contests of the nobles. Both these regulations, introduced first in France, were adopted by the other nations of Europe.—8. The evil, however, was so inveterate, that it did not yield to all these remedies. No sooner was publick peace established in any kingdom, than the barons renewed their private hostilities. They not only struggled to maintain this pernicious right, but to secure the exercise of it without any restraint. Upon the death of Philip the Fair, the nobles of different provinces in France formed associations, and presented remonstrances to his successor, demanding the repeal of several laws, by which he had abridged the privileges of their order. Among these, the right of private war is always mentioned as one of the most valuable; and they claim, that the restraint imposed by the truce of God, the royal truce, as well as that arising from the ordonance of the year 1296, should be taken off. In some instances, the two sons of Philip, who mounted the throne successively, eluded their demands; in others, they were obliged to make concessions. Ordon. tom. i. p. 551, 557, 561, 573. The ordonances to which I here refer, are of such length that I cannot insert them, but they are extremely curious, and may be peculiarly instructive to an English reader, as they throw considerable light on that period of English history, in which the attempts to circumscribe the regal prerogative were carried on, not by the people struggling for liberty, but by the nobles contending for power. It is not necessary to produce any evidence of the continuance and frequency of private wars under the successors of Philip the Fair.—9. A practice somewhat similar to the royal truce was introduced, in order to strengthen and extend it. Bonds of assurance, or mutual security, were demanded from the parties at variance, by which they obliged themselves to abstain from all hostilities, either during a time mentioned in the bond, or for ever; and became subject to heavy penalties, if they violated this obligation. These bonds were sometimes granted voluntarily, but more frequently exacted by the authority of the civil magistrate. Upon a petition from the party who felt himself weakest, the magistrate summoned his adversary to appear in court, and obliged him to give a bond of assurance. If, after that, he committed any farther hostilities, he became subject to all the penalties of treason. This restraint on private war was known in the age of St. Louis. Establissemens, liv. i. c. 28. It was frequent in Bretagne; and what is very remarkable, such bonds of assurance were given mutually between vassals and the lord of whom they held. Oliver de Clisson grants one to the Duke of Bretagne, his sovereign. Morice Mem. pour servir de preuves à l'hist. de Bret. tom. i. p. 846. ii. p. 371. Many examples of bonds of assurance in other provinces of France are collected by Brussel. tom. ii. p. 856. The nobles of Burgundy remonstrated against this practice, and obtained exemption from it as an encroachment on the privileges of their order. Ordon. tom. i. p. 558. This mode of security was first introduced in cities, and the good effects of it having been felt there, was extended to the nobles. See Note XVI.—10. The calamities occasioned by private wars became at some times so intolerable, that the nobles entered into voluntary associations, binding themselves to refer all matters in dispute, whether concerning civil property, or points of honour, to the determination of the majority of the associates. Morice Mem. pour servir de preuves à l'hist. de Bret. tom. ii. p. 728.—11. But all these expedients proving ineffectual, Charles VI. A. D. 1413, issued an ordonance expressly prohibiting private wars on any pretext whatsoever, with power to the judge ordinary to compel all persons to comply with this injunction, and to punish such as should prove refractory or disobedient, by imprisoning their persons, seizing their goods, and appointing the officers of justice, *Mangeurs & Gasteurs*, to live at free quarters on their estate. If those who were disobedient to this edict could not be personally arrested, he appointed their friends and vassals to be seized, and detained until they gave surety for keeping the peace; and he abolished all laws, customs, or privileges which might be pleaded in opposition to this ordonnance. Ordon. tom. x. p. 138. How slow is the progress of reason and of civil order! Regulations which to us appear so equitable, obvious, and simple, required the efforts of civil and ecclesiastical authority, during several centuries, to introduce and establish them. Even posterior to this period, Louis XI. was obliged to abolish private wars in Dauphiné, by a particular edict, A. D. 1451. Du Cange differt. p. 348.

This note would swell to a disproportional bulk, if I should attempt to enquire with the same minute attention into the progress of this pernicious custom in the other countries of Europe. In England, the ideas of the Saxons concerning personal revenge, the right of private wars, and the composition due to the party offended, seem to have been much the same with those which prevailed on the Continent. The law of Ina *de Vindicantibus*, in the eighth century, Lamb. p. 3; those of Edmund in the tenth century, *de homicidio*, Lamb. p. 72.

p. 72. & *de inimicitiis*, p. 76; and those of Edward the Confessor, in the eleventh century, *de temporibus & diebus pacis*, or Treuga Dei, Lamb. p. 126, are perfectly similar to the *ordonances* of the French Kings their contemporaries. The laws of Edward, *de pace regis*, are still more explicit than those of the French Monarchs, and, by several provisions in them, discover that a more perfect police was established in England at that period. Lambard. p. 128. fol. vers. Even after the conquest, private wars, and the regulations for preventing them, were not altogether unknown, as appears from Madox Formulare Anglicanum, N°. CXLV. and from the extracts from Domesday Book, published by Gale Scriptores hist. Britan. p. 759, 777. The well known clause in the form of an English indictment, which, as an aggravation of the criminal's guilt, mentions his having assaulted a person, who was in the peace of God and of the King, seems to be borrowed from the Treuga or Pax Dei and the Pax Regis which I have explained. But after the conquest, the mention of private wars among the nobility, occurs more rarely in the English history, than in that of any other European nation, and no laws concerning them are to be found in the body of their statutes. Such a change in their own manners, and such a variation from those of their neighbours, is remarkable. Is it to be ascribed to the extraordinary power which William the Norman acquired by right of conquest, and transmitted to his successors, which rendered the execution of justice more vigorous and decisive, five, and the jurisdiction of the King's court more extensive than under the Monarchs on the Continent? Or, was it owing to the settlement of the Normans in England, who having never adopted the practice of private war in their own country, abolished it in the kingdom which they conquered?. It is asserted in an ordonance of John King of France, that in all times past, persons of every rank in Normandy have been prohibited to wage war, and the practice has been deemed unlawful. Ordon, tom. ii. p. 407. If this fact were certain, it would go far towards explaining the peculiarity which I have mentioned. But as there are some English Acts of Parliament, which, according to the remark of the learned author of the *Observations on the Statutes, chiefly the more ancient*, recite falsehoods, it may be added, that this is not peculiar to the laws of that country. Notwithstanding the positive assertion contained in this publick law of France, there is good reason for considering it as a statute which recites a falsehood. This, however, is not the place for discussing that point. It is an inquiry not unworthy the curiosity of an English antiquarian.

In Castile, the pernicious practice of private war prevailed, and was authorised by the customs and law of the kingdom. Leges Tauri. tit. 76. cum commentario Anton. Gomezii, p. 551. As the Castilian nobles were no less turbulent than powerful, their quarrels and hostilities involved their
country

country in many calamities. Innumerable proofs of this occur in Mariana. In Aragon, the right of private revenge was likewise authorised by law; exercised in its full extent, and accompanied with the same unhappy consequences. Hieron. Blanca Comment. de rebus Arag. ap. Schotti. Hispan. illustrat. vol. iii. p. 733. Lex Jacobi I. A. D. 1247. Fueros & Observancias del Reyno de Aragon, lib. ix. p. 182. Several confederacies between the Kings of Aragon and their nobles, for the restoring of peace, founded on the truce of God, are still extant. Petr. de Marca. *Marca* sivi Limes Hispanic. App. 1303, 1388, 1418. As early as the year 1165, we find a combination of the King and court of Aragon, in order to abolish the right of private war, and to punish those who presumed to claim that privilege. Anales de Aragon por Zurita, vol. i. p. 73. But the evil was so inveterate, that Charles V. A. D. 1519. was obliged to publish a law enforcing all former regulations tending to suppress this practice. Fueros & Observanc. lib. ix. 183. b.

THE Lombards, and other northern nations who settled in Italy, introduced the same maxims concerning the right of revenge into that country, and these were followed by the same effects. As the progress of the evil was perfectly similar to what happened in France, the expedients employed to check its career, or to extirpate it finally, resembled those which I have enumerated. Murat. Ant. Ital. vol. ii. p. 306.

IN

PROOFS AND ILLUSTRATIONS.

In Germany the disorders and calamities occasioned by the right of private war were greater and more intolerable than in any other country of Europe. The Imperial authority was so much shaken and enfeebled by the violence of the civil wars, excited by the contests between the Popes and the Emperors of the Franconian and Suabian lines, that not only the nobility but the cities acquired almost independent power, and scorned all subordination and obedience to the laws. The frequency of these *faidæ* or private wars, are often mentioned in the German Annals, and the fatal effects of them are most pathetically described, Datt. de pace Imper. pub. lib. i. cap. v. n°. 30. & passim. The Germans early adopted the Treuga Dei, which was first established in France. This, however, proved but a temporary and ineffectual remedy. The disorders multiplied so fast, and grew so enormous, that they threatened the dissolution of society, and compelled the Germans to have recourse to the only remedy of the evil, viz. an absolute prohibition of private wars. The Emperor, William, published his edict to this purpose, A. D. 1255, an hundred and sixty years previous to the ordonance of Charles VI. in France. Datt. lib. i. cap. 4. n°. 20. But neither he nor his successors had authority to secure the observance of it. This gave rise to a practice in Germany, which conveys to us a striking idea both of the intolerable calamities occasioned by private wars, and of the feebleness of government during the twelfth and thirteenth centuries. The

cities

cities and nobles entered into alliances and affociations, by which they bound themfelves to maintain the publick peace, and to make war on fuch as fhould violate it. This was the origin of the league of the Rhine, of Suabia, and of many fmaller confederacies diftinguifhed by various names. The rife, progrefs, and beneficial effects of thefe affociations are traced by Datt with great accuracy. Whatever degree of publick peace, or of regular adminiftration was preferved in the Empire from the beginning of the twelfth century to the clofe of the fifteenth, Germany owes to thefe leagues. During that period, political order, refpect for the laws, together with the equal adminiftration of juftice, made confiderable progrefs in Germany. But the final and perpetual abolition of the right of private war was not accomplifhed until A. D. 1495. The Imperial authority was by that time more firmly eftablifhed, the ideas of men with refpect to government and fubordination were become more juft. That barbarous and pernicious privilege which the nobles had fo long poffeffed, was declared to be incompatible with the happinefs and exiftence of fociety. In order to terminate any differences which might arife among the various numbers of the Germanick body, the Imperial chamber was inftituted with fupreme jurifdiction, to judge without appeal in every queftion brought before it. That court has fubfifted fince that period, forming a very refpectable tribunal, of effential importance in the German

PROOFS AND ILLUSTRATIONS.

man conſtitution. Datt. lib. iii. iv. v. Pfeffel abregé de l'Hiſtoire du Droit, &c. p. 556.

NOTE XXII. Sect. I. p. 67. [Y].

It would be tedious and of little uſe to enumerate the various modes of appealing to the juſtice of God, which ſuperſtition introduced during the ages of ignorance. I ſhall mention only one, becauſe we have an account of it in a placitum or trial in the preſence of Charlemagne, from which we may learn the imperfect manner in which juſtice was adminiſtered even during his reign. In the year 775, a conteſt aroſe between the biſhop of Paris and the abbot of St. Denys, concerning the property of a ſmall abbey. Each of them exhibited deeds and records, in order to prove the right to be in them. Inſtead of trying the authenticity, or conſidering the import of theſe, the point was referred to the *judicium crucis*. Each produced a perſon, who, during the celebration of maſs, ſtood before the croſs with his arms expanded; and he whoſe repreſentative firſt became weary, and altered his poſture, loſt the cauſe. The perſon employed by the biſhop on this occaſion had leſs ſtrength or leſs ſpirit than his adverſary, and the queſtion was decided in favour of the abbot. Mabillon de re Diplomat. lib. vi. p. 498. If a Prince ſo enlightened as Charlemagne countenanced ſuch an abſurd mode of deciſion, it is no wonder that other monarchs

ſhould

PROOFS AND ILLUSTRATIONS.

should tolerate it so long. M. de Montesquieu has treated of the trial by judicial combat at considerable length. The two talents which distinguish that illustrious author, industry in tracing all the circumstances of ancient and obscure institutions, and sagacity in penetrating into the causes and principles which contributed to establish them, are equally conspicuous in his observations on this subject. To these I refer the reader, as they contain most of the principles by which I have endeavoured to explain this practice. De l'Esprit des Loix, lib. xxviii. It seems to be probable from the remarks of M. de Montesquieu, as well as from the facts produced by Muratori, tom. iii. Dissert. xxxviii. that the appeals to the justice of God by the experiments with fire and water, &c. were practised by the people who settled in the different provinces of the Roman Empire, before they had recourse to the judicial combat. The judicial combat, however, was the most ancient mode of terminating any controversy among the barbarous nations in their original settlements. This is evident from Velleius Paterculus, lib. ii. c. 118. who informs us, that all questions which were decided among the Romans by legal trial, were terminated among the Germans by arms. The same thing appears in the ancient laws and customs of the Swedes, quoted by Jo. O. Stiernhöök de Jure Sueonum & Gothorum vetusto. 4to. Holmiæ 1682. lib. i. c. 7. It is probable that when the various tribes which invaded the Em-

PROOFS AND ILLUSTRATIONS.

pire were converted to Christianity, the repugnance of the custom of allowing judicial combats to the precepts of religion, was so glaring, that, for some time, it was abolished, and by degrees, several circumstances which I have mentioned, led them to resume it.

It seems likewise to be probable from a law quoted by Stiernhöök in the treatise which I have mentioned, that the judicial combat was originally permitted, in order to determine points respecting the personal character, or reputation of individuals, and was afterwards extended not only to criminal cases, but to questions concerning property. The words of the law are, " if any man shall say to another these reproachful words, " you are not a " man equal to other men," or, " you have not " the heart of a man," and the other shall reply, " I am a man as good as you." Let them meet on the highway. If he who first gave offence appear, and the person offended absent himself, let the latter be deemed worse than he was called; let him not be admitted to give evidence in judgment either for man or woman, and let him not have the privilege of making a testament. If the person offended appear, and he who gave the offence be absent, let him call upon the other thrice with a loud voice, and make a mark upon the earth, and then let him who absented himself be deemed infamous, because he uttered words which he durst not support. If both shall appear

properly

properly armed, and the perfon offended fhall fall in the combat, let a half compenfation be paid for his death. But if the perfon who gave the offence fhall fall, let it be imputed to his own rafhnefs. The petulance of his tongue hath been fatal to him. Let him lie in the field without any compenfation being demanded for his death." Lex Uplandica ap. Stiern. p. 76. Martial people were extremely delicate with refpect to every thing that affected their reputation as foldiers. By the laws of the Salians, if any man called another a *bare*, or accufed him of having left his fhield in the field of battle, he was ordained to pay a large fine. Leg. Sal. tit. xxxii. § 4. 6. By the law of the Lombards if any one called another *arga*, i. e. a good for nothing fellow, he might immediately challenge him to combat. Leg. Longob. lib. i. tit. v. § 1. By the law of the Salians, if one called another *cenitus*, a term of reproach equivalent to arga, the fine which he was bound to pay was very high. Tit. xxxii. § 1. Paulus Diaconus relates the violent impreffion which this reproachful expreffion made upon one of his countrymen, and the fatal effects with which it was attended. De Geftis Longobard. lib. vi. c. 24. Thus the ideas concerning the point of honour, which we are apt to confider as a modern refinement, as well as the practice of duelling, to which it gave rife, are derived from the notions of our anceftors, while in a ftate of fociety very little improved.

As M. de Montesquieu's view of this subject did not lead him to consider every circumstance relative to judicial combats, I shall mention some particular facts necessary for the illustration of what I have said with respect to them. A remarkable instance occurs of the decision of an abstract point of law by combat. A question arose in the tenth century concerning the *right* of *representation*, which was not then fixed, though now universally established in every part of Europe. "It was a matter of doubt and dispute, (saith the historian) whether the sons of a son ought to be reckoned among the children of the family, and succeed equally with their uncles, if their father happened to die while their grandfather was alive. An assembly was called to deliberate on this point, and it was the general opinion that it ought to be remitted to the examination and decision of judges. But the Emperor following a better course, and desirous of dealing honourably with his people and nobles, appointed the matter to be decided by battle between two champions. He who appeared in behalf of the right of children to represent their deceased father was victorious; and it was established, by a perpetual decree, that they should hereafter share in the inheritance together with their uncles. Wittickindus Corbeins, lib. Annal. ap. M. de Lauriere Pref. Ordon. vol. i. p. xxxiii. If we can suppose the caprice of folly to lead men to any action more extravagant than this of settling a point in law by combat, it must be that of
referring

referring the truth or falsehood of a religious opinion to be decided in the same manner. To the disgrace of human reason, it has been capable even of this extravagance. A question was agitated in Spain in the eleventh century, whether the Musarabic Liturgy and ritual which had been used in the churches of Spain, or that approved of by the See of Rome, which differed in many particulars from the other, contained the form of worship most acceptable to the Deity. The Spaniards contended zealously for the ritual of their ancestors. The Popes urged them to receive that to which they had given their infallible sanction. A violent contest arose. The nobles proposed to decide the controversy by the sword. The king approved of this method of decision. Two knights in compleat armour entered the lists. John Ruys de Matanca, the champion of the Musarabic Liturgy, was victorious. But the Queen and Archbishop of Toledo, who favoured the other form, insisted on having the matter submitted to another trial, and had interest enough to prevail in a request, inconsistent with the laws of combat, which being considered as an appeal to God, the decision ought to have been acquiesced in as final. A great fire was kindled. A copy of each Liturgy was cast into the flames. It was agreed that the book which stood this proof, and remained untouched, should be received in all the churches of Spain. The Musarabic Liturgy triumphed likewise in this trial, and if we may believe Roderigo de Toledo, remained unhurt by the fire, when the other was reduced to ashes. The Queen and Archbishop had power or art sufficient to elude this decision also, and the use of the Musarabic form of devotion was permitted only in certain churches. A determination no less extraordinary than the whole transaction. Rodr. de Toledo, quoted by P. Orleans, Hist. de Revol. d'Espagne, tom. i. p. 217. Mariana, lib. i. c. 18. vol. i. p. 378.—A remarkable proof of the general use of trial by combat, and of the prædilection for that mode of decision occurs in the laws of the Lombards. It was a custom in the middle ages, that any person might chuse the law to which he would be subjected; and by the prescriptions of that law he was obliged to regulate his transactions, without being bound to comply with any practice authorized by other codes of law. Persons who had subjected themselves to the Roman law, and adhered to the ancient jurisprudence, as far as any knowledge of it was retained in those ages of ignorance, were exempted from paying any regard to the forms of proceedings established by the laws of the Burgundians, Lombards, and other barbarous people. But the Emperor Otho, in direct contradiction to this received maxim, ordained, " That all persons, under whatever law they lived, even although it were the Roman law, should be bound to conform to the edicts concerning the trial by combat." Leg. Longob. lib. ii. tit. 55. § 38. While the judicial combat subsisted,

subsisted, proof by charters, contracts, or other deeds, became ineffectual; and even this species of evidence, calculated to render the proceedings of courts certain and decisive, was eluded. When a charter or other instrument was produced by one of the parties, his opponent might challenge it, affirm that it was false and forged, and offer to prove this by combat. Leg. Longob. ib. § 34. It is true, that among the reasons enumerated by Beaumanoir, on account of which judges might refuse to permit a trial by combat, one is, " If the point in contest can be clearly proved or ascertained by other evidence." Coust. de Beauv. ch. 63. p. 323. But that regulation removed the evil only a single step. For the party who suspected that a witness was about to depose in a manner unfavourable to his cause, might accuse him of being suborned, give him the lie, and challenge him to combat; if the witness was vanquished in battle, no other evidence was admitted, and the party by whom he was summoned to appear lost his cause. Leg. Baivar. tit. 16. § 2. Leg. Burgund. tit. 45. Beauman. ch. 61. p. 315. The reason given for obliging a witness to accept of a defiance, and to defend himself by combat, is remarkable, and contains the same idea which is still the foundation of what is called the point of honour; " for it is just, that if any one affirms that he perfectly knows the truth of any thing, and offers to give oath upon it, that he should not hesitate to maintain the veracity of his affirmation in combat." Leg. Burgund. tit. 45.

PROOFS AND ILLUSTRATIONS.

That the trial by judicial combat was established in every country of Europe, is a fact well known, and requires no proof. That this mode of decision was frequent, appears not only from the codes of ancient laws which established it, but from the earliest writers concerning the practice of law in the different nations of Europe. They treat of this custom at great length; they enumerate the regulations concerning it with minute accuracy; and explain them with much solicitude. It made a capital and extensive article in jurisprudence. There is not any one subject in their system of law which Beaumanoir, Defontaines, or the compilers of the Assises de Jerusalem seem to have considered as of greater importance; and none on which they have bestowed so much attention. The same observation will hold with respect to the early authors of other nations. It appears from Madox, that trials of this kind were so frequent in England, that fines, paid on these occasions, made no inconsiderable branch of the King's revenue. Hist. of the Excheq. vol. i. p. 349. A very curious account of a judicial combat between Mesire Robert de Beaumanoir, and Mesire Pierre Tournemine, in presence of the duke of Bretagne, A. D. 1385, is published by Morice Mem. pour servir de preuves à l'hist. de Bretagne, tom. ii. p. 498. All the formalities observed in such extraordinary proceedings are there described more minutely, than in any ancient monument which I have had an opportunity of considering. Tournemine was accused by Beaumanoir of having
murdered

murdered his brother. The former was vanquished, but was saved from being hanged upon the spot, by the generous interceſſion of his antagoniſt. A good account of the origin of the laws concerning judicial combat, is publiſhed in the hiſtory of of Pavia, by Bernardo Sacci, lib. ix. c. 8. in Græv. Theſ. Antiquit. Ital. vol. iii. 743.

THIS mode of trial was ſo acceptable, that eccleſiaſticks, notwithſtanding the prohibitions of the church, were conſtrained not only to connive at the practice, but to authorize it. A remarkable inſtance of this is produced by Paſquier Recherches, lib. iv. ch. i. p. 350. The abbot Wittikindus, whoſe words I have produced in this note, conſidered the determination of a point in law by combat, as the beſt and moſt honourable mode of deciſion. In the year 978, a judicial combat was fought in the preſence of the Emperor Henry. The archbiſhop Aldebert adviſed him to terminate a conteſt which had ariſen between two noblemen of his court, by this mode of deciſion. The vanquiſhed combatant, though a perſon of high rank, was beheaded on the ſpot. Chronic. Ditmari Epiſc. Merſb. chez Bouquet Recueil des Hiſt. tom. x. p. 121. Queſtions concerning the property of churches and monaſteries, were decided by combat. In the year 961, a controverſy concerning the church of St. Medard, whether it belonged to the abbey of Beaulieu, was terminated by judicial combat. Bouquet Recueil des Hiſt. tom. ix. p. 729. Ibid. p. 612, &c. The Emperor Henry I. declares,

declares, that his law authorising the practice of judicial combats, was enacted with consent and applause of many faithful bishops. Ibid. p. 231. So remarkably did the martial ideas of those ages prevail over the genius and maxims of the canon law, which in other instances had such credit and authority with ecclesiastics. A judicial combat was appointed in Spain, by Charles V. A. D. 1522. The combatants fought in the Emperor's presence, and the battle was conducted with all the rites prescribed by the ancient laws of chivalry. The whole transaction is described at great length by Pontus Heuterus Rer. Austriac. lib. viii. c. 17. p. 205.

The last instance which occurs in the history of France, of a judicial combat authorised by the magistrate, was the famous one between M. Jarnac and M. de la Chaistaignerie, A. D. 1547. A trial by combat was appointed in England, A. D. 1571, under the inspection of the judges in the court of Common Pleas; and though it was not carried to the same extremity with the former, Queen Elizabeth having interposed her authority, and enjoined the parties to compound the matter, yet in order to preserve their honour, the lists were marked out, and all the forms previous to the combat were observed with much ceremony. Spelm. Gloss. voc. *Campus*, p. 103. In the year 1631, a judicial combat was appointed between Donald Lord Rea, and David Ramsay, Esq; by the authority of the Lord high Conſtable, and Earl Marſhal of England; but that quarrel likewiſe terminated without bloodſhed, being accommodated by Charles I. Another inſtance occurs ſeven years later. Ruſhworth in Obſervations on the Statutes, &c. p. 266.

NOTE XXIII. Sect. I. p. 74. [Z].

The text contains the great outlines which mark the courſe of private and public juriſdiction in the ſeveral nations of Europe. I ſhall here follow more minutely the various ſteps of this progreſs, as the matter is curious and important enough to merit this attention. The payment of a fine by way of ſatisfaction to the perſon or family injured, was the firſt device of a rude people, in order to check the career of private reſentment, and to extinguiſh thoſe *faidæ*, or deadly feuds which were proſecuted among them with the utmoſt violence. This cuſtom may be traced back to the ancient Germans, Tacit. de Morib. Ger. c. 21. and prevailed among other uncivilized nations. Many examples of this are collected by the ingenious and learned author of Hiſtorical Law-Tracts, vol. i. p. 41. Theſe fines were aſcertained and levied in three different manners. At firſt they were ſettled by voluntary agreement between the parties at variance. When their rage began to ſubſide, and they felt the bad effects of their continuing in enmity, they came to terms of concord, and the ſatisfaction made was called a *compoſition*, implying that it was fixed by mutual conſent. De l'Eſprit des Loix,

Loix, lib. xxx. c. 19. It is apparent from some of the more ancient codes of laws, that when these were compiled, matters still remained in that simple state. In certain cases, the person who had committed an offence, was left exposed to the resentment of those whom he had injured, until he should recover their favour, quoquo modo potuerit. Lex Frision. tit. 11. § 1. The next mode of levying these fines was by the sentence of arbiters. An arbiter is called in the Regiam majestatem amicabilis compositor, lib. xi. c. 4. § 10. He could estimate the degree of offence with more impartiality than the parties interested, and determine with greater equity what satisfaction ought to be demanded. It is difficult to bring an authentic proof of a custom previous to the records preserved in any nation of Europe. But one of the Formulæ Andegavenses compiled in the sixth century, seems to allude to a transaction carried on not by the authority of a judge, but by the mediation of arbiters. Bouquet Recueil des Histor. tom. iv. p. 566. But as an arbiter wanted authority to enforce his decisions, judges were appointed with compulsive power to oblige both parties to acquiesce in their decisions. Previous to this last step, the expedient of paying compositions was an imperfect remedy against the pernicious effects of private resentment. As soon as this important change was introduced, the magistrate, putting himself in place of the person injured, ascertained the composition with which he ought to rest satisfied. Every possible

injury

injury that could occur in the course of human society, was considered and estimated, and the compositions due to the person aggrieved were fixed with such minute attention as discovers, in most cases, amazing discernment and delicacy, in some instances, unaccountable caprice. Besides the composition payable to the private party, a certain sum, called a *fredum*, was paid to the King or state, as Tacitus expresses it, or to the fiscus, in the language of the barbarous laws. Some authors, blending the refined ideas of modern policy with their reasonings concerning ancient transactions, have imagined that the fredum was a compensation due to the community, on account of the violation of the publick peace. But it is manifestly the price paid to the magistrate for the protection which he afforded against the violence of resentment. The enacting of this was a considerable step towards improvement in criminal jurisprudence. In some of the more ancient codes of laws, the *freda* are altogether omitted, or so seldom mentioned, that it is evident they were but little known. In the latter codes, the fredum is as precisely specified as the composition. In common cases it was equal to the third part of the composition. Capitul. vol. i. p. 52. In some extraordinary cases, where it was more difficult to protect the person who had committed violence, the fredum was augmented. Capitul. vol. i. p. 515. These freda made a considerable branch in the revenues of the barons; and wherever territorial jurisdiction was granted, the royal judges were

prohibited

prohibited from levying any freda. In explaining the nature of the fredum, I have followed, in a great measure, the opinion of M. de Montesquieu, though I know that several learned antiquarians have taken the word in a different sense. De l'Esprit des Loix, liv. xxx. c. 20, &c. The great object of judges was to compel the one party to give, and the other to accept the satisfaction prescribed. They multiplied regulations to this purpose, and enforced them by grievous penalties. Leg. Longob. lib. i. tit. 9. § 34. Ib. tit. 37. § 1, 2. Capitul. vol. i. p. 371. § 22. The person who received a composition was obliged to cease from all farther hostility, and to confirm his reconciliation with the adverse party by an oath. Leg. Longob. lib. i. tit. 9. § 8. As an additional and more permanent evidence of reconciliation, he was required to grant a bond of security to the person from whom he received a composition, absolving him from all farther prosecution. Marculfus, and the other collectors of ancient writs, have preserved several different forms of such bonds. Marc. lib. xi. § 18. Append. § 23. Form. Sirmondicæ, § 39. The *Letters of Slanes*, known in the law of Scotland, are perfectly similar to these bonds of security. By the letters of Slanes, the heirs and relations of a person who had been murdered, bound themselves, in consideration of an *Assythment* or composition paid to them, to forgive, pass over, and for ever forget, and in oblivion inter all rancour, malice, revenge, prejudice, grudge and resentment, that they have or may conceive against the aggressor or

his

his posterity, for the crime which he had committed, and discharge him of all action, civil or criminal, against him or his estate, for now and ever. System of Stiles by Dallas of St. Martin's, p. 862. In the ancient form of letters of Slanes, the private party not only forgives and forgets, but pardons and grants remission of the crime. This practice, Dallas, reasoning according to the principles of his own age, considers as an encroachment on the rights of sovereignty, as none, says he, could pardon a criminal but the King. Ibid. But in early and rude times, the prosecution, the punishment, and the pardon of criminals, were all deeds of the private person who was injured. Madox has published two writs, one in the reign of Edward I. the other in the reign of Edward III. by which private persons grant a release or pardon of all trespasses, felonies, robberies, and murders committed. Formul. Anglican. N°. 702, 705. In the last of these instruments, some regard seems to be paid to the rights of the sovereign, for the pardon is granted *en quant que en nous est.* Even after the authority of the magistrate is interposed in punishing criminals, the punishment of criminals is long considered chiefly as a gratification to the resentment of the persons who have been injured. In Persia, a murderer is still delivered to the relations of the person whom he has slain, who put him to death with their own hands. If they refuse to accept of a sum of money as a compensation, the sovereign, absolute as he is, cannot pardon the murderer. Tavernier's Voyages, book v. c. 5 and 10. By a

law

law in the kingdom of Aragon as late as the year 1564, the punishment of one condemned to death cannot be mitigated but by consent of the parties who have been injured. Fueros & Obfervancias del Reyno de Aragon, p. 204. 6.

IF, after all the engagements to cease from enmity, which I have mentioned, any person renewed hostilities, and was guilty of any violence, either towards the person from whom he had received a composition, or towards his relations and heirs, this was deemed a most heinous crime, and punished with extraordinary rigour. It was an act of direct rebellion against the authority of the magistrate, and was repressed by the interposition of all his power. Leg. Longob. lib. i. tit. 9. § 8, 34. Capit. vol. i. p. 371. § 22. Thus the avenging of injuries was taken out of private hands, a legal composition was established, and peace and amity were restored under the inspection, and by the authority of a judge. It is evident, that at the time when the barbarians settled in the provinces of the Roman Empire, they had fixed judges established among them with compulsive authority. Persons vested with this character are mentioned by the earliest historians. Du Cange, voc. *Judices*. The right of territorial jurisdiction was not altogether an usurpation of the feudal barons. There is good reason to believe, that the powerful leaders who seized different districts of the countries which they conquered, and kept possession of them as *allodial* property, assumed at the same time the

right

PROOFS AND ILLUSTRATIONS.

right of jurisdiction, and exercised it within their own territories. This jurisdiction was supreme, and extended to all causes. The clearest proofs of this are produced by M. Bouquet. Le Droit publique de France eclairci, &c. tom. i. p. 206, &c. The privilege of judging his own vassals, appears to have been originally a right inherent in every baron who held a fief. As far back as the archives of nations can conduct us with any certainty, we find the jurisdiction and fief united. One of the earliest charters to a layman which I have met with, is that of Ludovicus Pius, A. D. 814. And it contains the right of territorial jurisdiction, in the most express and extensive terms. Capitul. vol. ii. p. 1405. There are many charters to churches and monasteries of a more early date, containing grants of similar jurisdiction, and prohibiting any royal judge to enter the territories of those churches or monasteries, or to perform any act of judicial authority there. Bouquet. Recueil des Hist. tom. iv. p. 628, 631, 633. tom. v. p. 703, 710, 752, 762. Muratori has published many very ancient charters containing the same immunities. Antiq. Ital. Dissert. lxx. In most of these deeds, the exacting of *Freda* is particularly prohibited, which shews that they constituted a valuable part of the publick revenue at that juncture. The expence of obtaining a sentence in a court of justice during the middle ages was so considerable, that this circumstance alone was sufficient to render men unwilling to decide any contest in judicial form. It appears from a charter in the thirteenth century, that the baron who had the right of justice, received the fifth part of the value of every subject, the property of which was tried and determined in his court. If, after the commencement of a law-suit, the parties terminated the contest in an amicable manner, or by arbitration, they were nevertheless bound to pay the fifth part of the subject contested to the court before which the suit had been brought. Hist. de Dauphiné. Geneve, 1722. tom. i. p. 22. Similar to this is a regulation in the charter of liberty granted to the town of Friburg, A. D. 1120. If two of the citizens shall quarrel, and if one of them shall complain to the superior Lord or to his judge, and after commencing the suit shall be privately reconciled to his adversary; the judge, if he does not approve of this reconciliation, may compel him to insist in his law-suit; and all who were present at the reconciliation shall forfeit the favour of the superior Lord. Historia Zaringo Badensis. Auctor. Jo. Dan. Schoepflinus. Carolsr. 1763. 4to. vol. v. p. 55.

WHAT was the extent of that jurisdiction which those who held fiefs possessed originally, we cannot now determine with certainty. It is evident that, during the disorders which prevailed in every kingdom of Europe, the great vassals took advantage of the feebleness of their Monarchs, and enlarged their jurisdictions to the utmost. As early as the tenth century, the more powerful barons had usurped the right of deciding all

causes,

caufes, whether civil or criminal. They had acquired the *High Juſtice* as well as the *Low.* Eſtabl. de St. Louis, lib. i. c. 24, 25. Their ſentences were final, and there lay no appeal from them to any ſuperior court. Several ſtriking inſtances of this are collected by Bruſſel. Traité des Fiefs, liv. iii. c. 11, 12, 13. Not ſatisfied with this, the more potent barons got their territories erected into *Regalities*, with almoſt every royal prerogative and juriſdiction. Inſtances of theſe were frequent in France. Bruſſ. ib. In Scotland, where the power of the feudal nobles became exorbitant, they were very numerous. Hiſtorical Law Tracts, vol. i. tract vi. Even in England, though the authority of the Norman Kings circumſcribed the juriſdiction of the barons more than in any feudal kingdom, ſeveral counties palatine were erected, into which the King's judges could not enter, and no writ could come in the King's name, until it received the ſeal of the county palatine. Spelman. Gloſſ. voc. *Comites Palatini*; Blackſtone's Commentaries on the Laws of England, vol. iii. p. 78. Theſe lords of regalities had a right to claim or reſcue their vaſſals from the King's judges, if they aſſumed any juriſdiction over them. Bruſſel, ubi ſupra. In the law of Scotland this privilege was termed the right of *repledging*; and the frequency of it not only interrupted the courſe of juſtice, but gave riſe to great diſorders in the exerciſe of it. Hiſt. Law Tracts, ib. The juriſdiction of the counties palatine

palatine was productive of like inconveniencies in England.

THE remedies provided by Princes against the bad effects of these usurpations were various, and gradually applied. Under Charlemagne and his immediate descendants, the regal prerogative still retained great vigour, and the *Duces, Comites*, and *Missi Dominici*, the former of whom were ordinary and fixed judges, the latter extraordinary and itinerant judges, in the different provinces of their extensive dominions, exercised a jurisdiction co-ordinate with the barons in some cases, and superior to them in others. Du Cange, voc. *Dux, Comites* & *Missi*. Murat. Antiq. Dissert. viii. & ix. But under the feeble race of Monarchs who succeeded them, the authority of the royal judges declined, and the barons usurped that unlimited jurisdiction which has been described. Louis VI. of France attempted to revive the function of the *Missi Dominici* under the title of *Juges des Exempts*, but the barons were become too powerful to bear such an encroachment on their jurisdiction, and he was obliged to desist from employing them. Henaut. Abregé Chron. tom. ii. p. 730. His successors (as has been observed) had recourse to expedients less alarming. The appeal *de defaute de Droit*, or on account of the refusal of justice, was the first which was attended with any considerable effect. According to the maxims of feudal law, if a baron had not as many vassals as enabled him

him to try by their peers, the parties who offered to plead in his court, or if he delayed or refused to proceed in the trial, the cause might be carried, by appeal, to the court of the superior lord of whom the baron held, and tried there. De l'Esprit des Loix, liv. xxviii. c. 28. Du Cange, voc. *defectus Justitiæ*. The number of Peers or assessors in the courts of Barons was frequently very considerable. It appears from a criminal trial in the court of the viscount de Lautrec, A. D. 1299, that upwards of two hundred persons were present, and assisted in the trial, and voted in passing judgment. Hist. de Langued. par D. D. De Vic & Vaisette, tom. iv. Preuves, p. 114. As the right of jurisdiction had been usurped by many inconsiderable barons, they were often unable to hold courts. This gave frequent occasion to such appeals, and rendered the practice familiar. By degrees, such appeals began to be taken from the courts of the more powerful barons, and it is evident, from a decision recorded by Brussel, that the royal judges were willing to give countenance to any pretext for them. Traité des Fiefs, tom. i. p. 235, 261. This species of appeal had less effect in abridging the jurisdiction of the nobles, than the appeal on account of the injustice of the sentence. When the feudal monarchs were powerful, and their judges possessed extensive authority, such appeals seem to have been frequent. Capitul. vol. i. p. 175, 180; and they were made in a manner suitable to the rudeness of a simple age. The persons aggrieved resorted to the palace of their sovereign, and with outcries and loud noise called to him for redress. Capitul. lib. iii. c. 59. Chronic. Lawierbergienfe ap. Mencken. Script. German. vol. ii. p. 284. b. In the kingdom of Aragon, the appeals to the *Justiza* or supreme judge were taken in such a form as supposed the appellant to be in immediate danger of death, or of some violent outrage; he rushed into the presence of the judge crying with a loud voice, *Avi, Avi, Fuerza, Fuerza,* thus imploring (as it were) the instant interposition of that supreme judge in order to save him. Hier. Blanca Comment. de rebus Aragon. ap. Script. Hispanic. Pistorii, vol. iii. p. 753. The abolition of the trial by combat facilitated the revival of appeals of this kind. The effects of this subordination which appeals established, in introducing attention, equity, and consistency of decision into courts of judicature, were soon conspicuous; and almost all causes of importance were carried to be finally determined in the King's courts. Bruffel, tom. i. 252. Various circumstances which contributed towards the introduction and frequency of such appeals are enumerated De l'Esprit des Loix, liv. xxviii. c. 27. Nothing, however, was of such effect as the attention which monarchs gave to the constitution and dignity of their courts of justice. It was the ancient custom for the feudal monarchs to preside themselves in their courts, and to administer justice in person. Marculf. lib. i. § 25. Murat. Differt. xxxi. Charlemagne, whilst he was dressing, used to call parties into his presence,

and

and having heard and confidered the fubject of litigation, gave judgment concerning it. Eginhartus vita Caroli magni cited by Madox Hift. of Exchequer, vol. i. p. 91. This could not fail of rendering their courts refpectable. St. Louis, who encouraged to the utmoft the practice of appeals, revived this ancient cuftom, and adminiftered juftice in perfon with all the ancient fimplicity. "I have often feen the faint," fays Joinville, "fit under the fhade of an oak in the wood of Vincennes, when all who had any complaint, freely approached him. At other times he gave orders to fpread a carpet in a garden, and feating himfelf upon it, heard the caufes that were brought before him." Hift. de St. Louis, p. 13. edit. 1761. Princes of inferior rank, who poffeffed the right of juftice, fometimes difpenfed it in perfon, and prefided in their tribunals. Two inftances of this occur with refpect to the Dauphines of Vienne. Hift. de Dauphiné, tom. i. p. 18. tom. ii. p. 257. But as Kings and Princes could not decide every caufe in perfon, nor bring them all to be determined in the fame court; they appointed *Baillis*, with a right of jurifdiction, in different diftricts of their kingdom. Thefe poffeffed powers fomewhat fimilar to thofe of the ancient *Comites*. It was towards the end of the twelfth century, and beginning of the thirteenth, that this office was firft inftituted in France. Bruffel, liv. ii. c. 35. When the King had a court eftablifhed in different quarters of his dominions, this invited his fubjects to have recourfe to it.

PROOFS AND ILLUSTRATIONS.

It was the private interest of the *Baillis*, as well as an object of publick policy, to extend their jurisdiction. They took advantage of every defect in the rights of the barons, and of every error in their proceedings, to remove causes out of their courts, and to bring them under their own cognizance. There was a distinction in the feudal law, and an extremely ancient one, between the high justice and the low. Capitul. 3. A. D. 812. § 4. A. D. 815. § 3. Establ. de St. Louis, liv. i. c. 40. Many barons possessed the latter jurisdiction who had no title to the former. The former included the right of trying crimes of every kind, even the highest; the latter was confined to petty trespasses. This furnished endless pretexts for obstructing, restraining and reviewing the proceedings in the baron courts. Ordon. ii. 457. § 25. 458. § 29.——A regulation of greater importance succeeded the institution of *Baillis*. The King's supreme court or parliament was rendered fixed as to the place, and constant as to the time of its meetings. In France, as well as in the other feudal kingdoms, the King's court of justice was originally ambulatory, followed the person of the monarch, and was held only during some of the great festivals. Philip Augustus, A. D. 1305, rendered it sedentary at Paris, and continued its terms during the greater part of the year. Pasquier Recherches, liv. ii. c. 2 and 3, &c. Ordon. tom. i. p. 366. § 62. He and his successors vested extensive powers in that court; they granted the members of it several privileges and distinctions which

which it would be tedious to enumerate. Pasquier, ib. Velly hist. de France, tom. vii. p. 307. Persons eminent for integrity and skill in law were appointed judges there. Ib. By degrees the final decision of all causes of importance was brought into the parliament of Paris, and the other parliaments which administered justice in the King's name, in different provinces of the kingdom. This jurisdiction, however, the parliament of Paris acquired very slowly, and the great vassals of the crown made violent efforts in order to obstruct the attempts of this parliament to extend its authority. Towards the close of the thirteenth century, Philip the Fair was obliged to prohibit his parliament from taking cognizance of certain appeals brought into it from the courts of the Count of Bretagne, and to recognize his right of supreme and final jurisdiction. Memoires pour servir de Preuves à l'Histoire de Bretagne par Morice, tom. i. p. 1037. 1074. Charles VI. at the end of the following century was obliged to confirm the rights of the Dukes of Bretagne in more ample form. Ibid. tom. ii. p. 580, 581. So violent was the opposition of the barons to this right of appeal which they considered as fatal to their privileges and power, that the authors of the *Encyclopedie* have mentioned several instances in which barons put to death, or mutilated, or confiscated the goods of such as ventured to appeal from the sentences pronounced in their courts, to the parliament of Paris, tom. xii. Art. *Parlement*, p. 25.

PROOFS AND ILLUSTRATIONS.

The progress of jurisdiction in the other feudal kingdoms was in a great measure similar to that which we have traced in France. In England, the territorial jurisdiction of the barons was both ancient and extensive. Leg. Edw. Conf. N° 5 and 9. After the Norman conquest it became more strictly feudal; and it is evident from facts recorded in the English history, as well as from the institution of Counties Palatine, which I have already mentioned, that the usurpations of the nobles in England were not inferior to those of their contemporaries on the continent. The same expedients were employed to circumscribe or abolish those dangerous jurisdictions. William the Conqueror established a constant court in the hall of his palace; from which the four courts now entrusted with the administration of justice in England took their rise. Henry II. divided his kingdom into six circuits, and sent itinerant judges to hold their courts in them at stated seasons. Blackstone's Commentaries on the Laws of England, vol. iii. 57. Justices of peace were appointed in every county by subsequent monarchs; to whose jurisdiction the people gradually had recourse in many civil causes. The privileges of the Counties Palatine were gradually limited; with respect to some points they were abolished; and the administration of justice was brought into the King's courts, or before judges of his appointment. The several steps taken for this purpose are enumerated in Dalrymple's History of Feudal Property, chap. vii.

IN Scotland the usurpations of the nobility were more exorbitant than in any other feudal kingdom. The progress of their encroachments, and the methods taken by the crown to limit or abolish their territorial and independent jurisdictions, both which I had occasion to consider and explain in a former work, differed very little from those of which I have now given the detail. History of Scotland, vol. i. p. 45.

I SHOULD perplex myself and my readers in the labyrinth of German jurisprudence, were I to attempt to delineate the progress of jurisdiction in the Empire, with a minute accuracy. It is sufficient to observe, that the authority which the Aulick council and Imperial chamber now possess, took its rise from the same abuse of territorial jurisdiction, and was acquired in the same manner that the royal courts attained influence in other countries. All the important facts with respect to both these particulars, may be found in Phil. Datt. de pace publica Imperii, lib. iv. The capital articles are pointed out in Pfeffel Abregé de l'Histoire & Droit publique d'Allemagne, p. 556, 581; and in Traité du Droit publique de l'Empire par M. le Coq. de Villeray. Both the two last treatises are of great authority, having been composed under the eye of M. Schoepflin of Strasburgh, one of the ablest publick lawyers in Germany.

PROOFS AND ILLUSTRATIONS.

NOTE XXIV. Sect. I. p. 78. [AA].

It is not eafy to fix with precifion the period at which Ecclefiafticks firſt began to claim exemption from the civil jurifdiction. It is certain, that during the early and pureſt ages of the church, they pretended to no fuch immunity. The authority of the civil magiftrate extended to all perſons, and to all caufes. This fact has not only been clearly eftabliſhed by Proteſtant authors, but is admitted by many Roman Catholicks of eminence, and particularly by the writers in defence of the liberties of the Gallican church. There are feveral original papers publiſhed by Muratori, which ſhew that, in the ninth and tenth centuries, caufes of the greateſt importance relating to ecclefiafticks were ſtill determined by civil judges. Antiq. Ital. vol. v. differt. lxx. Proofs of this are produced likewife by M. Howard, Anciennes Loix des François, &c. vol. i. p. 209. Ecclefiafticks did not ſhake off all at once their fubjection to civil courts. This privilege, like their other ufurpations, was gained flowly, and ſtep by ſtep. This exemption feems at firſt to have been merely an act of complaifance, flowing from veneration for their character. Thus from a charter of Charlemagne in favour of the church of Mans, A. D. 796, to which M. l'Abbe de Foy refers in his Notice de Diplomes, tom. i. p. 201, that monarch directs his judges, if any difference ſhould ariſe between the adminiftrators of the revenues

of

of that church and any perfon whatever, not to fummon the adminiftrators to appear in mallo publico; but firft of all to meet with them, and to endeavour to accommodate the difference in an amicable manner. This indulgence was in procefs of time improved into a legal exemption; which was founded on the fame fuperftitious refpect of the laity for the clerical character and function. A remarkable inftance of this occurs in a charter of Frederick Barbaroffa, A. D. 1172, to the monaftery of Altenburg. He grants them judicium non tantum fanguinolentis plagæ, fed vitæ & mortis; he prohibits any of the royal judges from difturbing their jurifdiction; and the reafon which he gives for this ample conceffion is, nam quorum, ex Dei gratia, ratione divini minifterii onus leve eft, & jugum fuave; nos penitus nolumus illius oppreffionis contumelia, vel manu Laica fatigari. Mencken. Script. rer. Germ. vol. iii. p. 1067.

It is not neceffary for illuftrating what is contained in the text, that I fhould defcribe the manner in which the code of the canon law was compiled, and fhew that the doctrines in it moft favourable to the power of the clergy, are founded on ignorance, or fupported by fraud and forgery. The reader will find a full account of thefe in Gerard. Van Maftricht, Hiftoria Juris Ecclefiaftici, & in Science de Government par M. Real, tom. vii. c. 1. & 3. § 2, 3, &c. The hiftory of the progrefs and extent of ecclefiaftical jurifdiction, with

an

an account of the arts which the clergy employed in order to draw causes of every kind into the spiritual courts, is no less curious, and would throw great light upon many of the customs and institutions of the dark ages; but it is likewise foreign from the present subject. Du Cange in his Glossary, voc. *Curia Christianitatis*, has collected most of the causes with respect to which the clergy arrogated an exclusive jurisdiction, and refers to the authors, or original papers, which confirm his observations. Giannonè in his Civil History of Naples, lib. xix. § 3. has ranged these under proper heads, and scrutinizes the pretensions of the church with his usual boldness and discernment. M. Fleury observes, that the clergy multiplied, at such a rate, the pretexts for extending the authority of the spiritual courts, that it was in their power to withdraw every person and every cause from the jurisdiction of the civil magistrate. Hist. Eccles. tom. xix. Disc. Prelim. 16. But how ill founded soever the jurisdiction of the clergy may be, or whatever might be the abuses to which their manner of exercising it gave rise, the principles and forms of their jurisprudence were far more perfect than that which was known in the civil courts. It is probable that ecclesiasticks never submitted, during any period of the middle ages, to the laws contained in the codes of the barbarous nations, but were governed entirely by the Roman law. They regulated all their transactions by such of its maxims as were

preserved

preserved by tradition, or were contained in the
Theodosian code, and other books extant among
them. This we learn from a custom which prevailed
universally in those ages. Every person was
permitted to chuse among the various codes of
laws then in force, that to which he was willing
to conform. In any transaction of importance, it
was usual for the persons contracting to mention
the law to which they submitted, that it might be
known how any controversy that should arise between
them was to be decided. Innumerable
proofs of this occur in the charters of the middle
ages. But the clergy considered it as such a valuable
privilege of their order to be governed by
the Roman law, that when any person entered into
holy orders, it was usual for him to renounce the
laws to which he had been formerly subject, and
to declare that he now submitted to the Roman
law. Constat me Johannem clericum, filium quondam
Verandi, qui professus sum, ex natione mea,
lege vivere Langobardorum, sed tamen, pro honore
ecclesiastico, lege nunc videor vivere Romana.
Charta, A. D. 1072. Farulfus presbyter qui professus
sum, more sacerdotii mei, lege vivere Romana.
Charta, A. D. 1075. Muratori Antichita
Estensi. vol. i. p. 78. See likewise Houard Anciennes
Loix des François, &c. vol. i. p. 203.

THE code of the canon law began to be compiled
early in the ninth century. Mem. de l'Acad.
des Inscript. tom. xviii. p. 346, &c. It was above
two centuries after that before any collection was
made

made of thofe cuftoms, which were the rule of judgment in the courts of the barons. Spiritual judges decided, of courfe, according to written and known laws; Lay judges, left without any fixed guide, were directed by loofe traditionary cuftoms. But befides this general advantage of the canon law, its forms and principles were more confonant to reafon, and more favourable to the equitable decifion of every point in controverfy, than thofe which prevailed in lay courts. It appears from Notes XXI. and XXII. concerning private wars, and the trial by combat, that the whole fpirit of ecclefiaftical jurifprudence was adverfe to thefe fanguinary cuftoms which were deftructive of juftice; and the whole force of ecclefiaftical authority was exerted to abolifh them, and to fubftitute trials by law and evidence in their room. Almoft all the forms in lay courts which contribute to eftablifh, and continue to preferve order in judicial proceedings, are borrowed from the canon law. Fleury Inftit. du droit canon. part iii. c. 6. p. 52. St. Louis in his Eftabliffemens confirms many of his new regulations concerning property, and the adminiftration of juftice, by the authority of the canon law, from which he borrowed them. Thus, for inftance, the firft hint of attaching moveables for the recovery of a debt, was taken from the canon law. Eftabl. liv. ii. c. 21 and 40. And likewife the ceffio bonorum, by a perfon who was infolvent. Ibid. In the fame manner, he eftablifhed new regulations with refpect to the effects of perfons dying inteftate, liv. i. c. 89. Thefe
and

PROOFS AND ILLUSTRATIONS.

and many other falutary regulations, the Canonifts borrowed from the Roman law. Many other examples might be produced of more perfect jurifprudence in the canon law than was known in lay courts. For that reafon it was deemed an high privilege to be fubject to ecclefiaftical jurifdiction. Among the many immunities, by which men were allured to engage in the dangerous expeditions for the recovery of the Holy Land, one of the moft confiderable was the declaring thofe who took the Crofs to be fubject only to the fpiritual courts. See Note XIII. and Du Cange, voc. *crucis privilegia*.

NOTE XXV. Sect. I. p. 80. [BB].

The rapidity with which the knowledge and ftudy of the Roman law fpread over Europe, is amazing. The copy of the Pandects was found at Amalphi, A. D. 1137. Irnerius opened a college of civil law at Bologne a few years after. Giann. Hift. book xi. c. 2. It began to be taught as a part of academical learning in different parts of France before the middle of the century. Vaccarius gave lectures on the civil law at Oxford, as early as the year 1147. A regular fyftem of feudal law, formed plainly in imitation of the Roman code, was compofed by two Milanefe lawyers about the year 1150. Gratian publifhed the code of canon law, with large additions and emendations, about the fame time. The earlieft collection of thefe cuftoms, which ferved as the rules of decifion in the courts of juftice, is the *Affifes de Jerufalem.*

PROOFS AND ILLUSTRATIONS.

Jerusalem. They were compiled, as the preamble informs us, in the year 1099, and are called Jus Consuetudinarium quo regebatur regnum orientale. Willerm. Tyr. lib. xix. c. 2. But peculiar circumstances were the occasion of this early compilation. The victorious Crusaders settled as a colony in a foreign country, and adventurers from all the different nations of Europe composed this new society. It was necessary on that account to ascertain the laws and customs which were to regulate the transactions of business, and the administration of justice among them. But there was at that time no collection of customs, and no attempt to render law fixed in any country of Europe. The first undertaking of that kind was by Glanville, Lord Chief Justice of England, in his Tractatus de Legibus & Consuetudinibus Angliæ, composed about the year 1181. The Regiam Majestatem in Scotland, ascribed to David I. seems to be an imitation, and a servile one of Glanville. Pierre de Fontaines, who tells us that he was the first who had attempted such a work in France, composed his *Conseil*, which contains an account of the customs of the country of Vermandois, in the reign of St. Louis, which began A. D. 1226. *Beaumanoir*, the author of the *Coustumes de Beauvoisis*, lived about the same time. The Establissemens of St. Louis, containing a large collection of the customs which prevailed within the royal domains, were published by the authority of that monarch. As soon as men became acquainted with the advantages of having written customs and

laws

laws to which they could have recourse on every occasion, the method of collecting them became common. Charles VII. of France, by an ordonance, A. D. 1453, appointed the customary laws in every province of France to be collected and arranged. Velley and Villaret. Histoire, tom. xvi. p. 113. His successor, Louis XI. renewed the injunction. But this salutary undertaking hath never been fully executed, and the French jurisprudence remains more obscure and uncertain than if these prudent regulations of their monarchs had taken effect. A practice was established in the middle ages, which affords the clearest proof that judges, while they had no other rule to direct their decrees but unwritten and traditionary customs, were often at a loss how to find out the facts and principles, according to which they were bound to decide. They were obliged in dubious cases to call a certain number of old men, and to lay the case before them, that they might inform them what was the practice or custom with regard to the point. This was called *Enquefte par tourbe.* Du Cange, voc. *Turba.* The effects of the revival of the Roman jurisprudence have been explained by M. de Montesquieu, liv. xxviii. c. 42, and by Mr. Hume, Hist. of England, vol. ii. p. 441. I have adopted many of their ideas. Who can pretend to review any subject which such writers have considered, without receiving from them light and information? At the same time I am convinced that the knowledge of the Roman law was not so entirely lost in Europe during the middle ages, as is commonly

monly believed. My subject does not require me to examine this point. Many striking facts with regard to it are collected by Donato Antonio d'Asti Dall' Uso e autorita della ragione civile nelle provincie dell' Imperio Occidentale. Nap. 1751. 2 vol. 8vo.

That the civil law is intimately connected with the municipal jurisprudence in several countries of Europe, is a fact so well known, that it needs no illustration. Even in England, where the common law is supposed to form a system perfectly distinct from the Roman code, and although those who apply in that country to the study of the common law boast, with affectation, of this distinction, it is evident that many of the ideas and maxims of the civil law are incorporated into the English jurisprudence. This is well illustrated by the ingenious and learned author of Observations on the Statutes, chiefly the more ancient. 2d edit. p. 66.

NOTE XXVI. Sect. 1. p. 62. [CC].

The whole history of the middle ages makes it evident, that war was the sole profession of gentlemen, and the only subject attended to in their education. Even after some change in manners began to take place, and the civil arts of life had acquired some reputation, the ancient ideas with respect to the accomplishments necessary for a person of noble birth, continued long in force. In the Memoirs de Fleuranges, p. 9, &c. we have an

account

account of the youthful exercises and occupations of Francis I. and they are altogether martial and athletic. That father of letters owed his relish for them, not to education, but to his own good sense, and good taste. The manners of the superior order of ecclesiastics during the middle ages, furnish the strongest proof that the distinction of professions was hardly known in Europe. The functions and character of the clergy are obviously very different from those of laymen; and among the inferior orders of churchmen, this constituted a distinct character, separate from that of their citizens. But the dignified ecclesiastics, who were frequently of noble birth, were above such a distinction; they retained the idea of what belonged to them as gentlemen, and in spite of the decrees of Popes, or the canons of councils, they bore arms, led their vassals to the field, and fought at their head in battle. Among them the priesthood was scarcely a separate profession; the military accomplishments which they thought essential to them as gentlemen, were cultivated; the theological science, and pacific virtues suitable to their spiritual function, were neglected and despised.

As soon as the science of law became a laborious study, and the practice of it a separate profession, such as rose to eminence in it obtained honours formerly appropriated to soldiers. Knighthood was the most illustrious mark of distinction during several ages, and conferred privileges to which rank or birth alone were not entitled. To this high

high dignity perfons eminent for their knowledge of law were advanced, and by that, were placed on a level with thofe whom their military talents had rendered confpicuous. *Miles Juſtitiæ*, *Miles Litteratus* became common titles. Matthew Paris mentions fuch knights as early as A. D. 1251. If a judge attained a certain rank in the courts of juſtice, that alone gave him a right to the honour of knighthood. Pafquier Recherches, liv. xi. c. 16. p. 130. Diſſertations hiſtoriques fur la Chevalerie par Honorè de Sainte Marie, p. 164, &c. A profeſſion which led to offices that ennobled ſuch as held them, grew into credit, and the people of Europe became accuſtomed to fee men rife to eminence by civil as well as military talents.

NOTE XXVII. Sect. I. p. 86. [DD].

The chief intention of thefe notes, was to bring at once under the view of my readers, fuch facts and circumſtances as tend to illuſtrate or confirm what is contained in that part of the hiſtory to which they refer. When thefe lay fcattered in many different authors, and were taken from books not generally known, or which it would be difagreeable to confult, I thought it would be of advantage to collect them together. But when every thing neceſſary for the proof or illuſtration of my narrative or reafonings may be found in any one book which is generally known, or deferves to be fo, I ſhall fatisfy myfelf with referring to it. This is the cafe with refpect to Chivalry. Almoſt every fact

fact which I have mentioned in the text, together with many other curious and inftructive particulars concerning this fingular inftitution, may be found in Memoires fur l'ancienne Chevalerie confiderée comme un eftabliffement politique & militaire, par M. de la Curne de St. Palaye.

NOTE XXVIII. SECT. III. p. 91. [EE].

THE fubject of my enquiries does not call me to write a hiftory of the progrefs of fcience. The facts and obfervations which I have produced, are fufficient to illuftrate the effects of its progrefs upon manners and the ftate of fociety. While fcience was altogether extinct in the weftern parts of Europe, it was cultivated in Conftantinople and other parts of the Grecian Empire. But the fubtile genius of the Greeks turned almoft entirely to theological difputation. The Latins borrowed that fpirit from them, and many of the controverfies which ftill occupy, and divide theologians, took their rife among the Greeks, from whom the other Europeans derived a confiderable part of their knowledge. See the teftimony of Æneas Sylvius ap. Conringium de antiq. academicis, p. 43. Hiftoire literaire de France, tom. vii. p. 113, &c. tom. ix. p. 151, &c. Soon after the Empire of of the Caliphs was eftablifhed in the Eaft, fome illuftrious Princes arofe among them, who encouraged fcience. But when the Arabians turned their attention to the literature cultivated by the ancient Greeks and Romans, the chafte and correct tafte of their works of genius appeared frigid and unanimated to a people of a more warm imagination. It was impossible for them to admire the poets and historians of Athens, or of Rome. But they were sensible of the merit of their philosophers. The operations of the intellect are more fixed and uniform than those of the fancy or taste. Truth makes an impression nearly the same in every place; the ideas of what is beautiful, elegant, or sublime, vary in different climates. The Arabians, though they neglected Homer, translated the most eminent of the Greek philosophers into their own language; and, guided by their precepts and discoveries, applied themselves with great ardour to the study of geometry, astronomy, medicine, dialectics and metaphysics. In the three former they made considerable and useful improvements, which have contributed not a little to advance those sciences to that high degree of perfection which they have attained. In the two latter, they chose Aristotle for their guide, and refining on the subtle and distinguishing spirit which characterizes his philosophy, they rendered it altogether frivolous or unintelligible. The schools established in the East for teaching and cultivating these sciences, were in high reputation. They communicated their love of science to their countrymen, who conquered Asia and Spain; and the schools instituted there were little inferior in fame to those in the East. Many of the persons who distinguished themselves by their proficiency in science

in

in the twelfth and thirteenth centuries, were educated among the Arabians. Bruckerus collects many inftances of this, Hiftor. Philof. v. iii. p. 681, &c. Almoft all the men eminent for fcience during feveral centuries, were inftructed in the fciences by the Arabians. The firft knowledge of the Ariftotelian philofophy in the middle ages, was acquired by tranflations of his works out of the Arabick. The Arabian commentators were deemed the moft fkilful and authentic guides in the ftudy of his fyftem. Conring. antiq. acad. Diff. iii. p. 95, &c. Supplem. p. 241, &c. Murat. antiquit. Ital. vol. iii. p. 932, &c. From them the Schoolmen derived the genius and principles of their philofophy, which contributed fo much to retard the progrefs of true fcience.

The eftablifhment of Colleges or Univerfities is a remarkable æra in literary hiftory. The fchools in cathedrals and monafteries confined themfelves chiefly to the teaching of grammar. There were only one or two mafters employed in that office. But in colleges, profeffors were appointed to teach all the different parts of fcience. The time that ought to be allotted to the ftudy of each was afcertained. A regular form of trying the proficiency of ftudents was prefcribed; and academical titles and honours were conferred on fuch as acquitted themfelves with approbation. A good account of the origin and nature of thefe is given by Seb. Bacmeifterus Antiquitates Roftochienfes, five, Hiftoria Urbis & Academiæ Roftoch.

ap. Monumenta inedita Rer. Germ. per E. J. de Westphalen, vol. iii. p. 781. Lipf. 1743. The first obscure mention of these academical degrees in the University of Paris (from which the other universities in Europe have borrowed most of their customs and institutions) occurs A. D. 1215, Crevier hist. de l'univ. de Paris, tom. i. p. 296, &c. They were completely established A. D. 1231. Ib. 248. It is unnecessary to enumerate the several privileges to which batchelors, masters, and doctors were entitled. One circumstance is sufficient to demonstrate the high degree of estimation in which they were held. Doctors in the different faculties contended with knights for precedence, and the dispute was terminated in many instances by advancing the former to the dignity of knighthood, the high prerogatives of which I have mentioned. It was even asserted, that a doctor had a right to that title without creation. Bartolus taught——doctorem actualiter regentem in jure civili per decennium effici militem ipso facto. Honoré de St. Marie Differt. p. 165. This was called Chevalerie de lectures, and the persons advanced to that dignity, milites Clerici. These new establishments for education, together with the extraordinary honours conferred on learned men, greatly encreased the number of scholars. In the year 1262, there were ten thousand students in the university of Bologna; and it appears from the history of that university, that law was the only science taught in it at that time. In the year 1340, there were thirty thousand in the university

of

of Oxford. Speed's Chron. ap. Anderson's Chronol. Deduction of Commerce, vol. i. p. 172. In the same century, ten thousand persons voted in a question agitated in the university of Paris; and as graduates alone were admitted to that privilege, the number of students must have been vastly great. Velly Hist. de France, tom. xi. p. 147. There were indeed few universities in Europe at that time; but such a number of students may nevertheless be produced as a proof of the extraordinary ardour with which men turned to the study of science in those ages; it shows likewise that they already began to consider other professions than that of a soldier as honourable and useful.

NOTE XXIX. Sect. I. p. 93. [FF].

THE great variety of subjects which I have endeavoured to illustrate, and the extent of this upon which I now enter, will justify my adopting the words of M. de Montesquieu, when he begins to treat of commerce. " The subject which follows would require to be discussed more at large; but the nature of this work does not permit it. I wish to glide on a tranquil stream; but I am hurried along by a torrent."

MANY proofs occur in history of the little intercourse between nations during the middle ages. Towards the close of the tenth century, Count Bouchard intending to found a monastery at St. Maur des Fosses, near Paris, applied to an abbot of Clugny in Burgundy, famous for his sanctity, intreating him to conduct the monks thither. The language in which he addressed that holy man is singular: He tells him, that he had undertaken the labour of such a great journey; that he was fatigued with the length of it, therefore hoped to obtain his request, and that his journey into such a distant country should not be in vain. The answer of the abbot is still more extraordinary: He refused to comply with his desire, as it would be extremely fatiguing to go along with him into a strange and unknown region. *Vita Burchardi venerabilis Comitis ap. Bouquet Rec. des Hist. vol. x. p. 351.* Even so late as the beginning of the twelfth century, the monks of Ferrieres in the diocese of Sens did not know that there was such a city as Tournay in Flanders; and the monks of St. Martin of Tournay were equally unacquainted with the situation of Ferrieres. A transaction in which they were both concerned, made it necessary for them to have some intercourse. The mutual interest of both monasteries prompted each to find out the situation of the other. After a long search, which is particularly described, the discovery was made by accident. *Herimannus Abbas de Restauratione St. Martini Tornacensis ap. Dacher. Spicel. vol. xii. p. 400.* The ignorance of the middle ages with respect to the situation and geography of remote countries was still more remarkable. The most ancient geographical chart which now remains as a monument of the state of that science in Europe during the middle ages,

ages, is found in a manuscript of the Chronique de St. Denys. There the three parts of the earth then known are so represented, that Jerusalem is placed in the middle of the globe, and Alexandria appears to be as near to it as Nazareth. Mem. de l'Acad. des Belles Lettres, tom. xvi. p. 185. There seem to have been no inns or houses of entertainment for the reception of travellers during the middle ages. Murat. Antiq. Ital. vol. iii. p. 581, &c. This is a proof of the little intercourse which took place between different nations. Among people whose manners are simple, and who are seldom visited by strangers, hospitality is a virtue of the first rank. This duty of hospitality was so necessary in that state of society which took place during the middle ages, that it was not considered as one of those virtues which men may practise or not, according to the temper of their minds, and the generosity of their hearts. Hospitality was enforced by statutes, and such as neglected this duty were liable to punishment. Quicumque hospiti venienti lectum, aut focum negaverit, trium solidorum inlatione mulctetur, Leg. Burgund. tit. xxxviii. § 1. Si quis homini aliquo pergenti in itinere mansionem vetaverit sexaginta solidos componat in publico. Capitul. lib. vi. § 82. This increase of the penalty, at a period so long after that in which the laws of the Burgundians were published, and when the state of society was much improved, is very remarkable. Other laws of the same purport are collected by Jo. Fred. Polac Systema Jurisprud. Germanicæ,

manicæ, Lipſ. 1733. p. 75. The laws of the Slavi were more rigorous than any that he mentions; they ordained, "that the moveables of an inhoſpitable perſon ſhould be confiſcated, and his houſe burnt. They were even ſo ſolicitous for the entertainment of ſtrangers, that they permitted the landlord to ſteal for the ſupport of his gueſt." Quod noctu furatus fueris, cras appone, hoſpitibus. Rerum Mecleburgicar. lib. viii. a Mat. Jo. Bechr. Lipſ. 1751. p. 50. In conſequence of theſe laws, or of that ſtate of ſociety which made it proper to enact them, hoſpitality abounded while the intercourſe among men was inconſiderable, and ſecured the ſtranger a kind reception under every roof where he choſe to take ſhelter. This, too, proves clearly, that the intercourſe among men was rare, for as ſoon as this increaſed, what was a pleaſure became a burden, and the entertaining of travellers was converted into a branch of commerce.

But the laws of the middle ages afford a proof ſtill more convincing of the ſmall intercourſe between different nations. The genius of the Feudal ſyſtem, as well as the ſpirit of jealouſy which always accompanies ignorance, concurred in diſcouraging ſtrangers from ſettling in any country. If a perſon removed from one province in a kingdom to another, he was bound within a year and a day to acknowledge himſelf the vaſſal of the baron in whoſe eſtate he ſettled; if he neglected

to

to do so, he became liable to a penalty; and if at his death he neglected to leave a certain legacy to the baron within whose territories he resided, all his goods were confiscated. The hardships imposed on foreigners settling in a strange country, were still more intolerable. In more early times, the superior lord of any territory in which a foreigner settled, might seize his person, and reduce him to servitude. Very striking instances of this occur in the history of the middle ages. The cruel depredations of the Normans in the ninth century, obliged many inhabitants of the maritime provinces of France to fly into the interior parts of the kingdom. But instead of being received with that humanity to which their wretched condition entitled them, they were reduced to a state of servitude. Both the civil and ecclesiastical powers found it necessary to interpose, in order to put a stop to this barbarous practice. Potgiesser. de Statu Servor. lib. i. c. 1. § 16. In other countries, the laws permitted the inhabitants of the maritime provinces to reduce such as were shipwrecked on their coast to servitude. Ibid. § 17. This barbarous custom prevailed in other countries of Europe. The practice of seizing the goods of persons who had been shipwrecked, and of confiscating them as the property of the lord on whose manor they were thrown, seems to have been universal. De Westphalen Monum. inedita Rer. Germ. vol. iv. p. 907, &c. et Du Cange, voc. *Laganum*, Beehr. Rer. Mecleb. lib. p. 512. Among the ancient Welsh, three sorts of persons, a madman,

PROOFS AND ILLUSTRATIONS.

man, a stranger, and a leper, might be killed with impunity. Leges Hoel Dda, quoted in Observat. on the Statutes, chiefly the more ancient, p. 22. M. de Lauriere produces several ancient deeds which prove that in different provinces of France, strangers became the slaves of the lord on whose lands they settled. Glossaire du Droit François, Art. *Aubaine*, p. 92. Beaumanoir says, " that there are several places in France, in which if a stranger fixes his residence for a year and day, he becomes the slave of the lord of the manor." Coust. de Beauv. ch. 45. p. 254. As a practice so contrary to humanity could not subsist, the superior lords found it necessary to rest satisfied with levying certain annual taxes from aliens, or imposing upon them some extraordinary duties or services. But when any stranger died, he could not convey his effects by a will, and all his real as well as personal estate fell to the King, or to the lord of the barony, to the exclusion of his natural heirs. This is termed in France Droit d'Aubaine. Pref. de Laurier. Ordon. tom. i. p. 15. Brussel. tom. ii. p. 944. Du Cange, voc. *Albani*. Pasquier Recherches, p. 367. This practice of confiscating the effects of strangers upon their death was very ancient. It is mentioned, though very obscurely, in a law of Charlemagne, A..D. 813. Capitul. Baluz. p. 507. § 5. Not only persons who were born in a foreign country were subject to the Droit d'Aubaine, but in some countries such as removed from one diocese to another, or from the lands of one baron to another. Brussel. vol. ii.

PROOFS AND ILLUSTRATIONS.

p. 947, 949. It is scarcely possible to conceive any law more unfavourable to the intercourse between nations. Something similar to it, however, may be found in the ancient laws of every kingdom in Europe. With respect to Italy, see Murat. Ant. vol. ii. p. 14. It is no small disgrace to the French jurisprudence, that this barbarous, inhospitable custom, should still remain in a nation so highly civilized.

THE confusion and outrage which abounded under a feeble form of government, incapable of framing or executing salutary laws, rendered the communication between the different provinces of the same kingdom extremely dangerous. It appears from a letter of Lupus, abbot of Ferrieres, in the ninth century, that the highways were so much infested by banditti, that it was necessary for travellers to form themselves into companies or caravans, that they might be safe from the assaults of robbers. Bouquet Recueil des Hist. vol. vii. 515. The numerous regulations published by Charles the Bald in the same century, discover the frequency of these disorders; and such acts of violence were become so common, that by many they were hardly considered as criminal. For this reason the inferior judges called Centenarii were required to take an oath, that they would neither commit any robbery themselves, nor protect such as were guilty of that crime. Capitul. edit. Baluz. vol. ii. p. 63, 68. The historians of the ninth and tenth centuries

give

give pathetic descriptions of these disorders. Some remarkable passages to this purpose are collected by Mat. Jo. Beerh Rer. Mecleb. lib. viii. p. 603. They became so frequent and audacious, that the authority of the civil magistrate was unable to repress them. The ecclesiastical jurisdiction was called in to aid it. Councils were held with great solemnity, the bodies of the saints were brought thither, and in presence of their sacred reliques, anathemas were denounced against robbers, and other violators of the publick peace. Bouquet Recueil des Hist. tom. x. p. 360, 431, 536. One of these forms of excommunication issued A. D. 988, is still preserved, and is so singular, and composed with eloquence of such a peculiar kind, that it will not perhaps be deemed unworthy of a place here. After the usual introduction, and mentioning the outrage which gave occasion to the anathema, it runs thus; "Obtenebrescant oculi vestri, qui concupiverunt; arescant manus, quæ rapuerunt; debilitentur omnia membra, quæ adjuverunt. Semper laboretis, nec requiem inveniatis, fructuque vestri laboris privemini. Formidetis, & paveatis, à facie persequentis, & non persequentis hostis, ut tabescendo deficiatis. Sit portio vestra cum Juda traditore Domini, in terra mortis et tenebrarum; donec corda vestra ad satisfactionem plenam convertantur.——Ne cessent a vobis hæ maledictiones, scelerum vestrorum persecutrices, quamdiu permanebitis in peccato pervasionis. Amen. Fiat, Fiat." Bouquet. Ib. p. 517.

NOTE XXX. Sect. I. p. 98. [GG].

With respect to the progress of commerce which I have described, p. 78, &c. it may be observed that the Italian states carried on some commerce with the cities of the Greek empire, as early as the age of Charlemagne, and imported into their own country the rich commodities of the east. Murat. Antiq. Ital. vol. ii. p. 882. In the tenth century, the Venetians had opened a trade with Alexandria in Egypt. Ibid. The inhabitants of Amalphi and Pisa had likewise extended their trade to the same ports. Murat. Ib. p. 884, 885. The effects of the Crusades in increasing the wealth and commerce of the Italian states, and particularly that which they carried on with the East, I have explained page 34th of this volume. They not only imported the Indian commodities from the East, but established manufactures of curious fabric in their own country. Several of these are enumerated by Muratori in his Dissertations concerning the *arts* and the *weaving* of the middle ages. Antiq. Ital. vol. ii. p. 349, 399. They made great progress, particularly in the manufacture of silk, which had long been peculiar to the eastern provinces of Asia. Silk stuffs were of such high price in ancient Rome, that only a few persons of the first rank were able to purchase them. Under Aurelian, A. D. 270, a pound of silk was equal in value to a pound of gold. Absit ut auro fila pensentur. Libra enim auri tunc libra serici fuit. Vopiscus in Aureliano.

Justinian,

PROOFS AND ILLUSTRATIONS.

Justinian, in the sixth century, introduced the art of rearing silk-worms into Greece, which rendered the commodity somewhat more plentiful, though still it was of such great value, as to remain an article of luxury or magnificence, reserved only for persons of the first order, or for publick solemnities. Roger I. King of Sicily, about the year 1130, carried off a number of artificers in the silk trade from Athens, and settling them in Palermo, introduced the culture of silk into his kingdom, from which it was communicated to other parts of Italy. Gianon. Hist. of Naples, b. xi. c. 7. This seems to have rendered silk so common, that about the middle of the fourteenth century, a thousand citizens of Genoa appeared in one procession clad in silk robes. Sugar is likewise a production of the East. Some plants of the sugar-cane were brought from Asia; and the first attempt to cultivate them in Sicily was made about the middle of the twelfth century. From thence they were transplanted into the southern provinces of Spain. From Spain they were carried to the Canary and Madeira isles, and at length into the new world. Ludovico Guicciardini, in enumerating the goods imported into Antwerp, about the year 1560, mentions the sugar which they received from Spain and Portugal as a considerable article. He describes that as the product of the Madeira and Canary islands. Descritt. de Paesi Bassi, p. 180, 181. The sugar-cane was either not introduced into the West-Indies at that time, or the cultivation of it was

not

not so considerable as to furnish an article in commerce. In the middle ages, though sugar was not raised in such quantities, or employed for so many purposes, as to become one of the common necessaries of life, it appears to have been a considerable article in the commerce of the Italian states.

These various commodities with which the Italians furnished the other nations of Europe, procured them a favourable reception in every kingdom. They were established in France in the thirteenth century with most extensive immunities. They not only obtained every indulgence favourable to their commerce, but personal rights and privileges were granted to them, which the natives of the kingdom did not enjoy. Ordon. tom. iv. p. 668. By a special proviso, they were exempted from the droit d'aubaine. Ibid. p. 670. As the Lombards engrossed the trade of every kingdom in which they settled, they became masters of its cash. Money of course was in their hands not only a sign of the value of their commodities, but became an object of commerce itself. They dealt largely as bankers. In an ordonance, A. D. 1295, we find them stiled *mercatores* and *campsores*. They carried on this as well as other branches of their commerce with somewhat of that rapacious spirit which is natural to monopolizers, who are not restrained by the concurrence of rivals. An absurd opinion, which prevailed in the middle ages, was, however, in some measure, the cause of their exorbitant demands, and may be pleaded in apology for them. Commerce cannot be carried on with advantage, unless the persons who lend a sum are allowed a certain premium for the use of their money, and as a compensation for the risk which they run in permitting another to traffick with their stock. This premium is fixed by law in all commercial countries, and is called the legal interest of money. But the Fathers of the church preposterously applied the prohibitions of usury in scripture to the payment of legal interest, and condemned it as a sin. The schoolmen, misled by Aristotle, whose sentiments they followed implicitly, and without examination, adopted the same error, and enforced it. Blackstone's Commentaries on the laws of England, vol. ii. p. 455. Thus the Lombards found themselves engaged in a traffick which was deemed criminal and odious. They were liable to punishment if detected. They were not satisfied, therefore, with that moderate premium, which they might have claimed if their trade had been open and authorised by law. They exacted a sum proportional to the danger and infamy of a discovery. Accordingly, we find that it was usual for them to demand twenty per cent. for the use of money in the thirteenth century. Murat. Antiq. Ital. vol. i. p. 893. About the beginning of that century, the Countess of Flanders was obliged to borrow money in order to pay her husband's ransom. She procured the sum requisite, either from Italian merchants or from Jews. The lowest interest which she paid to them was above twenty per cent. and some of them

them exacted near thirty. Martene and Durand. Thesaur. Anecdotorum. vol. i. p. 886. In the fourteenth century, A. D. 1311, Philip IV. fixed the interest which might be legally exacted in the fairs of Champagne at twenty per cent. Ordonan. tom. i. p. 484. The interest of money in Aragon was somewhat lower. James I. A. D. 1242, fixed it by law at eighteen per cent. Petr. de Marca. *Marca* five Limes Hispan. app. 1433. As late as the year 1490, it appears that the interest of money in Placentia, was at the rate of forty per cent. This is the more extraordinary, because at that time the commerce of the Italian States was become considerable. Memorie Storiche de Piacenza, tom. viii. p. 104. Piac. 1760. It appears from Lud. Guicciardini, that Charles V. had fixed the rate of interest in his dominions in the Low-Countries at twelve per cent. and at the time when he wrote about the year 1560, it was not uncommon to exact more than that sum. He complains of this as exorbitant, and points out its bad effects both on agriculture and commerce. Descritt. di Paesi Bassi, p. 172. This high interest of money, is alone a proof that the profits on commerce were exorbitant.—The Lombards were likewise established in England in the thirteenth century, and a considerable street in the city of London still bears their name. They enjoyed great privileges, and carried on an extensive commerce, particularly as bankers. See Anderson's Chronol. Deduction, vol. i. p. 137, 160, 204, 231, where the statutes or other authorities which confirm this are quoted.

PROOFS AND ILLUSTRATIONS.

But the chief mart for Italian commodities was at Bruges. Navigation was then so imperfect, that a voyage between the Baltick and Mediterranean could not be performed in one summer. For that reason, a magazine or storehouse half way between the commercial cities in the north, and those in Italy, became necessary. Bruges was pitched upon as the most convenient station. That choice introduced vast wealth into the Low-Countries. Bruges was at once the staple for English wool; for the woollen and linen manufactures of the Netherlands; for the naval stores, and other bulky commodities of the North; and for the Indian commodities, as well as domestick productions imported by the Italian States. The extent of its commerce in Indian goods with Venice alone, appears from one fact. In the year 1318, five Venetian galeasses laden with Indian commodities arrived at Bruges, in order to dispose of their cargoes at the fair. These galeasses were vessels of very considerable burden. L. Guic. Descritt. di Paesi Bassi, p. 174. Bruges was the greatest emporium in all Europe. Many proofs of this occur in the historians and records of the thirteenth and fourteenth centuries. But instead of multiplying quotations, I shall refer my readers to Anderson, vol. i. p. 12, 137, 213, 246, &c. The nature of this work prevents me from entering into any long details, but there are some detached facts, which give an high idea of the wealth both of the Flemish and Italian commercial states. The Duke of Brabant contracted his daughter to the Black Prince,

Prince, son of Edward III. of England, A. D. 1339, and gave her a portion which would amount to three hundred thousand pounds of our present money. Rymer's Fædera, vol. v. p. 113. John Galeazzo Visconti Duke of Milan concluded a treaty of marriage between his daughter and Lionel Duke of Clarence, Edward's third son, A. D. 1367, and granted her a portion equal to two hundred thousand pounds of our present money. Rymer Fæder. vol. vi. p. 547. These exorbitant sums so far exceeding what was then granted by the most powerful monarchs, and which appear extraordinary even in the present age, when the wealth of Europe is so much increased, must have arisen from the riches which flowed into these countries from their extensive and lucrative commerce. The first source of wealth to the towns situated on the Baltick sea, seems to have been the herring-fishery; the shoals of herring frequenting at that time the coasts of Sweden and Denmark, in the same manner as they now resort to the British coasts. The effects of this fishery are thus described by an author of the thirteenth century. The Danes, says he, who were formerly clad in the poor garb of sailors, are now cloathed in scarlet, purple and fine linen. For they abound with wealth flowing from their annual fishery on the coast of Schonen; so that all nations resort to them, bringing their gold, silver and precious commodities, that they may purchase herrings, which the divine bounty bestows upon them. Arnoldus Lubecensis ap. Conring. de Urbib. German. § 87.

The Hanseatick league is the most powerful commercial confederacy known in history. Its origin towards the close of the twelfth century, and the objects of its union, are described by Knipfcildt Tractatus Historico-Politico Juridicus de Juribus Civitat. Imper. lib. i. cap. 4. Anderson has mentioned the chief facts with respect to their commercial progress, the extent of the privileges which they obtained in different countries, their successful wars with several monarchs, as well as the spirit and zeal with which they contended for those liberties and rights without which it is impossible to carry on commerce to advantage. The vigorous efforts of a society of merchants attentive only to commercial objects, could not fail of diffusing new and more liberal ideas concerning justice and order in every country of Europe where they settled.

In England, the progress of commerce was extremely slow; and the causes of this are obvious. During the Saxon heptarchy, England, split into many petty kingdoms, which were perpetually at variance with each other, exposed to the fierce incursions of the Danes, and other northern pirates, and funk in barbarity and ignorance, was in no condition to cultivate commerce, or to pursue any system of useful and salutary policy. When a better prospect began to open by the union of the kingdom under one monarch, the Norman conquest took place. This occasioned such a violent shock, and such a sudden and total revolution of property, that the nation did not recover from it during

during several reigns. By the time that the constitution began to acquire some stability, and the English had so incorporated with their conquerors as to become one people, the nation engaged with no less ardour than imprudence in support of their monarch's pretensions to the crown of France, and long wasted its vigour and genius in its wild efforts to conquer that kingdom. When by ill success, and repeated disappointments, a period was at last put to this fatal frenzy, and the nation beginning to enjoy some repose, had leisure to breathe and to gather new strength, the destructive wars between the houses of York and Lancaster broke out, and involved the kingdom in the worst of all calamities. Thus, besides the common obstructions of commerce occasioned by the nature of the feudal government, and the state of manners during the middle ages, its progress in England was retarded by peculiar causes. Such a succession of events adverse to the commercial spirit was sufficient to have checked its growth, although every other circumstance had favoured it. The English were accordingly one of the last nations in Europe who availed themselves of their natural commercial advantages. Before the reign of Edward III. all the wool of England, except a small quantity wrought into coarse cloths for home consumption, was sold to the Flemings or Lombards, and manufactured by them. Though Edward, A. D. 1326, began to allure some of the Flemish weavers to settle in England, it was long before the English were ca-

pable

pable of fabricating cloth for foreign markets, and the export of unwrought wool still continued to be the chief article of their commerce. Anderson passim.—All foreign commodities were brought into England by the Lombard or Hanseatick merchants. The English ports were frequented by ships both from the north and south of Europe, and they tamely allowed foreigners to reap all the profits arising from the supply of their wants. The first commercial treaty of England on record, is that with Haquin King of Norway, A. D. 1217. Anderf. vol. i. p. 108. But they did not venture to trade in their own ships to the Baltick until the beginning of the fourteenth century. Ib. 151. It was after the middle of the fifteenth, before they sent any ship into the Mediterranean. Ib. p. 177. Nor was it long before this period that their vessels visited the ports of Spain or Portugal. But though I have pointed out the flow progress of the English commerce as a fact little attended to, and yet meriting consideration; the concourse of foreigners to the ports of England, together with the communication among all the different countries in Europe, which went on increasing from the beginning of the twelfth century, is sufficient to justify all the observations and reasonings in the text concerning the influence of commerce on the state of manners, and of society.

NOTE XXXI. Sect. III. p. 183. [HH].

I have not been able to discover the precise manner in which the Justiza was appointed. Among the

PROOFS AND ILLUSTRATIONS.

the claims of the *junta* or *union* formed against James I. A. D. 1264, this was one; that the King should not nominate any person to be Justiza, without the consent or approbation of the ricoshombres or nobles. Zurita Anales de Aragon, vol. i. p. 180. But the King in his answer to their remonstrance asserts, "that it was established by immemorial practice, and was conformable to the laws of the kingdom, that the King, in virtue of his royal prerogative, should name the Justiza." Zurita, Ibid. 181. Blanca, 656. From another passage in Zurita, it appears, that while the Aragonese enjoyed the privilege of *the union*, i. e. the power of confederating against their sovereign as often as they conceived that he had violated any of their rights and immunities, the Justiza was not only nominated by the King, but held his office during the King's pleasure. Nor was this practice attended with any bad effects, as the privilege of the union was a sufficient and effectual check to any abuse of the royal prerogative. But when the privilege of the union was abolished as dangerous to the order and peace of society, it was agreed that the Justiza should continue in office during life. Several Kings, however, attempted to remove the Justizas who were obnoxious to them, and they sometimes succeeded in the attempt. In order to guard against this encroachment, which would have destroyed the intention of the institution, and have rendered the Justiza the dependant and tool of the crown, instead of the guar-

dian

dian of the people, a law was enacted in the Cortes, A. D. 1442, ordaining that the Juſtiza ſhould continue in office during life, and ſhould not be removed from it unleſs by the authority of the Cortes. Fueros & Obſervancial del Reyno de Arag. lib. i. p. 22. By former laws the perſon of the Juſtiza had been declared ſacred, and he was reſponſible only to the Cortes. Ibid. p. 15. b. Zurita and Blanca, who both publiſhed their hiſtories while the Juſtiza of Aragon retained the full exerciſe of his privileges and juriſdiction, have neglected to explain ſeveral circumſtances with regard to the office of that reſpectable magiſtrate, becauſe they addreſſed their works to their countrymen, who who were well acquainted with every particular concerning the functions of a judge, to whom they looked up as to the guardian of their liberties. It is vain to conſult the later hiſtorians of Spain, about any point, with reſpect to which the excellent hiſtorians whom I have named are ſilent. The ancient conſtitution of their country was overturned, and deſpotiſm eſtabliſhed on the ruin of its liberties, when the writers of this and the preceding century compoſed their hiſtories, and on that account they had little curioſity to know the nature of thoſe inſtitutions to which their anceſtors owed the enjoyment of freedom, or they were afraid to deſcribe them with much accuracy. The ſpirit with which Mariana, his continuator Miniana, and Ferreras, write their hiſtories, is very different from that of the two hiſtorians of Aragon, from whom

I have

I have taken my account of the conſtitution of that kingdom.

Two circumſtances concerning the Juſtiza, beſides thoſe which I have mentioned in the text, are worthy of obſervation, 1. None of the ricoshombres, or noblemen of the firſt order, could be appointed Juſtiza. He was taken out of the ſecond claſs or cavalleros, who anſwer nearly to gentlemen or commoners in Great Britain. Fueros & Obſervanc. del Reyno, &c. lib. 1. p. 21. b. The reaſon was. By the laws of Aragon, the ricoshombres were not ſubject to capital puniſhment; but as it was neceſſary for the ſecurity of liberty, that the Juſtiza ſhould be accountable for the manner in which he executed the high truſt repoſed in him, it was a powerful reſtraint upon him to know that he was liable to be puniſhed with the utmoſt rigour. Blanca, p. 657, 756. Zurita, tom. ii. 229. Fueros & Obſervanc. lib. ix. p. 182. b. 183. It appears too from many paſſages in Zurita, that the Juſtiza was appointed to check the domineering and oppreſſive ſpirit of the nobles, as well as to ſet bounds to the power of the monarch, and therefore he was choſen from an order of citizens equally intereſted in oppoſing both.

2. A MAGISTRATE poſſeſſed of ſuch vaſt powers as the Juſtiza, might have exerciſed them in a manner pernicious to the ſtate, if he himſelf had been ſubject to no controul. A conſtitutional remedy,

PROOFS AND ILLUSTRATIONS.

remedy, however, was provided against this danger. Seventeen persons were chosen by lot in each meeting of the Cortes. These formed a tribunal called the court of inquisition into the office of Justiza. This court met at three stated terms in each year. Every person had liberty of complaining to it of any iniquity or neglect of duty in the Justiza, or in the inferior judges, who acted in his name. The Justiza and his deputies were called to answer for their conduct. The members of the court passed sentence by ballot. They might punish by degradation, confiscation of goods, or even with death. The law which erected this court, and regulated the forms of its procedure, was enacted A. D. 1461. Zurita Anales, iv. 102. Blanca Comment. Rer. Aragon. 770. Previous to this period, inquiry was made into the conduct of the Justiza, though not with the same formality. He was from the first institution of the office subject to the review of the Cortes. The constant dread of such an impartial and severe inquiry into his behaviour, was a powerful motive to the vigilant and faithful discharge of his duty. A remarkable instance of the authority of the Justiza when opposed to that of the King, occurs in the year 1386. By the constitution of Aragon, the eldest son or heir apparent of the crown possessed considerable power and jurisdiction in the kingdom. Fueros & Observan. del Reyno de Arag. lib. i. p. 16. Peter IV. instigated by a second wife, attempted to deprive his son of this, and enjoined his subjects to yield him no obedience.

dience. The Prince immediately applied to the Juſtiza; "the ſafe-guard and defence, ſays Zurita, againſt all violence and oppreſſion." The Juſtiza granted him the *firmo de derecho*, the effect of which was, that upon his giving ſurety to appear in judgment, he could not be deprived of any immunity or privilege, which he poſſeſſed, but in conſequence of a legal trial before the Juſtiza, and of a ſentence pronounced by him. This was publiſhed throughout the kingdom, and notwithſtanding the proclamation in contradiction to this which had been iſſued by the King, the Prince continued in the exerciſe of all his rights, and his authority was univerſally recognized. Zurita Anales de Aragon, tom. ii. 385.

NOTE XXXII. Sect. III. p. 184. [II].

I HAVE been induced, by the concurring teſtimony of many reſpectable authors, to mention this as the conſtitutional form of the oath of allegiance, which the Aragoneſe ſwore to their Sovereigns. I muſt acknowledge, however, that I have not found this ſingular oath in any Spaniſh author whom I have had an opportunity to conſult. It is mentioned neither by Zurita, nor Blanca, nor Argenſola, nor Sayas, who were all hiſtoriographers appointed by the Cortes of Aragon to record the tranſactions of the kingdom. All theſe writers poſſeſs a merit, which is very rare among hiſtorians. They are extremely accurate in tracing the progreſs of the laws and conſtitution

tion of their country. Their silence with respect to this, creates some suspicion concerning the genuineness of the oath. But as it is mentioned by so many authors, who produce the ancient Spanish words in which it is expressed, it is probable that they have taken it from some writer of credit, whose works have not fallen into my hands. The spirit of the oath is perfectly agreeable to the genius of the Aragonese constitution. Since the publication of the first edition, the learned M. Totze, Professor of History at Batzow in the Dutchy of Mecklenburgh, has been so good as to point out to me a Spanish author of great authority, who has published the words of this oath. It is Antonio Perez, secretary to the Philip II. a native of Aragon. The words of the oath are, "Nos, que valemos tanto como vos, os hazemos nuestro Rey y Señor, con tal que nos guandeys nuestros fueros, y libertades, y si No, No. Las Obras y Relaciones de Ant. Perez. 8vo. par Juan de la Planche 1631. p. 143."

THE privilege of Union, which I have mentioned in the preceding note, and alluded to in the next, is indeed one of the most singular which could take place in a regular government, and the oath that I have mentioned expresses nothing more than this constitutional privilege entitled the Aragonese to perform. If the King or his ministers violated any of the laws or immunities of the Aragonese, and did not grant immediate redress in consequence of their representations and remonstrances,

remonstrances, the nobles of the first rank, or *Ricos-bombres de natura, & de mesnada*, the equestrian order, or the nobility of the second class, called *Hidalgos* & *Infanciones*, together with the magistrates of cities, might, either in the Cortes, or in a voluntary assembly, join in union, and binding themselves by mutual oaths and the exchange of hostages to be faithful to each other, they might require the King, in the name and by the authority of his body corporate, to grant them redress. If the King refused to comply with their request, or took arms in order to oppose them, they might, in virtue of the privilege of union, instantly withdraw their allegiance from the King, refuse to acknowledge him as their Sovereign, and proceed to elect another Monarch; nor did they incur any guilt, or become liable to any prosecution on that account. Blanca Com. Rer. Arag. 661, 669. This union did not resemble the confederacies in other feudal kingdoms. It was a constitutional association, which pretended to legal privileges, which issued its mandates under a common seal, and proceeded in all its operations by regular and ascertained forms. This dangerous right was not only claimed, but exercised. In the year 1287, the Aragonese formed an union in opposition to Alfonso III. and obliged the King not only to comply with their demands, but to ratify a privilege so fatal to the power of the crown. Zurita Anales, tom. i. p. 322. In the year 1347, an union was formed against Peter IV. with equal success,

success, and a new ratification of the privilege was extorted. Zurita, tom. ii. p. 202. But soon after, the King having defeated the leaders of the union in battle, the privilege of union was finally abrogated in the Cortes, and all the laws or records which contained any confirmation of it, were cancelled or destroyed. The King, in presence of the Cortes, called for the act whereby he had ratified the union, and having wounded his hand with his poniard, he held it above the record, " That privilege, says he, which has been " so fatal to the kingdom, and so injurious to " royalty, should be effaced with the blood of a " King." Zurita, tom. ii. p. 229. The law abolishing the union is published. Fueros & Observanc. lib. ix. p. 178. From that period the Justiza became the constitutional guardian of publick liberty, and his power and jurisdiction occasioned none of those violent convulsions which the tumultuary privilege of the union was apt to produce. The constitution of Aragon, however, still remained extremely free. One source of this liberty was from the early admission of the representatives of cities into the Cortes. It seems probable, from Zurita, that burgesses were constituent members of the Cortes from its first institution. He mentions a meeting of Cortes, A. D. 1133, in which the *procuradores de las ciudades y villas* were present. Tom. i. p. 51. This is the constitutional language in which their presence is declared in the Cortes, after the journals of that court

were

were regularly kept. It is probable, that an historian so accurate as Zurita, would not have used these words, if he had not taken them from some authentick record. It was more than a century after this period before the representatives of cities formed a constituent part in the supreme assemblies of the other European nations. The free spirit of the Aragonese government is conspicuous in many particulars. The Cortes not only opposed the attempts of their Kings to increase their revenue, or to extend their prerogative, but they claimed rights and exercised powers which will appear extraordinary even in a country accustomed to the enjoyment of liberty. In the year 1286, the Cortes claimed the privilege of naming the members of the King's council and the officers of his houshold, and they seem to have obtained it for some time. Zurita, tom. i. p. 303, 307. It was the privilege of the Cortes to name the officers who commanded the troops raised by their authority. This seems to be evident from a passage in Zurita. When the Cortes, in the year 1503, raised a body of troops to be employed in Italy, it passed an act empowering the King to name the officers who should command them. Zurita, tom. v. p. 274; which plainly implies that without this warrant, it did not belong to him in virtue of his prerogative. In the Fueros & Observancias del Reyno de Aragon, two general declarations of the rights and privileges of the Aragonese are published; the one in the reign of Pedro I. A. D. 1283, the other in that of James II. A. D. 1325.

They

They are of such length, that I cannot insert them, but it is evident from these, that not only the privileges of the nobility, but the rights of the people, personal as well as political, were, at that period, more extensive, and better understood than in any kingdom in Europe. Lib. i. p. 7, 9. The oath by which the King bound himself to observe those rights and liberties of the people, was very solemn. Ibid. p. 14. b. & p. 15. The Cortes of Aragon discovered not only the jealousy and vigilance, which are peculiar to free states, in guarding the essential parts of the constitution, but they were scrupulously attentive to observe the most minute forms and ceremonies to which they were accustomed. According to the established laws and customs of Aragon, no foreigner had liberty to enter the hall in which the Cortes assembled. Ferdinand, in the year 1481, appointed his Queen, Isabella, regent of the kingdom, while he was absent during the course of the campaign. The law required that a regent should take the oath of fidelity in presence of the Cortes; but as Isabella was a foreigner, before she could be admitted, the Cortes thought it necessary to pass an act authorizing the serjeant-porter to open the door of the hall, and to allow her to enter; " so attentive were they, says Zurita, to observe " their laws and forms, even such as may seem " most minute." Tom. iv. p. 313.

The Aragonese were no less solicitous to secure the personal rights of individuals, than to maintain

tain the freedom of the conftitution; and the fpirit of their ftatutes with refpect to both was equally liberal. Two facts relative to this matter merit obfervation. By an exprefs ftatute in the year 1325, it was declared to be unlawful to put any native Aragonefe to the torture. If he could not be convicted by the teftimony of witneffes, he was inftantly abfolved. Zurita, tom. ii. p. 66. Zurita records the regulation with the fatisfaction natural to an hiftorian, when he contemplates the humanity of his countrymen. He compares the laws of Aragon to thofe of Rome, as both exempted citizens and freemen from fuch ignominious and cruel treatment, and had recourfe to it only in the trial of flaves. Zurita had reafon to beftow fuch an encomium on the laws of his country. Torture was at that time permitted by the laws of every other nation in Europe. Even in England, from which the mild fpirit of legiflation has long banifhed it, torture was not, at that time, unknown. Obfervations on the Statutes, chiefly the more ancient, &c. p. 66.

THE other fact fhows, that the fame fpirit which influenced the legiflature prevailed among the people. In the year 1485, the religious zeal of Ferdinand and Ifabella prompted them to introduce the inquifition into Aragon. Though the Aragonefe were no lefs fuperftitioufly attached than the other Spaniards to the Roman Catholick faith, and no lefs defirous to root out the feeds

of error and of herefy which the Jews and Moors
had fcattered, yet they took arms againft the in-
quifitors, murdered the chief inquifitor, and long
oppofed the eftablifhment of that tribunal. The
reafon which they gave for their conduct was,
That the mode of trial in the inquifition was in-
confiftent with liberty. The criminal was not
confronted with the witneffes, he was not acquainted with what they depofed againft him, he
was fubjected to torture, and the goods of perfons
condemned were confifcated. Zurita Anales, tom.
iv. p. 341.

The form of government in the kingdom of
Valencia, and principality of Catalonia, which
were annexed to the crown of Aragon, was likewife extremely favourable to liberty. The Valen-
cians enjoyed the privilege of *union* in the fame
manner with the Aragonefe. But they had no
magiftrate refembling the Juftiza. The Catalo-
nians were no lefs jealous of their liberties than
the two other nations, and no lefs bold in afferting
them. But it is not neceffary for illuftrating the
following hiftory to enter into any farther detail
concerning the peculiarities in the conftitution of
thefe kingdoms.

NOTE XXXIII. Sect. III. p. 185. [KK].

I have fearched in vain among the hiftorians
of Caftile for fuch information as might enable
me to trace the progrefs of laws and government

PROOFS AND ILLUSTRATIONS.

in Castile, or to explain the nature of the constitution with the same degree of accuracy wherewith I have described the political state of Aragon. It is manifest not only from the historians of Castile, but from its ancient laws, particularly the Fuero Juzgo, that its monarchs were originally elective, Ley 2, 5, 8. They were chosen by the bishops, the nobility, and the people, ibid. It appears from the same venerable code of laws, that the prerogative of the Castilian monarchs was extremely limited. Villaldiego, in his commentary on these laws, produces many facts and authorities in confirmation of both these particulars. Dr. Geddes, who was well acquainted with Spanish literature, complains that he could find no author, who gave a distinct account of the Cortes or supreme assembly of the nation, or who described the manner in which it was held, or mentioned the precise number of members who had a right to sit in it. He produces, however, from Gil Gonzales d'Avila, who published a history of Henry II, the writ of summons to the town of Abula, requiring it to chuse representatives to appear in the Cortes which he called to meet A. D. 1390. From this we learn, that Prelates, Dukes, Marquisses, the masters of the three military orders, Conde's and Riccos-hombres were required to attend. These composed the bodies of ecclesiasticks and nobles, which formed two members of the legislature. The cities which sent members to that meeting of the Cortes were forty-eight. The number of representatives, (for the cities had

right to chuse more or fewer according to their
respective dignity) amounted to an hundred and
twenty-five. Geddes Miscellaneous Tracts, vol. i.
331. Zurita having occasion to mention the
Cortes which Ferdinand held at Toro A. D. 1505,
in order to secure to himself the government of
Castile after the death of Isabella, records, with
his usual accuracy, the names of the members
present, and of the cities which they represented.
From that list it appears, that only eighteen cities
had deputies in this assembly. Anales de Aragon,
tom. vi. p. 3. What was the occasion of this
great difference in the number of cities represented
in these two meetings of the Cortes, I am unable
to explain.

NOTE XXXIV. Sect. III. p. 187. [LL].

A GREAT part of the territory in Spain was
engrossed by the nobility. L. Marinæus Siculus,
who composed his treatise de Rebus Hispaniæ during the reign of Charles V. gives a catalogue of
the Spanish nobility, together with the yearly rent
of their estates. According to his account, which
he affirms was as accurate as the nature of the
subject would admit, the sum total of the annual
revenue of their lands amounted to one million
four hundred and eighty-two thousand ducats. If
we make allowance for the vast difference in the
value of money in the fifteenth century from that
which it now bears, and consider that the catalogue of Marinæus includes only the *Titulados*, or
nobility

nobility whose families were distinguished by some honorary title, their wealth must appear very great. L. Marinæus ap. Schotti Scriptores Hispan. vol. i. p. 323. The Commons of Castile, in their contests with the crown, which I shall hereafter relate, complain of the extensive property of the nobility as extremely pernicious to the kingdom. In one of their manifesto's they assert that from Valladolid to St. Jago in Galicia, which was an hundred leagues, the crown did not possess more than three villages. All the rest belonged to the nobility, and could be subjected to no publick burden. Sandov. Vida del Emperor. Carl. V. vol. i. p. 422. It appears from the testimony of authors quoted by Bovadilla, that these vast possessions were bestowed upon the *Ricos-hombres, hidalgos,* and *cavalleros* by the Kings of Castile, in reward for the assistance which they had received from them in expelling the Moors. They likewise obtained by the same means a considerable influence in the cities, many of which anciently depended upon the nobility. Politica para Corregidores. Amb. 1750. fol. vol. i. 440, 442.

NOTE XXXV. Sect. III. p. 190. [MM].

I HAVE been able to discover nothing certain, as I observed Note XVIII. with respect to the origin of communities or free cities in Spain. It is probable, that as soon as these were recovered from the Moors, the inhabitants who fixed their residence in them, being persons of distinction and credit,

credit, had all the privileges of municipal government and jurisdiction conferred upon them. Many striking proofs occur of the splendour, wealth and power of the Spanish cities. Hieronymus Paulus wrote a description of Barcelona in the year 1491, and compares the dimensions of the town to that of Naples, and the elegance of its buildings, the variety of its manufactures, and the extent of its commerce to Florence. Hieron. Paulus ap. Scottum. Script. Hisp. ii. 844. Marinæus describes Toledo as a large and populous city. A great number of its inhabitants were persons of quality and of illustrious rank. Its commerce was great. It applied particularly to the manufactures of silk and wool; and the number of inhabitants employed in these two branches of trade amounted nearly to ten thousand. Marin. ubi supr. p. 308. I know no city, says he, that I would prefer to Valladolid for elegance and splendour. Ibid. p. 312. We may form some estimate of its populousness from the following circumstances. The citizens having taken arms in the year 1516, in order to oppose a measure concerted by cardinal Ximenes, they mustered in the city, and in the territory which belonged to it, thirty thousand fighting men. Sandov. Vida del Emper. Carl. V. tom. i. p. 81. The manufactures carried on in the towns of Spain were not intended merely for home consumption, they were exported to foreign countries, and that commerce was a considerable source of wealth to the inhabitants. The maritime laws of Barcelona are the foundation of mercantile jurisprudence

jurisprudence in modern times, as the Leges Rhodiæ were among the ancients. All the commercial states in Italy adopted these laws, and regulated their trade according to them. Sandi Storia Civile Veneziana, Vol. ii. 865. It appears from several ordonances of the Kings of France, that the merchants of Aragon and Castile were received on the same footing, and admitted to the same privileges with those of Italy. Ordonances des Roys, &c. tom. ii. p. 135, iii. 166, 504, 635. Cities in such a flourishing state became a respectable part of the society, and were entitled to a considerable share in the legislature. The magistrates of Barcelona aspired to the highest honour a Spanish subject can enjoy, that of being covered in the presence of their sovereign, and of being treated as grandees of the kingdom. Origin de la dignidad de Grande de Castilla por Don Alonso Carillo. Madr. 1657. p. 18.

NOTE XXXVI. Sect. III. p. 193. [NN].

The military order of St. Jago, the most honourable and opulent of the three Spanish orders, was instituted about the year 1170. The bull of confirmation by Alexander III. is dated A. D. 1176. At that time a considerable part of Spain was subject to the Moors, and the whole country much exposed to the depredations not only of the enemy, but of banditti. It is no wonder, then, that an institution, the object of which was to oppose the enemies of the Christian faith, and to

restrain

restrain and punish those who disturbed the publick peace, should be extremely popular, and meet with general encouragement. The wealth and power of the order became so great, that one historian says, that the Grand Master of St. Jago was the person in Spain of greatest power and dignity next to the King. Æl. Anton. Nebrissensis, ap. Schott. Scrip. Hisp. i. 812. Another observes, that the order possessed every thing in Castile that a King would most desire to obtain. Zurita Anales, v. 22. The knights took the vows of obedience, of poverty, and of conjugal chastity. By the former they were bound implicitly to obey the commands of their grand master. The order could bring into the field a thousand men at arms. Æl. Ant. Nebref. p. 813. If these men at arms were accompanied as was usual in that age, this was a formidable body of cavalry. There belonged to this order eighty-four commanderies, and two hundred priories and other benefices. Dissertations sur la Chevalerie par Hon. de St. Marie, p. 262. It is easy to see how formidable to his sovereign the command of these troops, the administration of such revenues, and the disposal of so many offices, must have rendered a subject. The other two orders, though inferior to that of St. Jago in power and wealth, were nevertheless very considerable. When the conquest of Granada deprived the knights of St. Jago of those enemies against whom their zeal was originally directed, superstition found out a new object, in defence

defence of which they engaged to employ their
courage. To their usual oath, they added the following clause: " We do swear to believe, to maintain, and to contend in publick and in private, that
the Virgin Mary, the mother of God, our Lady,
was conceived without the stain of original sin."
This singular addition was made about the middle
of the seventeenth century. Honorè de St. Marie
Dissertations, &c. p. 263.

NOTE XXXVII. SECT. III. p. 196. [OO].

I HAVE frequently had occasion to take notice
of the defects in police during the middle ages,
occasioned by the feebleness of government, and
the want of proper subordination among the different ranks of men. I have observed in a former
Note, that this greatly interrupted the intercourse
between nations, and even between different places
in the same kingdom. The description which the
Spanish historians give of the frequency of rapine,
murder, and every act of violence, in all the provinces of Spain, are amazing, and present to us the
idea of a society but little removed from the disorder and turbulence of that which has been called
a state of nature. Zurita Anales de Arag. i. 175.
Æl. Ant. Nebrissensis rer. a Ferdin. gestar. Hist.
ap. Schottum II. 849. Though the excess of these
disorders rendered the institution of the *Santa Hermandad* necessary, great care was taken at first to
avoid giving any offence or alarm to the nobility.
The jurisdiction of the judges of the Hermandad

was expresly confined to crimes that violated the publick peace. All other offences were left to the cognizance of the ordinary judges. If a perfon was guilty of the moſt notorious perjury, in any trial before a judge of the Hermandad, he could not puniſh him, but was obliged to remit the cafe to the ordinary judge of the place. Commentaria in Regias Hiſpan. Conſtitut. per Alph. de Azevedo, pars v. p. 220, &c. fol. Duaci, 1612. Notwithſtanding theſe reſtrictions, the barons were ſenſible how much the Hermandad would encroach on their juriſdiction. In Caſtile, ſome oppoſition was made to the inſtitution; but Ferdinand had the addreſs to obtain the conſent of the Conſtable to the introduction of the Hermandad into that part of the kingdom where his eſtate lay; and by that means, as well as the popularity of the inſtitution, he ſurmounted every obſtacle that ſtood in its way. Æl. Ant. Nebriſſen. 851. In Aragon, the nobles combined againſt it with greater ſpirit; and Ferdinand, though he ſupported it with vigour, was obliged to make ſome conceſſions in order to reconcile them. Zurita Anales de Arag. iv. 356. The power and revenue of the Hermandad in Caſtile ſeems to have been very great. Ferdinand, when preparing for the war againſt the Moors of Granada, required of the Hermandad to furniſh him ſixteen thouſand beaſts of burden, together with eight thouſand men to conduct them, and he obtained what he demanded. Æl. Ant. Nebriſſ. 881. The Hermandad has been found to be of ſo much uſe in preſerving peace, and reſtraining or detecting

ing crimes, that it is still continued in Spain, although it be no longer necessary either for moderating the power of the nobility, or extending that of the crown.

NOTE XXXVIII. Sect. III. p. 199. [PP].

NOTHING is more common among Antiquarians, and there is not a more copious source of error, than to decide concerning the institutions and manners of past ages, by the forms and ideas which prevail in their own times. The French lawyers in the seventeenth and eighteenth centuries, having found their sovereigns in possession of absolute power, seem to think it a duty incumbent on them, to maintain that such unbounded authority belonged to the crown in every period of their monarchy. " The government of France," says M. de Real very gravely, " is purely monarchical at this day, as it was from the beginning. Our Kings were absolute originally as they are at present." Science du Gouvernement, tom. ii. p. 31. It is impossible, however, to conceive two states of civil society more unlike to each other, than that of the French nation under Clovis, and that under Louis XV. It is evident from the codes of laws of the various tribes which settled in Gaul and the countries adjacent to it, as well as from the history of Gregory of Tours, and other early annalists, that among all these people the form of government was extremely rude and simple, and that they had scarcely begun to acquire the first rudiments of

PROOFS AND ILLUSTRATIONS.

that order and police which are necessary in extensive societies. The King or leader had the command of soldiers or companions, who followed his standard from choice, not by constraint. I have produced the clearest evidence of this, Note VI. An event related by Gregory of Tours, lib. iv. c. 14. affords the most striking proof of the dependence of the early French Kings on the sentiments and inclination of their people. Clotaire I. having marched at the head of his army, in the year 553, against the Saxons, that people, intimidated at his approach, sued for peace, and offered to pay a large sum to the offended monarch. Clotaire was willing to close with what they proposed. But his army insisted to be led forth to battle. The King employed all his eloquence to persuade them to accept of what the Saxons were ready to pay. The Saxons, in order to soothe them, increased their original offer. The King renewed his solicitations: But the army enraged, rushed upon the King, tore his tent in pieces, dragged him out of it, and would have slain him on the spot, if he had not consented to lead them instantly against the enemy.

If the early monarchs of France possessed such limited authority, even while at the head of their army, their prerogative during peace will be found to be still more confined. They ascended the throne not by any hereditary right, but in consequence of the election of their subjects. In order to avoid an unnecessary number of quotations, I refer my

readers

readers to Hottomanni Franco-gallia, cap. vi. p. 47. edit. 1573, where they will find the fullest proof of this from Gregory of Tours, Amoinus, and the most authentick historians of the Merovingian Kings. The effect of this election was not to invest them with absolute power. Whatever related to the general welfare of the nation, was submitted to publick deliberation, and determined by the suffrage of the people, in the annual assemblies called Les Champs de Mars and Les Champs de Mai. These assemblies were called *Champs*, because, according to the custom of all the barbarous nations, they were held in the open air, in some plain capable of containing the vast number of persons who had a right to be present. Jo. Jac. Sorberus de Comitiis veterum Germanorum, vol. i. § 19, &c. They were denominated Champs de Mars and de Mai, from the months in which they were held. Every free man seems to have had a right to be present in these assemblies. Sorberus, ibid. § 133, &c. The ancient annals of the Franks describe the persons who were present in the assembly held A. D. 788, in these words: In placito Ingelheimensi conveniunt pontifices, majores, minores, sacerdotes, reguli, duces, comites, præfecti, cives, oppidani, Apud Sorber. § 304. There every thing that concerned the happiness of their country, says an ancient historian, every thing that could be of benefit to the Franks, was considered and enjoined. Fredegarius ap. Du Cange Glossar. voc. *Campus Martii*. Chlotharius II. describes the business, and acknowledges the authority of these assemblies.

semblies. They are called, says he, that whatever relates to the common safety may be considered and resolved by common deliberation; and whatever they determine, to that I will conform. Amoinus de Gest. Franc. lib. iv. c. i. ap. Bouquet Recueil, iii. 116. The statutory clauses, or words of legislative authority in the decrees issued in these assemblies, run not in the name of the King alone. " We have treated, says Childebert, in a decree, A. D. 532, in the assembly of March, together with our Nobles, concerning some affairs, and we now publish the conclusion, that it may come to the knowledge of all." Childeb. Decret. ap. Bouquet Recueil des Histor. tom. iv. p. 3. We have agreed together with our vassals. Ibid. § 2. It is agreed in the assembly in which we were all united. Ibid. § 4. The Salic laws, the most venerable monument of French jurisprudence, were enacted in the same manner. Dictaverunt Salicam legem proceres ipsius gentis, qui tunc temporis apud eam erant Rectores. Sunt autem electi de pluribus viri quatuor—qui per tres Mallos convenientes, omnes causarum origines sollicité discurrendo, tractantes de singulis judicium decreverunt hoc modo. Præf. Leg. Salic. ap. Bouquet. Ibid. p. 122. Hoc decretum est apud regem & principes ejus, & apud cunctum populum christianum, qui infra regnum Merwingorum consistunt. Ibid. p. 124. Nay, even in their charters, the Kings of the first race are careful to specify that they were granted with the consent of their vassals. Ego Childebertus Rex unà cum consensu & voluntate Francorum,

Francorum, &c. A. D. 558. Bouquet, ibid. 622. Chlotharius III. unà cum patribus noſtris epiſcopis, optimatibus, cæteriſque palatii noſtri miniſtris, A. D. 664. Ibid. 648. De conſenſu fidelium noſtrorum. Mably Obſerv. tom. i. p. 239. The hiſtorians likewiſe deſcribe the functions of the King in the national aſſemblies in ſuch terms, as imply that his authority there was extremely ſmall, and that every thing depended on the court itſelf. Ipſe Rex (ſays the authors of Annales Francorum, ſpeaking of the Field of March) ſedebat in ſella regia, circumſtante exercitu, præcipiebatque is, die illo, quicquid a Francis decretum erat. Bouquet Recueil, tom. ii. p. 647.

That the general aſſemblies exerciſed ſupreme juriſdiction over all perſons, and with reſpect to all cauſes, is ſo evident as to ſtand in need of no proof. The trial of Brunehaut, A. D. 613, how unjuſt ſoever the ſentence againſt her may be, as related by Fredegarius, Chron. cap. 42. Bouquet, ibid. 430. is in itſelf ſufficient proof of this. The notorious violence and iniquity of the ſentence, ſerve to demonſtrate the extent of juriſdiction which this aſſembly poſſeſſed, as a Prince ſo ſanguinary as Clothaire II. thought the ſanction of its authority would be ſufficient to juſtify his rigorous treatment of the mother and grandmother of ſo many Kings.

With reſpect to conferring donatives on the Prince, we may obſerve, that among nations whoſe manners

manners and political institutions are simple, the publick, as well as individuals, having few wants, they are unacquainted with taxes, and free uncivilized tribes disdain to submit to any stated imposition. This was remarkably the case of the Germans, and of all the various people that issued from that country. Tacitus pronounces two tribes not to be of German origin, because they submitted to pay taxes. De Morib. Germ. c. 43. And speaking of another tribe according to the ideas prevalent in Germany, he says, " they were not degraded by the imposition of taxes." Ibid. c. 29. Upon their settlement in Gaul, we may conclude, that while elated with the consciousness of victory, they would not renounce the high-spirited ideas of their ancestors, or voluntarily submit to a burden which they regarded as a badge of servitude. The evidence of the earliest records and historians justify this conclusion. M. de Montesquieu, in the twelfth and subsequent chapters of the thirteenth book of l'Esprit des Loix, and M. de Mably Observat. sur l'Hist. de France, tom. i. p. 247. have investigated this fact with great attention, and have proved clearly that the property of freemen among the Franks was not subject to any stated tax. That the state required nothing from persons of this rank but military service at their own expence, and that they should entertain the King in their houses when he was upon any progress through his dominions, or his officers when sent on any publick employment, furnishing them with carriages and horses. Monarchs subsisted almost moft entirely upon the revenues of their own domains, and upon the perquifites arifing from the adminiftration of juftice, together with a few fmall fines and forfeitures exacted from thofe who had been guilty of certain trefpaffes. It is foreign from my fubject to enumerate thefe. The reader may find them in Obfervat. de M. de Mably, vol. i. p. 267.

WHEN any extraordinary aid was granted by free-men to their fovereign, it was purely voluntary. In the annual affembly of March or May, it was the cuftom to make the King a prefent of money, of horfes or arms, or of fome other thing of value. This was an ancient cuftom, and derived from their anceftors the Germans. Mos eft civitatibus, ultro ac viritim conferri principibus vel armentorum vel frugum, quod pro honore acceptum, etiam neceffitatibus fubvenit. Tacit. de Mor. Germ. c. 15. Thefe gifts, if we may form a judgment concerning them from the general terms in which they are mentioned by the ancient hiftorians, were confiderable, and made no fmall part of the royal revenue. Many paffages to this purpofe are produced by M. du Cange, Differt. iv. fur Joinville, 153. Sometimes a conquered people fpecified the gift which they bound themfelves to pay annually, and it was exacted as a debt if they failed. Annales Metenfes, ap. Du Cange, ibid. p. 155. It is probable that the firft ftep towards taxation was to afcertain the value of thefe gifts which were originally gratuitous, and to compel the people to pay the fum at which they were rated.

Still,

Still, however, some memory of their original was preserved, and the aids granted to monarchs in all the kingdoms of Europe were termed benevolences or free-gifts.

THE Kings of the second race in France were raised to the throne by the election of the people. Pepinus Rex pius, says an author who wrote a few years after the transaction which he records, per authoritatem Papæ, & unctionem sancti chrismatis, & electionem omnium Francorum in regni solio sublimatus est. Clausula de Pepini consecratione ap. Bouq. Recueil des Histor. tom. v. p. 9. At the same time, as the chief men of the nation had transferred the crown from one family to another, an oath was exacted of them, that they should maintain on the throne the family which they had now promoted; ut nunquam de alterius lumbis regem in ævo præsumant eligere. Ibid. p. 10. This oath the nation faithfully observed during a considerable space of time. The posterity of Pepin kept possession of the throne; but with respect to the manner of dividing their dominions among their children, Princes were obliged to consult the general assembly of the nation. Thus Pepin himself, A. D. 768, appointed his two sons, Charles and Carlomannus, to reign as joint sovereigns; but he did this, una cum consensu Francorum & procerum suorum seu & episcoporum, before whom he laid the matter in their general assembly. Conventus apud sanctum Dionysium. Capitular. vol. i. p. 187. This destination the French confirmed in

a sub-a subsequent assembly, which was called upon the death of Pepin; for, as Eginhart relates, they not only appointed them Kings, but by their authority they regulated the limits of their respective territories. Vita Car. Magni ap. Bouquet Recueil, tom. v. p. 90. In the same manner, it was by the authority of the supreme assemblies that any dispute which arose among the descendants of the royal family was determined. Charlemagne recognizes this important part of their jurisdiction, and confirms it in his charter concerning the partition of his dominions; for he appoints, that, in case of any uncertainty with respect to the right of the several competitors, he whom the people shall chuse, shall succeed to the crown. Capitular. vol. i. 442.

UNDER the second race of Kings, the assembly of the nation, distinguished by the name of Conventus, Malli, Placita, were regularly assembled once a year at least, and frequently twice in the year. One of the most valuable monuments of the history of France is the treatise of Hincmarus, archbishop of Rheims, de ordine Palatii. He died A. D. 882. only sixty-eight years after Charlemagne, and he relates in that short discourse the facts which were communicated to him by Adalhardus, a minister and confident of Charlemagne. From him we learn that this great monarch never failed to hold the general assembly of his subjects every year. In quo placito generalitas universorum majorum tam clericorum quam laicorum conveniebat.

conveniebat. Hincm. oper. edit. Sirmondi, vol. ii. c. 29. 211. In these assemblies, matters which related to the general safety and state of the kingdom were always discussed, before they entered upon any private or less important business. Ibid. c. 33. p. 213. His immediate successors imitated his example, and transacted no affair of importance without the advice of their great council.

UNDER the second race of Kings, the genius of the French government continued to be in a good measure democratical. The nobles, the dignified ecclesiastics, and the great officers of the crown, were not the only members of the national council; the people, or the whole body of free-men, either in person, or by their representatives, had a right to be present in it. Hincmarus, in describing the manner of holding the general assemblies, says, that if the weather was favourable, they met in the open air, but, if otherwise, they had different apartments allotted to them, so that the dignified clergy were separated from the laity, and the comites vel hujusmodi principes sibimet honorificabiliter a cætera multitudine segregarentur. Ibid. c. 35. p. 114. Agobardus, archbishop of Lyons, thus describes a national council in the year 833, wherein he was present. Qui ubique conventus extitit ex reverentissimis episcopis, & magnificentissimis viris inlustribus, collegio quoque abbatum & comitum, promiscuæque ætatis & dignitatis populo. The *cætera multitudo* of Hincmarus is the same with the *populus* of Agobardus,

and

and both describe the inferior order of freemen, the same who were afterwards known in France by the name of the third estate, and in England by the name of commons. The people, as well as the members of higher dignity, were admitted to a share of the legislative power. Thus, by a law, A. D. 803. it is ordained, " that the question shall be put to the people with respect to every new law, and if they shall agree to it, they shall confirm it by their signature." Capit. vol. i. 394. There are two capitularia which convey to us a full idea of the part which the people had in the administration of government. When they felt the weight of any grievance, they had a right to petition the sovereign for redress. One of these petitions, in which they desire that ecclesiasticks might be exempted from bearing arms, and from serving in person against the enemy, is still extant. It is addressed to Charlemagne, A. D. 803, and expressed in such terms as could have been used only by men conscious of liberty, and of the extensive privileges which they possessed. They conclude with requiring him to grant their demand, if he wished that they should any longer continue faithful subjects to him. That great monarch, instead of being offended or surprised at the boldness of their petition, received it in a most gracious manner, and signified his willingness to comply with it. But sensible that he himself did not possess legislative authority, he promises to lay the matter before the next general assembly, that such things as were of common concern to all might be there confidered and eftablifhed by common confent. Capitul. tom. i. p. 405.—409. As the people by their petitions brought matters to be propofed in the general affembly, we learn from another capitulare the form in which they were approved there, and enacted as laws. The propofitions were read aloud, and then the people were required to declare whether they affented to them or not. They fignified their affent by crying three times, " We are fatisfied," and then the capitulare was confirmed by the fubfcription of the monarch, the clergy and the chief men of the laity. Capitul. tom. i. p. 627. A. D. 822. It feems probable from a capitulare of Carolus Calvus, A. D. 851, that the fovereign could not refufe his affent to what was propofed and eftablifhed by his fubjects in the general affembly. Tit. ix. § 6. Capitul. vol. ii. p. 47. It is unneceffary to multiply quotations concerning the legiflative power of the national affembly of France under the fecond race, or concerning its right to determine with regard to peace and war. The uniform ftyle of the Capitularia is an abundant confirmation of the former. The reader who defires any farther information with refpect to the latter, may confult Les Origines ou l'Ancien Gouvernement de la France, &c. tom. iii. p. 87, &c. What has been faid with refpect to the admiffion of the people or their reprefentatives into the fupreme affembly merits attention, not only in tracing the progrefs of the French government, but on account of the light which it throws upon a fimilar

queftion

question agitated in England, concerning the time when the commons became part of the legiſlative body in that kingdom.

NOTE XXXIX. Sect. III. p. 201. [QQ].

That important change which the conſtitution of France underwent, when the legiſlative power was transferred from the great council of the nation to the King, has been explained by the French antiquarians with leſs care, than they beſtow in illuſtrating other events in their hiſtory. For that reaſon I have endeavoured with the greater attention to trace the ſteps which led to this memorable revolution. I ſhall here add ſome particulars which tend farther to illuſtrate it. The Leges Salicæ, the Leges Burgundionum, and other codes publiſhed by the ſeveral tribes which ſettled in Gaul, were general laws extending to every perſon, to every province and diſtrict where their authority was acknowledged. But they ſeem to have become obſolete; and the reaſon of their falling into diſuſe is very obvious. Almoſt the whole property of the nation was allodial when theſe laws were framed. But when the feudal inſtitutions became general, and gave riſe to an infinite variety of queſtions peculiar to that ſpecies of tenure, the ancient codes were of no uſe in deciding with regard to theſe, becauſe they could not contain regulations applicable to caſes which did not exiſt at the time when they were compiled. This conſiderable change in the nature of property

made

made it neceſſary to publiſh the new regulations contained in the *Capitularia*. Many of theſe, as is evident from the peruſal of them, were general laws extending to the whole French nation, in the general aſſembly of which they were enacted. The weakneſs of the greater part of the monarchs of the ſecond race, and the diſorder into which the nation was thrown by the depredations of the Normans, encouraged the barons to uſurp an independent power formerly unknown in France. The nature and extent of that juriſdiction which they aſſumed, I have formerly conſidered. The political union of the kingdom was at an end, its ancient conſtitution was diſſolved, and only a feudal relation ſubſiſted between the King and his vaſſals. The regal juriſdiction extended no further than the domains of the crown. Under the laſt Kings of the ſecond race, theſe were reduced almoſt to nothing. Under the firſt Kings of the third race, they comprehended little more than the patrimonial eſtate of Hugh Capet, which he annexed to the crown. Even with this acceſſion, they continued to be very narrow. Velly. Hiſt. de France, tom. iii. p. 32. Many of the moſt conſiderable provinces of France did not at firſt acknowledge Hugh Capet as a lawful Monarch. There are ſtill extant ſeveral charters, granted during the firſt years of his reign, with this remarkable clauſe in the form of dating the charter; " Deo regnante, rege expectante," regnante domino noſtro Jeſu Chriſto, Francis autem contra jus regnum uſurpante Ugone rege. Bouquet Recueil,

cueil, tom. x. p. 514. A Monarch whofe title was thus openly difputed, was not in a condition to affert the royal jurifdiction, or to limit that of the barons.

All thefe circumftances rendered it eafy for the barons to ufurp the rights of royalty within their own territories. The capitularia became no lefs obfolete than the ancient laws; local cuftoms were every where introduced, and became the fole rule by which all civil tranfactions were conducted, and all caufes were tried. The wonderful ignorance, which became general in France, during the ninth and tenth centuries, contributed to the introduction of cuftomary law. Few perfons, except ecclefiaftics, could read; and as it was not poffible for them to have recourfe to written laws, either as their guide in bufinefs, or their rule in adminiftering juftice, the cuftomary law univerfally prevailed.

During this period, the general affembly of the nation feems not to have been called, nor to have once exerted its legiflative authority. Local cuftoms regulated and decided every thing. A ftriking proof of this occurs in tracing the progrefs of the French jurifprudence. The laft of the Capitularia collected by M. Baluze, was iffued in the year 921, by Charles the Simple. An hundred and thirty years elapfed from that period to the publication of the firft ordonance of the Kings of the third race, contained in the great
collection

PROOFS AND ILLUSTRATIONS.

collection of M. Lauriere, and the first ordonance which appears to be an act of legislation extending to the whole kingdom, is that of Philip Augustus, A. D. 1190. Ordon. tom. i. p. 1, 18. During that long period of one hundred and sixty-nine years, all transactions were directed by local customs, and no addition was made to the statutory law of France. The ordonances, previous to the reign of Philip Augustus, contain regulations, the authority of which did not extend beyond the King's domains.

Various instances occur of the caution with which the Kings of France ventured at first to exercise legislative authority. M. l'Ab. de Mably produces an ordonance of Philip Augustus, A. D. 1206, concerning the Jews, who, in that age, were in some measure the property of the lord in whose territories they resided. But it is not so much an act of royal power, as a treaty of the King with the countess of Champagne, and the comte de Dampierre; and the regulations in it seem to be established not by his authority, but by their consent. Observat. sur l'hist. de France, ii. p. 355. In the same manner an ordonance of Louis VIII. concerning the Jews, A. D. 1223, is a contract between the King and his nobles, with respect to their manner of treating that unhappy race of men. Ordon. tom. i. p. 47. The Establissemens of St. Louis, though well adapted to serve as general laws to the whole kingdom, were not published as such, but only as a complete code

code of customary law, to be of authority within the King's domains. The wisdom, the equity and the order conspicuous in that code of St. Louis, procured it a favourable reception throughout the kingdom. The veneration due to the virtues and good intentions of its author, contributed not a little to reconcile the nation to that legislative authority, which the King began to assume. Soon after his time, the idea of the King's possessing supreme legislative power became common. If, says Beaumanoir, the King makes any establishment specially for his own domain, the barons may nevertheless adhere to their ancient customs; but if the establishment be general, it shall be current throughout the whole kingdom, and we ought to believe that such establishments are made with mature deliberation, and for the general good. Cout. de Beauvoisis, c. 48. p. 265. Though the Kings of the third race did not call the general assembly of the nation, during the long period from Hugh Capet to Philip the Fair, yet they seem to have consulted the bishops and barons who happened to be present in their court, with respect to any new law which they published. Examples of this occur Ordon. tom. i. p. 3 & 5. The practice seems to have continued as late as the reign of St. Louis, when the legislative authority of the crown was well established. Ordon. tom. i. p. 58. A. D. 1246. This attention paid to the barons facilitated the King's acquiring such full possession of the legislative power, as enabled

them

PROOFS AND ILLUSTRATIONS.

them afterwards to exercise it without observing that formality.

THE assemblies, distinguished by the name of the States General, were first called A. D. 1302, and were held occasionally from that period to the year 1614, since which time they have not been summoned. These were very different from the ancient assemblies of the French nation under the Kings of the first and second race. There is no point with respect to which the French antiquarians are more generally agreed, than in maintaining that the States General had no suffrage in the passing of laws, and possessed no proper jurisdiction. The whole tenor of the French history confirms this opinion. The form of proceeding in the States General was this. The King addressed himself to the whole body assembled in one place, and laid before them the affairs on account of which he had summoned them. The deputies of each of the three orders, of nobles, of clergy, and of the third estate, met apart, and prepared their *cahier* or memorial, containing their answer to the propositions which had been made to them, together with the representations which they thought proper to lay before the King. These answers and representations were considered by the King in his council, and generally gave rise to an ordonance. These ordonances were not addressed to the three estates in common. Sometimes the King addressed an ordonance to each of the estates

in

in particular. Sometimes he mentioned the assembly of the three estates. Sometimes mention is made only of the assembly of that estate to which the ordonance is addressed. Sometimes no mention at all is made of the assembly of estates, which suggested the propriety of enacting the law. Preface au tom. iii. des Ordon. p. xx. Thus the States General had only the privilege of advising and remonstrating; the legislative authority resided in the King alone.

NOTE XL. Sect. III. p. 206. [RR].

If the parliament of Paris be considered only as the supreme court of justice, every thing relative to its origin and jurisdiction is clear and obvious. It is the ancient court of the King's palace, new-modelled, rendered sedentary, and invested with an extensive and ascertained jurisdiction. The power of this court, while employed in this part of its functions, is not the object of present consideration. The pretensions of the parliament to controul the exercise of the legislative authority, and its claim of a right to interpose with respect to publick affairs and the political administration of the kingdom, lead to inquiries attended with greater difficulty. As the officers and members of the parliament of Paris were anciently nominated by the King, were paid by him, and on several occasions were removed by him at pleasure, (Chroniq. Scandaleuse de Louis XI. chez les Mem. de Comines, tom. ii. p. 51. Edit. de M. Lenglet

PROOFS AND ILLUSTRATIONS.

Lenglet de Frefnoy) they cannot be confidered as reprefentatives of the people, nor could they claim any fhare in the legiflative power as acting in their name. We muft fearch for fome other fource of this high privilege. The parliament was originally compofed of the moft eminent perfons in the kingdom. The peers of France, ecclefiaftics of the higheft order, and noblemen of illuftrious birth were members of it, to whom were added fome clerks and counfellors learned in the laws. Pafquier Recherches, p. 44, &c. Encyclopedie, tom. xii. Art. *Parlement,* p. 3, 5. A court thus conftituted was properly a committee of the States General of the kingdom, and was compofed of thefe barons and *fideles,* whom the Kings of France were accuftomed to confult with regard to every act of jurifdiction or legiflative authority. It was natural, therefore, during the intervals between the meetings of the States General, or during thofe periods when that affembly was not called, to confult the parliament, to lay matters of publick concern before it, and to obtain its approbation and concurrence, before any ordonance was publifhed, to which the people were required to conform. 2. Under the fecond race of Kings, every new law was reduced into proper form by the Chancellor of the kingdom, was propofed by him to the people, and when enacted, was committed to him to be kept among the publick records, that he might give authentick copies of it to all who fhould demand them. Hincm. de ord. palat. c. 16. Capitul. Car. Calv.

tit.

tit. xiv. § 11. tit. xxxiii. The chancellor presided in the parliament of Paris at its first institution. Encyclopedie, tom. iii. art. *Chancelier*, p. 88. It was therefore natural for the King to continue to employ him in his ancient functions of framing, taking into his custody, and publishing the ordonances which were issued. To an ancient copy of the Capitularia of Charlemagne, the following words are subjoined. Anno tertio Clementissimi domini nostri Caroli Augusti, sub ipso anno, hæc facta Capitula sunt, & consignata Stephano comiti, ut hæc manifesta faceret Parisiis mallo publico, & illa legere faceret coram Scabineis, quod ita & fecit, & omnes in uno consenserunt, quod ipsi voluissent observare usque in posterum, etiam omnes Scabinei, Episcopi, Abbates, Comites, manu propria subter signaverunt. Bouquet Recueil, tom. v. p. 663. *Mallus* signifies not only the publick assembly of the nation, but the court of justice held by the comes, or missus dominicus. Scabini were the judges, or the assessors of the judges in that court. Here then seems to be a very early instance, not only of laws being published in a court of justice, but of their being verified or confirmed by the subscription of the judges. If this was the common practice, it naturally introduced the verifying of edicts in the parliament of Paris. But this conjecture I propose with that diffidence, which I have felt in all my reasonings concerning the laws and institutions of foreign nations. 3. This supreme court of justice in

PROOFS AND ILLUSTRATIONS.

France was dignified with the appellation of parliament, the name by which the general assembly of the nation was distinguished towards the close of the second race of Kings; and men, both in reasoning and in conduct, are wonderfully influenced by the similarity of names. The preserving the ancient names of the magistrates established while republican government subsisted in Rome, enabled Augustus and his successors to assume new powers, with less observation, and greater ease. The bestowing the same name in France upon two courts, which were extremely different, contributed not a little to confound their jurisdiction and functions.

ALL these circumstances concurred in leading the Kings of France to avail themselves of the parliament of Paris, as the instrument of reconciling the people to their exercise of legislative authority. The French, accustomed to see all new laws examined and authorised before they were published, did not sufficiently distinguish between the effect of performing this in the national assembly, or in a court appointed by the King. But as that court was composed of respectable members, and well skilled in the laws of their country, when any new edict received its sanction, that was sufficient to dispose the people to implicit submission.

WHEN the practice of *verifying* and *registering* the royal edicts in the parliament of Paris became common, the parliament contended that this was

necessary

necessary in order to give them legal authority. It was established as a fundamental maxim in French jurisprudence, that no law could be published in any other manner; that, without this formality, no edict or ordonance could have any effect; that the people were not bound to obey it, and ought not to consider it as an edict or ordonance until it was verified in the supreme court, after free deliberation. Roche-flavin des Parlemens de France, 4to. Gen. 1621. p. 921. The parliament, at different times, hath with great fortitude and integrity opposed the will of their sovereigns; and notwithstanding their repeated and peremptory requisitions and commands, hath refused to verify and publish such edicts as it conceived to be oppressive to the people, or subversive of the constitution of the kingdom. Roche-flavin reckons, that between the year 1562, and the year 1589, the parliament refused to verify more than a hundred edicts of the Kings. Ibid. 925. Many instances of the spirit and constancy with which the parliaments of France opposed pernicious laws, and asserted their own privileges, are enumerated by Limnæus Notitiæ Regni Franciæ, lib. i. c. 9. p. 224.

But the power of the parliament to maintain and defend this privilege, bore no proportion to its importance, or to the courage with which its members asserted it. When any monarch was determined that an edict should be carried into execution, and found the parliament inflexibly resolved

PROOFS AND ILLUSTRATIONS.

not to verify or publish it, he could easily supply this defect by the plenitude of his regal power. He repaired to the parliament in person, he took possession of his seat of justice, and commanded the edict to be read, verified, registered and published in his presence. Then, according to another maxim of French law, the King himself being present, neither the parliament, nor any magistrate whatever, can exercise any authority, or perform any function. Adveniente Principe, cessat magistratus. Roche-flavin. ibid. p. 928, 929. Encyclopedie, tom. ix. Art. *Lit de Justice*, p. 581. Roche-flavin mentions several instances of Kings who actually exerted this prerogative, so fatal to the residue of the rights and liberties transmitted to the French by their ancestors. Pasquier produces some instances of the same kind. Rech. p. 61. Limnæus enumerates many others, which the length to which this note has swelled, prevents me from inserting at length, though they tend greatly to illustrate this important article in the French history, p. 245. Thus by an exertion of prerogative, which, though violent, seems to be constitutional, and is justified by innumerable precedents, all the efforts of the parliament to limit and controul the King's legislative authority, are rendered ineffectual.

I HAVE not attempted to explain the constitution or jurisdiction of any parliament in France, but that of Paris. All of them are formed upon the model of that most ancient and respectable tribunal, and all my observations concerning it will apply with full force to them.

NOTE XLI. Sect. III. p. 211. [SS].

The humiliating posture, in which a great Emperor implored absolution, is an event so singular, that the words in which Gregory himself describes it, merit a place here, and convey a striking picture of the arrogance of that Pontiff. Per triduum, ante portam castri, deposito omni regio cultu, miserabiliter, utpote discalceatus, & laneis indutus, persistens, non prius cum multo fletu apostolicæ miserationis auxilium, & consolationem implorari destitit, quam omnes qui ibi aderant, & ad quos rumor ille pervenit, ad tantam pietatem, & compassionis misericordiam movit, ut pro eo multis precibus & lacrimis intercedentes, omnes quidem insolitam nostræ mentis duritiem mirarentur; nonulli vero in nobis non apostolicæ sedis gravitatem, sed quasi tyrannicæ feritatis crudelitatem esse clamarent. Epist. Gregor. ap. Memorie della Contessa Matilda da Fran. Mar. Fiorentini, Lucca, 1756. vol. i. p. 174.

NOTE XLII. Sect. III. p. 222. [TT].

As I have endeavoured in the history to trace the various steps in the progress of the constitution of the Empire, and to explain the peculiarities in its policy very fully, it is not necessary to add much by way of illustration. What appears to be be of any importance, I shall range under distinct heads.

1. WITH respect to the power, jurisdiction and revenue of the Emperors. A very just idea of these may be formed by attending to the view which Pfeffel gives of the rights of the Emperors at two different periods. The first at the close of the Saxon race, A. D. 1024. These, according to his enumeration, were the right of conferring all the great ecclesiastical benefices in Germany; of receiving the revenues of them during a vacancy; of Mort-main, or of succeeding to the effects of ecclesiasticks who died intestate. The right of confirming or of annulling the elections of the Popes. The right of assembling councils, and of appointing them to decide concerning the affairs of the church. The right of conferring the title of King upon their vassals. The right of granting vacant fiefs. The right of receiving the revenues of the Empire, whether arising from the Imperial domains, from imposts and tolls, from gold or silver mines, from the taxes paid by the Jews, or from forfeitures. The right of governing Italy as its proper sovereigns. The right of erecting free cities, and of establishing fairs in them. The right of assembling the diets of the Empire, and of fixing the time of their duration. The right of coining money, and of conferring that privilege on the states of the Empire. The right of administering both high and low justice within the territories of the different states. Abregé, p. 160. The other period

period is at the extinction of the Emperors of the families of Luxemburg and Bavaria, A. D. 1437. According to the same author, the Imperial prerogatives at that time were the right of conferring all dignities and titles, except the privilege of being a state of the Empire. The right of *Preces primariæ*, or of appointing once during their reign a dignitary in each chapter or religious house. The right of granting dispensations with respect to the age of majority. The right of erecting cities, and of conferring the privilege of coining money. The right of calling the meetings of the diet, and of presiding in them. Abregé, &c. p. 507. It were easy to show that M. Pfeffel is well founded in all these assertions, and to confirm them by the testimony of the most respectable authors. In the one period, the Emperors appear as mighty sovereigns with extensive prerogatives; in the other, as the heads of a confederacy with very limited powers.

The revenues of the Emperors decreased still more than their authority. The early Emperors, and particularly those of the Saxon line, besides their vast patrimonial or hereditary territories, possessed an extensive domain both in Italy and Germany which belonged to them as Emperors. Italy belonged to the Emperors as their proper kingdom, and the revenues which they drew from it were very considerable. The first alienations of the Imperial revenue were made in this country. The Italian cities having acquired wealth, and aspiring at independence, purchased their liberty from different Emperors, as I have observed Note XV. The sums which they paid, and the Emperors with whom they concluded these bargains, are mentioned by Casp. Klockius de Ærario Norimb. 1671. p. 85, &c. Charles IV. and his son Wenceslaus, dissipated all that remained of the Italian branch of the domain. The German domain lay chiefly upon the banks of the Rhine, and was under the government of the Counts Palatine. It is not easy to mark out the boundaries, or to estimate the value of this ancient domain, which has been so long incorporated with the territories of different Princes. Some hints with respect to it may be found in the glossary of Speidelius, which he has intituled Speculum Juridico-Philologico-politico-Historicum Observationum, &c. Norimb. 1673. vol. i. 679. 1045. a more full account of it is given by Klockius de Ærario, p. 84. Besides this, the Emperors possessed considerable districts of land lying intermixed with the estates of the Dukes and barons. They were accustomed to visit these frequently, and drew from them what was sufficient to support their court during the time of their residence. Annalistæ, ap. Struv. tom. i. 611. A great part of these were seized by the nobles during the long interregnum, or during the wars occasioned by the contests between the Emperors and the court of Rome. At the same time that such encroachments were made on the fixed or territorial property of the Emperors, they were robbed almost entirely of their casual revenues. The

Princes

Princes and barons appropriating to themselves taxes and duties of every kind, which had usually been paid to them. Pfeffel Abregé, p. 374. The profuse and inconsiderate ambition of Charles IV. squandered whatever remained of the Imperial revenues after so many defalcations. He, in the year 1376, in order to prevail with the Electors to chuse his son Wenceslaus King of the Romans, promised each of them a hundred thousand crowns. But being unable to pay so large a sum, and eager to secure the election to his son, he alienated to the three ecclesiastical Electors, and to the Count Palatine, such countries as still belonged to the Imperial domain on the banks of the Rhine, and likewise made over to them all the taxes and tolls then levied by the Emperors in that district. Trithemius, and the author of the Chronicle of Magdeburgh, enumerate the territories and taxes which were thus alienated, and represent this as the last and fatal blow to the Imperial authority. Struv. Corp. vol. i. p. 417. From that period, the shreds of the ancient revenues possessed by the Emperors have been so inconsiderable, that, in the opinion of Speidelius, all that they yield would be so far from defraying the expence of supporting their houshold, that they would not pay the charge of maintaining the posts established in the Empire. Speidelii Speculum, &c. vol. i. p. 680. These funds, inconsiderable as they were, continued to decrease. Granvelle, the minister of Charles V. asserted in the year 1546, in presence of several of the German Princes, that his master drew no

money

money at all from the Empire. Sleid. History of the Reformation, Lond. 1689. p. 372. The same is the case at present. Traité de droit Publique de l'Empire par M. le Coq de Villeray, p. 55. From the reign of Charles IV. whom Maximilian called the pest of the Empire, the Emperors have depended entirely on their hereditary dominions, as the only source of their power, and even of their subsistence.

2. THE ancient mode of electing the Emperors, and the various changes which it underwent, require some illustration. The Imperial crown, as well as those of most monarchies in Europe, were originally attained by election. An opinion long prevailed among the antiquaries and publick lawyers of Germany, that the right of chusing the Emperors was vested in the archbishops of Mentz, Cologne and Treves, the King of Bohemia, the Duke of Saxony, the Marquis of Brandenburgh, and the Count Palatine of the Rhine, by an edict of Otho III. confirmed by Gregory V. about the year 996. But the whole tenor of history contradicts this opinion. It appears, that from the earliest period in the history of Germany, the person who was to reign over all, was elected by the suffrage of all. Thus Conrad I. was elected by all the people of the Franks, say some annalists; by all the princes and chief men, say others; by all the nation, say others. See their words, Struv. Corp. 211. Conringius de German. Imper. Repub. Acroamata Sex. Ebroduni 1654. p. 103. In the

year

year 1024, posterior to the supposed regulations of Otho III. Conrad II. was elected by all the chief men, and his election was approved and confirmed by the people. Struv. Corp. 284. At the election of Lotharius II. A. D. 1125, sixty thousand persons of all ranks were present. He was named by the chief men, and their nomination was approved by the people. Struv. ibid. p. 357. The first author who mentions the seven Electors is Martinus Polonus, who flourished in the reign of Frederick II. which ended A. D. 1250. We find, that in all the ancient elections to which I have referred, the Princes of the greatest power and authority were allowed by their countrymen to name the person whom they wished to appoint Emperor, and the people approved or disapproved of their nomination. This privilege of voting first is called by the German lawyers the right of *Prætaxation*. Pfeffel Abregé, p. 316. This was the first origin of the exclusive right which the Electors acquired. The Electors possessed the most extensive territories of any Princes in the Empire; all the great offices of the state were in their hands by hereditary right; as soon as they obtained or engrossed so much influence in the election as to be allowed the right of prætaxation, it became unnecessary for the inferior ecclesiastics and barons to attend, when they had no other function but that of confirming the deed of these more powerful Princes by their assent. During times of turbulence, they could not resort to the place of election without a numerous retinue of armed vassals, the expence

expence of which they were obliged to defray out
of their own revenues. The rights of the seven
Electors were supported by all the descendants and
allies of their powerful families, who shared in the
splendor and influence which they enjoyed by this
distinguishing privilege. Pfeffel Abregé, p. 376.
The seven Electors were considered as the representatives of all the orders which composed the
highest class of German nobility. There were three
archbishops, chancellors of the three great districts
into which the Empire was anciently divided; one
King; one Duke; one Marquis; and one Count.
All these circumstances contributed to render the
introduction of this considerable innovation into
the constitution of the Germanick body extremely
easy. Every thing of importance, relating to this
branch of the political state of the Empire, is well
illustrated by Onuphrius Panvinius, an Augustinian
Monk of Verona, who lived in the reign of Charles
V. His treatise, if we make some allowance for
that partiality which he expresses in favour of the
powers which the Popes claimed in the Empire,
has the merit of being one of the first works in
which a contraverted point in history is examined
with critical precision, and with a proper attention
to that evidence which is derived from records, or
the testimony of contemporary historians. It is
inserted by Goldastus in his Politica Imperialia, p. 2.

As the Electors have engrossed the sole right
of chusing the Emperors, they have assumed likewise that of deposing them. This high power the

Electors

Electors have not only presumed to claim, but have ventured, in more than one instance, to exercise. In the year 1298, a part of the Electors deposed Adolphus of Nassau and substituted Albert of Austria in his place. The reasons on which they found their sentence, show that this deed flowed from factious, not from publick-spirited motives. Struv. Corp. vol. i. 540. In the first year of the fifteenth century, the Electors deposed Wenceslaus, and placed the Imperial crown on the head of Rupert Elector Palatine. The act of deposition is still extant. Goldasti Constit. vol. i. 379. It is pronounced in the name and by the authority of the Electors, and confirmed by several prelates and barons of the Empire, who were present. These exertions of the electoral power demonstrate that the Imperial authority was sunk very low.

The other privileges of the Electors, and the rights of the electoral college are explained by the writers on the publick law in Germany.

3. With respect to the diets or general assemblies of the Empire, it would be necessary, if my object were to write a particular history of Germany, to enter into a minute detail, concerning the forms of assembling it, the persons who have right to be present, their division into several Colleges or Benches, the objects of their deliberation, the mode in which they carry on their debates or give their suffrages, and the authority of their

decrees

decrees or recesses. But in a general history it is sufficient to observe, that, originally, the diets of the Empire were perfectly the same with the assemblies of March and of May, held by the Kings of France. They met, at least, once a year. Every freeman had a right to be present. They were assemblies, in which a monarch deliberated with his subjects, concerning their common interest. Arumæus de comitiis Rom. German. Imperii, 4to, Jenæ. 1660, cap. 7. N°. 20, &c. But when the Princes, dignified ecclesiastics, and barons, acquired territorial and independent jurisdiction, the diet became an assembly of the separate states, which formed the confederacy of which the Emperor was head. While the constitution of the Empire remained in its primitive form, attendance on the diets was a duty, like the other services due from feudal subjects to their sovereign, which the members were bound to perform in person; and if any member who had a right to be present in the diet neglected to attend in person, he not only lost his vote, but was liable to an heavy penalty. Arumæus de Comit. c. 5. N°. 40. Whereas, from the time that the members of the diet became independent states, the right of suffrage was annexed to the territory or dignity, not to the person. The members, if they could not, or would not attend in person, might send their deputies, as Princes send ambassadors, and they were entitled to exercise all the rights belonging to their constituents. Ibid. N°. 42, 46, 49. By degrees, and upon the same principle of
considering

considering the diet as an assembly of independent states, in which each confederate had the right of suffrage, if any member possessed more than one of those states or characters which entitle to a seat in the diet, he was allowed a proportional number of suffrages. Pfeffel Abregé, 622. From the same cause the Imperial cities, as soon as they became free, and acquired supreme and independent jurisdiction within their own territories, were received as members of the diet. The powers of the diet extend to every thing relative to the common concern of the Germanick body, or that can interest or affect it as a confederacy. The diet takes no cognizance of the interior administration in the different States, unless that happens to disturb or threaten the general safety.

4. WITH respect to the Imperial chamber, the jurisdiction of which has been the great source of order and tranquillity in Germany, it is necessary to observe, that this court was instituted in order to put an end to the calamities occasioned by private wars in Germany. I have already traced the rise and progress of this practice, and pointed out its pernicious effects as fully as their extensive influence during the middle ages merited. In Germany, private wars seem to have been more frequent and productive of worse consequences than in the other countries of Europe. There are obvious reasons for this. The nobility of Germany were extremely numerous, and the causes of their dissention multiplied in proportion. The territorial

territorial jurisdiction which the German nobles acquired, was more compleat than that professed by their order in other nations. They became, in reality, independent powers, and they claimed all the privileges of that character. The long interregnum accustomed them to an uncontrouled licence, and led them to forget that subordination which is necessary in order to maintain publick tranquillity. At the time when the other monarchs of Europe began to acquire such an increase of power and revenues, as added new force to their government, the authority and revenues of the Emperors continued gradually to decline. The diets of the Empire, which alone had authority to judge between such mighty barons, and power to enforce its decisions, met very seldom. Conring. Acroamata, p. 234. The diets when they did assemble were often composed of several thousand members, Chronic. Constant. ap. Struv. Corp. i. p. 546, and were mere tumultuary assemblies, ill-qualified to decide concerning any question of right. The session of the diets continued only two or three days; Pfeffel Abregé, p. 244, so that they had no time to hear or discuss any cause that was in the smallest degree intricate. Thus Germany was left, in some measure, without any court of judicature, capable of repressing the evils of private war.

ALL the expedients which were employed in other countries of Europe in order to restrain this practice, and which I have described Note XXI.

were

were tried in Germany with little effect. The confederacies of the nobles and of the cities, and the division of Germany into various circles, which I mentioned in that Note, were found likewise insufficient. As a last remedy, the Germans had recourse to arbiters whom they called *Auſtregæ*. The barons and ſtates in different parts of Germany joined in conventions, by which they bound themſelves to refer all controverſies, that might ariſe between them, to the determination of *Auſtregæ*, and to ſubmit to their ſentences as final. Theſe arbiters are named ſometimes in the treaty of convention, an inſtance of which occurs in Ludewig Reliquæ Manuſcr. omnis ævi, vol. ii. 212.; ſometimes they were choſen by mutual conſent; ſometimes they were appointed by neutral perſons; and ſometimes the choice was left to be decided by lot. Datt. de Pace publica Imperii, lib. i. cap. 27. N° 60, &c. Speidelius Speculum, &c. voc. *Auſtrag.* p. 95. Upon the introduction of this practice, the publick tribunals of juſtice became, in a great meaſure, uſeleſs, and were almoſt entirely deſerted.

In order to re-eſtabliſh the authority of government, Maximilian inſtituted the Imperial chamber, at the period which I have mentioned. This tribunal conſiſted originally of a preſident, who was always a nobleman of the firſt order, and of ſixteen judges. The preſident was appointed by the Emperor, and the judges, partly by him, and partly by the States, according to forms which it is unneceffary to defcribe. A fum was impofed, with their own confent, on the States of the Empire, for paying the falaries of the judges, and officers in this court. The Imperial chamber was eftablifhed firft at Francfort on the Maine. During the reign of Charles V. it was removed to Spires, and continued in that city above a century and a half. It is now fixed at Wetzlar. This court takes cognizance of all queftions concerning civil right between the States of the Empire, and paffes judgment in the laft refort, and without appeal. To it belongs, likewife, the privilege of judging in criminal caufes, which may be confidered as connected with the prefervation of the publick peace. Pfeffel Abregé, 560.

ALL caufes relating to points of feudal right or jurifdiction, together with fuch as refpect the territories which hold of the Empire in Italy, belong properly to the jurifdiction of the Aulick council. This tribunal was formed upon the model of the ancient court of the palace inftituted by the Emperors of Germany. It depended not upon the States of the Empire, but upon the Emperor; he having the right of appointing at pleafure all the judges of whom it is compofed. Maximilian, in order to procure fome compenfation for the diminution of his authority, by the powers vefted in the Imperial chamber, prevailed on the diet A. D. 1512. to give its confent to the eftablifhment of the Aulick council. Since that time, it has been a great object of policy in the court of Vienna to

extend

extend the jurisdiction, and support the authority of the Aulick council, and to circumscribe and weaken those of the Imperial chamber. The tedious forms and dilatory proceedings of the Imperial chamber have furnished the Emperors with pretexts for doing so. Lites Spiræ, according to the witticism of a German lawyer, spirant, sed nunquam exspirant. Such delays are unavoidable in a court composed of members named by States, jealous of each other. Whereas the judges of the Aulick council, depending on one master, and being responsible to him alone, are more vigorous and decisive. Puffendorf. de Statu Imper. German. cap. v. § 20. Pfeffel Abregé, p. 581.

NOTE XLIII. Sect. III. p. 225. [UU].

THE description which I have given of the Turkish government is conformable to the accounts of the most intelligent travellers who have visited that Empire. The count de Marsigli, in his treatise concerning the military state of the Turkish Empire, ch. vi. and the Author of observations on the religion, laws, government and manners of the Turks, published at London 1768, vol. i. p. 81. differ from other writers who have described the political constitution of that powerful monarchy. As they had opportunity, during their long residence in Turkey, to observe the order and justice conspicuous in several departments of administration, they seem unwilling to admit that it should be denominated a despotism. But when the form of government in any country is represented to be despotick, this does not suppose that the power of the monarch is continually exerted in acts of violence, injustice and cruelty. Under governments of every species, unless when some frantick tyrant happens to hold the scepter, the ordinary administration must be conformable to the principles of justice, and if not active in promoting the welfare of the people, cannot certainly have their destruction for its object. A state, in which the sovereign possesses the absolute command of a vast military force, together with the disposal of an extensive revenue; in which the people have no privileges, and no part either immediate or remote in legislation; in which there is no body of hereditary nobility, jealous of their own rights and distinctions, to stand as an intermediate order between the Prince and the people, cannot be distinguished by any name but that of a despotism. The restraints, however, which I have mentioned, arising from the *Capiculy*, and from religion, are powerful. But they are not such as change the nature or denomination of the government. When a despotick Prince employs an armed force to support his authority, he commits the supreme power to their hands. The Prætorian bands in Rome dethroned, murdered, and exalted Princes, in the same wanton manner with the soldiery of the Porte at Constantinople. But notwithstanding this, the Roman Emperors have been considered by all political writers as possessing despotick power.

NOTE

NOTE XLIV. Sect. III. p. 227. [XX].

The inſtitution, the diſcipline, and privileges of the Janizaries are deſcribed by all the authors who give any account of the Turkiſh government. The manner in which enthuſiaſm was employed in order to inſpire them with courage is thus related by Prince Cantemir: "When Amurath I. had formed them into a body, he ſent them to Haji Bektaſh a Turkiſh Saint, famous for his miracles and prophecies, deſiring him to give them a banner, to pray to God for their ſucceſs, and to give them a name. The Saint, when they appeared in his preſence, put the ſleeve of his gown upon one of their heads, and ſays, Let them be called *Yengicheri*. Let their countenance be ever bright, their hands victorious, their ſword keen; let their ſpear always hang over the heads of their enemies, and wherever they go, may they return with a ſhining face." Hiſtory of the Ottoman Empire, p. 38. The number of Janizaries, at the firſt inſtitution of the body, was not conſiderable. Under Solyman, in the year 1521, they amounted to twelve thouſand. Since that time their number has greatly increaſed, Marſigli, Etat. &c. ch. 16. p. 68. Though Solyman poſſeſſed ſuch abilities and authority as to reſtrain this formidable body within the bounds of obedience, yet its tendency to limit the power of the Sultans was, even in that age, foreſeen by ſagacious obſervers. Nicolas Daulphinois, who accompanied M. D'Aramon ambaſſador from Henry II. of France

PROOFS AND ILLUSTRATIONS.

France to Solyman, published an account of his travels, in which he describes and celebrates the discipline of the Janizaries, but at the same time predicts that they would, one day, become formidable to their masters, and act the same part at Constantinople, as the Prætorian bands had done at Rome. Collection of Voyages from the Earl of Oxford's Library, vol. i. p. 599.

NOTE XLV. SECT. III. p. 229. [YY].

SOLYMAN the Magnificent, to whom the Turkish historians have given the firname of *Canuni*, or instituter of rules, first brought the finances and military establishment of the Turkish Empire into a regular form. He divided the military force into the *Capiculy* or foldiery of the Porte, which was properly the standing army, and *Serrataculy* or foldiers appointed to guard the frontiers. The chief strength of the latter consisted of those who held Timariots and Ziams. These were portions of land granted to certain persons for life, in much the same manner as the military fiefs among the nations of Europe, in return for which military service was performed. Solyman, in his *Canun-Nam?* or book of regulations, fixed with great accuracy the extent of these lands in each province of his Empire, appointed the precise number of foldiers each person who held a Timariot or a Ziam should bring into the field, and established the pay which they should receive while engaged in service. Count Marsigli and Sir Paul

Rycaut

Rycaut have given extracts from this book of regulations, and it appears, that the ordinary establishment of the Turkish army exceeded an hundred and fifty thousand men. When these are added to the soldiery of the Porte, they formed a military power which vastly exceeded what any Christian state could command. Marsigli Etat Militaire, &c. p. 136. Rycaut's state of the Ottoman Empire, book iii. ch. 2. As Solyman, during his active reign, was engaged so constantly in war, that his troops were always in the field, the *Serrataculy* became almost equal to the Janizaries themselves in discipline and valour.

It is not surprising, then, that the authors of the sixteenth century should represent the Turks as far superior to the Christians, both in the knowledge and in the practice of the art of war. Guicciardini informs us, that the Italians learned the art of fortifying towns from the Turks. Histor. lib. xv. p. 266. Busbequius, who was ambassador from Ferdinand to Solyman, and who had opportunity to observe the state both of the Christian and Turkish armies, published a discourse concerning the best manner of carrying on war against the Turks, in which he points out at great length the immense advantages which the Infidels possessed with respect to discipline, and military improvements of every kind. Busbequii opera edit. Elzevir. p. 393, &c. The testimony of other authors might be added, if the matter were, in any degree, doubtful.

PROOFS AND ILLUSTRATIONS.

BEFORE I conclude these Proofs and Illustrations, I ought to explain the reason of two omissions in them; one of which it is necessary to mention on my own account, the other to obviate an objection to this part of the work.

IN all my inquiries and disquisitions concerning the progress of government, manners, literature and commerce during the middle ages, as well as in my delineations of the political constitution of the different States of Europe at the opening of the sixteenth century, I have not once mentioned M. de Voltaire, who, in his *Essay sur l'histoire generale*, has reviewed the same period, and has treated of all these subjects. This does not proceed from inattention to the works of that extraordinary man, whose genius, no less enterprizing than universal, has attempted almost every different species of literary composition. In many of these he excels. In all, if he had left religion untouched, he is instructive and agreeable. But as he seldom imitates the example of modern historians in citing the authors from whom they derived their information, I could not, with propriety, appeal to his authority in confirmation of any doubtful or unknown fact. I have often, however, followed him as my guide in these researches; and he has not only pointed out the facts with respect to which it was of importance to inquire, but the conclusions which it was proper to draw from them. If he had, at the same time, mentioned the books which relate these particulars, a great part of my labour

PROOFS AND ILLUSTRATIONS:

bour would have been unneceffary, and many of his readers who now confider him only as an entertaining and lively writer, would find that he is a learned and well-informed hiftorian.

As to the other omiffion; every intelligent reader muft have obferved, that I have not entered, either in the hiftorical part of this volume, or in the Proofs and Illuftrations, into the fame detail with refpect to the ancient laws and cuftoms of the Britifh kingdoms, as concerning thofe of the other European nations. As the capital facts with regard to the progrefs of government and manners in their own country are known to moft of my readers, fuch a detail appeared to me to be lefs effential. Such facts and obfervations, however, as were neceffary towards completing my defign in this part of the work, I have mentioned under the different articles which are the fubjects of my difquifitions. The ftate of government, in all the nations of Europe, having been nearly the fame during feveral ages, nothing can tend more to illuftrate the progrefs of the Englifh conftitution, than a careful inquiry into the laws and cuftoms of the kingdoms on the Continent. This fource of information has been too much neglected by the Englifh antiquarians and lawyers. Filled with admiration of that happy conftitution now eftablifhed in Great Britain, they have been more attentive to its forms and principles, than to the condition and ideas of remote times, which, in almoft every particular,

particular, differ from the present. While engaged in perusing the laws, charters, and early historians of the continental kingdoms, I have often been led to think that an attempt to illustrate the progress of the English jurisprudence and policy, by a comparison with those of other kingdoms in a similar situation, would be of great utility, and might throw much light on some points which are now obscure, and decide others, which have been long contraverted.

INDEX.

INDEX

TO THE

FIRST VOLUME.

A

AFRICA, the shocking devastations made there by the Vandals, 258.

Alanus, his character of the clergy in his time, 279.

Alfred the Great, his complaint of the ignorance of the clergy, 279.

Allodial possession of land, explained, 256. How such possession became subject to military service, *ib.* Distinguished from beneficiary tenures, 257. How converted into feudal tenures, 265.

Allodium, the etymology of that word, 270.

Ammianus, his character of the Huns, 231, 247.

Amurath, Sultan, the body of Janizaries formed by him, 226.

Anathema, form of that denounced against robbers during the middle ages, 198.

Arabia, the ancient Greek philosophy cultivated there, while lost in Europe, 387, *Note* xxviii. The progress of philosophy from thence to Europe, 388.

Aragon, rise of the kingdom of, 175. Its union with Castile, *ib.* The constitution and form of its government, 180. The privileges of its Cortes, *ib.* Office and jurisdiction of the Justiza, 182. The regal power very confined, 131. Form of the allegiance swore to the Kings of, *ib.* The power of the nobility to control the regal power, 416. Their privilege of union taken away by Peter IV. *ib.* The establishment of the Inquisition opposed there, 420.

Armies, standing, the rise of, traced, 111. By what means they became more general in Europe, 114.

Arms, the profession of, the most honourable in uncivilized nations, 80.

Ass, an account of the antient Romish feast of, 281.

Assemblies, legislative, how formed, 43.

———— general, of France, their power under the first race of Kings, 197. Under the second and third, 198. At what period they lost their legislative authority, 199.

Attila,

INDEX TO THE

Attila, King of the Huns, account of his reception of the Roman ambassadors, 235, Note ib. Some account of his conquests, 242.

Avila, an assembly of Castilian nobles there, solemnly try and depose Henry IV. their King, 179.

Austria, the house of, by whom founded, 212.

B

Bailiis, in the old French law, their office explained, 371.

Balance of power, the first rise of, in Europe, 133. The progress of, 134.

Baltic, the first source of wealth, to the towns situated on that sea, 405.

Barcelona, its trade, riches, and privileges at the close of the fifteenth century, 424.

Barons, their independence, and mutual hostilities, under the feudal system, 19. How affected by the infranchisement of cities, 41. Acquire a participation in legislative government, 43. Their private wars for redress of personal injuries, 52. Methods employed to abolish these contentions, 54. Origin of their supreme and independent jurisdiction, 62. The bad effects resulting from these privileges, 69. The steps taken by Princes to reduce their courts, 71. How obliged to relinquish their judicial prerogatives, 81. Of Italy, subjected to municipal laws, 196, Note xv. Their right of territorial jurisdiction explained, 364. Their emoluments from causes decided in their courts, 360.

Benefices, under the feudal system, a history of, 260. When they became hereditary, 263.

Books, an inquiry into the materials of the ancient ones, 282. The loss of old manuscripts accounted for, ib. The great prices they sold for in antient times, 281.

Boroughs, representatives of, how introduced into national councils, 44.

Britons antient, their distress and dejection when deserted by the Romans, and harassed by the Picts and Caledonians, 233, Note i.

Brotherhood of God, an account of that association for extinguishing private wars, 118.

Bruges, how it became the chief mart for Italian commodities during the middle ages, 404.

Burgundy, Mary, heiress of, the importance with which her choice in a husband was considered by all Europe, 124. The treacherous views of Lewis XI. of France toward her, 127. Is married to the Archduke Maximilian, 128. The influence of this match on the state of Europe, ib.

Cæsar,

FIRST VOLUME.

C

Cæsar, his account of the antient Germans, compared with that of Tacitus, 247.

Cambray, treaty of, its object, 140. The confederacy diffolved, 142.

Canon Law, an inquiry into, 74. Progress of ecclefiaftial ufurpations, 75. The maxims of, more equitable than the civil courts of the middle ages, 76.

Caftile, rise of the kingdom of, 175. Its union with Aragon, *ib*. Its King Henry IV. folemnly tried and depofed in an affembly of the nobles, 179. The conftitution and government of that kingdom, 184. A hiftory of the Cortes of, and its privileges, *ib*. The kingdom originally elective, 421, *Note* xxxiii.

Catalonia, the fpirited behaviour of the people there in defence of their rights, againft their King John II. of Aragon, 179.

Cerefaales, a fpecies of the Oblati, or voluntary flaves, the obligations they entered into defcribed, 126.

Centenarii, or inferior judges in the middle ages, the extraordinary oath required from them, 398.

Champs de Mars, and *de Mai*, account of thofe affemblies of the antient Gauls, 431.

Charlemagne, his law to prevent private wars for redrefs of perfonal injuries, 54, 334. State of Germany under his defcendants, 207.

Charles IV. Emperor, diffipates the Imperial domains, 456.

——— V. Emperor, an emulator of the heroic conduct of his rival, Francis I. 86. His future grandeur founded on the marriage of the Archduke Maximilian with the heirefs of Burgundy, 121.

——— VII. of France, the firft who introduced ftanding armies in Europe, 112. His fuccefsful extenfion of the regal prerogative, 115.

——— VIII. of France, his character, 129. How induced to invade Italy, *ib*. His refources and preparations for this enterprize, 130. His rapid fuccefs, 131. A combination of the Italian ftates formed againft him, 133. Is forced to return back to France, *ib*. The diftreffed ftate of his revenues by this expedition, 139.

Charlevoix, his account of the North American Indians, made ufe of in a comparifon between them and the antient Germans, 256.

Charters, of immunity or franchife, an inquiry into the nature of thofe granted by the barons of France to the towns under their jurifdictions, 301, *Note* xvi. Of communities, granted by the Kings of France, how they tended to eftablifh regular government, 39, 302.

Chivalry, the origin of, 82. Its beneficial effects on human manners,

ners, 83. The enthusiasm of, distinguished from its salutary consequences, 85.

Christianity, corrupted when first brought into Europe, 88. Its influence in freeing mankind from the bondage of the feudal policy, 321, *Note* xx.

Circles of Germany, the occasion of their being formed, 214.

Cities, the antient state of, under the feudal policy, 36. The freedom of, where first established, 37. Charters of community, why granted in France by Louis le Gros, 39. Obtain the like all over Europe, 40. Acquire political consideration, 43.

Clergy, the progress of their usurpations, 75. Their plan of jurisprudence more perfect than that of the civil courts in the middle ages, 76. The great ignorance of, in the early feudal times of Europe, 279.

Clerica, slave to Willa, widow of Duke Hugo, extract from the charter of manomission, granted to her, 323.

Clermont, council of, resolves on the holy war, 28. See *Peter the hermit*, and *Crusades*.

Clotaire I. instance of the small authority he had over his army, 430.

Clotharius II. his account of the popular assemblies among the antient Gauls, 432.

Clovis, the founder of the French monarchy, unable to retain a sacred vase taken by his army, from being distributed by lot among the rest of the plunder, 254. *Note* vii.

Colleges, the first establishment of, in Europe, 389.

Combat, judicial, the prohibition of, an improvement in the administration of justice, 56. The foundation and universality of this mode of trial, 62. The pernicious effects of, 64. Various expedients for abolishing this practice, 65. The antient Swedish law of, for words of reproach, 350. Positive evidence, or points of proof, rendered ineffectual by it, 355. This mode of trial authorized by the ecclesiastics, 357. The last instances of, in the histories of France and England, 358.

Commerce, the spirit of crusading how far favourable to, at that early period, 34. The first establishment of free corporations, 38. Charters of community why granted by Louis le Gros, 39. The like practice obtains all over Europe, 40. The salutary effects of these institutions, *ib*. The low state of, during the middle ages, 92. Causes contributing to its revival, 93. Promoted by the Hanseatic league, 95. Is cultivated in the Netherlands, 96. Is introduced into England by Edward III. 97. The beneficial consequences resulting from the revival of, *ib*. The early cultivation of, in Italy, 399.

Common Law, the first compilation of, made in England by Lord Chief Justice Glanville, 382.

Communities, see *Charters*, *Cities*, *Commerce*, and *Corporations*.

Commerce,

FIRST VOLUME.

Comnena, Anne, her character of the Crusaders, 293.

Compass, mariner's, when invented, and its influence on the extension of commerce, 94.

Composition for personal injuries, the motive for establishing, 334. The custom of, deduced from the practice of the antient Germans, 359.

Compurgators, introduced as evidence in the jurisprudence of the middle ages, 58.

Condottieri, in the Italian policy, what, 162.

Conrad, count of Franconia, how he obtained election to the Empire, 207.

Conradin, the last rightful heir to the crown of Naples of the house of Swabia, his unhappy fate, 166.

Constance, treaty of, between the Emperor Frederic Barbarossa, and the free cities of Italy, 300.

Constantinople, its flourishing state at the time of the Crusades, 30. When first taken by the Turks, 223. The Crusaders how looked upon there, 293. The account given of this city by the Latin Writers, 294.

Constitutions, popular, how formed, 42.

Cordova, Gonsalvo de, secures the crown of Naples to Ferdinand of Aragon, 168.

Corporations, and bodies politic, the establishments of, how far favourable to the improvement of manners, 26. The privileges of, where first claimed, 38. Charters of community, why granted by Louis le Gros in France, 39. The institution of, obtains all over Europe, 40. Their effects, ib.

Cortes of Aragon, its constitution and privileges, 180, 417.

—— of Castile, a history of, and an account of its constitution and privileges, 184. The vigilance with which it guarded its privileges against the encroachments of the regal power, 185.

Crusades, the first motives of undertaking, 26. The enthusiastic zeal with which they were undertaken, 27. First promoted by Peter the hermit, 28. The success of them, 29. The consequences resulting from them, 30. Their effects on manners, ib. On property, 31. How advantageous to the enlargement of the regal power of the European princes, 32. The commercial effects of, 31, 93. The universal frenzy for engaging in these expeditions accounted for, 285, *Note* xiii. The privileges granted to those who engaged in them, 287. Stephen earl of Chartres and Blois, his account of them, 289. The expences of conducting them, how raised, 290. Character given of the Crusaders by the Greek writers, 293.

D

Debt, the first hint of attaching moveables for the recovery of, derived from the canon law, 380.

Delitors,

INDEX TO THE

Debtors, how considered in the rude and simple state of society, 305.

Diets of Germany, some account of, 462.

Doctors in the different faculties, dispute precedence with knights, 390.

E

Ecclesiastical jurisprudence, more perfect in its plan than the civil courts of the middle ages, 76.

Ecclesiastics, when, and by what degrees they claimed exemption from civil jurisdiction, 176. Military talents cultivated and exercised by those of the middle ages, 184.

Edward III. of England, his endeavours to introduce commerce into his kingdom, 96.

Electors of Germany, the rise of their privileges, 219.

Eloy, St. his definition or description of a good Christian, 283. *Note* xi.

Emperors of Germany, an inquiry into their power, jurisdiction, and revenue, 453, *Note* xlii. The antient mode of electing them, 458.

England, a summary view of the contests between, and France, 105. The consequences of its losing its continental possessions, 108. The power of the crown, how extended, 112. See *Henry* VII. Why so many marks of Saxon usages and language, in comparison with those of the Normans, to be found in, 236, *Note* iv. When corporations began to be established in, 316. Instances of the long continuance of personal servitude there, 327. Inquiry into the Saxon laws for putting an end to private wars, 340. The causes of the speedy decline of private wars there, proposed to the researches of Antiquarians, 344. The last instances of judicial combat recorded in the history of, 358. The territorial jurisdiction of the barons now abolished, 374. Cause of the slow progress of commerce there, 406. The first commercial treaty entered into by, 408.

Evidence, the imperfect nature of that admitted in law-proceedings during the middle ages, 57. Rendered ineffectual by the judicial combat, 355.

Europe, the alterations in, by the conquests of the Romans, 2. The improvements the nations of, received in exchange for their liberties, *ib*. Its disadvantages under this change of circumstances, 3. Inquiry into the supposed populousness of the antient northern nations, 5. The savage desolations exercised by the Goths, Vandals, and Huns, 11. The universal change occasioned by their irruptions and conquests, 12. The first rudiments of the present policy of, to be deduced from this period, 13. Origin of the feudal system, 14. See *Feudal System*. The general barbarism introduced with this policy, 21. At what time

government

FIRST VOLUME.

government and manners began to improve, 25. The causes and events which contributed to this improvement, 26. See *Crusades, Corporations, People*. The miseries occasioned by private wars in, 53. Methods taken to suppress them, 54. Judicial combats prohibited, 56. The defects of judicial proceedings in in the middle ages, 57. The influence of superstition in these proceedings, 59. The origin of the independent territorial jurisdictions of the barons, 67. The bad consequences of their judicial power, 68. The steps taken by princes to abolish their courts, 71. An inquiry into the canon law, 74. Revival of the Roman law, 79. Effects of the spirit of chivalry, 82. How improved by the progress of science and cultivation of literature, 86. Christianity corrupted when first received in, 88. Scholastic theology the first object of learning in, 89. Low state of commerce in, during the middle ages, 92. Commerce revives in Italy, 94. Is promoted by the Hanseatic league, 95. Is cultivated in the Netherlands, 96. The effects of the progress of commerce, on the polishing of manners, 97. The effects of the marriage of the heiress of Burgundy with the archduke Maximilian, on the state of, 128. By what means standing forces became general in, 134. Consequences of the league of Cambray to, 140. A view of the political constitution of the several states of, at the commencement of the sixteenth century, 146. Italy, 148. The papacy, 149. Venice, 159. Florence, 163. Naples, 164. Milan, 168. Spain, 172. France, 191. Germany, 206. Turkey, 223. Instances of the small intercourse among nations in the middle ages, 392.

F

Frodum, the etymology of that word, 171.
Ferdinand, King of Aragon, unites the Spanish monarchy, by his marriage with Isabella of Castile, 175. His schemes to exalt the regal power, 190. Resumes former grants of land from his barons, 191. Unites to the crown the grand masterships of the three military orders, 192. Why he patronized the association called the *Holy Brotherhood*, against the barons, 193.
Feudal system, the origin of, deduced, 15. The primary object of this policy, 16. Its deficiencies for interior government, 17. Tenures of land, how established under, *ib*. The rise of intestine discords among the barons under, 18. The servile state of the people, 19. The weak authority of the King, *ib*. Its influence on the external operations of war, 20. The general extinction of all arts and sciences effected by, 21. Its operation on religion, 22. Its influence on the character of the human mind, 23. At what time government and manners began to be improved, 25. The causes and events which contributed to this improvement, 25. See *Crusades*. The antient state of cities

under, 35. The frame of national councils under this policy, 41. How altered by the progress of civil liberty, 44. An inquiry into the administration of justice under, 49. Private war, 51. Judicial combat, 57. The independent jurisdictions of the barons, 58. The distinction between free men and vassals under, 358. How strangers were considered and treated under, 395.

Fiefs, under the feudal system, a history of, 260. When they became hereditary, 263.

Fitzstephens, observations on his account of the state of London, at the time of Henry II. 317.

Flanders. See *Netherlands*.

Florence, a view of the constitution of, at the commencement of the sixteenth century, 163. The influence acquired by Cosmo di Medici in, *ib*.

France, by what means the towns in, first obtained charters of community, 39. Ordinances of Louis X. and his brother Philip in favour of civil liberty, 48. Methods employed to suppress private wars, 54. St. Louis attempts to discountenance judicial combat, 65. A view of the contests between, and England, 106. The consequences of its recovering its provinces from England, 108. The monarchy of, how strengthened by this event, 110. The rise of standing forces in, 111. The regal prerogative strengthened by this measure, 113. The extension of the regal prerogative vigorously pursued by Louis XI. 116. See *Louis XI*. The effects of the invasion of Italy by Charles VIII. 129. See *Charles VIII*. National infantry established in, 138. League of Cambray formed against the Venetians, 141. Battle of Ghiaradadda, 142. An inquiry into its antient government and laws, 197. The power of the general assemblies under the first race of Kings, *ib*. Under the second and third, 198. The regal power confined to the King's own domains, 199. When the general assembly or states general lost their legislative authority, *ib*. When the Kings began to assert their legislative power, 201. When the government of, became purely monarchical, 202. The regal power nevertheless restrained by the privileges of the nobility, *ib*. An inquiry into the jurisdiction of its parliaments, particularly that of Paris, 204. How the allodial property of land there was altered into feudal, 267. The progress of liberty in that kingdom traced, 318. *Note* xiv. The attempts to establish liberty there unsuccessful, 320. The last instance of judicial combat recorded in the history of, 338. The present government of, compared with that of antient Gaul, 429. *Note* xxxviii. The States-general, when first assembled, 446.

Francis I. of France, his character influenced by the spirit of chivalry, 85. Is emulated by the Emperor Charles V. 86.

Frederick

FIRST VOLUME.

Frederick Barbarossa, Emperor, the free cities of Italy unite against him, 300. Treaty of Constance with them, *ib.* Was the first who granted privileges to the cities in Germany, 313.

Fredum, in the antient German usages explained, 361.

Freemen, how distinguished from vassals, under the feudal policy, 258, 275. Why often induced to surrender their freedom, and become slaves, 272.

Fulcherius Carnotensis, his character of the city of Constantinople, 294.

G

Gaul, how allodial property of land was changed into feudal there, 267. The government of, compared with that of modern France, 429. *Note* xxxviii. The small authority the Kings of, enjoyed over their armies illustrated in an anecdote of Clotaire I. 430. Account of the popular assemblies of, 431. The salic laws how enacted, 432. Were not subject to taxation, 434. See *France.*

Geoffrey de Villehardouin, his account of the magnificence of Constantinople at the time when taken by the Crusaders, 295.

Germans, antient, an account of their usages and way of life, 247. Their method of engaging in war, *ib.* A comparison between them and the North American Indians, 250. Why they had no cities, 312. *Note* xvii. The practice of compounding for personal injuries by fines, deduced from their usages, 362.

Germany, little interested in foreign concerns at the beginning of the fifteenth century, 107. National infantry established in, 137. State of under Charlemagne and his descendants, 206. Conrad, count of Franconia chosen Emperor, 207. His successors in the Imperial dignity, *ib.* How the nobility of, acquired independent sovereign authority, 208. The fatal effects of aggrandizing the clergy in, 209. The contests between the Emperor Henry IV. and Pope Gregory VII. 210. Rise of the factions of Guelfs and Ghibelines, 211. Decline of the Imperial authority, *ib.* The House of Austria, by whom founded, 212. A total change in the political constitution of the Empire, *ib.* The state of anarchy in which it continued to the time of Maximilian the immediate predecessor of Charles V. 213. Divided into circles, 214. The Imperial chamber instituted, *ib.* The Aulic council reformed, 215. A view of its political constitution at the commencement of the ensuing history, *ib.* Its defects pointed out, 216. The Imperial dignity and power compared, 217. Election of the Emperors, 219. The repugnant forms of civil policy in the several States of, 220. The opposition between the secular and ecclesiastical members of, 221. The united body hence incapable of acting with vigour, 222. When cities first began to be built in, 311. *Note* xvii. When the cities of, first

I i 2   acquired

acquired municipal privileges, 313. The artizans of, when infranchised, 314. *Immediate* cities in the German jurisprudence, what, 315. The great calamities occasioned there by private wars, 316. Origin of the league of the Rhine, 347. When private wars were finally abolished there, *ib*. Inquiry into the power, jurisdiction and revenue of its Emperors, 473. *Note* xlii. The antient mode of electing the Emperors, 458. Account of the diets, 462.

Ghibelines. See *Guelfs*.

Ghiarradadda, the battle of, fatal to the Venetians, 142.

Glanville, Lord Chief Justice, the first who compiled a body of common law, in all Europe, 382.

Goths, Vandals, and Huns, over-run the Roman empire, and precipitate its downfal, 4. The state of the countries from whence they issued, 5. The motives of their first excursions, 6. How they came to settle in the countries they conquered, 7. A comparison drawn between them and the Romans, at the period of their irruptions, 8. *& seq*. Compared with the native Americans, 10. The desolations they occasioned in Europe, 11. The universal change made by them in the state of Europe, 12. The principles on which they made their settlements, 14. Origin of the feudal system, 15. See *Feudal System*. An inquiry into the administration of justice among, 50. Their private wars, 51. Destroy the monuments of the Roman arts, 87. Their contempt of the Romans, and hatred of their arts, 214. *Note* li. Their aversion to literature, *ib*. No authentic account of their origin, or antient history existing, 235.

Government, how limited by the feudal policy, 18. The effects of the Crusades on, 33. How affected by the infranchisement of cities, 41. Legislative assemblies how formed, 43. Private wars destructive to the authority of, 54. Methods employed to abolish this hostile mode of redressing injuries, 55. How affected by the supreme independent jurisdictions of the barons, 68. The steps toward abolishing them, 71. The origin and growth of royal courts of justice, 75. How influenced by the revival of science and literature, 91. A view of, at the beginning of the fifteenth century, 100. The power of Monarchs then very limited, 101. Their revenues small, *ib*. Their armies unfit for conquest, 102. The Princes hence incapable of extensive plans of operation, 104. The kingdoms very little connected with each other, 105. How the efforts of, from this period became more powerful and extensive, 108. The consequences of England losing its provinces in France, 109. The schemes of Louis XI. of France to extend the regal power, 116. See *Louis* XI. The power of the English crown enlarged, 122. See *Henry* VII. As also that of Spain, 123. How the use of standing armies became general, 134. A view of the political constitution of the

several

several states of Europe, at the commencement of the sixteenth century, 148. In what respects the charters of communities granted by the Kings of France, tended to introduce a regular form of, 303.

Greece, the breeding of silk-worms, when introduced there, 400.

Greek Emperors, their magnificence at Constantinople, 293.

Gregory of Tours, remarks on the state of Europe during the period of which he wrote the history, 24.

———— the Great, Pope, his reason for granting liberty to his slaves, 322.

———— VII. Pope, the foundation of his contests with Henry IV. Emperor of Germany, 210. The mean submission he extorted from Henry, 211. His own account of this affair, 453.

Guelfs, and Ghibelines, rise of those factions in Germany, 211.

Guicciardini, the historian, instance of his superstitious reverence for Pope Clement VII. 159, *Note*.

Guntherus, a Monk, his character of Constantinople, at the time when taken by the Crusaders, 394.

H

Hanseatic league, when formed, and its influence on the extension of commerce, 95, 406.

Henry IV. of Castile, solemnly tried and deposed by an assembly of Castilian nobles, 179.

———— Emperor of Germany, the humiliating state to which he was reduced by Pope Gregory VII. 210, 453. *Note* xli.

———— VII. of England, his situation at his accession to the crown, 122. Enables his barons to break their entails and sell their estates, *ib.* Prohibits his barons keeping retainers, *ib.* Encourages agriculture and commerce, *ib.*

Herebannum, the nature of this fine under the feudal policy, explained, 259.

Hermandad, Santa, account of that institution, 428.

History, the most calamitous period of, pointed out, 11.

Holy Brotherhood, an association in Spain under that name, on what occasion formed, 195.

———— Land, the original inducements of the Christians to rescue it from the hands of the Infidels, 26. See *Crusades*, and *Peter the Hermit.*

Honour, points of the antient Swedish law for determining, 350.

Hospitality, enforced by statutes during the middle ages, 391.

Huns, instance of their enthusiastic passion for war, 235. *Note* iii. Some account of their policy and manners, 230, 247. See *Goths*.

INDEX TO THE

I

Janizaries, origin, and formidable nature of those troops, 226.

Imperial chamber of Germany, instituted, 214. The occasion of its institution, 425.

Indians, North American, a comparison drawn between them and the antient Germans, 250.

Industry, the spirit of, how excited by the infranchisement of cities, 41.

Infantry, the advantages of, beyond cavalry, taught to the rest of Europe by the Swiss, 137. National bodies of, established in Germany, *ib*. In France and Spain, 137.

Inheritance, and right of representation, between orphan grandsons and their uncles, how decided in the tenth century, 352.

Interest of money, the necessity of admitting, in a commercial view, 402. Preposterously condemned by the churchmen of the middle ages, *ib*. The cause hence, of the exorbitant exactions of the Lombard bankers, *ib*.

Italy, when the cities of, began to form themselves into bodies politic, 38. Commerce first improved there, and the reasons of it, 93. The revolutions in Europe occasioned by the invasion of, by Charles VIII. of France, 129. The state of, at the time of this invasion, 130. The rapid success of Charles, 132. A combination of the States of, drives Charles out of, and gives birth to the balance of power in Europe, 133. The political situation of, at the commencement of the sixteenth century, 148. The papacy, 149. Venice, 159. Florence, 163. Naples, 164. Milan, 168. Evidences of the desolation made there by the northern invaders of the Roman Empire, 242. How the cities of, obtained their municipal privileges, 296. *Note* xv. State of, under Frederick I. 297. Treaty of Constance between the free cities of, and the Emperor Frederick Barbarossa, 300.

Judgment of God, modes of acquittal by, in the law proceedings during the middle ages, 59, 348. *Note* xx I.

Judicium Crucis, method of trial by, 348.

Julius II. Pope, forms a confederacy against the Venetians at Cambray, 141. Seizes part of the Venetian territories, 142. The confederacy dissolved, *ib*. Turns his schemes against France, 143.

Jurisprudence, ecclesiastical, more perfect in its plan than the civil courts of the middle ages, 55. *See Law*.

Justice, an inquiry into the administration of, under the feudal policy, 50. The steps toward the improvement of, as civil liberty advanced, 51. Redress chiefly pursued by private wars, 52. Methods taken to suppress private wars, 54. Judicial combats prohibited, 56. The defects of judicial proceedings in the middle ages, *ib*. Compurgators, the nature of

that

FIRST VOLUME.

that kind of evidence, 58. Methods of trial by ordeal, or acquittal by Judgment of God, 59. Origin of the supreme independent jurisdictions of the feudal barons, 68. The extent and bad effects of their privileges, 69. The steps taken by monarchs to reduce the barons courts, 71. The growth of royal courts of justice, 72. Inquiry into the canon law, 74. How improved by the revival of the Roman law, 78. When the administration of, became a distinct profession, 81.

Justitia, or supreme judge of Aragon, his office and privileges, 181. An inquiry by whom this officer was elected, 409. Who was eligible to this office, 410. Nature of the tribunal appointed to controul his administration, 412. Instance of his extensive power, *ib*.

K

King, his power how circumscribed by the barons, under the feudal system, 19. By what means the Crusades tended to enlarge the regal authority, 13.

Koran, its influence in checking the Sultans of the Ottoman empire, 226.

L

Land, how held at the establishment of the feudal system, 17. See *Feudal system*.

——— the property of, how considered by the antient barbarous nations, 255. *Note* viii. Allodial possession of, explained, 256. The proprietors how subjected to military service, 257. Allodial and beneficiary possession distinguished, 258. Allodial property why generally converted into feudal, 266.

Law, when the study of it became a distinct employment, 81.

——— Canon, an inquiry into, 74. The maxims of, more equitable than the civil courts of the middle ages, 76. When first compiled, 379.

——— Roman, how it sunk into oblivion, 78. Circumstances which favoured the revival of it, 79. Its effects in improving the administration of justice, *ib*. Its rapid progress over Europe, 381. *Note* xxv.

Lawburrows, in the Scottish law, explained, 104.

Liberty, civil, the rise and progress of, traced, 18. How favoured by the ordinances of Louis X. of France, and his brother Philip, 48. The spirit of, how excited in France, 317. *Note* xix. The particular included in the charters of, granted to husbandmen, 321. *Note* xx. The influence of the Christian religion in extending, 322. The several opportunities of obtaining, 336.

Limoges, council of, its endeavours to extinguish private wars, 235.

Literature, the cultivation of, greatly instrumental in civilizing the nations of Europe, 86. Why the first efforts of, ill directed, 87. The good effects nevertheless of the spirit of inquiry exerted, 89. How checked in its progress, 90. Its influence on manners and government, 91.

Liturgy, the preference between the Musarabic, and Romish, how ascertained in Spain, 351.

Lombards, the first bankers in Europe, 401. The motive of their exacting exorbitant interest, 402.

London, its flourishing state at the time of Henry II. 317.

Louis le Gross, of France, his inducement to grant privileges to towns within his own domains, 39. See *Charters*.

——— VI. the great attention he paid to the administration of justice, in appeals which came before him, 371.

——— X. of France, his ordinances in favour of civil liberty, 48.

——— XI. of France, his character, 115. His schemes for depressing the nobility. *ib.* Sows divisions among them, 118. Increases the standing forces, *ib.* Enlarges the revenues of the crown, 119. His address in over ruling the assembly of states, *ib.* Extends the bounds of the French monarchy, 120. The activity of his external operations, 121. His treacherous baseness toward the heiress of Burgundy, 126, 127. The effects of his conduct, 128.

——— XII. his hesitation in carrying on war against the Pope, 169. *Note.* Asserts his right to the duchy of Milan, and retains Ludovico Sforza in prison, 171.

M

Manfred, his struggles for the crown of Naples, 165.

Mantua, the most calamitous period in the history of, pointed out, 110.

Manners, the barbarity of, under the feudal establishments, after the overthrow of the Roman empire, 21. When they began to improve, 24. Effects of the Crusades on, 30. How improved by the infranchisement of cities, 42. How improved by the erection of royal courts of justice, in opposition to the barons courts, 71. Effects of the revival of the Roman law on, 78. The beneficial tendency of the spirit of chivalry on, 82. How influenced by the progress of science, 86, 91. How polished by the revival of commerce, 97.

Manumission, particulars included in the charters of, granted to husbandmen or slaves, 321. *Note xx.* The form of, 323.

Maximilian, archduke of Austria, married to Mary heiress of Burgundy, 128. The influence of this match on the state of Europe, *ib.*

Maximilian,

FIRST VOLUME.

Maximilian, Emperor, institutes the Imperial chamber, 211. Reforms the Aulic council, *ib.*

Medici, Cosmo di, the first of the name, the influence he acquired in Florence, 161.

Milan, the state of the duchy of, at the commencement of the sixteenth century, 168. Rise and progress of the disputes concerning the succession to, 169.

Mind, the human, a view of, under the first establishment of the feudal policy in Europe, 24. The æra of its ultimate depression, and commencement of its improvement, *ib.* The progress of its operations, before the full exertion of it, 87.

Ministeriales, a class of the Oblati, or voluntary slaves, the pious motives of the obligations they entered into, 326.

Moors, make a conquest of Spain, 173. By what means weakened during their establishment there, 174. Remarks on their conduct in Spain, 176.

Municipal privileges, how obtained by the cities of Italy, 296. *Note* xv. Secured to them by the treaty of Constance, 302. The favourite state of, under the Roman government, 311.

N

Naples, a view of the constitution of that kingdom, at the commencement of the sixteenth century, 164. The turbulent unsettled state of that kingdom, 165. State of the disputes concerning the succession to the crown of, *ib.* The pretensions of the French and Spanish monarchs to the crown of, 167.

Narbonne, community of, preamble to the writ of summons of Philip the Long, to, 318. *Note* xix.

Navigation, proofs of the imperfect state of, during the middle ages, 40.

Netherlands, vigorous prosecution of the manufactures of hemp and flax there, on the revival of commerce in Europe, 96.

Normans, why so few traces of their usages and language, to be found in England, in comparison with those of the Saxons, 236. *Note* iv.

O

Oblati, or voluntary slaves, the classes of, specified, 325.

Ordeal, methods of trial by, during the middle ages, 59. The influence of superstition in dictating these means, 60.

Otto, Frisingensis, his account of the state of Italy under Frederic I. 297.

Ottoman empire, the origin, and despotic nature of, 223. Becomes formidable to the Christian powers, 229.

Papacy,

INDEX TO THE

P

Papacy. See *Popedom.*

Paper, when first made of the present materials, 281.

Paris, an inquiry into the pre-eminent jurisdiction of its parliament over the other parliaments of France, 104. Its origin traced, 447. *Note* xi. The royal edicts registered by, before admitted to be laws, 451.

Parliaments, or legislative assemblies, how formed under the feudal policy, 43. How altered by the progress of civil liberty, 44.

People, their wretched servile state under the feudal system, 19, 46. Released from their slavish state by the infranchisement of cities, 40. How they obtained a representation in national councils, 45. Those who lived in the country and cultivated the ground, an inquiry into their condition under the feudal policy, 272. *Note* ix.

Persia, murder in, how punished there, 363.

Peter the Hermit, excites the European Princes to undertake the Holy War, 24.

—— IV. King of Aragon, defeats the leaders of the Aragonese union, and destroys the privilege of these associations, 416.

Philip the Long, preamble to his writ of summons to the community of Narbonne, 316. *Note* xix.

Philosophy, cultivated by the Arabians, when lost in Europe, 387. *Note* xxviii. Its progress from them into Europe, 388.

Pilgrimages to the Holy Land, when first undertaken, 26. See *Crusades,* and *Peter the Hermit.*

Placentia, council of, the Holy war resolved on by, 28. See *Peter the Hermit,* and *Crusades.*

Plunder, how divided among the antient northern nations, 15. Illustrated in an anecdote of Clovis, 254. *Note* vii.

Popedom, the highest dignity in Europe at the commencement of the sixteenth century, 148. Origin and progress of the papal power, 149. The territories of the Popes unequal to the support of their spiritual jurisdiction, 150. Their authority in their own territories extremely limited, 151. The check they received from the Roman barons, 152. Nicolas Rienzo attempts to establish a democratical government in Rome, and to destroy the papal jurisdiction, 153. The papal authority considerably strengthened by the Popes Alexander VI. and Julius II. 154. See *Julius* II. The permanent nature of ecclesiastical dominion, 155. The civil administration of, not uniform or consistent, *ib.* Rome the school of political intrigue during the sixteenth century, 150. The advantages derived from the union of spiritual and temporal authority, 157. A view of the contests between the Popes and the Emperors of Germany, 210.

Populousness

FIRST VOLUME.

Populousness of the antient northern nations, an inquiry into, 5.
Priscus, extract from his account of the Roman embassy to Attila King of the Huns, 235. *Note* iii.
Procopius, his account of the cruel devastations made by the irruption of the northern nations, 236. *Note* v. 240, 241.
Property, the possession of, how secured by the French charters of communities, 305.
Proveditori, in the Venetian policy, their office, 160.

R

Religion, how corrupted by the northern nations established in Europe under the feudal policy, 22. Its influence in freeing mankind from the feudal servitude, 322.
Repledging, the right of, in the law of Scotland, explained, 267.
Reproach, words of, the antient Swedish law of satisfaction for, 350.
Revenues, royal, very small under the feudal policy, 102. By what means increased, 138.
Rhine, origin and intention of the league of, 147.
Rienzo, Nicola, endeavours to rescue Rome from the Papal authority, and establish a democratical form of government there, 153.
Robbers, the anathema pronounced against them during the middle ages, 198.
Rodulph of Hapsburgh, how he attained election to the Empire of Germany, 212.
Romans, an inquiry into those advantages which enabled them to conquer the rest of Europe, 2. The improvements they communicated in return for their conquests, *ib*. The disadvantages the provinces laboured under, from their dominion, 3. Their Empire overturned by the irruption of the barbarous nations, 4. The concurrent causes of their ruin, 6. A comparison drawn between them and the northern nations, 9. All the civil arts established by them obliterated, 21. The monuments of their arts industriously destroyed by their barbarous invaders, 86.
Rome, papal. See *Popedom*.
Royal truce, an account of, 339.

S

Salic laws, the manner in which they were enacted, 452.
Saxons, why so many traces of their laws, language and customs to be found in England, 236. *Note* iv. Inquiry into their laws for putting an end to private wars, 343.
Science, the revival and progress of, how far instrumental in civilizing the nations of Europe, 87. A summary view of the revival and progress of, in Europe, 327. *Note* xxviii.
Sforza, Francis, the foundation of his pretensions to the duchy of Milan, 170. Is murdered by his uncle Ludovico, *ib*.

Sforza,

Sforza, Ludovico, his private views in engaging Charles VIII. of France to invade Italy, 129. See *Charles* VIII. Murders his nephew Francis, and seizes Milan, 170. Is stripped of his dominions by Louis XII. of France, and dies in prison, 171.

Shipwrecks, the right, lords of manors claim to, whence derived, 395.

Silk, the rarity of, and the high price it bore in antient Rome, remarked, 399. The breeding of silk worms, when introduced into Greece, 400.

Slaves, letters of, in the law of Scotland, what, 362.

Slaves under the feudal policy, their wretched state, 270. *Oblati*, or voluntary slaves, the several classes of, 325.

Society, civil, the rude state of, under the feudal establishments after the downfal of the Roman Empire, 21. The influence of the Crusades on, 30. How improved by the establishment of municipal communities, 35. The effects the infranchisements of the people had on, 49. Private wars how destructive to, 53. These intestine hostilities, how suppressed, 54. The administration of justice improved by the prohibition of judicial combats, 56. The growth of royal courts of justice, in opposition to the barons courts, 71. How advanced by the revival of the Roman law, 78. The effects of the spirit of chivalry in improving, 82. The revival of commerce and its influences, 93.

Solyman, Sultan, his character, 228.

Spain, a summary view of its situation, at the commencement of the fifteenth century, 86. The power of the crown of, how extended by Ferdinand, 123. National infantry established in, 138. Is conquered by the Vandals, 172. and after by the Moors, 173. The empire of the Moors in, how weakened, 174. Rise of the kingdoms of Castile and Aragon, 175. Their union into the Spanish monarchy, *ib*. The antient customs still retained amidst all its revolutions, *ib*. Peculiarities in its constitution and laws remarked, 177. See *Aragon* and *Castile*. Various causes which contributed to limit the regal power in, 186. The cities of, how they attained their consideration and power, 188. The schemes of Ferdinand and Isabella, to exalt the regal power, 191. The grand masterships of the three orders, annexed to the crown, 192. The association of the *Holy Brotherhood*, on what occasion formed, 195. The tendency of this association to abridge the territorial jurisdictions of the barons, *ib*. The cruel devastations made by the Vandals, in the invasion of that province, 237. When the cities of, acquired municipal privileges, 315. *Note* xviii. The long continuance of the practice of private wars there, 344. The total annual revenue of the nobility, in the time of Charles V. 422. An inquiry into the origin of communities or free cities in, 423.

St. Jago,

FIRST VOLUME.

St. Jago, the military order of, when and on what occasion instituted, 425. *Note* xxxvi.
Standing armies. See *Armies*.
States general of France, causes which rendered their authority imperfect, 199. When they lost their legislative authority, *ib.* When first assembled, 446. The form of proceeding in them, *ib.*
Stephen earl of Chartres and Blois, his account of the progress of the Crusaders, 289.
Stiernhöök, his account of the antient Swedish law of satisfaction for words of reproach, 150.
Strangers, in what light confidered, and how treated during the middle ages, and under the feudal policy, 104.
Sugar canes, when first brought from Asia into Europe, and thence carried to America, 400.
Sultans, Turkish, their despotic power, 225. How nevertheless limited, 226.
Superstition, its influence in the legal proceedings during the middle ages, 60.
Swiss, the superior discipline of their troops, in the fifteenth century, 136. Teach other nations the advantages of infantry over cavalry, *ib.*

T

Tacitus, his account of the antient Germans compared with that of Cæsar, 246.
Tenures, feudal, the origin of, 17. See *Feudal System*, and *Land*.
Theology, scholastic, the first literary pursuits at the revival of learning in Europe, 88.
Truce of God, an account of, 136.
Turkey, origin of, its government, 223. The despotic genius of this government, 224. No hereditary nobility in, *ib.* The authority of the Sultans, how checked, 226. Origin of the Janizaries, *ib.* Becomes formidable to the Christian Princes, 229.

V

Vandals, their cruel devastations in the invasion of Spain, 238. The havock made by them in Africa, 239. See *Goths*.
Vassals under the feudal system, a view of their slavish condition, 19, 46. How they obtained infranchisement, 47. How antiently distinguished from freemen, 258. Their wretched state under their feudal masters, 270. *Note* Ix.
Venice, the long duration of its civil constitution, and its flourishing state at the time of the league of Cambray, 140. Its possessions dismembered by the confederates, 141. Dissolves the confede-

INDEX, &c.

racy, 142. Its rise and progress, 159. Defects in its constitution, 160. The excellency of its naval institutions, 161. Its extensive commerce, 162.

Visconti, rise of the family of, in Milan, 169.

Union of the Aragonese nobles to controul the undue exercise of regal power, explained, 414. This privilege abrogated by Peter IV. 416.

Universities, the first establishment of, in Europe, 389.

W

War, a comparison between the manner of carrying on, by barbarous and by civilized nations, 10. How rendered feeble in its operations by the feudal policy, 19. The profession of arms, the most honourable in uncivilized nations, 80. The rise of standing armies traced, 110. By what means standing forces became general, 134. The superiority of infantry in, how taught, 135.

Wars, private, for the redressing personal injuries, under the feudal policy, an inquiry into, 51. Methods taken to abolish this hostile practice, 54. Judicial combat prohibited, 56. Inquiry into the sources of these customs, 328. Note xxi. Who intitled to the privileges of exercising, 329. On what occasions undertaken, 330. Who included, or bound to engage in these disputes, 331. Who excluded from undertaking, 332. The cruel manner of prosecuting them, *ib*. A chronological account of the expedients made use of, to suppress them, 333. *Truce of God*, an account of, 336. *Brotherhood of God*, an account of, 338. *Royal truce*, what, 339. Saxon laws of England, for putting an end to them, 342. The obstinate attachment of the Spaniards to this practice, 344. The calamities occasioned in Germany by, 346.

Welsh, antient, strangers killed with impunity by them, 396.

Willa, widow of duke Hugo, extract from her charter of manumission, granted to Cleriza, one of her slaves, 323.

Willermus, archbishop of Tyre, his account of Constantinople, 293.

Wittikindus, abbot, his testimony in favour of the judicial combat, 357.

END OF THE FIRST VOLUME.

BOOKS printed for T. CADELL in the Strand.

QUARTO.

I. THE History of Scotland, during the Reigns of Queen Mary and of King James VI. till his Accession to the Crown of England, with a Review of the Scottish History previous to that Period; and an Appendix, containing original Papers, 2 Vols. By William Robertson, D. D. The 5th Edition. 1 l. 10 s.
The same in 2 Vols. 8vo. 12 s.

II. The History of the Reign of the Emperor Charles V. with a View of the Progress of Society in Europe, from the Subversion of the Roman Empire to the Beginning of the Sixteenth Century. By William Robertson, D. D. 3 Vols. 3 l. 3 s.

III. The History of England, from the Invasion of Julius Cæsar to the Revolution: A new Edition, printed on fine Paper, with many Corrections and Additions, and a complete Index. By David Hume, Esq; 8 Vols. Royal Paper. 7 l. 7 s.
    Another Edition on small Paper. 4 l. 10 s.
    Another Edition in 8 Vols. 8vo. 2 l. 8 s.

IV. Essays and Treatises on several Subjects, with an Index. By David Hume, Esq; 2 Vols. Royal Paper. 1 l. 16 s.
    Another Edition, 2 Vols. 8vo. 12 s.
    Another Edition, 4 Vols. small 8vo. 14 s.

V. Memoirs of England and Ireland, during the Revolution and the Reign of King William. By John Dalrymple, Esq; 1 l. 1 s.

VI. An Essay on the History of Civil Society. By Adam Ferguson, L.L. D. Professor of Moral Philosophy in the University of Edinburgh. 2d Edit. 15 s.

OCTAVOS and TWELVES.

VII. Memoirs of the Duke of Sully, Prime Minister of Henry the Great. Containing the History of the Life and Reign of that Monarch, and his own Administration under him. Translated from the French. To which is added, the Trial of Raviliac, for the Murder of Henry the Great. 4th Edit. 6 Vols. 18 s.

VIII. Plutarch's Lives. Translated from the Greek: with Notes Explanatory and Critical, from Dacier and others. To which is prefixed, the Life of Plutarch, written by Dryden. 6 Vols. 8vo. 1 l. 10 s. Or 8 Vols. 12mo. 1 l. 4 s. Or 9 Vols. Eighteens. 18 s.

BOOKS printed for T. CADELL.

IX. Reflections on the Rise and Fall of the Antient Republics, adapted to the present State of Great Britain. By Edward Wortley Montague, Esq; The 3d Edit. with Additions and Corrections. 5 s.

X. The History of England, from the earliest Accounts of Time to the Death of George II. adorned with Heads elegantly engraved. By Dr. Goldsmith. 4 Vols. 1 l. 4 s.

XI. The Parliamentary or Constitutional History of England, from the earliest Times to the Restoration of King Charles II. Collected from the Records, the Rolls of Parliament, the Journals of both Houses, the public Libraries, original MSS. scarce Speeches and Tracts. All compared with the several contemporary Writers, and connected throughout with the History of the Times. With a good Index, by several Hands. 24 Vols. 8vo. 7 l. 7 s.

XII. A Review of the Characters of the principal Nations in Europe. 2 Vols. 10 s.

XIII. The Roman History, from the Building of Rome, to the Ruin of the Common-Wealth. Illustrated with Maps and other Plates. By N. Hooke, Esq; a new Edition. 11 Vols. 3 l. 6 s.——The 10th and 11th Vols. may be had separate.

XIV. The Roman History, from the Foundation of the City of Rome to the Destruction of the Western Empire. By Dr. Goldsmith. 2 Vols. 12 s.

XV. The Works of Tacitus. With Political Discourses upon that Author. By Thomas Gordon, Esq; 5 Vols. 3d Edit. 15 s.

XVI. An Ecclesiastical History, Antient and Modern, from the Birth of Christ to the Beginning of the present Century. In which the Rise, Progress, and Variations of Church Power are considered, in their Connection with the State of Learning and Philosophy, and the political History of Europe, during that Period. By the late learned John Lawrence Mosheim, D. D. Translated, and accompanied with Notes and Chronological Tables, by Archibald Maclaine, D. D. To the whole is added, an accurate Index. The 2d Edit. corrected and improved by additional Notes, and several Appendixes. 5 Vols. 3 l. 10 s.

www.ingramcontent.com/pod-product-compliance
Lightning Source LLC
Chambersburg PA
CBHW051159300426
44116CB00006B/372